Montana Almanac

Second Edition

Andrea Merrill-Maker

INSIDERS' GUIDE®

GUILFORD, CONNECTICUT
AN IMPRINT OF THE GLOBE PEQUOT PRESS

INSIDERS' GUIDE ®

Copyright © 2006 by Morris Book Publishing, LLC.

Text design: Shirley Machonis
Maps © Morris Book Publishing, LLC.

Library of Congress Cataloging-in-Publication Data is available.
ISBN 0-7627-3655-0

Manufactured in the United States of America
Second Edition/First Printing

To all Montanans, past and present

Contents

Acknowledgments

In the acknowledgment for the first Montana Almanac, my co-author, Judy Jacobson, and I said that if we could name, individually, all the people who assisted us on the project, we would have another "almanac" just dedicated to outstanding Montanans. That is again true for this revision. It remains true, as well, that deepest appreciation goes to the many helpful, knowledgeable, and courteous people in government agencies and organizations who helped in a variety of ways. It is a special pleasure to spend time at the Montana Historical Society, especially with the fine staff at Photo Archives.

Since the first edition of this book, the Internet has developed beyond our imagining at that time, and Montana governmental agencies and organizations have made exemplary use of this incredible asset to make information gathering easier for all of us. While we hope you remain devoted to printed matter, we invite you to explore the many extensive, informative, and inviting websites we have listed in the book and thank those who keep these sites up to date.

I wish to thank my husband Fred Maker, my parents, children, grandchildren, and friends for again offering encouragement, ideas, and support during the writing of this book. A special thanks goes to my former co-author, Judy Jacobson, for her work on the first edition that remained valid for this version. I am most grateful to the many otherwise busy people who helped us locate just the right photo for a particular topic or biography: Please note the image credit lines to acknowledge the fine work of the many cooperative amateur and professional photographers who contributed to the edition.

Last but far from least, I wish to thank Editor Erin Turner and the other staff of The Globe Pequot Press. Erin is a joy to work with, as were others whom I may not have met but who deserve mention.

Andrea Merrill–Maker
Missoula, August 2005

CHAPTER ONE

This is Montana

$\mathcal{F}$ew have expressed what many feel about Montana better than John Steinbeck: "I am in love with Montana. For other states I have admiration, respect, recognition, even some affection, but with Montana it is love, and it's difficult to analyze love when you're in it."

An early Montana Highway Map captures the romance of the state.
MONTANA HISTORICAL SOCIETY

Images of Montana are tucked into the hearts of the people who live here or visit, and beckon those who hope to do one or the other someday. Some people just like to know that many icons of the Old West endure and thrive here. Montana still has ranches with front gates 20 miles from the ranch house porch, amber waves of grain, and majestic mountains under skies just like the ones that Charlie Russell painted. People here still share stories at cozy roadside saloons complete with glassy-eyed animal heads guarding the bar. And they still stop for deer, elk, and other creatures along the roadways.

Montana has its share of New West icons too. It is home to airfields seemingly in the middle of nowhere, golf courses with majestic views, corny roadside attractions, glittering casino lights, and 5-acre ranchettes along blue-ribbon trout streams. Freeways stretch across the 550 east-west miles of the state, and logging roads amble through its forests.

Old and new, there is much that is special about

Montana. For instance, did you know that, on the average, only six persons share each of the state's 145,552 square miles of land? (That's not counting 1,490 square miles of water, most of which we share as well.) Or that our state has forty-four state parks and more than six hundred campgrounds? The average working person in Montana earns less than the national average, but the state has about 12.5 million acres of wilderness to nourish the soul. Conveniently, we have only one area code: 406.

People work, create, and recreate in this place of awesome beauty, incredible dimensions, and great diversity, forging a pageant of events, institutions, and traditions.

People have been interested in statistical and essential information about Montana ever since explorers Meriwether Lewis and William Clark wrote the first travel journal about the West. But few know much about us here in what some still think is a hinterland. We hope this second edition of *Montana Almanac* will be a source of accessible, basic information about our state today, helping Montana students, government agencies, and citizens find the facts they need. We hope it imparts some of the love we feel for Montana, and that it serves as a suitable yardstick to measure its fascinating physical and social dimensions.

N O T A B L E

MONTANA HISTORICAL SOCIETY

Charles M. Russell (1864–1926)

"Charlie" Russell was one of America's best-known Western artists, but he was also a storyteller with first-hand knowledge of a large portion of Montana's history. Russell's drawings, paintings, and sculptures capture the spirit of life on the Western frontier. Though born in Oak Hill, Missouri, Charlie wandered to Montana to work at age 16 as a hunter and cowboy. With a photographic vision, he rendered vivid scenes of the West in the 1880s that gained fame outside Montana by the early 1900s. He is the only artist to be honored in Statuary Hall in the Capitol in Washington, D.C.

M O N T A N A N S

Big Sky Country in Brief

- **Admitted to the Union:** November 8, 1889, the 41st state
- **Population:** 917,621 (est. 2003)
  54.0% urban, 46.0% rural (1990)
  6.3 persons per square mile of land
  44th most populous state
- **Capital City:** Helena, in west-central Montana; population: 26,718 (est. 2003)
- **Largest City:** Billings, population: 95,200 (est. 2003)
- **State Name:** Derived from the Latin word *montaanus* which means "mountainous."
- **Nicknames:** Officially known as the Treasure State, Montana is also known as Big Sky Country. Other nicknames include Land of the Shining Mountains, Mountain State, and Bonanza State.
- **Size:** Total Area: 147,042 square miles (380,848 square km)
  Rank: 4th largest state
  Land Area: 145,552 square miles
  Inland Surface Water: 1,490 square miles
  Total Acres: 94,109,440
  Greatest Distance from East to West Boundary: approx. 559 miles
  Greatest Distance from North to South Boundary: approx. 321 miles in western Montana, app. 280 miles in eastern Montana
- **USGS Physiographic Regions:** Rocky Mountain region in the west, Great Plains in the east
- **Geographic Center:** In Fergus County, about 11 miles west of Lewistown
- **Number of Counties:** 56
- **Number of Incorporated Towns and Cities:** 129
- **Longitude and Latitude:** Between 44° 26' and 49° North Latitude and 104° 2' and 116° 2' West Longitude
- **Highest Point:** 12,799 feet (3,901 meters) above sea level at summit of Granite Peak in Park County near south-central boundary
- **Lowest Point:** 1,820 feet in Lincoln County in the northwest corner, where the Kootenai River enters Idaho
- **Mean Elevation:** 3,400 feet
- **Time Zone:** Mountain Standard
- **Area Code:** 406
- **Postal Abbreviation:** MT
- **Resident:** Montanan
- **Motto:** *Oro y Plata,* Spanish for "gold and silver"

Sources: The World Almanac and Book of Facts 2005. NY: World Almanac Books, 2004.

A Visitor's *Pronunciation* Guide

1. The town of **Glasgow** is pronounced like the Scottish city, GLAS-ko or GLAS-go, but in Montana, typically without the lilting Scottish brogue.

2. Don't say **Havre** like the French pronounce their city on the English Channel. For the town on Montana's Milk River, just say HAV-er.

3. Don't pronounce **Missoula** with a hard S. It should sound like a popular corn oil, but with an "oo" in the middle: Mizz-OO-luh.

4. Pronounce the county of **Pondera** pon-dur-AY. It is derived from the name of an Indian tribe, which is spelled Pend d'Oreille (French for "hanging ear"), also pronounced pon-dur-AY.

5. **Meagher** County is pronounced like the fourth planet from the sun, without the S: MAR.

6. Leave off the "X" when you pronounce the town and county of **Wibaux,** both along the North Dakota border. Just say WEE-bo.

7. **Butte,** the city and the landform, sounds like the word you might use to describe a nice-looking horse or pickup truck, as in "she's a BYOOT"; not the word to describe a backside.

8. Montana's state capital is pronounced HELL-un-uh. The common mispronunciation of hell-EE-nuh will attract unwanted attention in **Helena** and elsewhere in the state.

9 **Twodot** does not get a French pronunciation, as in two-DOE. Say it TOO-dott. Another numerical name that has caused problems is **Ninepipe,** a reservoir and wildlife refuge in the Mission Valley. You'll be met with smirks if you call it NINN-ee-pipp-ee. Just say 9-pype.

10. The town of **Choteau** and the county of **Chouteau,** both along the Rocky Mountain Front, are pronounced SHO-toe or SHO-doe.

Incidentally, you'll save yourself a lot of confusion by remembering that the town of **Choteau** is not in **Chouteau** County. It's in **Teton** (TEE-tawn) county. Likewise **Deer Lodge,** the town, is not in **Deer Lodge** County, but in **Powell** County. There is no town of Powell in Montana, but there is a **Power,** northwest of **Great Falls.** The town of **Lincoln,** which gained national attention when the Unabomber suspect was found there, is in **Lewis and Clark** county, about 200 miles from **Lincoln County,** which is in the northwest corner of the state. Clear?

Montana by County

County Names and Origins

- Population and people per square mile based on 2003 estimate
- Area listed in square miles of land

Beaverhead

Population: 8,919
Area: 5,542.6
People/Sq Mi: 1.6
Established: 1865

Not only is this county the largest, in terms of area, but it is also one of the largest counties in the United States, with more acres than Rhode Island and Connecticut combined. The county name is from the Shoshone, given by Sacagawea's people to a rock formation shaped like a beaver's head, along the Beaverhead River, 12 miles southwest of Twin Bridges. The county seat was the gold mining town of Bannack until 1881, when it was changed to Dillon. The Big Hole River, famous for its blue-ribbon trout fishing, runs through this county. Montana's sheep and cattle industries originated in this county, and today it remains the state's top cattle producing area.

Big Horn

Population: 12,894
Area: 4,994.8
People/Sq Mi: 2.6
Established: 1913

The dominant river, mountain range, and county were named for the Rocky Mountain bighorn sheep. John Bozeman blazed his pioneer trail through this area. Today, the Crow Indian Reservation dominates most of the county, where the Battle of the Little Bighorn was fought. Much of the Northern Cheyenne Indian Reservation lies in the eastern part of the county. Both Indians and non-Indians engage in the main industries of farming and cattle ranching. The county seat of Hardin was named for S. H. Hardin, a Texas cattleman. The Bighorn Canyon National Recreation Area offers stunning scenery and abundant recreational opportunities, including excellent trout fishing.

Blaine

Population: 6,729
Area: 4,226.2
People/Sq Mi: 1.6
Established: 1912

• Chinook

BLAINE

This county is mountainous in the south, the site of the Bears Paw Mountains, and dominated by prairie in the north. The county is named for James G. Blaine, a U.S. secretary of state from Maine. The county seat, Chinook, is named for the warm winds that sometimes blow across this area and throughout the state in winter. The Fort Belknap Indian Reservation, home to the Assiniboine and Gros Ventre Indians, are within this county's boundaries. The tribes operate Fort Belknap Tribal College, one of the state's seven tribal colleges. Agriculture is the main economic activity.

Broadwater

Population: 4,430
Area: 1,191.5
People/Sq Mi: 3.7
Established: 1897

Townsend
•

BROADWATER

Colonel C. A. Broadwater was a prominent figure in the early commerce of the state. He was president of the Montana Central Railroad and built Helena's Broadwater Hotel and Natatorium in 1889. Twenty-five miles of the Missouri River forms Canyon Ferry Lake, behind the Canyon Ferry Dam. The county seat of this mainly agricultural area is Townsend, named for an official of the Northern Pacific Railroad.

Carbon

Population: 9,770
Area: 2,048
People/Sq Mi: 4.8
Established: 1895

CARBON
•
Red Lodge

Coal deposits and coal mining gave this county its name and drew a workforce of many nationalities. There are several theories for the origin of the name of the county seat, Red Lodge. The generally accepted story is that the lodges of the Crow were colored by red clay found in the area. The county includes the Bear-tooth Plateau and Granite Peak, the highest elevation in the state. In 1915, the first commercial oil well was drilled in the Elk Basin field east of the mountains.

Carter

Population: 1,333
Area: 3,339.7
People/Sq Mi: 0.4
Established: 1917

Named for Montana's first U.S. Congressman,
Senator Thomas H. Carter, the territory was home to
the Sioux tribe before the arrival of non-Indians.
Ekalaka, the county seat, was named for an Indian woman
whose great-uncle was the Sioux leader Sitting Bull. The woman, whose name is
spelled Ijakalaka, meaning "swift one," was also the spouse of D. H. Russell, a famous
scout and frontier settler. Medicine Rocks State Park is in this county. For the past
century, this popular fossil hunting area has yielded many important dinosaur finds.

Cascade

Population: 79,561
Area: 2,698
People/Sq Mi: 29.5
Established: 1887

The county and the county seat of Great Falls were
named for the Great Falls of the Missouri River. This was
Blackfeet Indian territory at the time of Lewis and Clark's journey through the area in 1805–1806. The town of Great Falls was
founded and planned by engineer and entrepreneur Paris Gibson. Many Cascade
County residents work in agriculture. Malmstrom Air Force Base has contributed to
the economy of the county for the last half century. Some well-known natural features within the county include the Giant Springs State Park and Square Butte, often
depicted in Charlie Russell's paintings.

Chouteau

Population: 5,576
Area: 3,973.4
People/Sq Mi: 1.4
Established: 1865

As one of the original nine counties of the Montana
Territory, it once encompassed much of north-central
Montana. Even though several other counties were carved from its
boundaries, it is still one of the state's largest. The county was named for Auguste
and Pierre Chouteau, fur traders and founders of Fort Benton, today's county seat.
Fort Benton, named for U.S. Senator Thomas H. Benton of Missouri, was once an
important port on the Missouri River. The area was Blackfeet Indian territory and

home to vast herds of bison before the open-range cattle era. It is the state's largest wheat and barley producer, at the heart of the rich agricultural area in northcentral Montana known as the Golden Triangle.

Custer

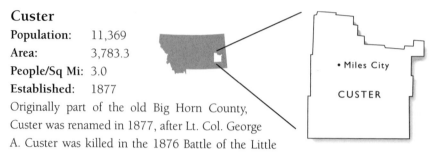

Population: 11,369
Area: 3,783.3
People/Sq Mi: 3.0
Established: 1877
Originally part of the old Big Horn County, Custer was renamed in 1877, after Lt. Col. George A. Custer was killed in the 1876 Battle of the Little Bighorn. The county seat of Miles City was named for General Nelson A. Miles, a veteran of the Civil War and campaigns against the Indians. The area was the range destination of many large Texas cattle drives and still hosts the world-famous Miles City Bucking Horse Sale each May. Today, it is cattle ranching, sugar beet, and dry land farming country.

Daniels

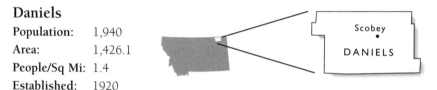

Population: 1,940
Area: 1,426.1
People/Sq Mi: 1.4
Established: 1920
This prairie county was named for Mansfield A. Daniels, a local pioneer, rancher, and storekeeper. Scobey, the county seat, is named for Major C. R. A. Scobey, an agent of the Fort Peck Indian Reservation. In the 1920s, there was an intense baseball rivalry between Scobey and Plentywood to the east in Sheridan County. The two towns hired professional baseball players, and for awhile, the competition between the towns was fierce. This area is cattle and dry land wheat country, and Scobey is a shipping and trade center for the alfalfa, livestock, wheat, and sugar beets produced in northeastern Montana.

Dawson

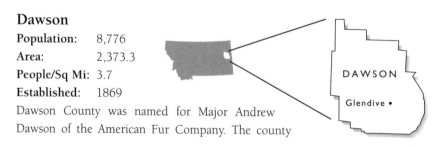

Population: 8,776
Area: 2,373.3
People/Sq Mi: 3.7
Established: 1869
Dawson County was named for Major Andrew Dawson of the American Fur Company. The county

seat of Glendive was named by the first Montana tourist, Sir St. George Gore, an Irish sportsman who was reminded of a stream named Glendale in Ireland. Gore came to hunt bison in 1854 and slaughtered so many it alarmed and irritated the area Indians. In the 1890s, the huge Texas cattle company, the XIT, staked a claim to much of the county's rich grassland. This area is now mostly dry land grain farming but also includes coal resources, gas and oil wells, and livestock ranches. In the 1950s, the county enjoyed the economic boom that came with the discovery of oil in the area. The Fort Peck Dam Interpretive Center and Museum holds some of the best dinosaur fossils in the world.

Deer Lodge

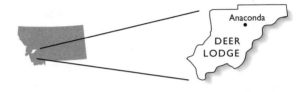

Population: 8,953
Area: 737
People/Sq Mi: 12.1
Established: 1865

Deer Lodge was one of the original nine territorial counties, once extending from the Beaverhead County line to the Canadian border. Much of the Deer Lodge valley was split off to create Powell County in 1901. Today it is the second-smallest county. The name "Deer Lodge" comes from a geothermal formation, at the site of present-day Warm Springs State Hospital, which resembled a large Indian lodge, and salt in the water attracted large numbers of deer.

Anaconda, the county seat, was platted in 1883 as the site for Marcus Daly's copper smelter. It was named to honor Daly's Anaconda Copper Mining Company in Butte. Anaconda/Deer Lodge County is a consolidated city-county government with executive management. Georgetown Lake and the Pintlar Wilderness Area are just a few of the many recreational attractions in the area.

Fallon

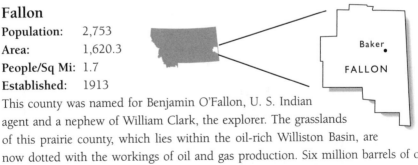

Population: 2,753
Area: 1,620.3
People/Sq Mi: 1.7
Established: 1913

This county was named for Benjamin O'Fallon, U. S. Indian agent and a nephew of William Clark, the explorer. The grasslands of this prairie county, which lies within the oil-rich Williston Basin, are now dotted with the workings of oil and gas production. Six million barrels of oil were extracted in 2001. The county seat of Baker, originally a train station called Lorraine, was named for A. G. Baker, an engineer with the Chicago, Milwaukee, St. Paul & Pacific Railroad.

Fergus

Population: 11,695
Area: 4,339.3
People/Sq Mi: 2.7
Established: 1885

This county was named for James Fergus, a pioneer, miner, cattleman, and territorial legislator. Some say its county seat, Lewistown, was named for Captain Meriwether Lewis of the Lewis and Clark Expedition, but more likely the name was taken from Camp Lewis, established in 1874 by Major William H. Lewis of the Seventh Infantry. Fergus County is home to three "island" mountain ranges, the Big Snowy, Judith, and Moccasin Mountains. The county is one of the most productive farm and ranch areas in the state.

Flathead

Population: 79,485
Area: 5,098.6
People/Sq Mi: 15.6
Established: 1893

This county and its famous river and large freshwater lake bear the name of the "Flathead" Indian tribe, so named by early explorers, but who were actually Salish Indians. These Indians called the area "the park between the mountains." The county seat of Kalispell, originally called Ashley, was named for the Kalispel, another Salish-speaking Indian group that inhabited the area. Big Mountain ski area at Whitefish and Glacier National Park are popular tourist attractions. The Columbia Falls Aluminum Company has been in operation since 1955. This county specializes in crops of peppermint, Christmas trees, cherries, barley, wheat, oats, and potatoes.

Garfield

Population: 1,233
Area: 4,668.2
People/Sq Mi: 0.3
Established: 1919

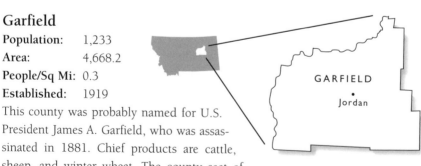

This county was probably named for U.S. President James A. Garfield, who was assassinated in 1881. Chief products are cattle, sheep, and winter wheat. The county seat of Jordan was founded by pioneer Arthur Jordan. This is one of the most isolated parts of the state, but not as isolated as it was before telephone service was established in 1935. The northern part of the county is called "The Breaks" because of the eroded landscape leading down to the Missouri River. It has been rich in dinosaur finds over the years, including the first discovery of a Tyrannosaurus rex.

Gallatin

Population: 73,243
Area: 2,605.8
People/Sq Mi: 28.1
Established: 1865

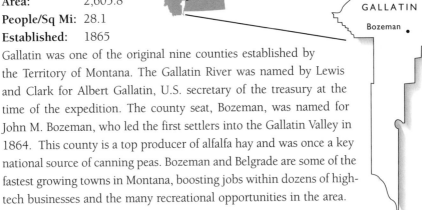

GALLATIN
Bozeman

Gallatin was one of the original nine counties established by the Territory of Montana. The Gallatin River was named by Lewis and Clark for Albert Gallatin, U.S. secretary of the treasury at the time of the expedition. The county seat, Bozeman, was named for John M. Bozeman, who led the first settlers into the Gallatin Valley in 1864. This county is a top producer of alfalfa hay and was once a key national source of canning peas. Bozeman and Belgrade are some of the fastest growing towns in Montana, boosting jobs within dozens of high-tech businesses and the many recreational opportunities in the area.

Glacier

Population: 13,250
Area: 2,994.7
People/Sq Mi: 4.4
Established: 1919

GLACIER
Cut Bank

Glacier National Park was the inspiration for the name for this county bordering the Park's eastern edge. The Blackfeet Indian Reservation covers much of the county. Cut Bank, the county seat, was named for a deep gorge made by the Cut Bank Creek. The Blackfeet described the creek as "the river that cuts into the white clay banks." Grain and livestock production are the basic industries today, but in the 1920s, the area enjoyed one of the state's first oil booms. The area is home to numerous Hutterite colonies, where members live simply and manage very successful agricultural operations.

Golden Valley

Population: 1,047
Area: 1,175.5
People/Sq Mi: 0.9
Established: 1920

GOLDEN VALLEY
Ryegate

This county was cut from parts of Musselshell and Sweet Grass Counties and given the picturesque name to attract settlers to the area. One possible source for the name of the county seat of Ryegate was the rich field of rye grass that was the building site for this homestead-era boom-town. The first settlers were English and Scottish cattle ranchers, many of whom established some of the state's most prosperous cattle operations.

Granite

Population: 2,892
Area: 1,727.5
People/Sq Mi: 1.7
Established: 1893

GRANITE

Philipsburg

Granite Mountain, whose mines produced more than $40 million worth of gold and silver in the 1880s, gives the county its name. The county seat, Philipsburg, was named for Philip Deidesheimer, the first superintendent of the St. Louis-Montana Gold and Silver Mining Company, later known as the Philipsburg Mining Company. Today, Philipsburg's restored main street highlights the glory of its mining past and is home to antique stores, gem shops, and a candy-making business that exports treats throughout the West. The forks of the blue-ribbon trout stream of Rock Creek meander through rich ranching country.

Hill

Population: 16,350
Area: 2,896.4
People/Sq Mi: 5.6
Established: 1912

HILL

Havre

This county was named for James J. Hill, builder of the Great Northern Railway and promoter of home-steading in Montana. Havre, the county seat, was named for the French seaport of Le Havre by railway officials, but in Montana, it is pronounced "HAV-er." Fort Assiniboine was constructed to police the Blackfeet and Assiniboine tribes in the late 1870s. The fort was maintained until 1911, when it was sold to the state for an agricultural experiment station. This county encompasses part of the Rocky Boy's Indian Reservation. Today, the county is a top producer of spring wheat.

Jefferson

Population: 10,499
Area: 1,656.7
People/Sq Mi: 6.3
Established: 1865

Boulder

JEFFERSON

One of the original nine counties of the Montana Territory, Jefferson County holds the Jefferson River, named by explorers Lewis and Clark in 1805 for President

Thomas Jefferson. The county seat was first at Jefferson City, then Radersburg, and finally, Boulder. Jefferson County boasts the well-preserved ghost town of Elkhorn, the site of a major silver mine in the 1880s. Today, the Golden Sunlight Mine and the Montana Tunnels Mine are large-scale, modern gold mining operations.

Judith Basin

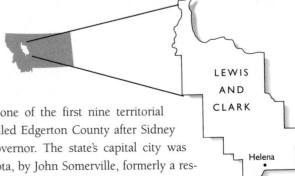

Population: 2,329
Area: 1,869.9
People/Sq Mi: 1.2
Established: 1920

Captain William Clark named the Judith River in 1805 to honor his cousin, Miss Judith (Julia) Hancock of Virginia, whom he later married. Although this county is known for the mining of Yogo sapphires, its mainstays are wheat and cattle. The county seat of Stanford was named for either Major James T. Stanford of Great Falls, or for Stanfordville, New York, the hometown of J. E. Bower, an early rancher and sheepman. Charles M. Russell, Montana's famous western artist, lived and created many of his paintings in this area during its heyday as rich open range cattle country.

Lake

Population: 26,507
Area: 1,493.8
People/Sq Mi: 17.7
Established: 1923

Flathead Lake inspired the name of this county, one of the last counties to be formed in Montana. The town of St. Ignatius was originally St. Ignatius Mission, founded by Jesuit missionaries in 1854. The county seat of Polson was named for David Polson, a stockman from the Mission valley. The area is famed for its annual crop of sweet cherries. Much of the southern half of the county is the Flathead Indian Reservation, home to the Confederated Salish and Kootenai Tribes.

Lewis and Clark

Population: 57,137
Area: 3,461
People/Sq Mi: 16.5
Established: 1865

When originally created as one of the first nine territorial counties, this county was called Edgerton County after Sidney Edgerton, first Territorial governor. The state's capital city was named after Helena, Minnesota, by John Somerville, formerly a resident of that Midwestern town. The site of early gold discoveries, the city was originally called Last Chance City; today, Main Street is also called Last Chance Gulch. The hills of Helena are home to some of the state's most stunning historical architecture—hundreds of stately Victorian-era homes, the Islamic minaret of the Helena Civic Center, the double spires of the Cathedral of St. Helena, the elegant Carroll College campus, and last but far from least, the copper doom and Lady Liberty of the newly renovated State Capitol.

Liberty

Population: 2,055
Area: 1,429.8
People/Sq Mi: 1.4
Established: 1920

LIBERTY

• Chester

The name most likely reflects the patriotic feelings of early settlers, who were stockmen, followed by homesteaders. Wheat growing and oil and gas production have been important industries. The county seat of Chester was named by a railroad telegrapher after his hometown of Chester, Pennsylvania. The Marias River winds for more than sixty miles through the county's rolling prairie, before spilling into Lake Elwell, a twenty-seven mile long lake formed behind Tiber Dam.

Lincoln

Population: 18,835
Area: 3,612
People/Sq Mi: 5.2
Established: 1909

LINCOLN

• Libby

This county was named for President Abraham Lincoln. Indians who lived in this area prior to non-Indian exploration and settlement were mostly members of the Kootenai tribe, who hunted, fished, and cultivated a native "tobacco" plant along the rivers. The first commerce of this area was fur trapping and trading during the early 1800s. For much of the 20th century, mining, logging operations, and sawmills were the dominant industries. In operation for nearly seventy years, the large vermiculite mine in Libby produced 80% of the world's supply of vermiculite and was a significant local employer. Since closure in 1990, the W. R. Grace mine has been blamed for dozens of deaths and illnesses among Libby residents due to exposure to the asbestos fibers in vermiculite. In recent years, the Environmental Protection Agency has been cleaning up the contamination. More than 90 percent of this county is within two national forests, Kootenai and a small part of Kaniksu.

McCone

Population: 1,818
Area: 2,642.6
People/Sq Mi: 0.7
Established: 1919

State Senator George McCone worked to create this county out of Dawson and Richland counties. Before the homesteading era, this was open range cattle country. Today, the area economy is based in wheat, ranching and oil production. Circle, the county seat, was named for the circle brand of the Cross and Twiggly cattle outfit. South of Circle are the Big Sheep Mountains, once home to the now-extinct Audubon mountain sheep.

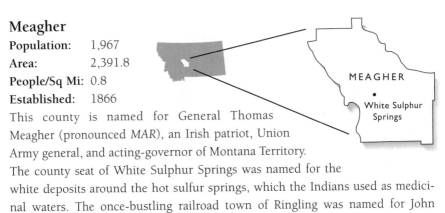

Madison

Population: 6,967
Area: 3,568.6
People/Sq Mi: 1.9
Established: 1865

Lewis and Clark named the Madison River in honor of then U.S. Secretary of State, James Madison. Virginia City, hub of the prosperous area gold fields, was incorporated as Montana's first town in 1864. First called Varina in honor of the spouse of Jefferson Davis, president of the Confederate South, the name was changed to Virginia by G. G. Bissell, a local judge and strong Unionist. The Old-West flavored county seat of Ennis offers fly-fishing outfitters, antique stores, and Western outfitting shops to help visitors enjoy the many recreational opportunities in the Madison Mountain Range and along the Madison River.

Meagher

Population: 1,967
Area: 2,391.8
People/Sq Mi: 0.8
Established: 1866

This county is named for General Thomas Meagher (pronounced *MAR*), an Irish patriot, Union Army general, and acting-governor of Montana Territory. The county seat of White Sulphur Springs was named for the white deposits around the hot sulfur springs, which the Indians used as medicinal waters. The once-bustling railroad town of Ringling was named for John Ringling, one of the "Ringling Bros." of circus fame. He also built a local railroad line that eventually became a branch of the "Milwaukee" railroad. In the 1900s, the family once considered establishing a circus headquarters on the over 100,000 acres they owned in area. The county boosts some of the best all-season recreation venues in Montana—hundreds of miles of trails for snowmobiling, cross-county skiing, and downhill skiing, in addition to the Smith River, one of the country's premier trout streams.

Mineral

Population: 3,884
Area: 1,219.9
People/Sq Mi: 3.2
Established: 1914

The many mines and mining prospects in this mountainous area inspired the name. In 1870, over 3,000 miners flocked to the Cedar Creek mining district, only to leave for more prosperous gold fields a few years later. Over 80 percent of the county is federally owned, mostly in forest lands. The 1910 fires destroyed much of those forests, but during the Great Depression, many Civilian Conservation Corp workers were employed to grow evergreen seedlings and to replant the area. The county economy was largely based on rail-roading, logging and lumber production until the mid-1990s.

Missoula

Population: 98,616
Area: 2,598.2
People/Sq Mi: 37.9
Established: 1865

Created as part of Washington Territory in 1860, Missoula became one of the orig-inal counties of Montana Territory in 1865. The source of the county name and its main town and county seat, Missoula, remain in dis-pute. One version says that Indians used to call Hellgate Canyon "Issoul," meaning horrible. *The Montana Almanac* of 1959 suggests it is a contraction of the Indian word, "Im-i-sul-e-etikee," meaning "by or near the place of fear or ambush." Another version says it is a Salish word meaning "River of Awe." While Missoula was Montana's timber industry center for more than a century, today it is a booming retail center and home to The University of Montana, the Northern Region headquarters for the U.S. Forest Service, and an ever-expanding medical community.

Musselshell

Population: 4,464
Area: 1,867.2
People/Sq Mi: 2.4
Established: 1911

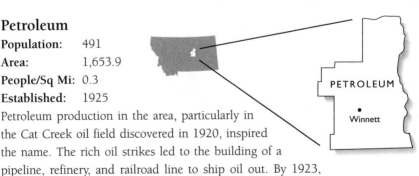

This county got its name from the Musselshell River, which was named by Lewis and Clark, who found mussel shells along the riverbank. This region was home to the Crow tribe before the arrival of white settlers. The county seat of Roundup was an annual gathering point for cattle that grazed on the open ranges of the valley. When the "Milwaukee" railroad arrived in Central Montana in 1907, it spurred not only homesteading in the area but also development of the area's rich coal deposits. The mines around Roundup soon became a main source of fuel for railroad steam locomotives throughout the northwest. Coal mining continues as a core economic activity today, with a railroad and power plant planned in conjunction with the Bull Mountain Mine.

Park

Population: 15,840
Area: 2,656.2
People/Sq Mi: 6.0
Established: 1887

Park County was named for its proximity to Yellowstone National Park. The area has played a key role in many of the major historical movements in Montana—as Indian hunting grounds, fur trading center, gold discovery, prosperous cattle grazing, lumbering, railroading, and tourism magnet, to name a few. The county seat is Livingston, named after Crawford, Charles, or Johnson Livingston, all directors of the Northern Pacific Railroad.

Petroleum

Population: 491
Area: 1,653.9
People/Sq Mi: 0.3
Established: 1925

Petroleum production in the area, particularly in the Cat Creek oil field discovered in 1920, inspired the name. The rich oil strikes led to the building of a pipeline, refinery, and railroad line to ship oil out. By 1923, Winnett had a population of 2,000 people. However, by 1933, the county seat of

Winnett had lost three-quarters of its population. It was named for Walter John Winnett, a local cattle owner, freighter, and store owner. The 2003 census counted fewer citizens here than in any other Montana county, 419. Today, the area's primary economic activity is ranching.

Phillips

Population: 4,271
Area: 5,139.9
People/Sq Mi: 0.8
Established: 1915

This county was carved from parts of Blaine and Valley counties and named for Ben D. Phillips, a well-known area cattle rancher and mine owner. An official of the Great Northern Railway named Malta, the county seat, after the Mediterranean island. From 1870 to 1900, the area was the hub of a cattle empire that reached from Glasgow to Havre and from the Missouri Breaks to Canada. Today, the county remains home to many ranchers, abundant wildlife, and unlimited outdoor recreation. The Phillips County Historical Museum in Malta offers outstanding dinosaur exhibits and local history.

Pondera

Population: 6,166
Area: 1,624.7
People/Sq Mi: 3.8
Established: 1919

The county was created from parts of Chouteau and Teton Counties. This was Blackfeet territory prior to fur traders, stock-raisers, and agricultural settlers; the Blackfeet Indian Reservation now occupies the northern corners of the county. Most of the available land was homesteaded by 1912. Wheat and barley production are the county's main industries today. The county seat, Conrad, was named for W. G. Conrad of the Conrad Investment Co., a major landowner, banker, and politician.

Powder River

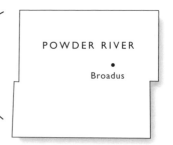

Population: 1,834
Area: 3,297.3
People/Sq Mi: 0.6
Established: 1919

The Powder River, running through the county that shares its name, is thought to be named for the gunpowder-colored sand on its banks. Lewis and Clark called it the Red Stone River because of the color of the streamside rocks. Said to be "a mile wide and an inch deep," it often runs dry. During World War I, the large contingent of Montana soldiers overseas were known by their battle cry of "Powder River, let 'er buck." The county seat, Broadus, is named for the Broaddus family. The current spelling is the result of a misspelling in Washington, D.C., when the town's post office was established. This is cattle and oil country.

Powell

Population: 7,066
Area: 2,326
People/Sq Mi: 3.0
Established: 1901

In this area, so important in Montana's earliest days of settlement, gold was discovered as early as 1852. A few years later, James and Granville Stuart claimed an official gold find that developed into a major placer mining operation, Gold Creek. While miners combed the many drainages and valleys of this area for their fortunes, others, such John Grant, saw treasure in the rich grass of the valleys. In 1897, the new smelter town of Anaconda won the county seat away from Deer Lodge, but in 1901, the citizens of Deer Lodge and the northern part of the county succeeded in splitting the county and named it for the major landmark, Mount Powell. The town is the site of the first territorial prison and the present-day state penitentiary.

POWELL

Deer Lodge

Prairie

Population: 1,154
Area: 1,736.6
People/Sq Mi: 0.7
Established: 1915

The name of this county well describes its terrain. Here, the Powder River joins with the Yellowstone River near the county seat of Terry. The town is named for General Alfred H. Terry, who commanded the 1876 expeditions against the Indians in connection with Custer's campaign. Sheep raising and coal mining are the main industries. The Cameron Gallery in Terry features the photographs of Evelyn Cameron, whose exceptional eye captured the everyday lives of eastern Montana homesteaders.

PRAIRIE

•Terry

Ravalli

Population: 38,662
Area: 2,394.3
People/Sq Mi: 16.1
Established: 1893

Formed from a portion of Missoula County, it was named for Father Anthony Ravalli, a Jesuit missionary who came to the region in 1845. Stevensville was the first county seat, but Hamilton replaced it in 1898. Hamilton probably got its name from J. W. Hamilton, an early pioneer from whom the right of way for the Northern Pacific Railroad was acquired. Some believe it was named after J. T. Hamilton, who surveyed the townsite for copper king, Marcus Daly's future lumber town. This basically rural county has experienced two decades of high population growth, attributed to the expansion of several bio-tech facilities and the attractiveness of a suburban life-style close to Missoula.

Richland

Population: 9,155
Area: 2,084.1
People/Sq Mi: 4.4
Established: 1914

Like other Montana counties created during the homesteading era, the name was chosen to attract settlers to the area. An important fur-trading area in the early 1800s, this county was first settled by stockmen, who were followed by homesteaders after the turn of the twentieth century. The county seat of Sidney was named for Sidney Walters, the son of a pioneer family in the area. This county is a top producer of sugar beets. The county also has dairy and grain farms and a sugar beet processing facility.

Roosevelt

Population: 10,455
Area: 2,355.6
People/Sq Mi: 4.4
Established: 1919

This county was cut from Sheridan County and named for Theodore Roosevelt, president of the United States and ranch owner in neighboring North Dakota. The Fort Peck Indian Reservation, home to Assiniboine and Sioux Indians, covers much of the county. The county seat is Wolf Point, whose name might have come from a stack of frozen gray wolf carcasses left by fur trappers along the river where the steamboats landed. During the steamboat era on the Missouri

River, Wolf Point was trading post and a refueling stop for the big wood burners. Today, it is a major storage center for Montana grains.

Rosebud

Population:	9,303
Area:	5,012.4
People/Sq Mi:	1.9
Established:	1901

The Rosebud River and the county were named for the profusion of wild rose bushes along the river banks. The county seat of Forsyth was named for Captain James W. Forsyth, one of the first U.S. Army officers to land in this area by steamer. The town of Colstrip grew up around what was once known as the largest "open pit" coal mine in the world. The strip mines near Colstrip remain one of the most productive and valuable coal mining operations in the nation.

Forsyth

ROSEBUD

Sanders

Population:	10,455
Area:	2,762.3
People/Sq Mi:	3.8
Established:	1905

Wilber Fisk Sanders, pioneer, vigilante, and U.S. senator from Montana inspired the name for this county. The county seat, Thompson Falls, was named for David Thompson, the man who surveyed much of the northern Rocky Mountain area for British fur interests. Wild horses once found good winter range in the protected areas near Plains, formerly call Horse Plains. The 35-mile-long Noxon Rapids Reservoir, located in this county, is a growing recreational area.

SANDERS

Thompson Falls

Sheridan

Population:	3,668
Area:	1,676.7
People/Sq Mi:	2.2
Established:	1913

Plentywood

SHERIDAN

This county was one of the last areas to be settled in Montana. It was named for General Phillip H. Sheridan, a Union cavalry leader. The county seat of Plentywood is said to have been named when a cattle outfit seeking wood as they crossed the treeless prairie was directed to a place of "plenty wood." The Sheridan County Museum features an extensive mural, depicting the colorful history of the county, which includes some "wild West" adventures along the Outlaw Trail to Canada. Sheridan County's main industries are wheat and oil production.

Silver Bow

Population: 33,208
Area: 718
People/Sq Mi: 46.2
Established: 1881

The county of Silver Bow and the city of Butte are consolidated under an elected-executive form of government. The name
might have originated from Silver Bow Creek, where legend has it that three prospectors saw a shaft of sun shining on the creek. The county seat, first called Butte City,
was known for a century as "the richest hill on earth." Miners named the city for the
peak called "Big Butte," which rises 6,369 feet above sea level. Although Silver Bow
is the smallest county in land area, it has been of great economic importance to the
state for over 100 years. The mines of the Atlantic Richfield Company (formerly the
Anaconda Copper Mining Company) were closed in 1983, but mining operations
were reopened in 1985 by Montana Resources, a division of the Washington
Corporation.

Stillwater

Population: 8,195
Area: 1,794.7
People/Sq Mi: 4.6
Established: 1913

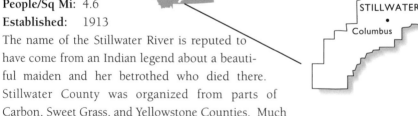

The name of the Stillwater River is reputed to
have come from an Indian legend about a beautiful maiden and her betrothed who died there.
Stillwater County was organized from parts of
Carbon, Sweet Grass, and Yellowstone Counties. Much
of the county was once an area favored by the Crow tribe. Stillwater's county seat
is Columbus, which began as a stage station on the Yellowstone Trail. It is a shipping center for the farm and ranch lands around it. The Columbus quarry furnished the stone for the state capitol in Helena. Today, the Russian-owned
Stillwater Mining Company is one of the world's top sources of chromium and palladium. In recent years, expansion of mining has made this county one of the
fastest growing in the state.

Sweet Grass

Population: 3,604
Area: 1,855.2
People/Sq Mi: 1.9
Established: 1895

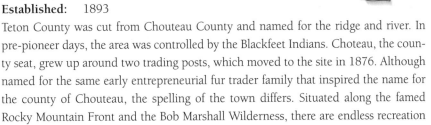

SWEET GRASS

Big Timber

This county, named for the rich grassland in the
area, was originally reserved for the Crow tribe, but
was opened to non-Indian settlement in 1891. The
county seat, Big Timber, was probably named for the
very large cottonwoods. This town gained fame in 1892
as the origin of the greatest single railroad shipment of wool. Like
its neighbor, Stillwater County, platinum mining has sparked population growth
since 2000. The county is framed on the northwest by the spectacular Crazy
Mountains and on the south by the Absaroka Beartooth Wilderness, with many of
the highest mountains in Montana.

Teton

Population: 6,369
Area: 2,272.6
People/Sq Mi: 2.8
Established: 1893

Choteau

TETON

Teton County was cut from Chouteau County and named for the ridge and river. In
pre-pioneer days, the area was controlled by the Blackfeet Indians. Choteau, the county seat, grew up around two trading posts, which moved to the site in 1876. Although
named for the same early entrepreneurial fur trader family that inspired the name for
the county of Chouteau, the spelling of the town differs. Situated along the famed
Rocky Mountain Front and the Bob Marshall Wilderness, there are endless recreation
opportunities nearby, including hiking, wildlife viewing, fishing, hunting and
dinosaur digging. It is also part of the rich Montana grain growing area called the
"Golden Triangle."

Toole

Population: 5,337
Area: 1,910.9
People/Sq Mi: 2.8
Established: 1914

TOOLE

• Shelby

Joseph K. Toole, the first governor of the State of
Montana, inspired the name for this county, which was formed
from parts of Hill and Teton counties. Wheat and oil are its main industries. The county seat of Shelby is named for Peter R. Shelby, an executive of the
Great Northern Railway. The Kevin-Sunburst oil field, discovered in 1920, turned

this homesteading area into a wild boom town. Shelby gained fame after it hosted a world championship heavyweight-boxing match in 1923 between Jack Dempsey and Tom Gibbons. Shelby is the site of a large private correctional facility.

Treasure

Population:	735
Area:	978.9
People/Sq Mi:	0.8
Established:	1919

This county, originally Sioux Indian territory, was named to attract settlers to the area. Two important early historic sites include Manuel Lisa's 1807 fur trading post near the mouth of the Bighorn and Fort Cass, the first fort built by the American Fur Company on the Yellowstone. The county seat of Hysham is named for Charles Hysham, a Texas trail herder with the Flying E Ranch. The main agricultural products of the county are cattle, hay, and sugar beets.

Valley

Population:	7,349
Area:	4,920.9
People/Sq Mi:	1.5
Established:	1893

Named for its location in the Milk River Valley, this county is one of the largest in the state. This region was a major homesteader destination in the early 1900s. Glasgow, the county seat on the Milk River, is one of the oldest communities in northeast Montana. During the building of the Fort Peck Dam, it was a bustling area. An official of the Great Northern Railway named it after Glasgow, Scotland. The Fort Peck Indian Reservation covers the eastern part of the county. Fort Peck Lake is the largest body of water in Montana, with a shoreline equal to the coast of California.

Wheatland

Population:	2,106
Area:	1,423.2
People/Sq Mi:	1.5
Established:	1917

Before the days of extensive wheat fields and sheep grazing, the area that is now Wheatland County was Crow Indian country. A gold find in the Little Belt Mountains brought prospectors to the area in 1870. Stock growing began in the early 1880s, and with the establishment of two railroads in the early 1900s, the homesteaders arrived. The county seat of Harlowton was named for Richard Harlow, who built the Montana Central Railroad, affectionately known to its riders as "The Jawbone."

Wibaux

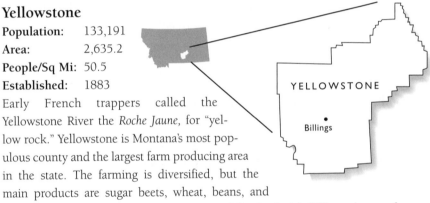

Population: 977
Area: 889.3
People/Sq Mi: 1.1
Established: 1914

An early Montana cattle baron, Pierre Wibaux (pronounced "WEE-bow"), inspired the name for this county and its county seat. In the late 1800s, the Northern Pacific Railroad built a stockyard here and stimulated the economy. Wibaux was originally known as Mingusville, supposedly after two early pioneers, Minnie and Gus. The area is a blend of badlands and rolling hills, offering a wide variety of prairie wildlife.

Yellowstone

Population: 133,191
Area: 2,635.2
People/Sq Mi: 50.5
Established: 1883

Early French trappers called the Yellowstone River the *Roche Jaune,* for "yellow rock." Yellowstone is Montana's most populous county and the largest farm producing area in the state. The farming is diversified, but the main products are sugar beets, wheat, beans, and livestock. Billings, the county seat, is named for Frederick Billings, lawyer, former president of the Northern Pacific Railroad, and philanthropist. As Montana's largest city, it is a major shipping center for cattle and other agricultural products. Captain William Clark spotted an unusual pillar of rock near Billings and called it "Pompy's Tower," for Sacagawea's son Jean Baptiste, whom he nicknamed "Little Pomp." Today it is known as Pompey's Pillar, renamed when the Lewis and Clark journals were published, and it is a national historic landmark.

Sources for population and land area figures from U.S. Bureau of the Census, compiled by Census and Economic Information Center, Montana Department of Commerce.

State Symbols

The following descriptions of Montana's state symbols appear in chronological order, according to when the legislature designated them as "official."

The Great Seal

The official Great Seal of the State of Montana is kept under the custody of the Secretary of State and is used to validate all official state documents. It is impressed or embossed directly on the documents.

The designing of the seal was one of the first acts of the Montana territorial government, established in 1864. After choosing "gold and silver" as the state motto, a special committee debated whether to denote the phrase in English or in Spanish. Unfortunately, the group's knowledge of the latter language was limited, and the selection of "Oro el Plata" had to be corrected to "Oro y Plata" before the final version of the Great Seal was approved by the territorial legislature.

The seal shows the Great Falls of the Missouri River; mountain scenery; a central depiction of a miner's pick, a shovel, and a plow; and the state motto along the bottom of the circle.

The seal pays tribute to major components of the history of the state. Agriculture, mining, mountains, water, and timber have been and will continue to be the source of wealth, controversy, and development in Montana.

Bitterroot

The bitterroot, *Lewisia rediviva,* was selected as Montana's first official symbol in 1895 and is the floral emblem of Montana. The state flower is a member of the purslane family of New World herbs and shrubs. It was highly valued for food by the Indians of the Northwest long before Meriwether Lewis and William Clark collected the exquisite lily-like, pink blossoms on their 1806 homeward trip through the valleys of western Montana.

Though universal suffrage was many years away, women were allowed to vote with the men on the question of the state flower in late 1894. It was no contest. The bitterroot garnered 3,621 votes. Evening primrose finished a distant second with 787, followed by wild rose with 668.

The bitterroot was such an important part of the diet of the Salish, Kootenai, Pend d'Oreille, Spokane, and Nez Perce tribes that spring tribal migrations were planned to find the plant along familiar riverbanks and hillsides. The women of the tribes used a digging stick to gather the root, prized for its starch and sugar content.

The bitterroot can be found on slopes and ridges on both sides of the continental divide of western Montana. It can thrive on little moisture through the summer but likes lots of sunshine. The low-set blossoms flower in late spring and early summer. The rosette of twelve to eighteen leaves ranges from deep rose-red to the more typical pink, and the blossoms turn white after a few days in the sun.

The Flag

In the spring of 1898, Colonel Harry C. Kessler mustered and trained a group of volunteers at Fort William Henry Harrison, west of Helena, for the war against Spain. Kessler commissioned a special banner to distinguish the First Montana Infantry, U.S.V., from other units in the "Philippine Insurrection." An unknown seamstress embroidered her interpretation of the state's Great Seal on the dark blue background of a 60- by 44-inch silk flag. The 1905 Legislative Assembly honored the First Montana Infantry by establishing an exact rendition of their flag as the official state flag.

In 1981, the word "Montana" was added to the flag, above the seal.

Western Meadowlark

Explorer Meriwether Lewis noted the western meadowlark, *Sturnella neglecta,* in the June 22, 1805, entry of his journal made while crossing what is now Montana. Lewis described the meadowlark's similarities with the eastern meadowlark of his homeland but commented that the song of the western cousin was richer and more varied. It consists of a loud, clear, melodic warble.

The chunky, brown-speckled bird has a bright yellow vest and black, V-shaped necklace. There is a patch of white on each side of its short, white tail. Its flight pattern consists of several short, rapid wing beats alternated with brief periods of sailing.

In 1930, Montana's schoolchildren were polled to select the bird that most represented their state. The responses overwhelmingly favored the western meadowlark. The 1931 Legislature agreed with the choice and declared the western meadowlark the official bird of Montana. The states of Kansas, Nebraska, North Dakota, Oregon, and Wyoming also designated the meadowlark as state bird.

Ponderosa Pine

The majestic ponderosa pine can be found on many hills and mountains of Montana. It is the dominant pine of the entire Rocky Mountain region, from Canada to Mexico. *Pinus ponderosa* was invaluable to settlers, who harvested millions of board feet of ponderosa lumber for railroad ties, mining braces, telegraph poles, bridges, and homes.

At maturity (about 150 years), a ponderosa pine is approximately 20 to 30 inches in diameter and from 60 to 200 feet tall. Its seed cones are 3 to 5 inches long, and its needles measure 8 to 10 inches. The species has a number of other popular names, including bull pine, black jack pine, western pitch pine, and western yellow pine.

In 1908, Helena's schoolchildren picked the ponderosa pine as the tree that best represented Montana, but it was not until the Montana Federation of Garden Clubs waged a yearlong campaign that the 1949 Legislature passed a resolution to officially honor this "king of the forest."

The largest known ponderosa pine in Montana stands at a Department of Fish, Wildlife & Parks viewing site about 3.4 miles up Fish Creek Road off Interstate 90 between Alberton and Superior. It measures 78 inches in diameter and is more than 194 feet tall.

Montana, The Song

The song "Montana" was virtually an overnight sensation when it was first introduced in 1910. A well-known songwriter and theatrical producer, Joseph Howard, had written several musical hits of the day, including "Shuffle Off to Buffalo" and "I Wonder Who's Kissing Her Now." He and his troupe were touring the state with a performance of *The Goddess of Liberty*. At an after-theater party in Butte, Howard accepted a challenge by his hostess to write a song about Montana. He retired to the music room and worked out a tune. Another guest, Charles C. Cohen, city editor for the *Butte Miner,* helped pen the lyrics.

When Howard got to Helena later that month with his troupe, he found an audience eager to hear the catchy "Montana" song. They requested twelve encores of the new song before proceeding with the play. At a social gathering following the performance, Governor Edwin L. Norris enthusiastically proclaimed the tune Montana's official song. The Legislature made it official in 1945.

The lyrics go, in part:

Tell me of that Treasure State,　　*Montana, Montana—*
story always new.　　*glory of the West,*
Tell of its beauties grand　　*Of all the states from coast to coast*
and its hearts so true . . . .　　*you're easily the best.*

Bluebunch Wheatgrass

Of the many official Montana symbols, the official grass—bluebunch wheatgrass—was the most important to Montana's first inhabitants as well as the later settlers. Both depended on the wildlife and domesticated animals that were nourished by this important native grass. The 1973 Legislature officially recognized the grass, with encouragement from a community development group from Havre.

Bluebunch wheatgrass (*Agropyron spicatum,* or pursh) also has the widest range of all Montana's official symbols. It is found from border to border in all types of soil. It greens up early in spring and peeks out from under the earliest fall snows to provide wildlife habitat, valuable forage for all types of animals, and protection of the watershed

Sapphire and Moss Agate

The 1969 Montana Legislature honored both the sapphire and the moss agate as the state gemstones.

Many variations of the exquisite moss agate are found in abundance along the Yellowstone River and are sought after by hobbyists and jewelry makers. Contrary to its name, a moss agate does not really contain fossilized moss. It also goes by the names landscape agate, scenic agate, Montana agate, plume agate, and Yellowstone River agate. The best spot to find the agate is in terraced gravel deposits on the hills above and on sand and gravel bars along the Yellowstone River, from Billings to Sidney.

The world-famous Yogo sapphires are one of Montana's most stunning exports, with over $40 million in precious gemstones over the years. The beautiful cornflower-blue gems even grace the Royal Crown Jewel Collection in London. The world's largest cut Yogo, 10.2 carats, is housed in the Smithsonian Institution in Washington, D.C.

The Yogo sapphire is unique for its ability to retain its brilliance under artificial light. Other types of sapphires generally absorb such light and appear black and lusterless.

Blackspotted Cutthroat Trout

A poll of the state's 200,000 resident fishing enthusiasts inspired the 1977 Legislature to designate the blackspotted cutthroat trout as the official Montana state fish.

The cutthroat species, *Oncorhynhus clarki,* bears the name of Captain William Clark. The taxonomy also honors his partner, Meriwether Lewis, by naming the westslope cutthroat *Oncorhynhus clarki lewisi.* The journals of the Lewis and Clark Expedition mention a "sumptuous" meal of 16- to 23-inch-long blackspotted cutthroat trout caught at the Great Falls of the Missouri River.

Today, the number of blackspotted cutthroat trout is depressed in much of the Upper Missouri River drainage, and it has been designated a sensitive species by the USDA Forest Service. The general decline of this fish is thought by many to be a serious indicator of wider ecosystem degradation.

Cutthroats have been overfished in many areas because they are generally easier to catch than other trout species. They are also highly vulnerable to competition from other species and to hybridization with rainbow trout.

The Grizzly Bear

In 1982, more than 55,000 students in 425 schools joined in the selection of an official state animal. They nominated seventy-four animals, compiled voter registration lists, conducted lively campaigns, and staged primary and general elections. In the final statewide tally of votes, the grizzly bear, *Ursus arctos horribilis,* won by a large margin over the runner-up, elk.

Montana Melody

A proposal was made in 1983 to replace "Montana" with a more recently composed song, "Montana Melody," written by Carleen Harvey and LeGrande Harvey. Lawmakers were reluctant to trade in the old song for the newer model, even though most state residents admit knowing only the refrain of the old one. As a compromise, "Montana Melody" was declared the official state ballad.

Duck-Billed Dinosaur

The duck-billed dinosaur, *Maiasaura peeblesorum*, was selected by the 1985 Legislature as the official Montana state fossil after middle school students from Livingston collected eight thousand petition signatures from sixty schools in the state.

The name Maiasaura means "good mother lizard"; peeblesorum honors the Peebles family, on whose Choteau-area ranch the discoveries were made. The area, known as Egg Mountain, has the world's largest known accumulation of dinosaur fossils.

The unearthing of the remains has provided valuable evidence that duck-billed dinosaurs nested in extensive colonies and had nests 6 feet in diameter that contained as many as 20 eggs. The duck-billed dinosaur, when newly hatched, was not quite 14 inches long and weighed about 1.5 pounds but matured to measure more than 30 feet long and weigh about 3 tons.

Mourning Cloak

The 2001 Legislature named the Mourning Cloak as the official state butterfly. Once again, schoolchildren and garden clubs had a role in promoting a state symbol. The Mourning Cloak, *Nymphalis antiopa,* is a sturdy, long-lived, and beautiful resident of Montana. It is a member of the butterfly sub-family called anglewings because of the ragged, angled edges on both their fore and hind wings. The mourning cloak has a broad, cream-colored band along the edge of its wings and sports an inside row of iridescent blue dots. When folded, the wings hide their beauty to resemble tree bark or twigs.

The winter-hardy Mourning Cloak can live as long as 11 months. They emerge from cocoons in July and eat heartily through the fall, preparing for hibernation. Come the first of March, you may see on fluttering through the woods or in your garden. They may be looking for sap on trees that were injured in winter storms.

LEGAL STATE HOLIDAYS

Each Sunday
New Year's Day, January 1
Martin Luther King Jr. Day, the third Monday in January
Presidents Day, the third Monday in February
Memorial Day, the last Monday in May
Independence Day, July 4
Labor Day, the first Monday in September
Columbus Day, the second Monday in October
Veterans' Day, November 11
Thanksgiving Day, the fourth Thursday in November
Christmas Day, December 25
State general election day, the first Tuesday after the first
   Monday in November

If any of the holidays above falls upon a Sunday, the Monday following is a legal holiday. All other days are business days, including the Friday before a holiday that occurs on a Saturday.

NOTABLE

Dorothy M. Johnson (1905–1984)

Born in Iowa, she grew up in Whitefish and became one of the most beloved portrayers of the history and heroes of the American West. The movies *The Man Who Shot Liberty Valance*, *The Hanging Tree*, and *A Man Called Horse* are based on Johnson's stories, which appeared regularly in many national magazines, including the *Saturday Evening Post*. After a 15-year career as a book and magazine editor in New York, she came home and worked as an editor at the *Whitefish Pilot*, later teaching journalism at The University of Montana in Missoula. She died at her home there.

MONTANANS

Gary Cooper
(1901–1961)

One of America's favorite movie stars was born Frank James Cooper in Helena. Cooper began as a silent film extra during the 1920s and by 1937 was America's highest-paid entertainer. He appeared in more than 90 movies and won Academy Awards for his performances in *Sergeant York* (1941) and *High Noon* (1952). One of his last roles as a Western hero was as Doc Frail in *The Hanging Tree*, in a script by Montana author Dorothy M. Johnson. Some of his other time-honored films include *The Virginian, For Whom the Bell Tolls, Mr. Deeds Goes to Town, The Pride of the Yankees,* and *A Farewell to Arms.*

COURTESY OF THE CASCADE COUNTY HISTORICAL SOCIETY

Bertha M. Bower
(1871–1940)

When Bertha Muzzey Bower's first serialized stories and novels were published in the early 1900s under the name B. M. Bower, few people would have believed the author was not a young, male ranch hand like her key character Chip and the rest of the "Happy Family" bunkhouse gang portrayed in her stories. With the publication of *Chip of the Flying U* in 1906, B. M. Bower launched a long and successful career in writing popular Westerns. Between 1904 and 1940, she published more than 68 novels, some 200 short stories, and numerous screenplays for silent films. Most were set in her central-Montana home "stomping grounds" in the Big Sandy area and other parts of the West where she later lived. Between 1914 and 1939, Hollywood produced four different film versions of her "Chip" stories. Some reviewers credited her with a realistic view of western life, and others criticized her books as attempts to spice up western adventures with love stories aimed a female audience. Bower's books have remained popular and collectible, with a reprint of *Chip of the Flying U* in 1995, complete with the 1906 illustrations by her good friend, Charles M. Russell.

Further Reading

Ashby, Norma B., and Rex C. Myers. *Symbols of Montana*. Helena: Montana Historical Society, 1989.

Bradshaw, Glenda Clay, comp. *Montana's Historical Highway Markers*. Helena: Montana Historical Society, revised edition, 1994.

Cheney, Roberta Carkeek. *Names on the Face of Montana: The Story of Montana's Place Names*. Missoula: Mountain Press Publishing Company, 1983.

Conklin, Dave. *Montana History Weekends: 52 Adventures in History*, Guilford, Conn.: The Globe Pequot Press, 2002.

DeSanto, Jerry. *The Montana State Flower Bitterroot*. Babb, Mont.: LERE Press, 1993.

Federal Writers' Project of the Work Projects Administration. *Montana: A State Guide Book*. New York: Hastings House, 1949. Reissued by The University of Arizona Press as *The WPA Guide to 1930s Montana*.

Fritz, Harry W. *Montana, Land of Contrast, An Illustrated History*. Sun Valley: American Historical Press, 2001.

Gilluly, Bob. *One Man's Montana*. Missoula, Mont: Heartland Journals, 1999.

Guthrie, A. B., Jr. *The Big Sky*. Boston: Houghton Mifflin, 1947.

Kittredge, William and Annick Smith, eds. *The Last Best Place: A Montana Anthology*. Helena: Montana Historical Society Press, 1988.

Malone, Michael P., Richard B. Roeder, and William L. Lang. *Montana: A History of Two Centuries*. Seattle: University of Washington Press, revised edition, 1991.

McRae, W. C. and Judy Jewell. *Montana Handbook*, fifth edition. Chico, Calif.: Moon Publications, Inc., 2004.

McCoy, Michael. *Montana Off the Beaten Path, A Guide to Unique Places*. Guilford, Conn.: The Globe Pequot Press, 2004.

Montana: The Last Best Place. Helena: Falcon Press, 1993.

Montana On My Mind. Helena: Falcon Press, 1991. A book for the coffee table. Color photos by Michael S. Sample and quotes from A. B. Guthrie, Chet Huntley, Jeannette Rankin, Mike Mansfield, and other Montanans.

Murphy, Alexandra. *Graced by Pines*. Missoula: Mountain Press Publishing Company, 1994. Essays on the cultural and natural history of the ponderosa pine.

Spritzer, Don. *A Roadside History of Montana*. Missoula: Mountain Press Publishing Company, 1999.

Tirrell, Norma. *Montana*, fifth edition. Oakland: Compass American Guides, Inc., 2004. A thoughtful description of Montana culture and places.

Toole, K. Ross. *Twentieth Century Montana: A State of Extremes*. Norman, Okla.: University of Oklahoma Press, 1972.

Vasapoli, Salvatore, with essay by Pat Williams. *Montana. Photography*. Portland, Ore.: Graphic Arts Center Publishing Company, 2003.

Van West, Carroll. *A Traveler's Companion to Montana History*. Guilford, Conn.: The Globe Pequot Press, 1986.

Voynick, Stephen M. *The Great American Sapphire*. Missoula: Mountain Press Publishing Company, 2004.

For Reference

Montana Atlas and Gazetteer. Freeport, Maine: DeLorme Mapping Co., fourth edition, 2001.

Montana 2004–2005 Highway Map. Montana Department of Transportation.

CHAPTER TWO

Climate and Weather

*M*ontana historian Harry Fritz declared Montana to be a "land of contrasts," and nowhere are those contrasts more apparent than in the state's diverse topography and the vicissitudes of weather caused by the terrain.

The boundary of Montana forms a rough rectangle that contains parts of two major physiographic regions

Floods in the Great Falls area, June 10, 1964.
MONTANA HISTORICAL
SOCIETY

of North America. The western third of the state (about 49,000 square miles) contains the Rocky Mountain region. Montana's portion of the Rockies consists of long, roughly parallel mountain chains oriented along a northwest-to-southeast axis. This area of the state is covered with forests, mountain ranges, lakes, basins, and valleys. The largest of the valleys are from 10 to 20 miles wide, and from 25 to 100 miles long. The Continental Divide meanders along ridges of the western mountains, entering from the north in Glacier National Park, continuing south, then taking a slow arc to the west near Helena and Butte before heading along the Anaconda and Pintler mountains to the Idaho border. Half of the state rises over 4,000 feet above sea level.

The eastern edge of Montana's Rockies gives way to the central portion of the state: some isolated or "island" mountain ranges (the Big Belts, the Big Snowies, the Crazies), broad benchlands and valleys, and an expanse of prairie—the Great Plains—that extends through eastern Montana and beyond the state's eastern, northeastern, and southeastern borders.

The size and topography of Montana contribute to wide climatic variations across the state. The barrier created by the high elevations of the Rocky Mountains has an inescapable effect on Montana's weather.

Montana's weather has a reputation for being extreme and unpredictable. Our temperature extremes certainly are noteworthy, with the lows dipping below minus 35 degrees (all temperatures in this chapter are given in Fahrenheit) in the high mountains and the northeast in winter, and the highs topping 100 degrees, most often in the middle and lower Yellowstone Valley. Hot spells are rarely oppressive, as the summer nights almost invariably are cool and pleasant—between 50 and 60 degrees. In addition to a temperate summer climate, Montana's northern latitude offers the advantage of long days—as much as 15 hours of daylight.

In measurable reality, though, Montana's temperatures are no more severe than in other states along the northern tier of the United States. Duluth and Minneapolis/St. Paul, Minnesota, for example, are on average colder than most of Montana's major cities. Although Montana weather can be temperamental any given day in any season, our overall climate is generally milder than the extremes reported from some of the state's more infamous recording stations such as West Yellowstone, which often records the lowest temperature in the continental U.S. on national weather charts.

Compared to the U.S. average, the state's relatively low precipitation and low relative humidity take the edge off the hottest days of summer and the coldest days of winter.

Generally, adequate moisture contributes to rapid plant and crop growth during most growing seasons. Despite what may indicate winters on the cold side, growing seasons (freeze-free periods) are four months or more in length in much of the valleys and agricultural areas of the state. In parts of the Yellowstone Valley, the freeze-free period runs as long as 150 days.

HOTTEST READINGS

The mercury rose to 117 degrees in Glendive on July 20, 1893, and again in Medicine Lake, in the northeastern corner of the state, on July 5, 1937.

The Big Skies

The following pie charts represent 365 days of weather (sunrise to sunset) and are divided into the mean number of days of each condition—clear (white), partly cloudy (gray), and cloudy (black).

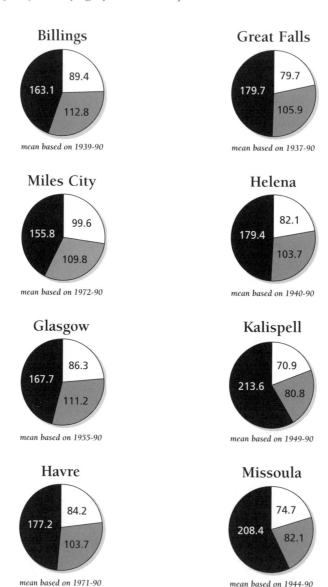

Billings

89.4 / 112.8 / 163.1

mean based on 1939-90

Great Falls

79.7 / 105.9 / 179.7

mean based on 1937-90

Miles City

99.6 / 109.8 / 155.8

mean based on 1972-90

Helena

82.1 / 103.7 / 179.4

mean based on 1940-90

Glasgow

86.3 / 111.2 / 167.7

mean based on 1955-90

Kalispell

70.9 / 80.8 / 213.6

mean based on 1949-90

Havre

84.2 / 103.7 / 177.2

mean based on 1971-90

Missoula

74.7 / 82.1 / 208.4

mean based on 1944-90

Source: Joseph M. Caprio and Gerald A. Nielsen. Climate Atlas of Montana—1992. Bozeman: Montana State University Extension Service.

Hottest Places in Montana

Location	County	Average Daily High in July (°F)*
1. Hardin	Big Horn	90.2
2. Crow Agency	Big Horn	90.1
3. Ballantine	Yellowstone	90.1
4. Yellowtail Dam	Big Horn	89.6
5. Jordan	Garfield	89.6
6. Birney	Rosebud	89.5
7. Lame Deer	Rosebud	89.2
8. Hysham	Treasure	88.9
9. 11 miles northeast of Ingomar	Rosebud	88.9
10. Billings water plant	Yellowstone	88.9

* Based on monthly average maximum temperatures for periods of record ranging from 100+ to 50+ years up to 2002 for reporting weather stations. *Source: Western Regional Climate Center.* Historical Climate Infornation, 2002. www.wrcc.dri.edu/.

Rain and Snowfall

As a consequence of its interior position on the continent, and because the west winds lose moisture over the mountains, Montana has relatively light precipitation. The annual average precipitation (rain and melted snow) for the entire state is 15 inches.

In the valleys on the westward side of the Continental Divide, the annual average is just under 20 inches. The annual average for the eastern side of the divide is about 13 inches, but local averages vary widely.

Most parts of Montana were plagued by drought since 1999, leading to several severe wildfire seasons during the period. While many parts of the state experienced above average spring rains in 2005; the soggy weather was not enough to bring the water year up to average. For example, the Flathead Valley recorded the wettest in June in 100 years but was still below normal for annual precipitation.

The wettest months in Montana also vary across the state: December and January in the mountains either side of the Continental Divide, May and June for the plains and valleys. The driest months are January and February in the eastern plains and valleys, and July in the west and in the mountains east of the divide.

Summit, on U.S. Highway 2 south of Glacier Park, holds several records for moisture. It received 55.5 inches of precipitation in 1953. Summit was

Wettest Places in Montana

Location	County	Annual Average Precipitation (in inches)*
1. 18 miles north of Troy	Lincoln	35.61
2. 12 miles northeast of Bozeman	Gallatin	34.62
3. 2 miles northwest of Heron	Sanders	33.58
4. Hungry Horse Dam	Flathead	33.07
5. 3 miles east of Haugan	Mineral	29.71
6. West Glacier	Flathead	29.34
7. East Glacier	Glacier	28.88
8. Swan Lake	Lake	28.87
9. Trout Creek Ranger Station	Sanders	28.79
10. Hebgen Dam	Gallatin	28.35

* Based on monthly average precipitation for periods of record ranging from 40+ years up to 2002, for reporting weather stations near populated areas. *Source: Western Regional Climate Center.* Historical Climate Information, 2002. *www.wrcc.dri.edu/*.

also hit by Montana's greatest snowfall ever, in January 1972. The storm lasted six days and dropped more than six feet of snow (77.5 inches), including a one-day record of 44 inches on January 20. Summit normally gets about 40 inches of precipitation a year. The record for 24-hour rainfall belongs to Circle, where 11.5 inches fell on June 20, 1921.

For total snowfall during one winter, Cooke City is tops. Almost 35 feet (418.1 inches) of the white stuff fell during the winter of 1977–1978. The largest snowflakes ever recorded in the world fell across Fort Keogh in Montana on January 28, 1887. The flakes were measured at a massive 15 inches across by 8 inches thick.

Winter

The truth is the infamous Montana winter rarely settles in for keeps. Montana's cold spells, blasts of arctic air that can bring blizzards and whose chill can hang in the valleys for days, are frequently broken up by a sunny mildness and refreshingly warm, dry chinook winds from the west.

Winters in the Great Plains are generally colder than in the west. North-central and eastern Montana are subject to waves of that frigid arctic air from six to twelve times each winter; the entire state can become enveloped by such cold waves about twice each winter. Some of the cold waves, often referred to as the "Siberian Express," can push temperatures to 50 below zero, but extremes like that do not occur in most winter seasons.

WINTER '96

A few weeks in January and February 1996 illustrate the weather extremes that are possible during a Montana winter. On January 14, much of the state experienced a tropical heat wave. Winter heat records fell with readings like 61 degrees at Billings and 52 degrees at Butte. A few days later, a blizzard buried much of the state in more than 10 inches of snow. The following near record low temperatures were recorded February 2:

Helena	-42	Cut Bank	-37
Belgrade	-40	Great Falls	-35

By February 5, warm winds blew in, and two days later, most of the snow in the valleys was all but melted. The downside of the balmy weather was a destructive four days of flooding.

Coldest Places in Montana

Location	County	Average Daily Low in January (°F)*
1. Westby	Sheridan	-5.0
2. 10 miles north of Opheim	Valley	-3.2
3. 3 miles southeast of Medicine Lake	Sheridan	-3.1
4. Redstone	Sheridan	-2.8
5. Glasgow	Valley	-2.6
6. Culbertson	Roosevelt	-2.4
7. Scobey	Daniels	-2.1
8. border station at Raymond	Sheridan	-2.0
9. 1 mile northwest of Saco	Phillips	-1.9
10. 2 miles east of Poplar	Roosevelt	-1.7

Source: Western Regional Climate Center. Historical Climate Information, 2002. www.wrcc.dri.edu/.

COLDEST READING

The state record cold temperature also stands as the lowest temperature ever recorded in the lower 48 states: 70 degrees below zero. It was recorded January 20, 1954, by an unpaid observer for the United States Weather Bureau who saw the mercury plummet to 69.7 degrees below zero at a mining camp just west of Rogers Pass along the Continental Divide. Based on the observer's written remarks about the condition of the thermometers, and subsequent laboratory tests in Washington, D.C., the official temperature was pegged at 70 below. The previous record of minus 66 degrees was recorded at West Yellowstone, Montana.

Normal Precipitation and Growing Season

County	Station	Normal Precipitation*	Annual Precip. (inches) 2003	Length of Growing Season (days)**
Beaverhead	Dillon	11.65	8.37	103
Big Horn	Hardin	12.07	10.85	133
Blaine	Chinook	13.0	12.87	119
Broadwater	Townsend	10.67	8.44	120
Carbon	Joliet	15.77	12.20	120
Carter	Ekalaka	17.25	18.34	123
Cascade	Great Falls	14.89	14.99	120
Chouteau	Ft. Benton	13.69	11.46	131
Custer	Miles City	13.49	11.01	143
Daniels	near Scobey	12.48	11.18	108
Dawson	Glendive	13.62	12.06	144
Deer Lodge	N/A			
Fallon	Plevna	14.69	13.74	114
Fergus	Lewistown	17.85	13.86	116
Flathead	Kalispell	17.21	12.30	91
Gallatin	Bozeman	19.29	19.34	120
Garfield	Jordan	12.90	9.79	122
Glacier	Cut Bank	12.51	5.00	113
Golden Valley	N/A			
Granite	N/A			
Hill	Havre	11.46	9.81	125
Jefferson	N/A			
Judith Basin	Stanford	17.13	15.75	109
Lake	near Bigfork	21.87	16.96	152
Lewis & Clark	Helena	11.32	9.34	121
Liberty	Chester	10.58	8.62	108
Lincoln	N/A			
Madison	Virginia City	15.82	13.90	85
McCone	Circle	13.28	16.04	120
Meagher	N/A			
Mineral	N/A			
Missoula	Missoula	13.82	14.55	117
Musselshell	Roundup	13.25	—	131
Park	Livingston	15.73	15.06	105
Petroleum	near Flatwillow	13.30	12.92	118
Phillips	near Malta	12.88	12.18	122
Pondera	Valier	12.22	10.44	117
Powder River	Broadus	13.59	14.22	119
Powell	N/A			
Prairie	Terry	11.85	—	126
Ravalli	Hamilton	13.54	13.39	129
Richland	Sidney	14.31	—	125

Normal Precipitation and Growing Season (cont.)

County	Station	Normal Precipitation*	Annual Precip. (inches) 2003	Length of Growing Season (days)**
Roosevelt	Culbertson	13.58	16.12	117
Rosebud	Forsyth	14.08	16.64	131
Sanders	Thompson Falls	23.07	17.14	133
Sheridan	Plentywood	13.15	11.45	116
Silver Bow	Butte	12.78	9.67	73
Stillwater	Columbus	15.67	12.12	125
Sweet Grass	Big Timber	16.11	16.63	126
Teton	Fairfield	12.50	9.05	133
Toole	N/A			
Treasure	Hysham	14.37	16.13	135
Valley	Glasgow	11.23	10.80	133
Wheatland	Harlowton	14.08	—	111
Wibaux	near Wibaux	14.27	15.04	113
Yellowstone	Billings	14.77	12.18	150

* Normal for period 1971–2000. ** Average frost-free days for period 1991–2002.
N/A - data not available
Growing season = days between last frost (32 degrees) in spring to first frost after June 30. *Source: National Weather Service, National Oceanic and Atmospheric Administration, Great Falls, Montana.*

GROWING SEASON

The growing season varies from 39 days a year in the high mountain valleys of the southwest to 150 in scattered areas of the Yellowstone River basin.

High Winds

The eastern region tends to be windier than the region west of the divide (excluding mountain ridge areas), with Whitehall, Livingston, and Judith Gap recording average daily wind speeds of 14.4 to 15.7 mph.

Great Falls holds the official state record for the strongest wind at a National Weather Service station, where it raced at 82 mph in December 1956. It is widely accepted that wind speeds have unofficially beaten this record at several locations east of the divide. On December 5, 1995, hurricane-force winds were recorded on both sides of the divide, with 110 mph clocked by a weather observer at Plains and 100 mph at Ulm, near Great Falls. In the first few days of February 1989, wind gusts of 124 mph were clocked at Choteau; that same day, wind gusts were as high as 117 mph at Browning. Twelve railroad cars were blown over in Shelby, another town in that area along the eastern slopes of the Rocky Mountain Front. In 1973, an observer in Big Timber clocked the wind at 120 mph. These observations remain unofficial.

Chinooks occur most often in the "chinook belt," a zone from Browning and Shelby in the north, along the Front Range, 75 to 100 miles to the Yellowstone Valley and Billings to the southeast.

THE CHINOOKS

Severe winter temperatures east of the Continental Divide are sometimes modified by warm chinook winds from the eastern slopes of the Rockies. Indians called these winds "snow eaters," and it's true that the warm winds can gobble up the snowdrifts of the most severe storms within days or even hours.

This weather phenomenon begins over the Pacific Ocean and moves east as a warm, moist air mass. As the air moves up and over the mountains, it cools and causes the moisture to condense. Now here's the weird part. While cooling causes condensation, condensation generates heat—thus the air that slides down the east side of the mountains is warmer than it was at a similar elevation on the west side, plus the rush downhill further warms the air.

—from *Trail of the Great Bear*
by Bruce Weide

Historic Weather Disasters

One cowboy described the winter of 1886–1887 as "hell without the heat." It all started when there wasn't enough rain during the spring and summer of 1886. The grass, streams, and water holes dried up, but cattlemen kept on bringing in more herds from Texas, Washington, and Oregon. The summer was abnormally hot. Vegetation shriveled in the searing wind. Prairie fires roared across the land. The scant water remaining in the shallow streams was so foul with alkali that thirsty horses refused to drink it. There were signs of a hard winter to come. Wild geese and ducks flew south early, and the cattle grew shaggy coats. Winter came, and it was a hard one, with snowfall drifted by wild blizzards. Cold bit down, and strong young steers froze to death in a series of bitter storms between mid-November and March, one of which lasted for ten days without a letup. When a thaw came, cold followed it, so that everything was topped by a sheet of ice.

THE TEMPERATURES, THEY ARE A-CHANGING

Sudden and dramatic temperature changes under the Big Sky are tall tales come true. One of the quickest changes in the United States occurred in Great Falls, when on January 11, 1980, the temperature rose from 32 below zero to 15 above—a change of 47 degrees—in only seven minutes. Loma, north of Great Falls, now holds the records for the biggest, 24-hour temperature swing in the United States. On January 14, 1972, Loma climbed from bone-chilling 54 below zero to a balmy 49 above the following day, a change of 103 degrees. It replaces the existing records of a 100-degree temperature swing in January 23–24, 1916 in Browning, Montana. The temperature dropped from 44 degrees above zero to 56 degrees below zero in a 24-hour period.

When a March chinook melted the snow and ice like magic, cattlemen surveyed their losses and it wasn't a pretty picture. The coulees were filled with rotting carcasses of cattle that had starved or frozen. Some stockmen lost two-thirds of their herds; a few lost 90 percent. To add to the ruin, the price of beef bottomed out because so many owners had to sell their diminished herds to raise money. There were bankruptcies. The dream of the open range ended in a nightmare.

We're Not in Kansas Anymore, Toto

Tornados touch down in Montana more often than many people think. However, the sightings are generally in sparsely populated areas and the effects are minimal. There have been an average of a dozen sightings per year in recent years. Since record keeping began in the early 1920s, six people have been killed by tornados. In July 1983, a tornado south of Wolf Point was responsible for the death of a Terry woman, Marjorie Grist. The twister picked up the truck she and her husband were riding in and she was ejected as they spun through the air.

Other Weather-Related Disasters

March 24, 1869   Seventeen soldiers returning with supplies to Fort Shaw from Fort Benton die near present-day Vaughn in a severe blizzard that lasts only a few hours.

June 19, 1938	A flash flood weakens a trestle, causing a Milwaukee Road passenger train to plunge into Custer Creek; 49 people are killed, 65 injured.
January 25, 1962	Severe winds along the Rocky Mountain Front are blamed for the crash of a National Guard C-47 near Wolf Creek. Governor Donald Nutter loses his life in the crash.
June 7–8, 1964	After a week of heavy rains, dams fail and devastating floods along the Rocky Mountain Front claim thirty-four lives and inundate towns from the Flathead Valley to Great Falls.
April 24, 1969	More than 100,000 livestock are killed in freezing rain and snow in southeastern Montana.

Weather Reports

Montana residents and visitors can call the following numbers to receive updated regional weather reports.

Statewide	449-5204
Billings	652-1916
Glasgow	228-9625
Great Falls	453-5469, or 453-5460
Helena	449-5204
Kalispell	755-4829
Missoula	721-3939

The following website has many links to current and historical weather reports for all parts of the state, including severe weather and flood warnings: http://www.mdt.state.mt.us/travinfo/weather/weather.shtml.

UNDER ICE

In the past five decades, Flathead Lake has frozen over only seven times—
in 1946,
1962, 1969,
1972, 1985,
1986, and 1989.

Weather Radio

The National Weather Service maintains a nationwide network of weather radio transmitters known as NOAA Weather Radio (NWR), which broadcasts weather information twenty-four hours a day, 365 days a year. The broadcasts, including local forecasts and observations and severe weather watches and warnings, can be received over much of Montana with a special radio receiver available at many electronics stores on the following frequencies.

Great Falls	162.55	Helena	162.40	Havre	162.40
Butte	162.55	Kalispell	162.55	Missoula	162.40
Glasgow	162.40	Miles City	162.40	Billings	162.550

Further Reading

Caprio, Joseph M., and Gerald A. Nielsen. *Climate Atlas of Montana: Mapping Montana's Weather.* Bozeman: Montana State University Extension Service, 1992. *For those intently interested in mean temperatures, annual potential evaporation, solar radiation in langleys per day, etc., these maps tell the story of Montana's climate.*

Searl, Molly. *Montana Disasters, Fires, Floods, and Other Catastrophes.* Boulder, Colo.: Pruett Publishing, 2001.

For Gardeners

Gough, Bob, Cheryl Moore-Gough, and Laura Peters. *Best Garden Plants for Montana.* Lone Pine Publications, 2005.

Hackett, Molly, and Georgianna Taylor. *The Compleat Gardener.* Missoula: The Missoulian, 1995.

Perrin, Sandra. *Organic Gardening in Cold Climates.* Missoula: Mountain Press Publishing, 1991.

CHAPTER THREE

Natural Treasures

$\mathcal{M}$ontana is a vast treasure trove of mountains, canyons, river valleys, forests, grassy plains, and badlands. As the 4th largest state in the nation, the 147,042 square miles (land and water) of Big Sky Country account for about 4 percent of the total U.S. land area. Montana's borders are big enough to fit Connecticut, Delaware, New Hampshire, Vermont, Massachusetts, Maine, South Carolina, and Ohio within them. If we had 23 more square miles, we could also squeeze in Rhode Island. Montana's boundary with the provinces of Saskatchewan, Alberta, and British Columbia spans one-seventh of the international border between Canada and the lower 48 states.

"Great Falls of the Missouri River, MT."
Summer 1880.
HAYNES FOUNDATION
COLLECTION, MONTANA
HISTORICAL SOCIETY

The eastern two-thirds of the state consists of high plains cut by numerous major rivers, several isolated mountain ranges, badlands and rolling hills. The western third is mountainous, with broad, fertile valleys, watered by streams and rivers. It is this geography that makes Montana's history so interesting. This raw land influenced the exploits of those who came here and shaped the currents of life in this area. To conquer the elements and topography, it took nerve, knowledge, and perseverance. The steep mountains and impassable rivers made discovery difficult but yielded great resources like beaver pelts, gold, and water power. The oceans of grass that attracted the buffalo later lured the cattlemen and farmers. Even the great expanses of drier plains proved to be passable grazing for sheep.

Montana is famous for its endless blue skies and a landscape painted with many other hues of nature's palette. In fall, its forests may not flaunt all the gaudy colors of the eastern woodlands, but its tamaracks are bright yellow against the evergreens, and its aspen groves are a dazzling gold. In winter, the bare branches of red-osier dogwood retain their tint along streambeds. Sagebrush provides subtle grays, greens, and whites all year long. Spring brings wildflowers of all hues, set against the stark white of bear grass in high mountain meadows. In summer, there are all the tones of green in a giant box of crayons. And to be sure, there are purple mountains, full of majesty, and amber waves of grain.

Geology

Montana's remarkable and varied landscape contains evidence of many geologic events. The earth under the prehistoric Big Sky was vastly different than it is today, at times roamed by dinosaurs or covered by shallow seas.

During the Paleozoic Era, which lasted from 544 to 248 million years ago, much of the northern Rocky Mountain area was flooded by shallow seas at various intervals. The rise and fall of great seas occurred again during the Mesozoic era, which lasted from 248 million years ago to until

LACCOLITHS

Many of Charlie Russell's paintings feature flat-topped buttes' which the artist could see for miles south and southwest of Great Falls—Cascade Butte, Square Butte, Fort Shaw Butte, and Crown Butte. These formations are technically known as laccoliths. They form when magma rises into a volcano but cannot break through to the surface. The magma hardens into rock, which is slowly revealed by erosion.

Russell's beloved buttes remain, on his canvasses and on the landscape. Laccoliths can be found east of the Rocky Mountain Front and north of Helena along the Missouri River and in the Adel, Highwood, Bears Paw, and northern Crazy mountains. The laccoliths contain shonkinite, a very rare rock similar to basalt, named for Shonkin, a small settlement between Great Falls and Geraldine.

about 65 million years ago. The shallow seas, sometimes stretching from northern Canada to Mexico, laid down thick layers of sediment that hardened to rock. Dinosaurs of many types inhabited this area during the Mesozoic time. The chalky sediment deposited during this era, between about 135 and 65 million years ago, contain bones of many kinds of dinosaurs.

Around 80 million years ago, masses of molten rock rose beneath western North America and lifted, stretched, and heated the continental crust. The crust broke up into the long, narrow blocks of mountains that run north and south throughout much of the western and southwestern parts of Montana. Large volumes of volcanic rock erupted in western Montana.

Volcanoes erupted and molten magma rose upward into the earth's crust and, about 50 million years ago, created many of the isolated mountain ranges that dot the prairies well into the eastern half of the state. Great swamps flooded and dried, compacting the remains of vegetation into the great coal seams of today. Montana's coal beds are part of what may be the largest coal basin on earth, the Fort Union formation. Reaching into parts of Wyoming, North Dakota, and Saskatchewan, it is between 60 and 65 million years old.

Throughout the Tertiary period, from about 65 million years ago until the great ice ages began some 2 million years ago, there were long periods of dry, desert climate. There may have been enough precipitation to assist with erosion, but not enough to flush away the gravels and mud we can see today in many road cuts of the broader valleys. The eastern plains and badlands of Montana are remnants of high, smooth expanses of water-washed surfaces, where deposits of gravel tell a tale of great flash floods. Streams continue to cut through the rock layers.

When the Tertiary period ended about 2 million years ago, the great Pleistocene ice ages began. Part of Montana's modern landscape has been carved by glacial ice and the subsequent movement of great quantities of glacial meltwater. At least twice during the last 150,000 years, great glaciers blanketed northern Montana east of the Rocky Mountains and north of the Missouri River. It was not so much a time of intense cold, as many suppose, but a time when the winter snowfalls were so heavy that they could not melt during the summer. Glaciers covered the mountain peaks and scoured the Seeley, Swan, Flathead, and Bull Lake valleys. They blocked northerly flowing rivers like the Missouri to create ancient glacial lakes near Great Falls, Cut Bank, Roundup, Jordan, and Glendive. The great rivers of glacial melt

BEFORE THE FLOOD

Dams of glacial ice once held back the Clark Fork River to a depth of 2,000 feet near the present site of Lake Pend Oreille in Idaho. A giant lake, 1,000 feet deep in many places, such as present-day Missoula, formed recurrently throughout the Clark Fork River drainage, it spread east into the lower Deer Lodge Valley, beyond Darby, and north to the ice that filled the Seeley-Swan Valley. Evidence of Glacial Lake Missoula can be seen in the horizontal shorelines etched into Mount Sentinel and Mount Jumbo, the two mountains that flank Interstate 90 as it enters Missoula, and on hundreds of other mountains.

Between 15,000 and 12,000 years ago, the ice dam formed and broke at least forty times, sending the contents of the giant lake down the Columbia River to the Pacific Ocean in what geologists think may have been the world's greatest floods.

scoured sediments on the valley floors that had been building for eons. The climate and vegetation between the glacial periods probably resembled those of modern times.

The glacial age of 10,000 years ago was the last. It left moraines that can be seen in the rolling hills of Blaine, Phillips, and Hill counties, and at the southern end of Flathead Lake; and across the Ovando Valley floor south of the Bob Marshall and Scapegoat wilderness areas. A moraine is a low ridge made by mud, sand, gravel, and boulders, deposited at the edge of a receding glacier.

The glaciers that ventured onto the northern third of eastern Montana did not change the landscape to a great degree. The ice was not thick enough or moving fast enough to do much eroding. As the last of the ice melted, shallow lakes disappeared and the Missouri River flowed in a new easterly course along the former front of the glacier. Modern types of vegetation adapted to the new conditions, and ice-free corridors allowed great prehistoric mammals and humans to migrate throughout the plains. The woolly mastodon roamed through portions of the state during the last ice age, as did the imperial mammoth and saber-toothed tiger.

Today, the northern Rocky Mountains are still subject to intense geological activity. Streams practice the art of erosion on a daily basis. In Yellowstone National Park, hot mud bubbles up and geysers erupt over the top of an enormous volcano. Though it has been decades since a serious earthquake struck, the earth is moving under us more often than we think.

Earthquakes

Montana is the fourth most geologically active state, behind Alaska, California, and Hawaii. A narrow strip of the state, from Yellowstone Park to Kalispell, is at high risk of earthquake damage. The historic earthquakes of Montana are among the largest recorded on the continental United States.

A series of 1,200 shocks struck Helena and western Montana in 1935, beginning in October and lasting into December. Another round of about six hundred more shocks hit in February 1936. Two of the October quakes were particularly powerful. One, on October 12, shook half of Montana. The most severe was centered near Helena. It occurred the evening of October 18 and was recorded as a magnitude of 6.3 on the Richter scale. Four people were killed and total property damage reached $3.5 million. The new Helena High School, completed in August, suffered the greatest damage. The Kessler Brewery and St. Joseph's Orphanage were also damaged.

The earthquake at Hebgen Lake on August 17, 1959, was one of the most severe ever recorded in the United States, with a magnitude variously reported between 7.1 and 7.5. It was felt throughout the Pacific Northwest and southwestern Canada. The world feels only about ten quakes of this magnitude each year.

The Madison River valley in the Hebgen Lake area near West Yellowstone dropped by as much as 22 feet. The quake also triggered a landslide of some

Montana's Major Earthquakes

Date	Center	Magnitude	Effects
05/22/1869	Helena	6.7	Only minor damage
12/10/1872	8 mi. east of Deer Lodge	—	Buildings shaken violently; shocks in Philipsburg, Helena, and Blackfoot Valley
06/27/1925	Three Forks area	6.75	Rock slides block railroad tracks and dam stream; slight damage to chimneys and buildings
10/12/1935	Helena	—	Very minor damage
10/18/1935	Helena	6.3	Four people killed; extensive property damage
11/23/1947	Madison-Beaverhead county line	6.2	No reported damage
08/17/1959	West of Yellowstone National Park	7.5	28 people killed
06/30/1975	Yellowstone National Park	6.4	No reported damage

80 million tons of rock and earth. The slide filled 1.5 miles of the Madison River Canyon, backing up the river to create Quake Lake. Large waves rolled across Hebgen Lake and sloshed over the top of Hebgen Dam. As many as 250 people were thought to have been camping in the area, and 28 of them lost their lives in the earthquake.

Visitors to the area, about 40 miles south of Ennis on U.S. Highway 287, can see the effects of this earthquake on the mountains and surroundings. At the top of the slide is a visitor center with educational exhibits. The USDA Forest Service has built a new campground nearby.

Many Are Better Than One

Consider us lucky that every year, frequent small earthquakes lightly jostle the state's populated areas within the earthquake belts of western Montana. Although these may be unsettling, the positive view holds that the seismic energy is being released in many small shocks instead of suddenly—in one large, destructive earthquake.

In 1995, the largest quake for nearly a decade occurred on May 2 near Kila in northwest Montana and registered a magnitude of 4.5 on the Richter scale. On August 20, 1999, a 5.3 magnitude quake rocked a relatively unpopulated area near the Red Rock Valley south of Dillon.

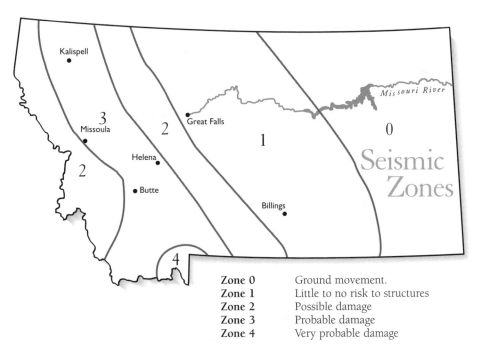

Zone 0	Ground movement.
Zone 1	Little to no risk to structures
Zone 2	Possible damage
Zone 3	Probable damage
Zone 4	Very probable damage

WHERE THE GLACIERS ARE

Some sources count only twenty-six small glaciers in Glacier National Park today. These are not part of the ancient glaciers that the park was named for, but formed later. Many have shrunk to half or one-third of the size they were a century ago. Many others have disappeared during that time.

Grinnell Glacier is the largest glacier in the park. It can be reached at the head of Grinnell Valley on a physically demanding trail, 5.5 miles from the Many Glacier campground. Gem and Salamander Glaciers can also be seen from the trail. Sperry Glacier is similar in size to Grinnell. It can be seen from the Sperry Chalet Trail, a 6.2-mile hike from the trailhead at Lake McDonald Lodge. Like the walk to Grinnell Glacier, it is somewhat strenuous.

In the Absaroka-Beartooth Wilderness Area, one of the largest ice fields in the United States, Grasshopper Glacier is named for millions of grasshoppers frozen beneath its surface. The insects, whose species is now extinct, can only be seen when snow melts enough to expose the ice on an 80-foot cliff.

Seismic Zones

The U.S. Geological Survey ranks the part of Montana near Yellowstone National Park in Zone 4, the highest seismic risk category. Parts or all of sixteen counties are in Zone 3, which are high-risk seismic areas. The risk of earthquakes is nearly insignificant in eastern Montana.

For more information on Montana earthquakes and seismic zones, call the Earthquake Studies Office, Montana Bureau of Mines, Butte, at 496-4332, or Montana Disaster and Emergency Services, Helena, at 444-6982.

Dinosaurs and Fossils

The first dinosaur fossil discovered and described in the western hemisphere was a single tooth found in beds near the mouth of the Judith River, east of Fort Benton, in 1854. The creature was given the name of Troödon. In 1902, the first fossil remains of a Tyrannosaurus rex were found in a dig near Hell Creek, outside of Jordan. The remains suggested an animal 40 feet long, weighing about 16,000 pounds. Based on the size of the teeth, Tyrannosaurus rex was thought to be a vicious predator. Montana's own dinosaur expert, Jack Horner, the director of paleontology for the Museum of the Rockies, suggests the creature was an opportunistic scavenger. T. rex would have been hard pressed to catch anything with its small arms, but it had strong legs for going great distances to find animals that were wounded or dead. With a good sense of smell, it could follow the duck-billed dinosaurs, or "cows of the Cretaceous period," which roamed the same areas in large herds.

At Egg Mountain near Choteau in north-central Montana, nests and eggs of the duck-billed dinosaur, Maiasaura peeblesorum, and the small plant-eater Orodromeus makelai have been found. In 1978, Marion Brandvold, a life-long fossil hunter and owner of a rock shop in nearby Bynum, made the first discovery of baby dinosaurs. Later that year, she showed the site to Jack Horner, who undertook further excavations and christened the species. Horner helped convince other paleontologists that dinosaurs built vast colonies in order to better care for their young in a manner similar to birds. It is now widely believed that all dinosaurs reproduced by laying eggs. The fossils of numerous other plant-eating dinosaurs have been discovered in herds made up of both adults and young. Inside many of these dinosaur nests were found fossilized eggshell fragments that were thoroughly crushed, as by the feet of baby dinosaurs, leading Horner to conclude that the babies stayed in the nests and were fed and cared for by their parents. If the young had left the nests immediately after hatching, the eggshells would have stayed more intact.

Recent finds suggest there may be as many as thirty fossilized bones per square yard in the area of Egg Mountain. This site has yielded the largest collection of dinosaur remains in the world.

"Best Dinosaur Graveyard in the World"

In recent years, the following fossil finds have earned Montana recognition as the "dinosaur capital of the world" and added to a long and impressive history of discoveries. Some of the rarest discoveries include dinosaur skeletons with nearly every bone in place. Other finds have yielded impressions of skin and evidence of internal organs and the beast's last meal. Many amateur fossil hunters have made some of the most amazing discoveries.

- Leonardo, the world's best-preserved dinosaur, was found north of Malta in 2001 by a volunteer who was helping paleontologist Nate Murphy. The remains of this nearly 2 ton, 77-million-year-old mummified Brachylophosaurus reveal fossilized scales and pads on the bottom of his three-toed foot. Exhibits of Leonardo and another near-perfect duck-bill named Elvis can be viewed at the Phillips County Museum.
- Twelve-year-old Bobby Wells found the nearly complete remains of another Brachylophosaurus, named Roberta, in his honor.

MUSEUM OF THE ROCKIES/BRUCE SELYEM

John R. "Jack" Horner (1946–)

Though recognized all over the world as a paleontologist, Jack Horner did not have to go far from his hometown of Shelby for his most important find. Near Choteau, he excavated and studied the first dinosaur nests ever uncovered. The discovery enabled Horner to solve truly ancient mysteries and change long-held ideas about dinosaur behavior. He is the recipient of major research grants from the National Science Foundation, the MacArthur Foundation, and other sources. He serves as curator of paleontology for the Museum of the Rockies in Bozeman. When he's not on a dig, he keeps busy conducting other research, lecturing, or writing articles and books. He was an advisor to Steven Spielberg's production of Jurassic Park.

M O N T A N A N S

- Peck's Rex, an unusually well preserved Tyrannosaurus rex, was discovered by a volunteer fossil hunter near Fort Peck in 1997. This 70-million-year-old critter had sharp, banana-sized teeth and was 40 feet from nose to tail.
- Giffen, a 150-million-year-old stegosaurus, was found buried in the backyard of a family in Stockett.
- On a ranch north of Billings, the remains were found of a 150-million-year-old, four ton, plant-eating Sauropod, one of the largest land animals ever.
- The remains of a Triceratops, discovered by an amateur paleontologist, Ken Olson, near Glendive in 1991, indicated that it had been gnawed on by a T. rex.
- In 2001, the world's largest dinosaur skull, that of a 5,000-pound, pronghorned Torosaurus, had to be air lifted out of the Hell Creek area near Jordan by an Army National Guard helicopter. The process was shown live on NBC's "Today Show."
- In May 1997, the Great Falls Civic Center hosted the premier showing of "The Lost World," the sequel to the 1993 hit, "Jurassic Park."

FOSSIL

Vertebrate fossils and other fossils of "recognized scientific interest" are protected by federal law. Removing them from federal lands is prohibited, unless authorized by the agency that manages the land in question. It is also illegal to destroy "any historic or prehistoric ruin or monument, or any object of antiquity."

When exploring the state's geological and archaeological wonders, respect all natural resources as well as the rights of private property owners.

Dig Those Dinos

You can visit these places to see many world record-setting dinosaur discoveries. Or you can don a big-brimmed hat, gloves, and sunscreen, and join one of the amateur digs offered by some of the following resources:

Carter County Museum, Ekalaka, 775-6886

Dinosaur Field Station, Malta, 654-5300

Fort Peck Interpretive Center, Fort Peck, 526-3539

Garfield County Museum, Jordan

Judith River Dinosaur Institute, Malta, 654-2323
    www.montanadinosaurdigs.com

Makoshika State Park Visitor Center, Glendive, 377-6256

Museum of the Rockies, Montana State University-Bozeman, has the
    largest collection of dinosaur fossils in the United States, 994-3170.

Old Trail Museum, Choteau, 466-5332 www.oldtrailmuseum.org

Phillips County Museum, Malta, 1-800-704-1776 or 654-1037

Two Medicine Dinosaur Center, Bynum, 800-238-6873 or 469-2211
    www.tmdinosaur.org

Mountains

Depending on who's counting and how they're counting, Montana contains between 25 and 30 mountain peaks higher than 12,000 feet, all in the Beartooth Range, west of Red Lodge and south of Big Timber. Granite Peak (12,799 feet) and the next 56 highest peaks in Montana are in the Beartooths. Hundreds of peaks in the western part of the state rise higher than 10,000 feet.

Numerous isolated mountain ranges, associated plateaus, and buttes dot the central and eastern plains. Examples of these mountains include the Pryor Range, the Crazy Mountains, and the Little Belts.

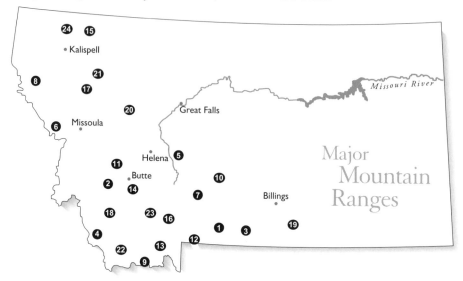

Major Montana Mountain Ranges

1 – Absaroka Range

This range west of the Beartooths has more than 65 peaks over 10,000 feet. The Absarokas are considered the most rugged mountains in Montana—128 major summits in the range have no official names.

2 – Anaconda Range

This range rises south of Anaconda and makes the Continental Divide for 40 miles. It borders the eastern side of the Big Hole. Two-thirds of the many 10,000-foot peaks of this range lie within the Anaconda-Pintler Wilderness Area on the western side of the range.

3 – Beartooth Range

This is the only range in the state with peaks over 12,000 feet—almost 30 of them. Eleven plateaus reach higher than 10,000 feet. The easy way to see these peaks is along the Beartooth Highway, a National Forest Scenic Byway between Red Lodge and Cooke City. Rocks over 3.3 billion years old are exposed in this range.

4 – Beaverhead Mountains

This range borders Idaho, running between the Bitterroot Range and the Big Hole Valley.

5 – Big Belt Mountains

The range features limestone cliffs and other rock formations above the Missouri River and Canyon Ferry Reservoir.

6 – Bitterroot Range

Montana's longest mountain range, it extends into Idaho. Eighteenmile Peak is the highest peak on the Continental Divide in Montana, at 11,125 feet.

7 – Bridger Range

The crest of this range to the north of Bozeman towers nearly 10,000 feet. Bridger Bowl Ski Area is famous for its excellent powder skiing.

8 – Cabinet Mountains

The Cabinets are the dominant range of northwestern Montana, extending along the Idaho border. Within this range is the 100,000-acre Cabinet Mountain Wilderness Area. The highest point, Snowshoe Peak, is only 8,738 feet, but the range appears stunningly high because surrounding areas are some of the lowest elevations in Montana.

9 – Centennial Mountains

The spine of these east-west oriented mountains forms the Continental Divide and the Montana-Idaho border. The Centennials are noted for diversity of flora and fauna.

10 – Crazy Mountains

This west-central Montana range rises abruptly from ranchlands north of Big Timber and features 23 majestic peaks above 10,000 feet. Fifteen of these do not have names.

11 – Flint Creek Range

The Flint Creeks separate the Deer Lodge Valley on the eastern side from the Philipsburg Valley on the western edge. The highest of these peaks is Mount Powell, which reaches higher than 10,000 feet.

12 – Gallatin Range

The Gallatins stretch for 60 miles south of Bozeman into Yellowstone National Park. The range's highest point, Electric Peak (10,992 feet), lies just inside the park. Also includes the Gallatin River and its canyon, waterfalls, lakes, and creeks.

13 – Gravelly Range

The Gravelly Range, south of Virginia City, is an imposing plateau with several 10,000-foot peaks.

14 – Highland Mountains

This small range, just south of Butte, includes a 10,000-foot plateau known as Table Mountain.

15 – Lewis Range

The forested lower slopes of these mountains in Glacier National Park lead to magnificent heights. The road that winds among many of these peaks and through spectacular Logan Pass is aptly called Going-to-the-Sun.

16 – Madison Range

With six peaks over 11,000 feet, this range is considered the second highest in the state. Only 48 of its 122 peaks that exceed 10,000 feet have names. The 11,316-foot Hilgard Peak is the loftiest peak outside the Beartooth Range, yet it is only the 61st highest in the state. The range runs from south of Bozeman for 50 miles to the western entrance to Yellowstone National Park. It includes the Spanish Peaks at its northern end.

17 – Mission Range

This 60-mile-long wall of rugged peaks separates the Swan Valley from the Mission and Flathead Valleys. The Mission Mountains rise sharply from the valley floors and appear higher than they are. There are remnants of several small glaciers and more than one hundred high lakes. Much of the range is in the Mission Mountains Tribal Wilderness, managed by the Kootenai-Salish Indians.

18 – Pioneer Mountains

These mountains have a western and eastern flank, split by the Wise River and

---

THE GREAT DIVIDE

The Continental Divide enters the state at the Canadian border, bisecting Glacier National Park. It then winds through the state's western counties. It defines the border of Montana and Idaho from Lost Trail Pass in southwestern Montana to the Wyoming border at Yellowstone National Park.

Every land mass has divides—a ridge of land from which water sheds in different directions. The Continental Divide is also known as the Great Divide, since it separates the continent's mass into its major watersheds.

From Triple Divide in Glacier National Park, raindrops that fall only a few feet apart take widely differing routes to the seas. Depending on which side of the three-sided point of land they fall on, the raindrops flow east into the Missouri and Mississippi rivers, the Gulf of Mexico, and the Atlantic Ocean; west to the Columbia River and the Pacific, or north and east into the rivers that lead to Hudson Bay.

a National Forest Scenic Byway, which provides access to trailheads leading into the backcountry. Fifty summits in the Pioneers reach higher than 10,000 feet.

19 – Pryor Mountains

This unglaciated range is characterized by flat benches, high deserts, mesas, buttes, and deep limestone canyons. Portions of the range, much of which is on the Crow Indian Reservation, are desert-like and only partially forested.

20 – Rocky Mountain Front

This range is sometimes known as the Sawtooths and aptly so. Its sharp, often irregular peaks rise abruptly from the plains on the far eastern border of the Bob Marshall and Scapegoat wilderness areas. The range features many precipitous limestone cliffs and deep canyons.

N O T A B L E

James Willard Schultz (1859-1947)

Schultz came to Montana from the state of New York at the age of 17 and worked at the Fort Conrad Trading Post. He soon was living with the Blackfeet. He married a Piegan woman, was given the Piegan name *Apikuni*, meaning "Far Off White Robe," and even participated in raids against other tribes. Schultz shared his knowledge of Indian life, hunting, and the Montana wilderness by writing about them. He published more than thirty books, including *My Life As An Indian* (1907) and *Blackfeet Tales of Glacier National Park* (1916).

MONTANA HISTORICAL SOCIETY

In 1885, the naturalist George Bird Grinnell read one of Schultz's articles in Forest and Stream magazine after visiting northwestern Montana. Grinnell soon returned to the area and, with Apikuni as his guide, visited the lakes, rivers, and peaks that inspired Grinnell to crusade for their preservation. In 1910, the area that Schultz wrote of was designated x. Apikuni Mountain, north of Lake Sherburne in the park, was named in his honor. Schultz's son, Hart Merriam Schultz, also known as "Lone Wolf," became a respected painter and provided a visual equivalent of his father's documentation of life as a Blackfeet Indian.

M O N T A N A N S

21 – Swan Range

This rugged range borders the western side of the Bob Marshall and Scapegoat wilderness areas for over 100 miles. The abrupt rise of much of the range limits access but provides several spectacular waterfalls.

22 – Tendoy Mountains

In the southwestern corner of the state, this range stretches more than 30 miles west of Interstate 15. Its eastern canyons drain into the Red Rock River.

23 – Tobacco Root Mountains

This range rises like a fortress on the plains south of Whitehall. Its deeply glaciated high peaks contain dozens of sparkling glacial lakes.

24 – Whitefish Range

Extends northwest from the town of Whitefish and Big Mountain ski resort to the Canadian border. Woodland caribou have been seen in the Ten Lakes area, northeast of Ksanka Peak (7,505 feet).

Highs and Lows

Montana's elevations, measured from sea level, range from 1,820 feet, where the Kootenai River exits the state in the northwest corner, to 12,799-foot Granite Peak, near the south-central border. Almost all of the plains area of the state is 4,500 feet or less, with most locations below 3,000 feet. Most agricultural activities west of the Continental Divide are confined to areas under 4,500 feet.

Source: Joseph Caprio and Gerald Nielsen, Climate Atlas of Montana. *Bozeman: Montana State University Extension Service, 1992.*

Highest Peaks in Selected Ranges

Peak	Elevation (in feet)	Range
Granite Peak	12,799	Beartooth Range
Hilgard Peak	11,316	Madison Range
Crazy Peak	11,214	Crazy Mountains
Mount Cowan	11,206	Absaroka Range
Tweedy Mountain	11,154	East Pioneer Mountains
Eighteenmile Peak	11,141	Bitterroot Range
Electric Peak	10,992	Gallatin Range
West Goat Peak	10,793	Anaconda Range
Mount Jefferson	10,604	Tobacco Root Mountains
Sunset Peak	10,581	Gravelly Range
Mount Cleveland	10,466	Lewis Range
Table Mountain	10,223	Highland Mountains
Mount Powell	10,164	Flint Creek Range

Elevations of Selected Mountain Passes

Pass	Location	Elev. (in feet)
Colter Pass	US 212, east of Cooke City	8,000
Chief Joseph Pass	MT 43, west of Wisdom	7,264
Targhee Pass	US 20, west of West Yellowstone	7,072
Lost Trail Pass	US 93, Montana-Idaho border	7,014
Monida Pass	I-15, Montana-Idaho border	6,870
Raynolds Pass	MT 87, southwest of Hebgen Lake	6,836
Logan Pass	Going-to-the-Sun Road, Glacier National Park	6,646
Homestake Pass	I-90, east of Butte	6,375
Elk Park Pass	I-15, north of Butte	6,368
MacDonald Pass	US 12, west of Helena	6,320
Flesher Pass	County 279, northwest of Helena	6,130
Bozeman Pass	I-90, east of Bozeman	5,760
Rogers Pass	MT 200, northeast of Lincoln	5,710
Marias Pass	US 2, west of East Glacier	5,280
Lolo Pass	US 12, southwest of Missoula	5,235
Lookout Pass	I-90, Montana-Idaho border	4,700

Source: Montana Department of Commerce, Official Montana Highway Map, 2004.

Rivers

Montana has within its borders portions of three major river drainage systems of North America.

- West of the Continental Divide, the streams eventually drain into the Columbia River, which flows into the Pacific Ocean. Major rivers of this system within the state are the Kootenai, Clark Fork, Blackfoot, Bitterroot, and Flathead.
- East of the divide, the Missouri River collects numerous tributaries, including the Marias, Milk, and Yellowstone rivers. From its headwaters at Three Forks, the Missouri flows 2,546 miles to the Mississippi River, and joins waters emptying into the Gulf of Mexico.
- In parts of Glacier National Park and Teton County, streams drain via the Belly and St. Mary rivers into Canada's Saskatchewan-Nelson drainage, flowing northeastward into Hudson Bay.

Whitefish
2,998 ft

Kalispell
2,984 ft

Polson
2,930 ft

Havre
2,493 ft

Glasgow
2,088 ft

Missoula
3,232 ft

Deer Lodge
4,609 ft

Anaconda
5,239 ft

Great Falls
3,389 ft

Lewistown
3,963 ft

Glendive
2,053 ft

Miles City
2,362 ft

Hamilton
3,625 ft

Helena
4,068 ft

Livingston
4,557 ft

Bozeman
4,806 ft

Billings
3,153 ft

City
Elevations

Dillon
5,118 ft

West Yellowstone
6,670 ft

Source: Natural Resource Information Center, Montana State Library.

The Missouri River is 2,546 miles long, a distance longer than the main stem (2,340 miles) of the Mississippi River into which it flows near St. Louis, Missouri. Had surveyors considered the Missouri River to be the upper stem of the Mississippi, what are today considered two rivers would be one, stretching 3,710 miles from Beaverhead County to the Louisiana Delta. It would rank as the fourth longest river in the world after the Nile (4,160 miles), the Amazon (4,000 miles), and China's Chang Jiang (3,964 miles). Instead, surveyors took Lake Itasca, Minnesota, as the source of the Mississippi. The Upper and Lower Mississippi total 2,340 miles and form the world's twelfth largest river.

The waters of the Missouri begin their journey in the Red Rock River, flowing into the Beaverhead River, a tributary of the Jefferson. The Jefferson, Gallatin, and Madison rivers merge around Three Forks to form the main stem of the Missouri. The Missouri River receives the Yellowstone River near the Montana-North Dakota border. Other great Montana rivers that join the Missouri flow include: the Dearborn, Teton, Sun, Marias, Musselshell, Smith, Judith, Milk, and Poplar rivers, to name a few.

Montana cannot claim all of the great Yellowstone River, as it begins some 30 miles south of Yellowstone National Park in Wyoming before it winds its 670 miles to the Missouri River. Along the Yellowstone's 570-mile course through Montana, it collects water from the Shields, Boulder, Stillwater, Clarks Fork (of the Yellowstone), Tongue, Powder, and Bighorn rivers. It is the nation's longest of free-flowing river.

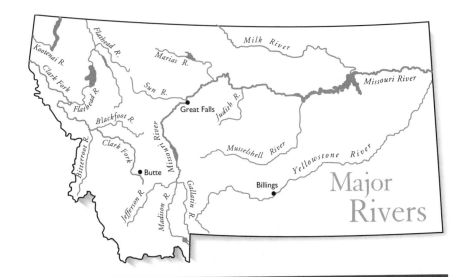

Major Rivers

The Clark Fork (of the Columbia) River is the major drainage of western Montana. It begins as Silver Bow Creek near Butte and flows northwestward to the Idaho border near Noxon, Montana, and Sandpoint, Idaho. On its deep and relentless course through Montana to the Columbia, it collects Rock Creek and the Blackfoot, Bitterroot, Flathead, and Thompson rivers. The Kootenai River, a tributary of the Columbia, makes a short loop through the northwestern corner of Montana. When it enters at the Canadian border near Eureka, it is as Lake Koocanusa, a 40-mile-long reservoir behind Libby Dam. The Kootenai leaves at the state's lowest elevation—1,820 feet.

There are 49,643 miles of perennial streams in Montana, 117,065 miles of intermittent and ephemeral waterways and 7,094 miles of manmade ditches and canals.

In an average year, 44 million acre-feet of water flow out of Montana and 64 percent of this amount originates within the state's borders.

Source: United States Department of Agriculture, Natural Resources Conservation Service.

National Wild and Scenic Rivers

Montana has 368 miles of federally designated Wild and Scenic Rivers. The federal Wild and Scenic Rivers Act of 1968 preserves these waters in their free-flowing condition for the "enjoyment of present and future generations." A stretch of river may be granted status as "Wild and Scenic" if it is free-flowing and contains at least one "outstandingly remarkable value." This standard can include scenery, recreational potential, wildlife, fisheries, or cultural, historic or geological significance. It takes an act of Congress or the Secretary of the Interior, upon a request by a state governor, to declare a river "Wild and Scenic."

Upper Missouri	149 miles, from Fort Benton to the Fred Robinson Bridge on US 191
North Fork of the Flathead	58 miles, from the Canadian border to its confluence with the Middle Fork
Middle Fork of the Flathead	101 miles, from the confluence of Strawberry and Bowl Creeks to its confluence with the South Fork
South Fork of the Flathead	60 miles, from the confluence of Young's and Danaher Creeks downstream to Hungry Horse Reservoir

Lakes

Montana has over 1,400 square miles of inland water. Much of this is held in the hundreds of natural and man-made lakes that dot the high mountain terrain, valley bottoms, and "potholes" on the prairies. Most of the natural lakes are in the Rocky Mountain region, but there are a few in the north-central and northeastern parts of the state.

Flathead Lake, in the mountain valley south of Glacier National Park, is the state's largest natural lake, with 188 square miles of surface area. Ice age glaciers carved the trench that now holds Flathead Lake. The year-round mild weather that backs up against the Mission Mountains to the east of the lake, along with fertile glacial soils, have created an excellent environment for growing the famous Flathead sweet cherries.

Tally Lake, west of Whitefish, has been determined to be the deepest natural lake in Montana, with a depth of 492 feet.

Lake McDonald, in Glacier National Park, is 10 miles long and 400 feet at its deepest. Medicine Lake, in northeastern Montana, is what remains of an ancient channel of the Missouri River.

Other large natural lakes include Big, Kintla, Mary Ronan, Placid, Seeley, Salmon, Swan, Whitefish, and Georgetown. Lakes have formed behind twenty-five dams in Montana.

Native Plants and Trees

The Lewis and Clark Expedition compiled the first catalogue of Montana flora and fauna along its route to the Pacific Ocean. Today, more than 2,500 species of wildflowers and non-flowering plants can be found in Montana.

Great expanses of native grasslands on public and private lands in Montana provide some of the best cattle and sheep grazing opportunities in the nation.

There are 15 species of flowering plants that occur only in this state.

The Montana Natural Heritage Program identifies 330 Plant Species of Concern in Montana (2003). There are no federally listed endangered plant species in Montana. The two federally listed threatened plant species are: water howellia (Howellia aquatilis), an annual aquatic plant, which can occur in glacial potholes and former river oxbows; and Ute ladies'-tresses (Spiranthes diluvialis), a native, perennial, white-flowered orchid, which can occur in low elevation wetlands.

Huckleberry Heaven

On August 14, 1805, Meriwether Lewis and his party of explorers held off starvation with huckleberry pancakes while waiting to meet up with Captain William Clark after crossing the Continental Divide into Idaho. While most of us think of huckleberries as a delightful treat, they may have served as Lewis and his corps' salvation.

The Indians they met knew all about the purple treasures. The berries held an important place in Kootenai and Salish Indian tradition. Well into the 20th century, the Salish had a ceremony in July, around powwow time, in which two sisters would go into the woods and pick a bucket of berries. The berries would be passed among tribal members until everyone had two berries. It was then deemed the appropriate time for everyone to go picking. The Indians dried huckleberries for use in stew with venison and bitterroot.

In general, huckleberries are pea-sized, with smooth skin, an indent on their base, and seeds no bigger than a pepper flake. The bushes are knee to chest high and the green leaves are occasionally tinged with red.

The berries grow best on a north slope, with a preference for elevations of 3,500 to 7,000 feet. They require moisture and the acidic soil typical to coniferous forests. Hand-picking is the preferable way to harvest the berry. Other means can damage the plant.

Throughout the 1930s and 1940s, the legendary huckleberry crops of western Montana provided a free food supply and critical economic activity during tough times. Old-timers tell of the great "huckleberry camps," where Indian and non-Indian families would bring camping and canning equipment into woods and stay until the berries were gone. In certain good drainages, there were sometimes five hundred tepees, an improvised store, and a general boomtown atmosphere.

Morel Mushrooms

The coveted morel mushroom flourishes in recently burned areas of the forest. In the severe fire seasons since 2000, thousands of acres in the Lolo, Bitterroot, Flathead, and Kootenai national forests have been designated for commercial mushroom harvesting from mid-May through July. A permit is required for commercial picking.

The morel mushroom looks like a cross between a brain and a cow pie, but it is a high-class delicacy that is fetching top dollar across the United States and the world. Morels sprout when conditions of moisture, sunlight, and soil disturbance are just right. They seem to like the edges of forests, though morels can be found in a variety of conditions.

Weeds

The spread of noxious weeds is a big problem in Montana. Each person who engages in activities in the forests and recreation areas is a potential "carrier" of destructive weed seeds, like those of knapweed. Seeds can be transported long distances before they shake loose and become buried in the soil to germinate in a future weed patch that edges out native wild grasses, flowers, and other plants. Knapweed is one of Montana's most undesirable noxious weeds. One plant can send out as many as 100,000 seeds. Its root system puts chemicals into the nearby ground that kill native plants. The spread of this noxious weed has ruined extensive public and private pasture lands.

It is illegal to permit certain weeds to grow on private land. Landowners are considered in noncompliance with the law if they make no attempt to control the following weeds:

Canada thistle	field bindweed	dyers woad
whitetop	leafy spurge	purple loosestrife
Russian knapweed	spotted knapweed	yellow toadflax
diffuse knapweed	Dalmatian toadflax	orange hawkweed
St. Johnswort	sulfur cinquefoil	meadow hawkweed
perennial pepperwood	oxeye daisy	hounds tongue
common tansy	tansy ragwort	tall buttercup
tamarisk		

Source: http://www.montana.edu/wwwpt/pubs/

Forests and Trees

Nearly one fourth of Montana, 22.4 million acres, is forested. Nearly 11.4 million acres of forest are administered by the USDA Forest Service and 3.4 million acres are protected in wilderness areas, national parks, and monuments. Six million acres are privately owned timberlands.

Most of the forests occur west of the Continental Divide, where the moist Pacific Coast air mass and the mountainous topography provide favorable climatic conditions for the growth of some twenty-seven types of forest trees and other vegetation. East of the divide, the drier climate results in more scattered forests, mainly found at elevations of 6,000 feet or more. At lower elevations in eastern Montana, there are considerable areas of open "coniferous woodland" along the outer margins of the forests. Douglas-fir is the predominant forest type.

Our forests provide the timber for the lumber and wood-products industries. They also serve an important function as a watershed, storing and releasing water for irrigation, hydroelectric power, and industrial and domestic uses. Annual precipitation on forested land is considerably greater than it is on nonforested. Seventy percent of the state's runoff or stream flow originates in forested areas.

Montana's Most Common Trees

Conifers: Douglas-fir (40%)
Subalpine fir (11%)
Grand fir
Mountain hemlock
Western hemlock
Rocky Mountain juniper
Utah juniper
Subalpine larch
Western larch
Limber pine
Lodgepole pine
Ponderosa pine (20%)
Western white pine
Whitebark pine
Western redcedar
Engelmann spruce
White spruce

Deciduous: Quaking aspen
Paper birch
Black cottonwood
Narrowleaf cottonwood
Plains cottonwood
Willow
Thinleaf alder
Black chokecherry
Black hawthorn
Bigtooth maple
Rocky Mountain maple
Western mountain ash
Curlleaf mountain
mahogany

Arnold Bolle (1912–1994)

A forester, conservationist, educator, and avid bird watcher, Bolle served as dean of The University of Montana Forestry School in the 1960s and 1970s. With six colleagues, he offered scientific evidence of the destruction wrought by clearcutting in the Bitterroot National Forest, paving the way for passage of the National Forest Management Act of 1976. Consequently, extraction of our natural resources was subjected to much closer scrutiny by public officials and lawmakers. Bolle was well liked by students and respected by his peers and many of his opponents for the knowledge and wisdom that support-

MONTANA HISTORICAL SOCIETY

ed his strong defense of wild lands. Of his many honors, Bolle is said to have most prized the Bob Marshall Award, the highest honor bestowed by The Wilderness Society.

Rutledge Parker (1877–1969)

Parker was a forester and administrator. He was appointed state forester in 1925 and served for twenty-eight years. In 1929, with the support of Montana's Kiwanis Clubs, he proposed a state park system to the Legislature, which responded with little enthusiasm to the idea. It was the eve of the Great Depression and Montana already had seventeen national forests and two national parks. Many officials thought the state could not afford to reserve more land, removing it from possible agricultural use and requiring an agency to manage the parks.

It took years of determination and compromise to get what Parker (and many others) wanted.

In 1936 Lewis and Clark Caverns became Montana's first state park. The land around the caverns was set aside through trades and donations, with little help from the Legislature, which had given Parker the additional title of Director of State Parks but made no appropriations for acquisition and development of land for parks. Parker kept the park system afloat and, in 1947, the Legislature finally appropriated funds for Montana's state parks.

Montana's Trophy Trees

Montana has the nation's largest western larch. It stands at 155 feet, in Missoula County. Our other national champion is a 142-foot tall quaking aspen, which has a trunk diameter of 30 inches. It lives near Troy.

Forest Fires

Prior to modern settlement, the forests and prairies were naturally "cleaned and groomed" by periodic forest fires, in a cycle that many believe to be beneficial to the health of the forest. But for decades, Montanans were hard pressed to find anything positive about the terrible forest fires of 1910—the

Major Forest Fires

Fire Name	Year	Location	Cause	Acres Burned	Deaths/ Damage
Mann Gulch	1949	Gates of the Mountains	lightning	5,000+	12 smokejumpers 1 FS employee killed
Sleeping Child	1965	Darby		28,000	
Pattee Canyon	1977	Missoula			6 homes destroyed
Hawk Creek	1984	near Roundup		180,000	44 homes destroyed
North Hills	1984	N.E. of Helena		27,000	cabins burned, 2 towns threatened
Canyon Creek	1988	Scapegoat Wilderness-Augusta	lightning	247,000	outbuildings and cattle burned; fire-fighters receive burns
Storm Creek	1988	Yellowstone Park-Custer NF-Absaroka Wilderness	lightning	107,000	Cooke City and Silver Gate evacuated
Red Bench	1988	Flathead NF		37,500	Polebridge evacuated; firefighter killed by falling snag
Warm Springs	1988	Elkhorn Mountains	human-caused	47,000	2 homes destroyed, others burned
Shephard Mtn.	1996	East Rosebud Lake	lightning	12,800	$2 million in property damage; 32 homes destroyed; Luther and Roscoe evacuated
Valley Complex Skalkaho Complex Wilderness Complex Blodgett and Little Blue acres	2000	Bitterroot NF	lightening; human-caused	356,000	70 residences and 170 other structures destroyed
Canyon Ferry	2000	north of Helena	human-caused	43,922	250 residents evacuated; 50 structures lost
Wedge Canyon	2003	north of Columbia Falls, Glacier National Park	lightning	53,515	36 structures lost

worst on record for the northern Rocky Mountains. The fires that raged all across western Montana and northern Idaho that year destroyed 2.6 billion board feet of timber in Montana alone and have come to be remembered as "The Great Burn."

After that frightening event, and for the rest of the century, the public policy on forest fires was to extinguish wild fires as quickly as possible, even in remote areas. The new United States Department of Agriculture's Forest Service, created in 1905, began to develop better fire detection systems — a network of lookout towers, forest roads, wilderness trails, and telephone stations. After World War II, the Forest Service teamed up with the Army Air Patrol to locate and extinguish fires by using aircraft and "smokejumpers." The agency also initiated the "Smokey Bear" and "Keep Montana Green" fire protection programs. Today, fires are fought with smoke jumpers, bulldozers, portable pumps, helicopters and aircraft, and fire retardant drops.

Even with an impressive arsenal of fire fighting equipment and prevention measures, Montana and the West have experienced some fearsome forest fire seasons in recent years. In 1988, almost 600,000 acres burned in various locations across the state, including much of Yellowstone National Park. In the summers of 2000 and 2003, many Montana counties endured some of the worst fire seasons on record. In both years, hundreds of separate fires burned millions of acres of Montana's forests and prairie lands. At times, up to 10,000 firefighters battled to save people, livestock, towns, wildlife, and historic landmarks. Nearly 20 percent of the Bitterroot National Forest

SMOKEJUMPERS

More than 5,000 smokejumpers have learned to fight forest fires at the Missoula Smokejumper Base. They have made hundreds of thousands of jumps to make quick initial attacks on wild land fires in remote areas.

Twelve smokejumpers and a USDA Forest Service employee lost their lives in the Mann Gulch fire of August 1949. The fire burnt 5,000 acres near the Gates of the Mountains on the Missouri River. The 1952 movie Red Skies Over Montana is based on the tragedy. Norman Maclean's book Young Men and Fire (1992) is an exhaustive, painstakingly researched account of the blaze and its aftermath.

burned in 2000. In addition to over 980,000 acres burned statewide in thousand of separate fires, some 13 percent of Glacier National Park was lost to fire in 2003. The combined state and federal costs of firefighting in 2003 exceeded $122 million.

Wildlife

In 1805, when the Lewis and Clark Expedition first reached Montana, they noted vast herds of buffalo, elk, and antelope on the prairies along the Missouri River. The number and varieties of waterfowl and other birds astonished them. In one journal entry, Captain Clark vowed to stop talking about the quantity of game and other animals, as no one would believe the claims.

They encountered the fearsome grizzly bear near the present-day North Dakota border. They saw moose as far east as the Milk River. By the time the Corps of Discovery got to the area that would become Montana, its members had to subsist on the bounty of the land, but Captain Lewis would not allow the party to kill more animals than were needed. Captain Clark noted that it required four deer, or an elk and a deer, or one buffalo to supply the troop for 24 hours.

The Indians who made Montana home had always counted on wildlife for food, shelter, clothing, and trade items, and so did those adventurers who followed on the heels of Lewis and Clark. When the golden age of fur trapping ended in the 1850s, the beaver population was all but gone, and interest turned to a thriving trade in elk, deer, and buffalo hides. When the gold strikes of the early 1860s brought in a flood of prospectors, game was still plentiful near the mining camps and became an important source of food. That would soon change.

After the 1870s, the Indian tribes could no longer protect their hunting grounds from the buffalo hunters who slaughtered the bison for sport and profit. In addition, stockmen valued the verdant plains as rangeland for cattle driven up from Texas.

By the turn of the century, Montana's wildlife resources presented a sorry picture. Only a few bands of elk remained in the high mountains, and deer were diminishing in areas where they had formerly flourished. Mountain sheep and antelope diminished, some herds all but disappearing. Millions of buffalo had been reduced to a few stragglers in the Yellowstone National Park region. Fur-bearing animals of any importance to man were becoming rare. The people of Montana finally realized that an important resource of the state could be wiped out. Some of the first laws enacted in the new state of Montana were aimed at protecting big game, waterfowl, fur-bearing animals, birds, and fish.

Research by wildlife biologists has advanced our understanding of habitat, ecology, and population control. Combined with law enforcement, that research has helped improve the state of most of our wildlife populations. Today, Montana is one of the best places in the lower forty-eight states for wildlife watching and hunting opportunities.

The Montana Department of Fish, Wildlife & Parks website is www.fwp.state.mt.us. The site includes information on fishing, hunting, wildlife, parks, education, a kid's page, and resources. In addition, the site provides links to Travel Montana, the U.S. Fish and Wildlife Service, the National Park Service, Trout Unlimited, Ducks Unlimited, and various news and weather links.

Bison

The bison once roamed over one-third of the North American continent, in numbers exceeding any other large mammal of recent times. Montana's Indian tribes pursued the great beasts on their southward migration to the central Great Plains in the late fall and met them with bows and arrows on their return to the rich grasslands of the state in the spring. Scattered across Montana are a number of the "pishkuns," or cliffs where Indians killed large portions of the herds by driving them over the edge.

The skilled hunters and their tribes used nearly every part of the bison. Bison meat was a food staple, the hides became clothing and tepees, and the bones were used for knives and scraping tools. The white men who came to the plains of the West slaughtered all but a few of this species from the 1870s to 1883. In 1881–1882, one steamship captain claimed that he hauled over 250,000 hides from Montana to Bismarck, North Dakota, for further dispersion. The hides sold for three or four dollars, and there was some market demand for the horns as Victorian-era hat racks and other decorations.

The bison in Montana were the last of the nation's great herds to be slaughtered. They survived longer than their counterparts in other western states because the cold winters and the hostile Blackfeet discouraged many buffalo hunters. Also, the railroads were comparatively late in coming to Montana and providing a means of exporting hides and other parts. After the greatest animal annihilation ever documented, some of the dried and bleached bison bones were gathered up and sold as fertilizer for $5 a ton. A

A Montana Mammal Sampler

Here is a listing of some of the 110 mammals that can be found, in varying habitats, within the state's borders.

Common Name	Scientific Name	Habitat & Occurrence
Badger	*Taxidea taxus*	Throughout the state, common.
Beaver	*Castor canadensis*	Along streams and lakes throughout the state, common.
Bighorn sheep	*Ovis canadensis*	In scattered bands in the western half of the state.
Bison	*Bison bison*	Formerly occurred throughout the state, now confined to Yellowstone Park, the National Bison Range, and in scattered bands on private ranches.
Black bear	*Ursus americanus*	Forested areas, rather common.
Black-footed ferret	*Mustela nigripes*	Originally across most of E. MT; reintroduced at UL Bend NWR.
Black-tailed prairie dog	*Cynomys ludovicianus*	Formerly abundant in eastern Montana, now much reduced by poisoning and the plague.
Bobcat	*Lynx rufus*	In many areas of the state, common.
Big brown bat	*Eptesicus fuscus*	Throughout the state; may hibernate in buildings during the winter.
Little brown bat	*Myotis lucifugus*	Throughout the state, common.
Canada lynx	*Lynx canadensis*	Heavily forested areas in western part of the state, rare.
Coyote	*Canis latrans*	Throughout the state, common.
Elk	*Cervus canadensis*	Certain areas in central and western Montana, common.
Fisher	*Martes pennanti*	Northwestern portion of the state, very rare.
Gray wolf	*Canis lupus*	Originally present throughout the state; recently reintroduced in Yellowstone Park; found in Glacier National Park and locally in NW Montana, rare.
Grizzly bear	*Ursus arctos horribilis*	Remote wilderness areas; originally throughout state, rare.
Hoary marmot	*Marmota caligata*	Above timberline in Glacier National Park and neighboring high mountain ranges, rare.
Montane vole	*Microtus montanus*	Dry grasslands of western and central Montana, uncommon.
Moose	*Alces americana*	Suitable areas in western half of the state, fairly common.
Mountain goat	*Oreamnos americanus*	High mountain ranges of western Montana; successfully transplanted in the Crazy Mountains.
Mountain lion	*Felix concolor*	Western counties, uncommon, rare in the eastern half of the state.
Mule deer	*Odocoileus hemionus*	Suitable habitats throughout the state, common.
Northern bog lemming	*Synaptomys borealis*	Only in wet meadows locally in western Montana, rare.
Northern flying squirrel	*Glaucomys sabrinus*	Dense forest in western counties, common.
Northern grasshopper mouse	*Onychomys leucogaster*	Grasslands of eastern mountains.
Norway rat	*Rattus norvegicus*	Known only in some of the cities.
Otter	*Lutra canadensis*	On large streams, mostly in western portion, uncommon.
Pygmy rabbit	*Sylvilagus idahoensis*	Found locally in sagebrush of SW Montana, rare.
Pika	*Ochotona princeps*	Slide rock areas in higher mountains, common.

A Montana Mammal Sampler (cont.)

Common Name	Scientific Name	Habitat & Occurrence
Porcupine	*Erethizon dorsatum*	Throughout the state, common.
Prairie jumping mouse	*Zapus hudsonius*	Known only in southeast Montana, rare.
Pronghorn antelope	*Antilocapra americana*	Most of eastern and central Montana, common.
Red fox	*Vulpes fulva*	Across most of the state, common.
Sagebrush mouse	*Lagurus curtatus*	Sagebrush areas in eastern and central Montana, rare.
Snowshoe hare	*Lepus americanus*	Forested areas in western half of the state, common.
Western jumping mouse	*Zapus princeps*	High mountain meadows and wet woods near water in the western half of the state.
White-tailed deer	*Odocoileus virfinianus*	Forested areas in western Montana and brushy river bottoms in eastern Montana.
White-tailed prairie dog	*Cynomys leucurus*	Known only in Carbon County.
Wolverine	*Gulo luscus*	Wilder portions of western mountains, very rare.
Yellow-bellied marmot	*Marmota flaviventris*	Rocky areas and mountains of most of the western part of the state, uncommon.

A HOME ON A RANGE

The bison, the largest mammal native to North America, was almost extinct in the early years of the twentieth century when the American Bison Society collected forty-one of them from private herds in Montana and elsewhere to stock the National Bison Range near Moiese. The U.S. government bought 18,540 acres on the Flathead Indian Reservation, and the reserve opened in 1908. The number of bison in the herd has increased over the years. The calves that are born there every spring can bring the herd's population to about four hundred by October. Some of the bison are sold after a fall roundup.

In 1933, a remarkable bison calf was born at the National Bison Range. He was almost an albino, white except for a dark brown "hat" between his horns. White buffalo are very rare, and Montana's Indians considered them sacred, so this one was given an Indian name: Big Medicine. At full maturity, he weighed 1,900 pounds and measured 12 feet long. You can still see him, but not at the refuge. He died at the great age of 26 and is now on display in the state Historical Society Museum in Helena, on the second floor. The taxidermy is the work of Bob Scriver, who was also a renowned bronze sculptor.

Bison are large animals and a close encounter with one is likely to be very dangerous, perhaps fatal. Visitors to the refuge at Moiese can observe them from the safety of a motor vehicle on a 19-mile self-guided tour open during the summer months.

The National Bison Range is also home to mule and white-tailed deer, elk, bighorn sheep, and pronghorns.

Check out http://bisonrange.fws.gov/nbr/.

few wild bison remained in Yellowstone National Park, forming the only wild herd left in the United States

The bison, *Bison bison,* is a member of the cattle family and is not accurately a "buffalo," which has no hump and is found mainly in Asia and Africa. A mature bull bison can weigh close to 2,000 pounds, stand 6 feet high at the shoulder, and measure up to 121/2 feet from his nose to the end of his tail. Calves are born in May and are a brick-red color for the first year of life. The animal sheds its shaggy, winter-damaged coat each March and can appear relatively trim and sleek until the new coat grows in.

In 2004, the Yellowstone National Park bison population was estimated to be around 4,200. More than 460 bison were captured in that winter as they wandered near the boundary of the Park in search of forage. About 260 were sent to slaughter, after testing positive for the cattle disease brucellosis.

Elk

Montana is home to more than 150,000 Rocky Mountain elk. The elk, sometimes referred to by its Shawnee name, "wapiti," is a large, grazing and browsing animal that prefers coniferous forests and mountain meadows. Bull elk can weigh from 700 to 850 pounds. Cows generally weigh in around 400 pounds. Mature bulls drop their antlers in March. By July, their new antlers may weigh up to 40 pounds.

By the turn of the last century, the Montana elk population was nearly decimated by loss of habitat, food hunters, and collectors of the "ivory teeth." In 1910, 6,000 elk from Yellowstone National Park were transplanted to suitable habitat across the state. Since that time, the state has been dedicated to protecting and increasing elk habitat, especially appropriate winter range. Montana is one of the premier hunting grounds for this most prized big game animal.

ROCKY MOUNTAIN ELK FOUNDATION

Founded in 1984, the Rocky Mountain Elk Foundation is a nonprofit wildlife conservation organization that works to ensure the future of elk, other wildlife, and their habitat. The RMEF has completed over 3,600 conservation projects in North America and has helped protect and enhance nearly 4 million acres of habitat, including 91,630 acres in Montana.

The RMEF Visitor Center and Gift Shop attracts more than 75,000 visitors each year. A new facility opened in late 2005, near the Reserve Street exit of Interstate 90.

The foundation can be reached by phone at (900) CALL ELK. Check out www.elkfoundation.org.

Wolves

Most of the wolves in Montana had been exterminated by the early 1900s. From 1870 to 1877, an estimated 700,000 wolves were shot, trapped, or poisoned. While those estimates may be overstated, records suggest that some 80,000 wolves were killed from 1883 to 1918 by the bounty-hunting "wolfers" or "wolf-getters" in the service of livestock owners eager to see their industry thrive. Federal government predator control programs removed another 24,000 from 1915 to 1942.

Several wolf packs, with members numbering from fifteen to thirty, did survive in Glacier National Park and the extreme northwestern corner of Montana. In 1989, wildlife biologists studied the first pack known to den outside Glacier National Park in 60 years. By the mid 1990s, there were as many as nine natural wolf packs in Montana, ranging as far south as the Deer Lodge and Boulder valleys.

Intense public debate and legal wrangling arose over plans for the reintroduction of breeding packs to Yellowstone National Park and central Idaho. In March 1995, twenty-nine Canadian wolves were finally released into the wilds of those areas. In January and April 1996, another seventeen Canadian wolves were set free in Yellowstone and nine were released in central Idaho. By that spring, the wolves released in Yellowstone had produced nine pups. Two of the original wolves had been killed—one by a truck; the other was illegally shot.

By the end of 2002, officials estimated Montana had over 180 wolves in 35 packs, and sixteen breeding pairs.

Troubled Species

The following species, which occur in Montana, are considered by the U.S. Fish and Wildlife Service to be endangered (in danger of extinction throughout all or a significant part of its range) or threatened (likely to become endangered in the foreseeable future) and are protected under the Federal Endangered Species Act.

Endangered
Black-footed ferret, *Mustela nigripes*
Pallid sturgeon, *Scaphirhynchus albus*
Whooping crane, *Grus americana*
Interior least tern, *sterna antillarum athalasso*
White sturgeon, *Acipenser transmontanus*
(Kootenai River population)

National Wildlife Refuges in Montana

Refuge Name Address/Phone	Location	Size (in acres)	Terrain	Wildlife Viewing
Benton Lake NWR 922 Bootlegger Trail Great Falls, MT 59404 727-7400	10 mi north of Great Falls on US 87, the Bootlegger Trail	Land: 12,383 Water: 5,000	marshy glacial lake bed on semiarid shortgrass prairie; low hills, coulees	nesting waterfowl, inc. tundra and whistling swan, snow geese, ibis, peregrine falcon; deer and smaller prairie mammals
Bowdoin NWR HC65, Box 5700 Malta, MT 59538 654-2863	7 mi east of Malta off old US 2	Land: 15,500 Water: 3,700	prairie pothole marshes on semiarid plain	on Central Flyway; duck nesting groups; over 200 bird species, antelope, and white-tailed deer
Charles M. Russell NWR P.O. Box 110 Lewistown, MT 59457 538-8706	Between MT 24 and US 191, south of Glasgow and Malta, north of Jordan	1,009,000 Fort Peck Lake	35 mi of Missouri River and Breaks	upland game birds; 45 species of mammals inc. elk, bighorn sheep, prairie dogs
Hailstone NWR P.O. Box 110 Lewistown, MT 59457	35 mi west of Billings, N of Rapelje	Land: 1,988 Water: 660	prairie marshes, sagebrush, native grasses, some private land	breeding grounds for grouse, shorebirds, and waterfowl; antelope, mule deer
Halfbreed NWR P.O. Box 110 Lewistown, MT 59457	5 mi south of Hailstone NWR	Land: 3,886	prairie marshes, sagebrush, native grasses, some private land	breeding grounds for grouse, shorebirds, and waterfowl; antelope, mule deer
Lake Mason NWR P.O. Box 110 Lewistown, MT 59457	6 mi NW of Roundup	Land: 18,600	marshes, open water, riparian habitat, shortgrass prairie	waterfowl, shorebirds, and upland game bird nesting area; peregrine falcon, bald eagle; prairie dog, rattlesnakes, lizards
Lee Metcalf NWR Box 257 Stevensville, MT 59870 777-5552	East of Stevensville, off US 93	Land: 2,800	forested river bottom in mountain valley	waterfowl, raptors, shorebirds, falcon, bald eagle, osprey, owls, muskrats, black bear, river otter
Lost Trail NWR National Bison Range Moeise, MT 59824 858-2216	25 miles west of Kalispell	Land: 9,325	shallow wetland, prairie grasslands, wooded slopes	variety of bird and mammal species, inc. endangered grizzly bear and grey wolf
Medicine Lake NWR 223 North Shore Rd. Medicine Lake, MT 59247 789-2305	24 mi N of Culbertson, off MT 16	Land: 31,457 Water: 21,500+	prairie potholes (glacially-formed lakes)	white pelicans nesting area; other waterfowl and upland, whooping and sandhill cranes, cormorants, gulls, heron; small prairie and game mammals

National Wildlife Refuges in Montana (cont.)

Refuge Name Address/Phone	Location	Size (in acres)	Terrain	Wildlife Viewing
Ninepipe NWR National Bison Range Moiese, MT 59824 644-2211	49 mi N of Missoula on US 93	Land: 2,062 Water: 1,770	over 800 potholes in marshes upland grasses, W of Mission Mtns.	migratory waterfowl, nesting area; 180 species, inc. Canada geese, heron, avocets, gulls
Pablo NWR National Bison Range Moiese, MT 59824 644-2211	49 mi N of Missoula on US 93	2,542	pothole marshland, upland grass W of Mission Mtns.	migratory waterfowl, nesting area; Canada geese, heron, whistling swan, avocets, gulls
National Bison Range 132 Bison Range Rd. Moiese, MT 59824 644-2211	N of Missoula on US 93 to Ravalli west 6 miles	18,541	steep hills, canyons, upland grasslands, river bottomland	some 500 American bison; mule deer, elk, bighorn sheep, mountain goat, and antelope
Red Rock Lakes NWR Monida Star Rt. Box 15 Lima, MT 59739 276-3536	I 15 to N of Idaho border	Land: 42,525 Water: 9,000	6,600 elev., N of Centennial Mtns., lake marshes	resident trumpeter swans, 250 species of birds, inc. sandhill crane; wide range of large and small mammals
Swan River NWR National Bison Range Moiese, MT 59824 644-2211	south end of Swan Lake off MT 83	1,569	wooded bottomlands, marshes	best viewing from canoe; 171 species of birds, inc. great blue heron, bald eagle, waterfowl; moose, grizzly and black bear
UL Bend NWR P. O. Box 110 Lewistown, MT 59457 538-8706	40 mi south of Malta on country roads	56,049	within Charles M. Russell NWR	elk in their native prairie habitat; prairie dogs, sage grouse, pronghorn, deer, and bighorn sheep
War Horse NWR P.O. Box 110 Lewistown, MT 59457 538-8706	40 mi east of Lewistown on MT 200	Land: 3,192 Water: 900	marshy lakes in upland grasslands and sagebrush	waterfowl and upland game bird habitat, bald eagle, antelope, mule deer

Threatened	Gray wolf, *Canis lupus*
	Grizzly bear, *Ursus arctos horribilis*
	Piping plover, *Charadrius melodus*
	Bald eagle, *Haliaeetus leucocephalus*
	Canadian lynx, *lynx Canadensis*
	Bull trout, *Salvelinus confluentus*

In an effort to maintain biological diversity in our state, the Montana Natural Heritage Program conducts an inventory of plant and animal populations, focusing on species and communities that are rare, threatened, endangered, or vulnerable throughout their range in Montana. The list is constantly updated and is accessible at http://nhp.nris.state.mt.us/. MNHP can be contacted at 444-3009.

Birds of Montana

The following 294 species have been documented as reliably occurring in Montana.

Common Loon
Pied-billed Grebe
Horned Grebe
Red-necked Grebe
Eared Grebe
Western Grebe
Clark's Grebe
American White Pelican
Double-crested Cormorant
American Bittern
Great Blue Heron
Snowy Egret
Black-crowned Night-Heron
White-faced Ibis
Turkey Vulture
Tundra Swan
Trumpeter Swan
Mute Swan
Greater White-fronted Goose
Snow Goose
Canada Goose
Wood Duck
Green-winged Teal
Mallard
Northern Pintail
Blue-winged Teal
Cinnamon Teal
Northern Shoveler
Gadwall

Eurasian Wigeon
American Wigeon
Canvasback
Redhead
Ring-necked Duck
Greater Scaup
Lesser Scaup
Harlequin Duck
Oldsquaw
Surf Scoter
White-winged Scoter
Common Goldeneye
Barrow's Goldeneye
Bufflehead
Hooded Merganser
Common Merganser
Red-breasted Merganser
Ruddy Duck
Osprey
Bald Eagle
Northern Harrier
Sharp-shinned Hawk
Cooper's Hawk
Northern Goshawk
Broad-winged Hawk
Swainson's Hawk
Red-tailed Hawk
Ferruginous Hawk
Rough-legged Hawk
Golden Eagle
American Kestrel
Merlin
Peregrine Falcon

Gyrfalcon
Prairie Falcon
Gray Partridge
Chukar
Ring-necked Pheasant
Spruce Grouse
Blue Grouse
White-tailed Ptarmigan
Ruffed Grouse
Sage Grouse
Sharp-tailed Grouse
Wild Turkey
Virginia Rail
Sora
American Coot
Sandhill Crane
Whooping Crane
Black-bellied Plover
Lesser Golden Plover
Semipalmated Plover
Piping Plover
Killdeer
Mountain Plover
Black-necked Stilt
American Avocet
Greater Yellowlegs
Lesser Yellowlegs
Solitary Sandpiper
Willet
Spotted Sandpiper
Upland Sandpiper
Whimbrel
Long-billed Curlew

Marbled Godwit
Ruddy Turnstone
Sanderling
Western Sandpiper
Least Sandpiper
Baird's Sandpiper
Pectoral Sandpiper
Dunlin
Stilt Sandpiper
Short-billed Dowitcher
Long-billed Dowitcher
Common Snipe
Wilson's Phalarope
Red-necked Phalarope
Franklin's Gull
Bonaparte's Gull
Ring-billed Gull
California Gull
Herring Gull
Caspian Tern
Common Tern
Forster's Tern
Least Tern
Black Tern
Rock Pigeon
Mourning Dove
Black-billed Cuckoo
Yellow-billed Cuckoo
Eastern Screech-Owl
Western Screech-Owl
Great Horned Owl
Snowy Owl
Northern Pygmy-Owl
Burrowing Owl
Barred Owl
Great Gray Owl
Long-eared Owl
Short-eared Owl
Boreal Owl
Northern Saw-whet Owl
Common Nighthawk
Common Poorwill
Black Swift
Chimney Swift
Vaux's Swift
White-throated Swift
Ruby-throated Hummingbird
Black-chinned Hummingbird
Calliope Hummingbird
Broad-tailed Hummingbird
Rufous Hummingbird
Belted Kingfisher
Lewis' Woodpecker

Red-headed Woodpecker
Red-naped Sapsucker
Williamson's Sapsucker
Downy Woodpecker
Hairy Woodpecker
Three-toed Woodpecker
Black-backed Woodpecker
Northern Flicker
Pileated Woodpecker
Olive-sided Flycatcher
Western Wood-Pewee
Willow Flycatcher
Least Flycatcher
Hammond's Flycatcher
Dusky Flycatcher
Cordilleran Flycatcher
Say's Phoebe
Cassin's Kingbird
Western Kingbird
Eastern Kingbird
Horned Lark
Tree Swallow
Violet-green Swallow
Northern Rough-winged
   Swallow
Bank Swallow
Cliff Swallow
Barn Swallow
Gray Jay
Steller's Jay
Blue Jay
Pinyon Jay
Clark's Nutcracker
Black-billed Magpie
American Crow
Common Raven
Black-capped Chickadee
Mountain Chickadee
Boreal Chickadee
Chestnut-backed Chickadee
Red-breasted Nuthatch
White-breasted Nuthatch
Pygmy Nuthatch
Brown Creeper
Rock Wren
Canyon Wren
House Wren
Winter Wren
Sedge Wren
Marsh Wren
American Dipper
Golden-crowned Kinglet
Ruby-crowned Kinglet

Eastern Bluebird
Western Bluebird
Mountain Bluebird
Townsend's Solitaire
Veery
Swainson's Thrush
Hermit Thrush
American Robin
Varied Thrush
Gray Catbird
Northern Mockingbird
Sage Thrasher
Brown Thrasher
American Pipit
Sprague's Pipit
Bohemian Waxwing
Cedar Waxwing
Northern Shrike
Loggerhead Shrike
European Starling
Plumbeous Vireo
Cassin's Vireo
Blue-headed Vireo
Warbling Vireo
Red-eyed Vireo
Tennessee Warbler
Orange-crowned Warbler
Nashville Warbler
Yellow Warbler
Yellow-rumped Warbler
Townsend's Warbler
Blackpoll Warbler
Black-and-white Warbler
American Redstart
Ovenbird
Northern Waterthrush
MacGillivray's Warbler
Common Yellowthroat
Wilson's Warbler
Yellow-breasted Chat
Western Tanager
Rose-breasted Grosbeak
Black-headed Grosbeak
Lazuli Bunting
Indigo Bunting
Green-tailed Towhee
Rufous-sided Towhee
American Tree Sparrow
Chipping Sparrow
Clay-colored Sparrow
Brewer's Sparrow
Field Sparrow
Vesper Sparrow

Lark Sparrow
Lark Bunting
Savannah Sparrow
Baird's Sparrow
Grasshopper Sparrow
Le Conte's Sparrow
Sharp-tailed Sparrow
Fox Sparrow
Song Sparrow
Lincoln's Sparrow
White-throated Sparrow
White-crowned Sparrow
Harris' Sparrow
Dark-eyed Junco
McCown's Longspur

Lapland Longspur
Chestnut-collared Longspur
Snow Bunting
Bobolink
Red-winged Blackbird
Western Meadowlark
Yellow-headed Blackbird
Rusty Blackbird
Brewer's Blackbird
Common Grackle
Brown-headed Cowbird
Orchard Oriole
Northern Oriole
Rosy Finch
Pine Grosbeak

Purple Finch
Cassin's Finch
House Finch
Red Crossbill
White-winged Crossbill
Common Redpoll
Hoary Redpoll
Pine Siskin
American Goldfinch
Evening Grosbeak
House Sparrow

Source: Montana Bird Distribution, 2003, Montana Audubon

Public Lands

Approximately 26.14 million acres (28 percent) of Montana's 93.156 million acres are owned, held in trust, or leased by the federal government for use by all U.S. citizens. The USDA Forest Service and the Bureau of Land Management together administer nearly 25 million acres.

State land accounts for more than 5 million acres (5.4 percent).

The diverse values of public lands include recreation, range, timber, minerals, watershed, fish and wildlife, and wilderness. Other values placed on public lands include scenic, scientific, and cultural resources.

National Forests

The USDA Forest Service, Northern Region, manages nine national forests in Montana, containing 16.8 million acres—18 percent of all lands in the state. USDA Forest Service lands are located throughout the state, though most are

MONTANA'S NEW NATIONAL MONUMENTS

Montana has two of the nation's newest National Monuments: the Upper Missouri River Breaks National Monument, spanning 149 miles of central Montana's Upper Missouri River and the surrounding badlands; Pompeys Pillar National Monument is a sandstone formation that the sits on 51 acres along the Yellowstone River, 28 miles east of Billings. It is named for Sacagawea's son, nicknamed Pomp by Captain William Clark. Clark carved his name on the landmark on his way eastward to meet Meriwether Lewis on their homeward trek in 1806.

in western Montana. National forests were established on conservation principles, based on wise use of natural resources. By congressional mandate, they are managed for multiple use, the combination of interests that best serves the public.

USDA Forest Service Offices
Northern Region Headquarters
Federal Bldg., 200 East Broadway
P.O. Box 7669
Missoula, MT 59807
329-3511
http://www.fs.fed.us.r1/

Beaverhead-Deerlodge National Forest 3.3 million acres

Dillon Supervisor's Office
420 Barrett Street
Dillon, MT 59725
683-3900

Deerlodge Supervisor's Office
Federal Building
P.O. Box 400
Butte, MT 59703
496-3400

Butte Ranger District 494-0200
Dillon Ranger District 683-3900
Madison Ranger District 682-4253
Deerlodge Ranger District 846-1770

Jefferson Ranger District 287-3223
   or (800) 433-9206
Philipsburg Ranger District 859-3211
Wise River Ranger District 832-3178
Wisdom Ranger District 689-3243

Bitterroot National Forest 1.6 million acres
1801 North 1st Street
Hamilton, MT 59840
363-7161

Stevensville Ranger District 777-5461
Darby Ranger District 821-3913

Sula Ranger District 821-3201
West Fork Ranger District 821-3269

Custer National Forest 1.1 million acres
1310 Main Street
Billings, MT 59105
657-6200

Beartooth Ranger District 446-2103
Ashland Ranger District 784-2344
(other ranger districts in North and South Dakota)

Flathead National Forest 2.35 million acres
1935 Third Ave. East
Kalispell, MT 59901
758-5200

Spotted Bear Ranger District
   758-5376 (Summer) 387-5243 (Winter)
Swan Lake Ranger District 837-7500

Hungry Horse Ranger District 387-3800
Glacier View Ranger District 892-4372
Tally Lake Ranger District 863-5400

Gallatin National Forest 1.8 million acres
Federal Bldg., 10 East Babcock
P.O. Box 130
Bozeman, MT 59771
587-6701

Big Timber Ranger District 932-5155   Bozeman Ranger District 522-2520
Livingston Ranger District 222-1892   Hebgen Lake Ranger District 823-6961
Gardiner Ranger District 848-7375 or -7376

Helena National Forest 975,407 acres
2880 Skyway Drive
Helena, MT 59601
449-5201

Townsend Ranger District 266-3425   Lincoln Ranger District 362-4265
Helena Ranger District 449-5490

Kootenai National Forest 1.8 million acres
506 U.S. Highway 2 West
Libby, MT 59923
293-6211

Rexford Ranger District 296-2536   Libby Ranger District 293-7773
Fortine Ranger District 882-4451   Cabinet Ranger Station 827-3533
Three Rivers Ranger District 295-4693

Lewis and Clark National Forest 1.9 million acres
1101 15th Street North
P.O. Box 869
Great Falls, MT 59403
791-7700

Rocky Mountain Ranger District 466-5341   Kings Hill Ranger District 547-3361
Judith Ranger District 566-2292   Belt Creek Ranger District 236-5511
Musselshell Ranger District 632-4391

Lolo National Forest 2.1 million acres
Building 24, Fort Missoula
Missoula, MT 59804
329-3750

Missoula Ranger District 329-3814   Seeley Lake Ranger District 677-2233
Ninemile Ranger District 626-5201   Superior Ranger District 822-4233
Plains/Thompson Falls Ranger District 826-3821

Bureau of Land Management

Within Montana, the Bureau of Land Management (BLM) administers more than 7,964,023 acres of federal lands, mostly in the eastern and southwestern parts of the state. That's about 8.6 percent of the land in the state.

Lands managed by the BLM extend across a varied geography, including mountains, forests, and plains, and afford extensive recreational opportunities—hunting, fishing, boating, camping, snowmobiling, and bird watching. The bureau protects numerous archaeological and historic sites and oversees 448,863 acres of wilderness study areas and hundreds of miles of federally designated Back Country Byways and Wild and Scenic Rivers.

The Bureau of Land Management maintains the Pryor Mountain Wild Horse Range south of Billings. It is home to about 150 horses, some of which are rare descendants of old Spanish stock.

Montana State Office
5001 Southgate Dr.
Billings, MT 59107
896-5013
www.mt.blm.gov

Butte Field Office
106 North Parkmont
Butte, MT 59702
494-5059

Dillon Field Office
1005 Selway Dr.
Dillon, MT 59715
683-2337

Lewistown Field Office
Airport Road
Lewistown, MT 59457
538-7461

Malta Field Office
501 South 2nd Street E.
Malta, MT 59538
654-1240

Miles City Field Office
111 Garyowen Road
Miles City, MT 59301
232-4333

Missoula Field Office
3225 Ft. Missoula Rd.
Missoula, MT 59804
329-3914

Havre Field Station 265-5891
Glasgow Field Station 228-4316
Great Falls 727-0503

Wilderness Areas

Less than 150 years ago Montana was one immense wilderness. Today, there are 15 major tracts of wild land in the state, 3,372,000 acres, formally protected by the federal Wilderness Act of 1964. These wilderness areas constitute 3.7 percent of the land in the state.

Approximately 9 percent of Montana is still considered roadless wild land, and the 89 areas are under temporary study or preservation status.

Montana wilderness areas are valuable homes for wildlife and watershed protection. They are not game preserves; hunting and fishing are permitted in accordance with state law.

"THE BOB"

The Bob Marshall Wilderness Area was named to honor a major advocate for wilderness preservation during the 1930s. Bob Marshall is also considered the catalyst for The Wilderness Society. While Marshall worked in and promoted wild places all over the United States, he got his start in Montana in 1925, when he went to work for a USDA Forest Service Range Experiment Station. He is remembered as a world-class hiker, often walking 40 or more miles in a day. He died of a heart condition in 1939, at the age of 38.

Wilderness Area	Year Designated	Acres	Location
Absaroka-Beartooth	1978	920,377	Custer/Gallatin NF
Anaconda-Pintler	1964	157,874	Beaverhead-Deerlodge/ Bitterroot NF
Bob Marshall	1978	1,009,356	Flathead/Lewis & Clark NF
Cabinet Mountains	1964	94,272	Kootenai/Kaniksu NF
Gates of the Mountains	1964	28,562	Helena NF
Great Bear	1978	286,700	Flathead NF
Lee Metcalf	1983	259,000	Beaverhead-Deerlodge/ Gallatin NF
Mission Mountains	1974	73,877	Flathead NF
Rattlesnake	1980	32,976	Lolo NF
Scapegoat	1974	239,936	Helena/Lolo/ Lewis & Clark NF
Selway-Bitterroot	1964	251,441	Bitterroot/Lolo NF
Welcome Creek	1978	28,135	Lolo NF

Source: Montana Wilderness Society.

Further Reading

Alt, David. *Glacial Lake Missoula and Its Humongous Floods.* Missoula, Montana: Mountain Press Publishing Company, 2001.

Alt, David D., and Donald W. Hyndman. *Roadside Geology of Montana.* Missoula: Mountain Press Publishing Company, ninth printing, 2000.

Bass, Rick. *The Ninemile Wolves.* New York: Ballantine Books, 1992.

Bowen, "Asta. *The Huckleberry Book.* Helena, Mont.: American Geographic Publishing, 1988.

Cunningham, Bill. *Wild Montana: A Guide to 55 Roadless Recreation Areas.* Helena: Falcon Press, 1995.

Elias, Thomas S., and Peter A. Dykeman. *A Field Guide to North American Edible Wild Plants.* New York: Outdoor Life Books, Times Mirror Magazines, Inc., 1982.

Fischer, Carol, and Hank Fischer. *Montana Wildlife Viewing Guide,* revised edition. Helena: Falcon Press, 1995.

Fischer, Hank. *Wolf Wars.* Helena: Falcon Press, 1995.

Foresman, Kerry. *Wild Mammals of Montana.* Special Publication No. 12, American Society of Mammalogists, Allen Press Inc., 2001.

Graetz, Rick and Susie. *This Is Montana.* Helena, Montana: Northern Rockies Publishing, 2003.

Hart, Jeff. *Montana Native Plants and Early Peoples.* Helena: Montana Historical Society Press, 1996 reprint.

Horner, Jack. *Dinosaurs Under the Big Sky.* Missoula, Mont.: Mountain Press Publishing Company, 2001.

Krumm, Bob. *The Rocky Mountain Berry Book.* Helena: Falcon Press, 1994.

Lange, Ian. *Ice Age Mammals of North America: A Guide to the Big, the Hairy, and the Bizarre.* Mountain Press Publishing Co., 2002.

Magley, Beverly. *Montana Wildflowers: A Beginner's Guide to the State's Most Common Flowers.* Helena: Falcon Press, 1992.

McMillion, Scott. *Mark of the Grizzly: True Stories of the Recent Bear Attacks and the Hard Lessons Learned.* Helena, Mont.: Falcon Publishing, Co., 1998.

Rocky Mountain Elk Foundation. *Majesty: Visions from the Heart of Elk Country.* Helena: Falcon Press, 1995.

Strickler, Dee. *Alpine Wildflowers.* Columbia Falls, Mont.: The Flower Press, 1990. *This title is an excellent guide, with color photos, covering the alpine and subalpine areas of the Rocky Mountain states. There are two other guides in Strickler's series,* Forest Wildflowers *and* Prairie Wildflowers, *both by the same publisher.*

Thompson, Larry S. *Distribution of Montana Amphibians, Reptiles and Mammals.* Helena: Montana Audubon Council, 1982.

Unforgettable Day Afield, Montana Hunting. Helena: Riverbend Publishing. 2002.

Werner, J. Kirwin, Bryce A. Maxell, Paul Hendricks, and Dennis L. Flath. *Amphibians and Reptiles of Montana.* Missoula, Mont.: Mountain Press Publishing Company, 2004.

CHAPTER FOUR

Montana's Past

$\mathcal{M}$ontana was described as a "land of shining mountains" by early explorers who may have seen only the far eastern edges of the majestic Rocky Mountains. Like adventurer and storyteller Andrew Garcia, these early visitors probably thought that roaming through nineteenth-century Montana was a "tough trip through paradise." Many years later, distinguished state historian K. Ross Toole named this place "an uncommon land" and declared twentieth-century Montana to be a "state of extremes." Other respected historians, such as Harry W. Fritz, Michael P. Malone, Richard B. Roeder, and William L. Lang, have

Huckleberry camp on the West Fisher River, ca., 1939, Kootenai National Forest.
PHOTO BY K. D. SWAN, U.S.D.A. FOREST SERVICE

written the complex political and cultural history of two centuries of Montana—a story so rich in events and so full of colorful characters that it is almost a sacrilege to compress the saga into the few pages allotted in this book. This history is supplemented by a chronology of major events, some significant figures from the past, and a brief bibliography of excellent sources on the story of Montana and its people.

The First Montanans

It is hard to know how many early hunting groups and later Indian tribes trekked through or made a home in this part of North America prior to the steady entry of non-Indians to the area. Some archaeologists believe the first people arrived here via what is now called the Old North (or Great North) Trail along the eastern front of the Rocky Mountains. These earliest immigrants, termed Paleo-Indians, lived in the region we now know as Montana between 11,500 and 7,500 years ago and hunted large mammals such as mammoth and ancestors of the modern bison.

Archaeologists have found projectile points and primitive tools of these people in the south-central part of the state near Alder, Montana City, and Whitehall, and in eastern Montana near Lindsay. During a thousand-year dry period in the Great Plains that began about 5,000 B.C., the early hunting groups were forced to seek smaller animals and plant foods along edges of the mountainous regions. The prehistoric people who lived here two thousand years ago pursued migrating buffalo as a staple of the culture. Bison could supply most items in the life of the people—clothing, shelters, tools, fuel, and food. The hunting bands often drove the buffalo herds off cliffs, or pishkuns, and perfected the use of the bow and arrow. Like earlier inhabitants, these bands of people were nomadic or semi-nomadic, moving their camps regularly to find shelter and food. Art made by these early hunters can be found on cave walls and cliffs throughout Montana—most notably at Pictograph Cave near Billings and along the Smith River.

The ancestors of today's Montana Indians arrived in this area in the 1600s and 1700s. Some historians believe that the Kootenai (or Kutenai) may have been the first of the present-day tribes to live in Montana, arriving as long ago as the 1500s. Tribal histories and other accounts suggest that in the late 1700s the principal tribes in the Montana area included the Kalispel, Salish, Pend d'Oreille, Shoshone, Gros Ventre, and Nez Perce. At some time in the early 1700s, the horses brought to the New World by Spanish explorers made their way into Indian culture, and life for all Plains and Plateau tribes changed dramatically. The mobile tribal groups could move into new territories within the northern Great Plains.

The Blackfeet, Crow, and Assiniboine later established themselves as plains dwellers after being pushed westward ahead of the pressures of eastern settlement. The Sioux, Northern Cheyenne, Chippewa, and Cree people arrived in the 1800s. By the time of their encounter with the first Euroamerican explorers, these tribes had each established hunting territories. Different tribes and bands had distinct traditions, beliefs, and cultures.

The tepee was the typical means of shelter used by the first Montanans (Paleo-Indians) and later Plains Indian tribes. Many "tepee rings"—circles of rocks that may have marked the outer edge of the lodges—remain in place today and are one of the most common types of archaeological sites found in Montana, mainly in the eastern part of the state.

Explorers and Fur Traders

A few parties of Spanish, French, and British fur traders may have made their way into parts of the region as early as the mid- or late 1700s, but none left extensive documentation. Louis and François de la Verendrye, brothers exploring ever westward from eastern Canada for their father's fur trade grant, are credited with being the first white men to glimpse the land that would become Montana. They turned back from a long walk across the Dakotas after describing "shining mountains" in the distance. Historians believe they probably saw the southeastern Montana range known as the Bighorns.

In 1803, President Thomas Jefferson commissioned an exploration to trace the Missouri River to its source and find a water route to the Pacific Ocean, under the leadership of Meriwether Lewis and William Clark. These adventurous young men and their Corps of Discovery covered almost 8,000 miles from St. Louis, Missouri, to the mouth of the Columbia River, returning two years later. They journeyed westward across Montana from April 1805 to September of that year. On the return trip to St. Louis in the summer of 1806, the leaders crossed the state in two separate routes. Their extensive scientific journal entries revealed to the world the geography and many resources that were to attract the attention of those eager to capitalize on the newly opened land.

The Corps of Discovery's return coincided with the search for a source for beaver pelts—a demand made necessary by the fashion for beaver-pelt top hats. Over the next four decades of the nineteenth century, British and American fur trading companies combed the streams of Montana for precious furs, all but destroying the beaver population in the process. Many of these companies constructed posts for conducting business and for protection from the elements and Indians. Fort Benton, built on the Missouri River by the American Fur Company, became an important center for trading and shipping goods and furs. The steamboat was introduced to Missouri River traffic in 1819 and eventually replaced the keelboats and mackinaws the first traders used. Steamboats could navigate with a full load of 500 tons of freight on only 50 inches of water. This relatively inexpensive mode of travel prompted many persons with capital to make the 2,000-mile river trip from St. Louis to Fort Benton. From 1847 to the 1870s, more than six hundred steamboats arrived at what was then the world's most remote inland port.

In the mid-1800s, the beaver-skin hat fell out of fashion, but interest in leather hides for clothing, machinery belts, and animal tack accompanied the westward expansion. A new tanning process in the 1870s rendered bison hides suitable for much-needed leather goods. Montana's fur and hide hunters chased down bison and other prairie game almost as relentlessly as they had trapped the beaver.

The Missionaries

Catholic priests were some of the first Europeans to be formally invited to Montana by the native inhabitants. When the few Catholic Iroquois Indians who accompanied fur companies to western Montana intermarried with the Kootenai, Salish, and other Indians of the area, they were eager to have the "Blackrobes" sanctify those marriages and baptize their offspring. In the 1830s, four delegations of Indians walked the great distance to St. Louis to entice Jesuit priests to the Northwest. From this initial contact, Father Pierre Jean DeSmet came west to establish St. Mary's Mission in the Bitterroot Valley in 1841, the first permanent white settlement in Montana. Father DeSmet introduced interested tribal members to the practices of farming and irrigation. The multitalented Father Anthony Ravalli, who arrived later, brought the first European medicine and surgery to the Montana tribes and started the first sawmill and gristmill near St. Mary's Mission.

Wagons and Trails

In the fevered drive for westward expansion of the United States, Congress arranged for a number of wagon trail and railway surveys. An 1853 expedition led by Isaac I. Stevens, the governor of Washington Territory, recorded the most thorough descriptions of the area since Lewis and Clark. Modern-day rail lines still follow much of the route. The northernmost of these surveys led to the construction of four major wagon trails for overland traffic into Montana.

The Fisk wagon trailsWagon Trail, running from St. Paul, Minnesota, to Fort Benton, connected with the Mullan Road. John Mullan, veteran of the Stevens trek, had completed his namesake 624-mile route over the Continental Divide in 1862, connecting the inland west to the Pacific by means of steamboat navigation on the Columbia River near Fort Walla Walla. The Bozeman Trail pointed travelers northward off the famous Oregon Trail, providing a cutoff from Fort Laramie, Wyoming, to the mining boomtown of Virginia City, Montana. From the railhead at Corinne, Utah, the Corinne Road passed through Virginia City and went as far north as Helena.

These wagon trails trespassed on the Indian territories that had been formally established by the Fort Laramie Treaty of 1851. More than a few hostile confrontations prompted the establishment of a number of military forts and outposts in an attempt to ensure safe passage on these routes. Even with several routes into Montana, the region remained isolated, with few settlers until the mid-1860s.

Gold and Its By-Products

Wagon roads proved useful when gold was discovered in the gravels along Montana streams. Although reports of gold finds in the Deer Lodge Valley had been made as early as 1858, it was the rich strike on a small tributary of the Jefferson River in southwestern Montana in 1862 that set the first big gold rush in motion. Within a year or two, thousands of miners stampeded

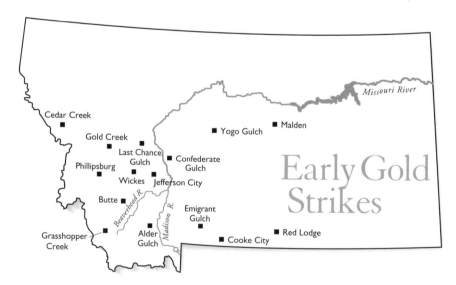

to the major strikes at Grasshopper Creek (1862), Alder Gulch (1863), Last Chance Gulch (1864), and Confederate Gulch (1864). Many came to apply themselves to the hard work of placer mining, but some came to get their gold mininggold the easy way—through robbery and trickery. Incidents ranged from minor thefts to brutal murders, resulting in the organization of the extralegal "Vigilantes." This secret society vowed to destroy the reign of terror and to establish law and order. In the first month of 1864, vigilantes hanged twenty-one supposed outlaws and chased off many who had reputations as road agents and criminals.

Trading and mercantile centers sprang up to serve the gold camps. Fort Benton served as an inland port for the people, machinery, and supplies

N O T A B L E

Mattie Castner (?–1920)

"The Mother of Belt." Enslaved until she was eight years old, Mattie came west, landed in Fort Benton, and got a job in a hotel. She and her husband, John C. Castner, built the first log cabin in Belt—it became the town's first hotel. They later opened the first store in town. Mattie also worked in the coal mine her husband developed and, above ground, grew vegetables to sell in Fort Benton, 40 miles away. Both she and her husband gave selflessly to a variety of charities and causes.

Thomas Francis Meagher (1823–1867)

This Irish revolutionary leader was convicted of treason and exiled by the British to a penal colony in Tasmania, but managed to escape and make his way to New York City. He volunteered to serve in the Civil War, and organized an Irish brigade. In 1865, he accepted a post as Montana's territorial secretary and wound up serving two stints as acting governor. Historians William L. Lang and Rex C. Myers suggest Meagher "created more problems than he solved."

MONTANA HISTORICAL SOCIETY

Others consider him a hero. He is believed to have drowned in the Missouri River after being seen drinking on a boat at Fort Benton. Whether he fell, jumped, or was pushed remains a mystery.

M O N T A N A N S

destined for the gold fields. The Whoop-Up Trail led from this port on the Missouri north to isolated settlements on the Canadian prairie. More than a few enterprising pioneers saw that mining gold was not the only way to become prosperous in the boomtowns of Bannack, Virginia City, and Helena. Extensive and varied agricultural ventures developed in the southwestern mountain valleys, particularly the Deer Lodge, Beaverhead, and Gallatin Valleys, to meet the needs of the placer mining boom. Several flour mills operated by the late 1860s. Of the more than five hundred mining camps that dotted the western mountains, only a few, such as Butte and Helena, survived to become modern towns.

Cattle and Stockmen

Stockmen also made their fortunes on hungry miners and the need for horses and oxen. In 1850, Richard Grant and his sons, Johnny and James, began acquiring worn-out cattle from travelers along the Oregon Trail. After grazing and fattening them on the rich Montana grasses, they drove them back to the trail to trade one fresh animal for two weary ones. Conrad Kohrs bought the Johnny Grant ranch in the Deer Lodge Valley in 1865 and became one of Montana's leading stockmen. Dan Floweree brought a herd of cattle into Montana from Missouri in 1865. Nelson Story, another early cattle king, brought the first trail herd of Texas longhorns to Montana, settling in the Paradise and Gallatin valleys.

Montana as a Territory

For the sixty years prior to establishment of the territory of Montana in 1864, the area had been governed from afar within numerous early divisions of the western U.S. territories. The part of Montana located east of the Continental Divide belonged, in succession, to Louisiana Territory (purchased from France in 1803), Missouri Territory (1812–1821), the so-called "Indian Country" (1821–1854), Nebraska Territory (1854–1861), and Dakota Territory (1861–1863). The western portion was acquired from Great Britain in 1846 and belonged to the Oregon (1848–1853) and Washington (1853–1863) territories until the entire future state was included in Idaho Territory in 1863.

When gold seekers began flooding into southwestern Montana in the 1860s, the law-abiding populace knew it would be wise to create a government close to the action around the gold fields near Bannack, Virginia City, and Helena. The gold strikes and improved transportation routes swelled the population to the five thousand male citizens needed to ask the U.S. government for territorial status. Bad winter weather in 1864 kept Sidney Edgerton, chief justice of the newly created Idaho Territory, from leaving Bannack to travel elsewhere in the territory. He viewed firsthand the vigilante efforts to control criminal activity in that raw land and volunteered to head back to Washington, D.C., in March 1864 to appeal to Congress to divide the territory. As proof of the mineral riches of the area, Edgerton carried gold ingots sewn into the lining of his coat. Congress passed the Organic Act, making Montana a territory in May 1864, and it was approved by President Abraham Lincoln.

The election of delegates to the First Territorial Legislative Assembly took place in October 1864. The body met in December in a dirt-roofed cabin in Bannack. During the next sixty days, the Assembly passed seven hundred pages of laws and chose nearby Virginia City as the first territorial capital. At the time, the Civil War raged and Montana's early politics suffered from the same strongly held allegiances as did the rest of the country. Yankees wanted to make sure that Confederate sympathizers would not gain an edge in the new Montana territory, either by law or lawlessness. Although many Montana settlers were former Southerners, the territory's population was largely pro-Union Democrats, and government lay in the hands of appointed Union Republicans.

The ink was hardly dry on the papers creating the new territory before the followers of Thomas Meagher, Democratic territorial secretary, started clamoring for statehood. When the first Republican territorial governor, Sidney Edgerton, was out of the region, Acting Governor Meagher called a constitutional convention in April 1866 on the petition of a number of citizens but without the desirable invitation of Congress. One of the greatest unsolved mysteries of Montana is just what happened to this first Montana constitution. Supposedly, a delegate lost the papers while they were in transit to St. Louis for printing. Another unsolved mystery is what happened to Meagher later that year, when he not only fell from grace with many citizens but also apparently fell from the deck of a Missouri

River steamboat after a night on the town in Fort Benton. He was never seen again.

Indian Treaties

Treaties with some Montana Indian tribes in 1851 and 1855 had parceled parts of Montana into tribal reserves, giving tribes the right to approve transportation routes through them. A liberal interpretation of the 1855 treaties permitted American settlement in the mountain valleys. U.S. policy was meant to protect the miners, merchants, and settlers, confining Indians within specified boundaries. From 1866 onward, fourteen forts were established by the U.S. Army along transportation routes and near the gold fields.

The Sioux closed the extralegal Bozeman Trail in 1868 and gathered with Cheyenne and other allies in their hunting grounds along the Powder River country of eastern Montana. The army thought it could control the largest gathering of Plains Indians ever recorded. After many years of confrontation, the result was a lose-lose situation—the U.S. Army lost the Battle of the Little Bighorn in 1876, but Indians knew they would lose the next round. Disputes over a treaty regarding the Wallowa Indian Reservation in Oregon resulted in an 1877 attempt by some eight hundred Nez Perce to journey across Montana Territory and head for Canada. In several encounters, the Nez Perce outwitted and outfought soldiers sent to intercept them. Poor winter weather enabled the U.S. military, under General Nelson A. Miles, to thwart this march to freedom, and the exhausted Indian survivors and their famous chief, Joseph, surrendered after the Battle of the Bears Paw Mountains.

Booms and Busts: In the Mines, On the Range, Along the Rails

In addition to conflicts between whites and Indians, the two decades preceding statehood saw the expansion of mining. By the 1870s, the great gold camps had begun to play out and with them went Montana's first boom period. Placer gold mining operations were replaced with hardrock mining for silver and copper. These potentially more profitable but technical operations required corporate organization, tremendous capital, better transportation and facilities, and legal services. This activity determined the centers of settlement and influenced Montana transportation and politics for years to come. Banks and lumber companies prospered with the silver mines. Helena became the territorial capital and a center of commerce in 1875. From 1870 to 1890, silver mining ruled the economy, but in 1893 the bottom fell out of this market. Mines closed and thousands were out of work.

New cities emerged as the Northern Pacific Railroad built westward across Montana in 1883. The railroads reduced the need for river and wagon trade and subjected Montana to more outside economic control, but also made rapid development possible. With the coming of other railroads, Montana's population again showed significant gains.

Along with the rush for the mineral treasures of Montana, a four-legged stampede ensued. Stockmen drove thousands of cattle from Texas and elsewhere to feed on the rich grasslands of central Montana. After the final Indian confrontations in the late 1870s, the virtual extermination of the buffalo, and the arrival of railroad transportation, the high plains opened to profitable grazing for the cattle ranchers and sheepmen. By the early 1880s, the cattle industry had claimed the public lands of central Montana as one enormous pasture and gained power and wealth within the new territory.

The boom days of the open range came to an abrupt end after the hard winter of 1886–1887, when many cattle perished. The ranching industry steadily recovered by fencing the open range and planting dependable supplies of feed. But the open-range era had introduced to Montana the colorful cowboy, whose exploits and lifestyle were romanticized in the art and literature of the day. The paintings, sketches, sculptures, and writings of Charlie Russell portrayed and perpetuated the cowboy life.

Statehood

To set the stage for statehood, a second constitutional convention was convened at Helena in January 1884, and the resulting document was ratified by the people in November of that year. But Congress failed to take any action on the subject of Montana's admission to the Union, partly because of political high jinks involved in making sure Montana (and other western territories) did not have more Democrats than Republicans at the time. The admission to the Union of other western states was stalled not only by national political tensions but also by the jockeying for positions of advantage in the Great Plains and Intermountain West by railroads and mining interests.

The Enabling Act of 1889 required Montana to create a state constitution, so a third and successful constitutional convention was called. Delegates met in Helena in July and, except for a controversy over mining taxation, worked with speed to produce the constitution in about six weeks. The 1889 constitution, patterned after constitutions of other western states, was ratified in an election held October 1, 1889. After a little more than twenty-five years as a territory, Montana was admitted into the Union as the forty-first state on November 8, 1889, by proclamation of President Benjamin Harrison.

Buried Treasures

It was no wonder that Montana came to be known as the Treasure State. The Butte area produced thousands of tons of copper annually. The refining of silver, zinc, lead ore, and by-products of copper were also important industries in Montana well into the twentieth century. Antimony was mined near Thompson Falls. Large reserves of chromium were mined in Stillwater County. Fluorspar mining was a significant commercial industry in Ravalli County. Gems such as sapphires, moss agate, amethyst, garnet, and rhodochrosite were found in scattered areas throughout Montana with varying commercial value. The coming of the transcontinental railroads (Northern Pacific, 1881–1883; Great Northern, 1887–1893; Milwaukee Road, 1907–1909) created demands for fuel from vast coal deposits in Carbon and Cascade counties and then later in Musselshell, Rosebud, and Richland counties.

As Montanans clamored for statehood, one of the most widely known chapters of Montana history was taking place in Butte—the infamous "War of the Copper Kings." The city was thought to be the "richest hill on earth." By 1887, Montana led the nation in the production of silver and copper. Proof of this economic power was a provision exempting unmined ore from taxation in the 1889 constitution. The "war" culminated in the corporate growth of the Anaconda Copper Mining Company, founded by Marcus Daly.

Daly had built a smelter at Anaconda in the early 1880s. After he enlisted the backing of some of the West's most powerful capitalists, the syndicate incorporated and, in 1895, reorganized its holdings as the Anaconda Copper Mining Company. Daly's rival, William Andrews Clark, poured his money into mines, smelters, a bank in Deer Lodge, and other businesses and properties. Fanning the flame of their intense industrial rivalry, Daly used his power to thwart Clark's bid for a U.S. Senate seat in 1889 and 1893. The Copper Kings also battled over selection of the official state capital. In that battle, Daly and the town of Anaconda lost to Clark's choice of Helena in 1894.

From the 1870s to well into the twentieth century, unions and other civic reformers tried to curb the power and excesses of the powerful copper industry. These efforts were somewhat successful in mitigating unfair working conditions and excessive legislative influence by the mining industry, but the greatest legacy was probably heightened citizen involvement in the affairs of the workplace and in government in general.

The Homesteaders

In the 1890s, farmers began to follow cattle ranchers and sheepmen onto the eastern Montana plains. The population of Montana in 1890 was more than 142,000, and by 1900 it was more than 243,000, with a large share of the increase in the plains area. By 1920, that population had doubled. The great boom in homesteading began about 1909 and lasted through World War I.

Three railroads, particularly Jim Hill's Great Northern Railway, promoted Montana farming opportunities to the world. Whereas the Northern Pacific was a land grant railroad and could sell land to build its line, the Great Northern counted on moving people and products along its northern Montana route. The Chicago, Milwaukee, St. Paul and Pacific Railroad hoped to lure settlement along its central Montana holdings. Opportunistic land speculators, the state of Montana, and dry land farming proponents also convinced thousands of hopeful homesteaders that diversified farming was possible where native shortgrass had rooted in shallow soil. Neither homesteaders nor federal officials realized how many acres were needed to support a family on the semi-arid grasslands, and this lack of foresight caused one of the most devastating periods in the state's history.

Under the Enlarged Homestead Act of 1909, the head of a family or anyone over the age of 21 could claim 320 acres of public land. A homesteader was required to build a house (a shack would do) and cultivate part of the acreage for grain production. In the years between 1909 and 1917, the homesteaders, for the most part, did well, but most were unaware that these were unusually wet years for the area. Some of the settlers were experienced farmers, but many were not. Hundreds of single women took up claims, and hired help to do the required improvement work. Some homesteaders expected to sell the land at good prices after they "proved up" on it. Towns boomed along the railroad to supply the farmers' needs. In the 10 years following 1909, the cultivated land in Montana increased from 258,000 acres to 3,417,000 acres. Some one hundred new towns had sprouted on the prairie. In 1916, farmers in one area raised 80 bushels of wheat to the acre when an average crop was 25.

Then disaster struck. In 1917, the first of the drought years hit some parts of the state, just as the U.S. government encouraged farmers to plow as much land as possible for food production during wartime. Banks were encouraged to lend money to the farmers to buy equipment, but many of the banks lost their investment. By 1919, the drought had become widespread throughout the state, and wheat lands averaged only 2.4 bushels an acre. The dry soil blew away on the unending wind. By 1925, half of Montana's farmers had lost their farms because they could not repay money they had borrowed. Half of the state banks eventually went out of business. Between 1920 and 1930, Montana was the only state in the Union to lose population, and much of this loss was from the eastern counties.

The Depression, the New Deal, and World War II

Montana did not escape the drought and the Great Depression of the 1930s. Climate and economics conspired to exacerbate already tough times. Fire, winds, and insects took a toll on the plains. The price of copper dropped, leaving thousands out of work. Cattle and wheat prices also dropped dramatically.

The building of Fort Peck Dam was Montana's greatest New Deal project, but thanks to Montana's powerful Democratic congressional delegation, the federal government aided the state with hundreds of other public works projects. Federal funding made rural electrification possible, and the Civilian Conservation Corps reforestation program employed 25,600 men in 40 camps across the state. As elsewhere in the nation, the provisions of the National Labor Relations Act enabled unions to win concessions. These New Deal programs benefited Montana well beyond the years of the Great Depression.

During World War II, the weather cooperated with the need for an abundant national food supply. Copper, timber, oil, and gas output soared. There were few defense industry jobs here, so nearly ninety thousand people left the state, with forty thousand of those enlisting in the armed services. In the years after the war, Montana's population increased by 121,000. Along with returning soldiers, growth was fueled by federal defense projects—including expansion of Malmstrom Air Force Base and the housing of much of the nation's cold war nuclear missile force beneath the fields of central Montana.

The Last Half Century

During the 1960s, the economic power of the state shifted toward development of coal, oil, and gas resources on the eastern plains. The most important economic change in Montana in the 1970s and 1980s was the decline of the Anaconda Company. For a century, the copper giant had ruled state politics and the press, expanded into lumbering and smelting, and shared power projects with the Montana Power Company. After buying other mines in the U.S., Chile, and Mexico, the company controlled one-fourth of the world's copper. By the 1970s, fiber optic cable was replacing copper in phone lines, environmental laws were strengthened, and the Chilean properties were nationalized. Just three years after the oil giant Atlantic Richfield Company (ARCO) purchased the Anaconda Company, it closed most smelter and refinery operations, and in 1983 stopped all its mining in Butte. In 1985, Dennis Washington, a construction company owner from Missoula, purchased the copper mining interests and resumed open pit mining activity, though at a lesser scale.

In the 1970s and 1980s, the rising influence of oil, gas, and coal interests coincided with the waning copper interests in the western half of the state. The Montana Power Company became the state's number one industrial employer but had to answer to growing environmental concerns over its coal-fired generating plants in southeastern Montana. The homegrown environmental movement that had its genesis in the 1970s continued to advocate government policies and economic growth that did not sacrifice a healthy environment and the Montana way of life. Other economic changes in the 1980s and 1990s included the rise of tourism and the trucking and construction industries and the decline of labor unions and the timber industry. Also in the 1980s, most banks in the state were drawn into various regional banking networks. While the 1980s were tough years for agriculture, brought on by drought and low farm prices, crop and livestock producers experienced better times in much of the 1990s.

Montana in the 21st Century

Agriculture remains the state's number one economic activity. Although Montana continues to suffer from a drought cycle, some crops have experi-

PHOTO BY GRACE AMBROSE ZAKEN

Stephen A. Ambrose (1936–2002)

Stephen Ambrose was one of America's most widely read and respected historians and lecturers. He authored more than 30 books that focused on the American West, America's political leaders, and World War II. In addition to his multi-volume biographies of presidents Nixon and Eisenhower, his most popular works include *Undaunted Courage: Meriwether Lewis, Thomas Jefferson, and the Opening of the American West; Citizen Soldiers: The U.S. Army From the Normandy Beaches to the Bulge to the Surrender of Germany, June 7, 1944–May 7, 1945; D-Day June 6, 1944: The Climactic Battle of World War II; Crazy Horse and Custer: the Parallel Lives of Two American Warriors.* Ambrose was a consultant for the film *Saving Private Ryan* and his 1992 book *Band of Brothers: E Company, 506th Regiment, 101st Airborne, from Normandy to Hitler's Eagle Nest,* was the basis for a cable TV miniseries. He taught at the University of New Orleans for 24 years. While Ambrose made Montana his home for only part of the last decade of his life, he was warmly thought of as a "native," not only because many of his five children lived in the Helena area but because he contributed to many Montana projects that will memorialize his love of what he like to call "this special place."

M O N T A N A N S

enced bumper yields in recent years. Tourism continues to be the next most important economic activity. State and local governments and private developers continue to expand recreation and visitor opportunities in all corners of the state.

Montana remains a state rich in natural resources, and the potential exists for growth in the traditional areas of hydro-electric power, timber, mining and mineral production. Limited access to federal timber supplies and cut backs in operations due to summer wildfires have forced many lumber mills to curtail or close. Mills that can obtain timber supplies are enjoying high prices and demand for their products. After closing for a few years, Montana Resources reopened its open pit mining operations in Butte in 2004. Oil and gas businesses are reaping some benefit from rising energy prices. The state's economy has diversified in the past fifteen years and economic growth is expected to average 2 percent a year through 2007. Stronger connections to the global economy have made it easier for Montanans to market their products.

Montanans continue to earn significantly less per capita than the rest of the nation, especially those whose educational background would garner much higher wages elsewhere. Yet, most native Montanans stay and newcomers and former residents arrive on a steady basis. Surveys reveal that most residents, new and old, place a higher value on the quality of life here that they do more monetary concerns.

Politics

For a remote and sparsely populated state, Montana has quite frequently sent representatives to Washington who have made remarkable contributions to the national political scene. Among them have been Thomas H. Carter, Thomas J. Walsh, Burton K. Wheeler, James E. Murray, Lee Metcalf, Max Baucus, and Mike Mansfield, all powerful figures in the United States Senate. Jeannette Rankin was the first woman elected to the House of Representatives, where she served separate terms during both world wars and voted against participation in both. Also in top political ranks was Joseph M. Dixon, who gained prominence in national Republican and Progressive Party politics before returning to Montana to serve from 1921 through 1924 as a Republican governor.

The governorship was in the hands of the Democratic party from 1925 through 1940, and again from 1949 through 1952. From 1941 through 1948, and in the years from 1953 through 1968, Republicans held the governorship. Democratic governors were returned to office from 1969 through 1988. For the next sixteen years, Republican governors were elected to lead the state, through the administrations of Stan Stephens, Marc Racicot (two terms) and Judy Martz. Republicans controlled both houses of the legislature from 1993 through 2004. In the 2005 legislative session, Democrats held a majority in the Senate and an even split with Republicans in the House. Democrat Brian Schweitzer was sworn in as governor, along with his Republican running mate Lt. Governor John Bohlinger.

Most frequently, Montanans send liberal Democrats to Washington, D.C., but elect more conservative Democrats or Republicans to run state government. Since direct election of senators began in 1913, only Zales N. Ecton in 1946 and Conrad Burns in 1988 have won Montana's U.S. Senate seats as

Republicans. It is also common in Montana for the executive branch and one or more of the legislative houses to be dominated by opposite political parties. Often, the two houses of the legislature have been evenly split between political parties. Republicans controlled both houses of the legislature since 1995.

Montana has led the nation in a number of worthy governmental reforms. The state's voters adopted the initiative and referendum process in 1906 and woman suffrage in 1914. Lawmakers passed the first worker's compensation law in 1915.

By the end of the 1960s, the original 1889 constitution contained much that was outdated. Rather than revising a document that had been amended forty-one times over the years, the people affirmed the need for a new constitution by voting in November 1970 to call a constitutional convention. One hundred elected delegates met in Helena on January 17, 1972, and by March 22 of that year had created one of the most modern state constitutions in the nation. The voters approved the new constitution on June 6, 1972, and it became effective July 1, 1973. Some progressive tenets of the 1972 constitution include the recognition of the people's right to a clean and healthy environment, an open meeting law, and liberalization of the people's right to enact legislation.

Chronology: It Happened in Montana, 1743 to 2005

1743   On a westward trek that ends near the southeast corner of modern Montana, the Verendrye brothers, French explorers, describe the "land of shining mountains" to the west.

1762   The province of Louisiana, including that part of Montana east of the Rocky Mountains, passes from French to Spanish control.

1802   Napoleon forces Spain to cede Louisiana back to France.

1803   United States purchases Louisiana from France for what amounts to three cents an acre. It becomes known as Louisiana Territory.

1805   After departing from the mouth of the Missouri in May 1804, Meriwether Lewis, William Clark, and their expeditionary Corps of Discovery cross the Montana Rockies on their way to the Pacific Ocean.

        François Larocque explores southeast Montana for the Canadian North West Company and is first to describe what is later named Pompeys Pillar, a 200-foot isolated rock on the south bank of the Yellowstone River. William Clark will name it in 1806.

1806	Lewis and Clark reach Bitterroot Valley July 1 on return trip from the Pacific. After splitting up, Lewis meets Clark at mouth of the Yellowstone River in August.
1807	American fur trade begins with Manuel Lisa's construction of the Missouri Fur Company's trading post at the confluence of the Bighorn and Yellowstone rivers.
1808	Explorer David Thompson, representing British fur interests (NorthWest Company), enters Montana via "Kootenay" River and, in 1809, erects Saleesh House at present-day Thompson Falls.
	John Colter, a veteran of the Lewis and Clark Expedition, is stripped, disarmed, and forced to run for his life from a band of Blackfeet near the Three Forks of the Missouri River. He escapes and makes his way back to Fort Manuel Lisa.
1812	Territory of Louisiana is renamed Missouri Territory. It includes the eastern two-thirds of what is now Montana.
1818	Land east of Continental Divide and south of the 49th parallel is conceded to U.S. by Great Britain; west of divide subject to joint claim by both nations.
1821	Eastern Montana becomes part of the Great Plains "Indian Country."
	Merger of North West Company and the British Hudson's Bay Company strengthens latter.
1822	Andrew Henry builds a trading post on the Yellowstone River for Rocky Mountain Fur Company.
1823	Blackfeet ambush and kill Missouri Fur Company trappers (Jones–Immel party) on Yellowstone River near Billings and steal large fur cache, discouraging expansion.
1827	Under the leadership of Pierre Chouteau, John Jacob Astor's American Fur Company attempts monopoly of Upper Missouri fur trade by forcing out other companies.
1828	Fort Union, an American Fur Company post, is built near mouth of Yellowstone River.
1831	Nez Perce and Salish delegation visits St. Louis to encourage missionaries to travel to Montana and the Northwest.
1832	First steamboat to navigate upper reaches of the Missouri, the Yellowstone, reaches Fort Union near border of Montana and Dakota, with artist George Catlin, noted portrayer of Indian culture, as a passenger.
1834	Hudson's Bay Company dominates fur trade west of Continental Divide, while American Fur Company controls the trade east of the divide.
1837	Smallpox epidemic ravages the Blackfeet and weakens their power in the area.
1840	Fur trade begins serious decline due to change in style of men's hats, no longer requiring beaver pelts.
1841	Jesuit priest Pierre Jean DeSmet establishes St. Mary's Roman Catholic Mission in the vicinity of present-day Stevensville.

1842	First crops are planted at St. Mary's Mission.
1846	Western Montana is ceded to United States by Great Britain as the international border is extended to Pacific along 49th parallel.
1848	Congress creates the Oregon Territory, which includes Montana west of the Continental Divide.
1850	St. Mary's Mission is leased by John Owen, who constructs trading post.
1851	Eastern Montana's Indian tribes are included in federal treaty system with first Fort Laramie Treaty.
1852	François Findlay, known as "Benetsee," finds first gold in Montana on a creek near present-day Garrison.
1853	Montana considered as site for transcontinental railroad by Isaac I. Stevens, governor of Washington Territory.
	John Grant starts first cattle herd in Deer Lodge Valley.
	Montana west of Continental Divide included in newly created Washington Territory.
1854	Montana east of Continental Divide included in newly created Nebraska Territory.
	Roman Catholic mission is established at St. Ignatius, south of Flathead Lake.
1855	Governor Stevens, of Washington Territory, signs treaty with western tribes at Council Grove near Missoula. In Lame Bull's treaty, Blackfeet people and their allies, the Gros Ventre, accept reservation that encompasses the northern two-thirds of eastern Montana. By 1888, this huge reserve would be incrementally reduced and divided until it resembled the present-day boundaries of the Fort Peck, Fort Belknap, and Blackfeet reservations.
1858	James and Granville Stuart spread the word about their significant gold find northwest of the Deer Lodge valley on Benetsee Creek, later named Gold Creek.
1860	Steamboat Chippewa is first to reach Fort Benton, head of navigation on the Missouri River.
1861	Montana east of Continental Divide is included in creation of Dakota Territory.
1862	Mullan Wagon Road built between Walla Walla and Fort Benton.
	James Liberty Fisk begins years of leading wagon trains over the Minnesota–Montana Road, connecting upper Midwest to Fort Benton.
	Gold rush draws thousands to Grasshopper Creek diggings, later called Bannack.
	First local elections are held in Missoula County, part of Washington Territory.

1863	Gold rush draws thousands to Alder Gulch. Virginia City springs up almost overnight on a tributary of Alder Creek.
	Idaho Territory is organized, including all of future Montana.
1864	Montana Territory is created on May 26, with capital at Bannack. Sidney Edgerton, former chief justice of Idaho Territory, is appointed first territorial governor.
	Bannack–Virginia City vigilantes hunt down and hang twenty-one members of Sheriff Henry Plummer's alleged gang of robbers and killers, including Plummer.
	The "Four Georgians" find gold in Last Chance Gulch, site of future Helena.
	John M. Bozeman leads first wagon train over Bozeman Trail.
	First newspaper, the Montana Post, is published in Virginia City.
	Miners rush to Confederate Gulch (Diamond City) near present-day Townsend.
1865	Virginia City becomes territorial capital, replacing Bannack.
	Thomas Francis Meagher, acting governor and former Union Army general, stirs up extreme political partisanship and Civil War sentiments when he switches allegiance from Union Democrat-Republican leanings to pro-Southern Democrats.
1866	Virginia City is connected by telegraph with Salt Lake City in November. First public school is opened in Virginia City.
	Fort C. F. Smith is constructed on Bighorn River to protect Bozeman Trail.
	Nelson Story brings first longhorns into Gallatin Valley, traveling 1,800 miles from Texas.
1867	All acts of second and third Montana legislative sessions annulled by U.S. Congress.
	Acting Governor Thomas Meagher disappears (a supposed drowning) at Fort Benton, under mysterious circumstances.
	First band of sheep in Montana is brought to Prickly Pear Valley.
1868	U.S. cedes land east of Bighorns to Sioux and other tribes; Fort C. F. Smith burned by Indians; Bozeman Trail abandoned.
	Indians are considered to be born into a foreign nation and are not included in the extension of U.S. citizenship in ratification of the Fourteenth Amendment to the U.S. Constitution.
1869	Washburn–Langford expedition is first official exploration of future Yellowstone National Park area.
1870	U.S. Army troops massacre 173 non-hostile Piegan Indians, a tribe of the Blackfeet Nation.
	First federal census shows 20,595 people in territory.

1872	Congressman James A. Garfield bargains with Salish tribe for compensation and resettlement. Salish are directed to leave Bitterroot Valley; Chief Arlee moves, but Chief Charlot refuses to sign agreement.
	Yellowstone becomes the first national park.
1875	Helena becomes territorial capital, replacing Virginia City.
1876	More than two hundred sixty men of the Seventh U.S. Cavalry, led by Lieutenant Colonel George Armstrong Custer, are killed on Little Bighorn by a combined force of Sioux and Cheyenne.
1877	Nez Perce elude U.S Army, in last great Indian military success, by fleeing to Montana. Forced to surrender at Bears Paw Mountains.
1878	Butte Workingmen's Union organizes as first Montana labor group.
	Northern Cheyenne Indians begin a six-week march back to Montana from exile in Oklahoma.
1880	Utah & Northern Railroad reaches Dillon from Ogden, Utah, and is completed to Garrison in 1881.
	Census lists 39,159 citizens. There are about five men to every two women.
1881	Northern Pacific Railroad stretches west to Miles City.
	Slaughter of buffalo reaches peak.
1882	Marcus Daly's Anaconda Mine at Butte is found to contain the richest cache of copper ore in the world.
	Successful sheepman Paris Gibson envisions great city on the banks of the Missouri River and files claim for townsite of Great Falls. The city incorporates in 1888.
1883	Former President Grant attends "last spike" ceremony at Gold Creek when Northern Pacific Railroad is completed from Lake Superior to the Pacific.
1884	Montana denied statehood by U.S. Congress after meeting of constitutional convention in Helena.
	Stockmen form vigilante group to protect cattle from rustlers in central Montana; fifteen rustlers are killed.
	Marcus Daly builds copper smelter and town of Anaconda.
1885	Montana Stockgrowers Association is formed at peak of the cattle boom.
1886	Open-range grazing in Montana reaches peak, with 700,000 cattle and nearly one million sheep.
1887	Severe winter blizzards kill at least half the cattle on open range.
	Federal Dawes Act requires division of Indian reservations into individual allotments for tribal members and into certain trust lands held by federal government.

1888	"War of the Copper Kings" intesifies as Marcus Daly fights the election of rival William A. Clark to Congress.
1889	Third constitutional convention is held in Helena on July 4. Voters ratify constitution on October 1.
	Montana is admitted to Union as forty-first state on November 8, along with Washington, North Dakota, and South Dakota.
	First legislative session ends in disgrace with claims of election fraud, and rival Houses of Representatives are organized. Each party of each house elects a senator to send to Washington, D.C., where a Republican-controlled Senate sends the two Democrats home.
	Montana is the nation's top copper-producing state; it is second in silver production.
1890	Steamboat traffic on the Missouri River declines as roads and railroads offer reliable transportation.
1891	Second legislative assembly begins constructive work on creating state government.
1893	Great Northern Railway is completed across state.
	Electoral irregularities prompt Legislature to refuse to elect William A. Clark to U.S. Senate. Copper kings buy state newspapers.
	Legislature establishes state university at Missoula, college at Bozeman, School of Mines at Butte, and Normal College at Dillon.
	Western Federation of Miners established in Butte.
1894	Voters choose Helena as state capital in hard-fought battle with Anaconda.
1897	Bitterroot National Forest is established as first in state and one of the first in the nation.
1899	Standard Oil Company buys Anaconda Copper Mining Company and other Butte mines and creates holding company, Amalgamated Copper Company.
	William A. Clark is accused of bribery in run for U.S. Senate; Senate disallows his election.
1900	Six million sheep in Montana make the state first in nation in wool growing.
	In the struggle for dominance over the copper ore beneath Butte and in state politics, copper kings F. A. Heinze and William A. Clark align against Amalgamated Copper Company, Daly's former copper empire. The state judiciary is corrupted and the legislature overrun by corporate interests.
1902	State Capitol is completed in Helena.
1905	Industrial Workers of the World battle other unions in Butte.

1906	Chicago, Milwaukee, St. Paul and Pacific Railroad (the Milwaukee Road) enters Montana and is completed with golden spike ceremony at Gold Creek in 1909.
1909	Industrial Workers of the World foments lumber strikes at Somers and Kalispell; "free-speech" strike breaks out in Missoula.
	Mount St. Charles College (Carroll College) is formed in Helena.
1910	Glacier National Park is established by an act of Congress.
	Homesteading boom is in full swing, eventually resulting in over 30 million acres of public land opened to sodbusting; number of Montana farms has doubled since 1900. Agriculture replaces mining as Montana's top industry.
	"The Big Blowup" forest fire burns more than three million acres of western Montana and Idaho panhandle.
1911	Socialists join forces with Industrial Workers of the World to elect socialist city government in Butte.
1912	State Capitol is expanded; two wings are added.
	Voters initiate and approve Progressive Era reforms to clean up politics, including direct election of U.S. senators.
	County-busting craze in Montana begins, resulting in twenty-five new counties by 1920.
	Cromwell Dixon makes first flight over the Continental Divide, from Helena to Blossburg.
1913	State Highway Commission is created.
	Northern Montana College in Havre and Eastern Montana College of Education in Billings are established.
	First Montana gas well is drilled, near Glendive.
1914	Montana grants women suffrage, five years before amendment to U.S. Constitution.
	Labor violence in Butte ends recognition for the miners' unions.
1915	Anaconda Copper Mining Company disengages from Standard Oil and remains the world's biggest copper company.
	Oil is found in Elk Basin.
	Homesteading is encouraged by record yield of 60 million bushels of wheat.
1916	Republican Jeannette Rankin is elected as first woman to serve in the U.S. Congress.
	Nonpartisan League and other progressive labor and civic groups call for sweeping taxation and social reforms.

K. Ross Toole (1920–1991)

Toole was one of Montana's favorite and most outspoken historians. He was the kind of teacher whose lectures drew rapt, standing-room-only audiences. For his students, he made history come alive. He encouraged a critical look at the state's past as prologue to the treatment of resource development of the 1970s and 1980s. He was also the first director of the Montana Historical Society and led creation of the society's museum and art galleries, founding a quarterly magazine, *Montana, The Magazine of Western History.* Toole left the state to become director of the Museum of the City of

MONTANA HISTORICAL SOCIETY

New York and directed the Museums of New Mexico before returning in 1965 to teach at The University of Montana, Missoula, where he was Hammond Professor of Western History. He authored eleven books and many articles on the American West and *Montana, including Montana: An Uncommon Land* and *The Rape of the Great Plains: Northwestern America, cattle and coal.*

MONTANA HISTORICAL SOCIETY

Anne McDonnell (1884–1977)

Some called her "an encyclopedia of Montana history." From 1924 until 1953, McDonnell served as a librarian at the Montana Historical Society, contributing to innumerable research efforts to unearth the region's past. Born in Minnesota and raised by her grandparents in Butte, where her father worked in the mines, she worked briefly at the Butte Public Library and also taught school before taking the job at the historical society. Though the title of "librarian" belonged to the chief administrative officer of the society, McDonnell knew the library and archives better than anyone and earned the chief post shortly before her retirement.

Greatest year in copper mining, with $97 million in value.

State voters approve prohibition of alcoholic beverages by overwhelming margin; state becomes "dry" at end of 1918.

Milwaukee Road completes 438 miles of electrified rail operation.

1917   The death of 164 Butte miners in Speculator Mine fire sparks strike by 15,000 workers. Federal troops intervene. Industrial Workers of the World leader Frank Little is lynched by masked vigilantes in Butte.

Census miscalculation results in overdraft of Montana men for wartime service; more than forty thousand leave for duty.

First of drought years that eventually halt decade-long boom in agriculture.

1918   Wave of ultra-patriotism sweeps state; state Sedition Act is model for federal law.

Statewide influenza epidemic.

1919   Drought and low crop prices persist through 1925, leading 20 percent of Montana farms to stop production; half of all farm mortgages foreclose, and half of commercial banks fail.

1922   Grasshopper plague destroys crops in eastern Montana.

Kevin-Sunburst oil field is discovered.

Oil boomtown of Shelby hosts world heavyweight title fight between Jack Dempsey and Tommy Gibbons.

1924   U.S. Senator Thomas J. Walsh of Montana exposes Teapot Dome scandal in Washington, D.C., and chairs National Democratic Convention.

U.S. Senator Burton K. Wheeler of Montana is vice-presidential candidate for Progressive Party.

Indian Citizenship Act extends citizenship to those Indians who had not become citizens through the allotment process.

Northern Pacific Railroad begins coal strip-mining near Colstrip.

Voters override Legislature and increase the mines tax.

1930   Census shows population of 537,606 and 10 percent fewer farms than in 1920.

1933   Senator Thomas Walsh dies on his honeymoon trip to Washington, D.C., where he was to take office as U.S. attorney general.

1934   Indian Reorganization Act (Wheeler-Howard Act) is passed, providing for tribal self-government, land and resource conservation and development, and other reforms.

1935   Helena suffers devastating earthquake that kills four people and does $3.5 million damage.

1936	More than 10,500 workers are employed in building of Fort Peck Dam.
	Montana ranks second in nation per capita for federal aid during 1930s.
1938	Milwaukee Road passenger train plunges into Custer Creek, killing forty and injuring eighty people.
1939	Fort Peck Dam, world's largest earth-filled dam, is completed.
1940	Jeannette Rankin is elected to Congress for a second time.
1941	Representative Rankin casts the sole vote against U.S. entry into World War II; many Montanans react bitterly.
1943	Smith mine disaster kills seventy-four coal miners.
1949	Foundation Program Act of 1949 establishes most advanced school funding equalization mechanism in the nation.
1951	Oil boom begins in Williston Basin, a deep and productive oil field lying beneath western North Dakota, southern Saskatchewan, and eastern Montana.
1955	Columbia Falls aluminum plant opens, fueled by power from Hungry Horse Dam.
	Anaconda Copper Mining Company begins digging for copper ore in what will become Butte's Berkeley Pit.
1959	Earthquake near Yellowstone National Park results in twenty-eight deaths and formation of Quake Lake.
	Anaconda Company sells its Montana newspapers to Lee Newspapers, Inc.
1960	Malmstrom Air Force Base is nation's first operative Minuteman intercontinental ballistic nuclear missile site.
1962	Governor Donald Nutter and several associates are killed in airplane crash.
1964	State celebrates Territorial Centennial by sending twenty-five-car Centennial Train to World's Fair in New York City.
	Congress passes Wilderness Act, establishing five major reserves in Montana.
	In early June, record rainfall and melting snow combined to bring life threatening floods to areas east and west of Glacier National Park, and many other parts of Montana. Towns were evacuated, large sections of highway were washed away, and the Swift Dam failed, leaving 30 drown and 400 residents homeless on the Blackfeet Reservation.
1965	When Montana Legislature fails to act, federal district court reapportions Legislative Assembly and both congressional districts to achieve "one-person, one-vote."
1967	Montana Legislature passes Clean Air Act.
1968	Longest and costliest strike in Montana's history ends March 29; 7,200 copper workers are unemployed for 250 days, with $34 million in lost wages.

Yellowtail Dam on the Bighorn River is completed; construction begins on Libby Dam on the Kootenai River.

Timber industry peaks with 1.5 billion board feet harvested.

1969   Large scale strip mining of coal begins at Colstrip.

1970   Three major railroads—Northern Pacific, Great Northern, and Burlington—merge as Burlington Northern.

1972   Voters narrowly approve a new state constitution and approve side issues allowing the Legislature or the voters, by initiative, to authorize gambling and the death penalty.

1973   Major Utility Siting Act, Strip Mining and Reclamation Act, and Water Use Act are enacted, providing strongest state environmental protection laws in the nation.

1975   Montana adopts a coal severance tax of up to 30 percent, as the first Colstrip power plant is completed.

1977   Oil giant Atlantic Richfield Company (ARCO) buys Anaconda Company.

1980   ARCO closes copper smelter in Anaconda and refinery in Great Falls, putting more than one thousand employees out of work.

Government, schools, and many businesses close for a day as ash from the eruption of Mount St. Helens covers much of the state.

1981   Milwaukee Road declares bankruptcy.

1982   Controversy rages over placing of MX missiles with nuclear warheads in Montana.

After more than 100 years of mining operations and $4 billion in mineral production, ARCO closes all its mines in Butte.

Dispute rages over the web of power lines being strung through western Montana to the Pacific Northwest.

1985   The Washington Corporation purchases Butte mining operations from ARCO, and mining resumes in 1986.

1986   Burlington Northern Railroad closes Livingston repair shops and announces it will sell its southern line through the state.

1987   A voter-approved Montana lottery begins selling tickets.

1988   Helena District Court declares Montana school finance system to be unconstitutional in school funding lawsuit initiated by sixty-five underfunded districts.

Worst wildfires since 1930s sweep across Montana forests, and drought devastates crops.

1989   On a 40-degree-below-zero February night, a runaway freight train crashes and explodes near Helena's Carroll College.

Montana celebrates centennial year with cattle drives, wagon trains, and other festivities.

Bison hunt along Yellowstone National Park border sparks state and national controversy.

1990   Reapportionment of the U.S. House, based on 1990 census, reduces Montana's two seats to one.

1994   Tax revolt flares, then fizzles as constitutional amendments defeated.

Hi-line farmers protest new free-trade Canadian grain imports. Agreement reached on limiting imports.

1995   First execution of a Montana death row inmate in fifty-two years as Duncan Peder McKenzie, Jr., is given lethal injection at Montana State Prison.

Republicans control both houses of the Legislature and the governor's office for the first time since 1968.

Montana draws worldwide attention as home to various militia and "patriot" white supremacist groups.

Wolves are reintroduced to Yellowstone National Park.

1996   Theodore Kaczynski, suspected "Unabomber" serial bomber, is arrested at his Lincoln cabin. He has since been tried and received four consecutive life sentences in a maximum security facility.

A Montana Rail Link train carrying chlorine gas derails near Alberton, causing evacuation of more than five hundred area residents and closure of a stretch of Interstate 90 for more than two weeks.

Self-designated "Freemen" and FBI face off near a Jordan-area ranch. After an 81-day standoff, Freemen surrender and are jailed.

State Senator Chet Blaylock, running for governor, suffers fatal heart attack while driving to a Missoula debate less than two weeks before the general election. His running mate, Judy Jacobson, assumes his role, appearing on ballots as the candidate for governor and lieutenant governor, but loses to Republican incumbent Marc Racicot.

1997   Montana legislature allows deregulation of electrical power industry.

B-1 bomber crashes, killing four Air Force officers aboard.

Lawmakers kill a 4 percent state sales tax.

More than eight hundred Yellowstone National Park bison killed or sent to slaughter for fear of spreading brucellosis outside Park boundaries.

1998   Montana Supreme Court strikes down voter-approved constitutional amendment CI-75, which would have required voter approval any new or increased taxes.

Pegasus Gold Corporation files for bankruptcy.

Voter initiative bans use of cyanide in new or expanding gold mines.

Atlantic Richfield Co. agrees to pay state $420 million to repair damages of mining and smelting in Anaconda and Butte area.

Mentally-ill Rimini resident, Russell Weston, shoots two police officers in the U.S. Capitol building.

Leaders of Montana Freemen convicted in federal court for criminal acts associated with their antigovernment actions and 1996 standoff with federal agents.

1999   Montana Power Company sells generation assets and divests of electric energy infrastructure in order to transform into Touch America, a telecommunications company.

After much public outcry, state ends contract with beleaguered out-of-state company hired to manage public mental health services.

Republican Judy Martz is elected as Montana's first female governor.

Montana reinstates a daytime speed limit of 70 mph on two-lane paved roads and 75 mph on interstates.

2000   Butte's Montana Resources mine closes, resulting in the lay-off of 175 workers.

In what has been termed Montana's greatest natural disaster, summer fires burn nearly 1 million acres, including 320 structures and homes, mostly in Ravalli County.

Beaverhead County is site of weeklong campout by 23,000 members of the counterculture group, Rainbow Family of Living Light.

Missoula police reaction to summer visit of the Hells Angels Motorcycle Club sparks arrests of non-members.

2001   Montana reacts to national tragedies of September 11, 2001, with public memorial gatherings in many towns and churches, increased displays of patriotism, blood donations, and donations of money and other forms of assistance to victim and their families.

Washington D.C. staff of U.S. Senator Max Baucus exposed to anthrax in Hart Senate Office Building.

High power prices lead to shutdowns of many mining and timber businesses.

Montana's most famous son, former U.S. Senator, Mike Mansfield dies at age 98.

House Majority Leader Paul Slater dies in car crash in which Shane Hedges, top aide of Governor Martz, is the driver.

2002   Illegal methamphetamine production and related arrests proliferate in both rural and urban Montana.

Citing unfair allegations about his past, Republican candidate Mike Taylor abandons campaign for U.S. Senate against incumbent Democratic Senator Max Baucus, who easily wins re-election.

MONTANANS IN WAR

In World War II, Montanans suffered the second highest percentage of combat deaths per capita in the nation, with the loss of 1,869 lives. More than 57,000 Montanans served their country in active military service during the war; 69,000 others left the state to take jobs in defense plants. For the World War II effort, 1,400 men of the 163rd Infantry Battalion of the Montana National Guard were deployed to the South Pacific. They stayed in the Pacific theater until 1945, fighting in some of the toughest jungle battles of the war.

The Vietnam Veterans Memorial in Washington, D.C., honors the 267 Montanans who died in the Vietnam conflict. Montana has about 108,000 veterans, with nearly one-third of them Vietnam-era veterans.

When 700 soldiers with the 1-163rd Infantry Battalion of Montana National Guard were mobilized in June 2004, it was the largest single call-up of Montana troops since 1941. By January 2005, sixty-two percent of the National Guard's total force of 2,500 soldiers were mobilized for service related to the conflicts in Iraq and Afghanistan. Since September 11, 2001, approximately 500 of the state's 800 Army Reservists were called to active duty. Hundreds of airmen from the Malstrom Air Force Base 341st Space Wing were also sent overseas.

As of August 2005, seven Montanans in various branches of the armed forces has lost their lives while in Iraq on active duty. Montana National Guard soldier Sgt. 1st Class Robbie McNary, of Lewistown, was killed in Iraq on March 31, 2005.

Falling state revenues force two special legislative sessions, only to leave huge deficit for 2003 Legislature.

Governor Martz is implicated in the suspected cover-up of the role of her top aide, Shane Hedges, in the 2001 car crash death of House Majority Leader Paul Slater.

Montana Power Company, one of the state's most prominent, longtime businesses, sells its electrical generating and natural gas utilities to South Dakota-based NorthWestern Corp. for $1.1 billion.

Libby is added to federal Environmental Protection Agency's Superfund cleanup list due to residual effects of asbestos contamination by defunct W.R. Grace and Co. vermiculite mine.

2003   Touch America and NorthWestern Energy, two companies that emerged from the breakup of the Montana Power Company, file for bankruptcy. Most of Touch America's telecommunications assets sold to Canadian company.

Summer wildfires blacken more than 650,000 acres of Montana, including 140,000 acres of Glacier National Park. Dozens of major fires forced temporary evacuations of residents near Lincoln, Missoula, and Condon.

Granville Stuart
(1834–1918)

MONTANA HISTORICAL SOCIETY, HELENA

Even during his lifetime, Granville Stuart was considered one of the "founding fathers" of Montana. After he and his brother James worked a gold discovery at Gold Creek in 1862, Stuart set up a store in Bannack to supply goods to miners. By the 1880s, he was a partner and manager in one of the largest cattle operations in central Montana. In an attempt to curtail the growth of cattle rustling, he organized a group of "vigilantes, known as "Stuart's Stranglers." In 1884, he became the first president of the Montana Stockgrowers Association.

Stuart helped found the state historical society in 1865 and wrote an early guidebook and Indian language dictionary entitled, *Montana As It Is*. Posthumously published, his book *Forty Years of the Frontier* is considered one of the cornerstones of Montana history.

Stuart served several terms as a Democrat in the territorial legislature, and in 1894, President Cleveland appointed him Foreign Minister to Uruguay and Paraguay. When he returned to Montana in 1898, he became head librarian at the Butte Public Library, where he dedicated himself to documenting the history of Montana Territory. Though he never achieved the business and financial success he hoped for, Stuart lived a long full life amid the primary events of early Montana History.

Federal government declares thirty-five Montana counties as primary drought disaster areas. Similar declarations have been made for all or parts of Montana since 2000.

Discovery of mad cow disease in Alberta closes U.S.-Canadian border to live cattle importation.

2004   Marc Racicot, former governor, becomes head of National Republican Party and chair of the Bush-Cheney 2004 re-election campaign.

Montana Supreme Court upholds a District Court ruling that state funding for public education is inadequate to provide a "basic, quality education system," as required by the Montana Constitution.

Five persons are believed to be dead in a Forest Service airplane crash in wilderness near Kalispell, but two seriously injured survivors walk to safety two days later.

SELECTED MONTANA HISTORY EVENTS

Bannack Days, Bannack State Park, Dillon, third weekend in July, 834-3413

Big Hole National Battlefield Day, Wisdom, August, 689-3155

Black Powder Shoot, Havre, late May, 265-2483

Burnt Hole Rendezvous Reenactment, West Yellowstone, August, 646-7110

Central Montana Wagon Train, Lewistown, July, 538-3915

Chief Victor Days, Victor, July, 961-3037

Christmas at the Daly Mansion, Hamilton, December, 755-2166

Custer's Last Stand Reenactment, Hardin, third week of June, 655-3577

Fort Owen Day, Stevensville, July, 542-5500

Fort Union Rendezvous, Sidney, June 443-1916

Infantry Encampment, Miles City, July, 232-2182

Lewis and Clark Festival and Encampment, Giant Springs State Park, Great Falls, third week of June, 727-8733

Milk River Wagon Train, Malta, September, 654-1200

Montana Historical Society Annual Conference, October, 444-2694

Mullan Day, Superior, May, 822-4891

Museum Without Walls, Billings, Summer, 246-6809

Polson Living History Day, Polson, July, 883-6804

Powder River Wagon Train and Cattle Drive, Broadus, July, 436-2404

Red Lodge Mountain Man Rendezvous, Red Lodge, late July, 446-1718

Sandcreek Clydesdale Wagon Train, Jordan, July, 557-2865

Sidney Living History Weekend, September. 443-1916

St. Mary's Heritage Celebration, Stevensville, June, 777-3773

Sun-Child Reenactment Camp, East Glacier, July, (800) 350-2882

Two Medicine Culture and Language Camp, Browning, July, 338-2882

Vanderburg Camp, Arlee, June, 675-0160

Virginia City Heritage Days, Virginia City, August, 843-5833

Wagon Train and Trail Ride, Culbertson, September, 787-5559

Western Days, Billings, June, 652-8494 or 256-6961

Western Heritage Days, Grant-Kohrs Ranch National Historic Site, Deer Lodge, July, 846-2070

The federal Environmental Protection Agency and State officials approve final plan for cleanup and restoration of the Clark Fork River Basin Superfund site, including removal of the aging Milltown Dam near Missoula.

2005   For the first time in twenty years, Democrats gain a majority in both houses of the Montana Legislature, led by Democratic Governor Brian Schweitzer the first Democratic governor in 16 years.

On February 2, President George W. Bush holds a "town hall meeting" at the Four Seasons Arena in Great Falls to promote his plan to revamp the federal Social Security Program.

Summer wildfires threaten the towns of Plains and Alberton.

Further Reading

Though some of the following titles are out of print, most can be found in Montana's public or school libraries.

Ambrose, Stephen E. *Undaunted Courage, Meriwether Lewis, Thomas Jefferson, and the Opening of the American West*. New York: Simon & Schuster, 1996.

Bennion, Jon. *Big Sky Politics, Campaigns and Elections in Modern Montana*, Missoula, Mont.: Five Valleys Publishing, 2004.

Bradshaw, Glenda Clay, comp. *Montana's Historical Highway Markers*. Helena: Montana Historical Society, revised edition, 1994.

Burlingame, Merrill C. *The Montana Frontier*. Bozeman: Big Sky Books, 1942.

Cheney, Roberta C. *Names on the Face of Montana*. Missoula, Mont.: Mountain Press, 1983.

Conklin, Dave. *Montana History Weekends, 52 Adventures in History*, Guilford, Conn.: The Globe Pequot Press, 2002.

Crutchfield, James A. *It Happened in Montana*. Helena: The Globe Pequot Press, 1994.

Dimsdale, Thomas J. *The Vigilantes of Montana, or Popular Justice in the Rocky Mountains*. Virginia City, Mont.: Montana Post, 1866.

Ewers, John C. *The Blackfeet: Raiders on the Northwestern Plains*. Norman: University of Oklahoma Press, 1958.

Fifer, Barbara. *Along the Trail with Lewis and Clark*. Helena: Farcountry Press, 2004.

Fifer, Barbara. *Montana Battlefields, 1806–1877, Native Americans and the U.S. Army at War*. Helena, Mont.: Farcountry Press, 2004.

Fritz, Harry W. *Montana, Land of Contrasts, An Illustrated History*. Sun Valley, Calif.: American Historical Press, 2001.

Garcia, Andrew. *Tough Trip Through Paradise, 1878–1879*. Edited by Ben Stein. Boston: Houghton, 1967.

Gilluly, Bob. *One Man's Montana. Bob Gilluly's Best Newspaper Yarns. Great Falls Tribune 1983 to 1999*. Missoula, Mont.: Heartland Journals 1999.

Glasscock, Carl B. *The War of the Copper Kings: Builders of Butte and Wolves of Wall Street*. Indianapolis: Bobbs-Merrill, 1935.

Hedren, Paul L., ed. *The Great Sioux War, 1876–77*. Helena: Montana Historical Society Press, 1991.

Howard, Joseph Kinsey. *Montana: High, Wide, and Handsome*. New Haven, Conn.: Yale University Press, 1943.

———. *Strange Empire: A Narrative of the Northwest*. New York: William Morrow and Co., 1952.

Johnson, Dorothy M. *The Bloody Bozeman*. New York: McGraw-Hill, 1971.

Lang, William L., and Rex C. Myers. *Montana Our Land & People*, revised edition. Boulder, Colo.: Pruett Publishing Company, 1989.

Langford, Nathaniel Pitt. *Vigilante Days and Ways*. (2 vols.) Boston: J. G. Cupples, 1890.

Linderman, Frank Bird. *Montana Adventure*. Edited by H. G. Merriam. Lincoln: University of Nebraska Press, 1968.

Malone, Michael P. *The Battle for Butte: Mining and Politics on the Northern Frontier, 1864–1906*. Helena: Montana Historical Society Press, 1993.

Malone, Michael P., Richard B. Roeder, and William L. Lang. *Montana, A History of Two Centuries*, revised edition. Seattle: University of Washington Press, 1991.

Merrill-Maker, Andrea. *Montana People and Their Stories*. Carson City, Nev.: The Grace Dangberg Foundation, Inc., 2004.

Montana Historical Society. *Not in Precious Metals Alone: A Manuscript History of Montana.* Helena: Montana Historical Society Press, 1976.

Montana, The Magazine of Western History. Published by the Montana Historical Society, Box 201201, Helena, MT 59620. Subscriptions $29 per year (4 issues, $6.50 each).

Murphy, May. *Hope in Hard Times, New Deal Photographs of Montana 1936–1942.* Helena: Montana Historical Society Press, 2003.

O'Brien, Mary Barmeyer. *Jeannette Rankin: Bright Star in the Big Sky.* Helena: Falcon Publishing Co., 1995.

Parry, Ellis Roberts. *Montana Dateline.* Guilford, Conn.: The Globe Pequot Press, 2001.

Petrik, Paula. *No Step Backward: Women and Family on the Rocky Mountain Mining Frontier, Helena, Montana 1865–1900.* Helena: Montana Historical Society Press, 1987.

Schultz, James Willard. *My Life As an Indian.* Boston: Houghton Mifflin, 1907.

Shirley, Gayle C. *Charlie's Trail: The Life and Art of C. M. Russell.* Helena: Falcon Press, 1996.

———. *More Than Petticoats: Remarkable Montana Women.* Helena: The Globe Pequot Press, 1995.

Small, Lawrence F., ed. *Religion in Montana: Pathways to the Present.* Vols. 1 and 2. Billings: Rocky Mountain College, 1995.

Smith, Phyllis. *Bozeman and the Gallatin Valley: A History.* Helena: The Globe Pequot Press, 1996.

Spritzer, Don. *A Roadside History of Montana.* Missoula: Mountain Press Publishing Company, 1999.

Stuart, Granville. *Forty Years on the Frontier: As Seen in the Journals and Reminiscences of Granville Stuart, Gold-Miner, Trader, Merchant, Rancher and Politician.* Edited by Paul C. Phillips. (2 vols.) Cleveland: Arthur J. Clark, 1925.

Swartout, Robert R., Jr., and Harry W. Fritz, eds. *The Montana Heritage: An Anthology of Historical Essays.* Helena: Montana Historical Society Press, 1992.

Toole, K. Ross. *Montana: An Uncommon Land.* Norman: University of Oklahoma Press, 1959.

———. *Twentieth Century Montana: A State of Extremes.* Norman: University of Oklahoma Press, 1972.

———. *The Rape of the Great Plains: Northwest America, Cattle and Coal.* Boston: Little, Brown and Co., 1976.

Tubbs, Stephenie Ambrose, with Clay Straus Jenkinson. *The Lewis and Clark Companion, An Encyclopedic Guide to the Voyage of Discovery.* New York: Henry Holt and Company, 2003.

Vasapoli, Salvatore, Photography, with Essay by Pat Williams. *Montana.* Portland, Ore.: Graphic Arts Center Publishing Company, 2003.

Wilson, Gary. *Outlaw Tales of Montana,* second edition. Guilford, Conn.: The Globe Pequot Press, 2003.

Writers Project of Montana. *Copper Camp, Stories of the World's Greatest Mining Camp, Butte, Montana.* First published in 1943. Reissued by Riverbend Publishing, Helena, Mont., 2002.

CHAPTER FIVE

People

Montana's big sky covers 145,552 square miles of land, but there are only about 6 people per square mile to hold up that much heaven, 6.30 to be precise. So much space may be the paramount reason so many former Montanans are moving back to the state, and so many newcomers establish homes here.

Blossom T. Neff and Robert Yellowtail.
MONTANA HISTORICAL SOCIETY

Montana's original residents were numerous tribal groups who inhabited the area for various periods over thousands of years. Most of today's modern tribal groups started arriving in the 1700s, finding the refuge and bounty they needed to survive hostile tribes in other homelands, and later, the encroachment of European civilization from the east. In the early 1800s, the various Indian tribes in the area may have numbered over 30,000, before widespread devastation by smallpox epidemics. The wave of settlers to Montana from the 1860s to early 1900s, though, combined with efforts of the U.S. government during that time to contain the Indians within designated boundaries, soon guaranteed that people of mainly European stock would outnumber the various tribes. Native Americans now account for over 6 percent of the state's population, the second largest ethnic group under the Big Sky.

From the Lewis and Clark Expedition onward, many different ethnic groups have found their way to Montana. Following on the heels of the French-Canadian and British fur traders were white Americans, most of them from southern and midwestern states and other parts of the settled West. The Montana gold rush of the 1860s also attracted immigrants from Ireland, England, Scandinavia, and Germany. Chinese immigrants, who came to labor in the earliest towns and to rework the placer mines, made up the largest foreign-born population in the 1870 census. There were 1,949 Chinese counted.

The industrial copper mines brought many more diverse groups to the Butte area, the largest of these ethnic groups being the Irish, the Welsh, and the Cornish, or "Cousin Jacks." After 1900, immigrants from Italy, Poland, and other European countries—mainly Greece, Austria, and Yugoslavia—added to the populations of Butte, Anaconda, and Great Falls. In the heyday of mining, you could hear as many as thirty languages on the streets of these mining and smelting towns.

In the early 1900s, tens of thousands of homesteaders were lured by the railroads' advertisements and the promise of free land along the Hi-Line, Montana's northern tier. These eager settlers were mainly from the midwestern states, Scandinavia, and Germany. Many Scandinavian Lutherans still enjoy lutefisk and lefse dinners in Montana churches and grange halls around Christmas time. The dozens of Hutterite colonies scattered across Montana represent only a portion of the state's heavy percentage of German ancestry. In the 1940s, Mexican laborers were imported to work the sugar beet fields of the Yellowstone Valley. The latest group of immigrants to Montana include Hmong refugees and other Southeast Asian peoples who came mainly to the Missoula area in the 1970s.

The population growth rate has never been as dramatic as in the years from 1870 to 1920. In the 1920s, the state lost 2 percent of its population. From 1980 to 1990, Montana's population grew by a modest 1.6 percent, less than most other states. From 1990 to 2000, the population gain was an impressive 12.9 percent. Yet, when the 435 seats in the U.S. House of Representatives were reapportioned based on the 2000 census, for the second decade in a row, Montana was just shy of the population needed to retain two representatives in that body.

The 2000 U.S. census count was 902,195, making Montana forty-fourth among the fifty states in population.

HOW CROWDED IS MONTANA?

	Population	Sq. Mi.*	Person/sq.mi.
Alaska	648,818	570,374	1.1
Wyoming	501,242	97,105	5.2
Montana	917,621	145,552	6.3
Colorado	4,550,688	103,729	43.8
California	35,484,453	155,973	227.5
Los Angeles	3,819,951	469	8,144.9
San Francisco	751, 682	47	15,993.2
New York City	8,085,742	303	26,685.6

*Square miles in land area only (i.e., excluding lakes, rivers, etc.)
Source: U.S. Bureau of the Census, 2003 Population Estimates. Washington, D.C., 2004.

Population Density

2003   6.30 persons per square mile

1890   .91 persons per square mile

Montana's small population and vast size account for one of the lowest rankings for population density in the nation, historically among the bottom five states; in 2000, Montana was the forty-eighth most densely populated state. Only ten counties in the state have population densities of more than ten people per square mile. Eight Montana counties have less than one person per square mile.

Who We Were

The Montana of 100 years ago looked quite different than it does today. The 1890 census counted only 142,924 people within the state's borders, only about a sixth of today's population. In addition to 10,765 Indians on reservations in the state in 1890, there were 89,063 U.S.-born and 43,096 foreign-born residents of Montana.

Who We Are

The 2003 census estimated a total of 917,621 people in Montana. There are not only a lot more people than 100 years ago, there are many different kinds of people here, too. Today's diverse population is a reflection of the Treasure State's colorful history. You'll find descendants of Montana's early Indian inhabitants as well as those who can trace their roots back to early fur traders

Racial Makeup of Montana, 2000

Race	Number of Persons	% of Total MT Population
White	817,229	90.6%
American Indian or Alaska Native	56,068	6.2%
Hispanic or Latino	18,081	2.0%
Black	2,692	0.3%
Asian	5,161	0.6%
Native Hawaiian and Other Pacific Islander	470	0.1%
Some other race	5,315	0.6%

Source: U.S. Census Bureau, Census 2000

Montanans Born in State

Year	Percentage
1960	59.7%
1970	59.7%
1980	56.9%
1990	60.0%
2000	56.1%

or immigrants farmers and miners. You'll also find folks from all over the world who have only recently become residents of Big Sky Country; many of these people have moved here looking for that special lifestyle that make Montana unique.

Because of changing census policies that reflect changing attitudes toward race and ethnicity, the census breaks the population down into more specific categoreies of race than it did 100 years ago, making direct comparison difficult.

Montana's Indians

Eleven principal tribal groups of Indians live on seven reservations in Montana. Three reservations are shared by more than one principal tribal group. While a majority of Montana's 66,000 people of Indian extraction live on the reservations, over 25,000 live throughout the state, in all sizes of communities. Most, however are concentrated in the larger cities of Billings, Missoula, Great Falls, Helena, and Butte. While most of the Indian population of Montana are members of state's principal tribal groups, the 2000 census reports that over 80 Indian tribes are represented in the state. Indian

Montana Population Growth—1870 to 2000

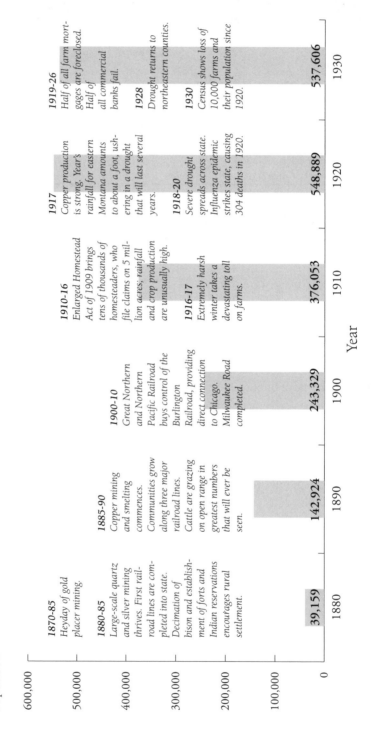

Population

1870-85
Heyday of gold placer mining.

1880-85
Large-scale quartz and silver mining thrives. First railroad lines are completed into state. Communities grow along three major railroad lines. Decimation of bison and establishment of forts and Indian reservations encourages rural settlement.

1885-90
Copper mining and smelting commences.

1900-10
Great Northern and Northern Pacific Railroad buys control of the Burlington Railroad, providing direct connection to Chicago. Milwaukee Road completed.

1910-16
Enlarged Homestead Act of 1909 brings tens of thousands of homesteaders, who file claims on 5 million acres; rainfall and crop production are unusually high.

1916-17
Extremely harsh winter takes a devastating toll on farms.

1917
Copper production is strong. Year's rainfall for eastern Montana amounts to about a foot, ushering in a drought that will last several years.

1918-20
Severe drought spreads across state. Influenza epidemic strikes state, causing 304 deaths in 1920.

1919-26
Half of all farm mortgages are foreclosed. Half of all commercial banks fail.

1928
Drought returns to northeastern counties.

1930
Census shows loss of 10,000 farms and their population since 1920.

Year	Population
1880	39,159
1890	142,924
1900	243,329
1910	376,053
1920	548,889
1930	537,606

Population axis: 0, 100,000, 200,000, 300,000, 400,000, 500,000, 600,000

Year

Montana Population Growth—1870 to 2000 (cont.)

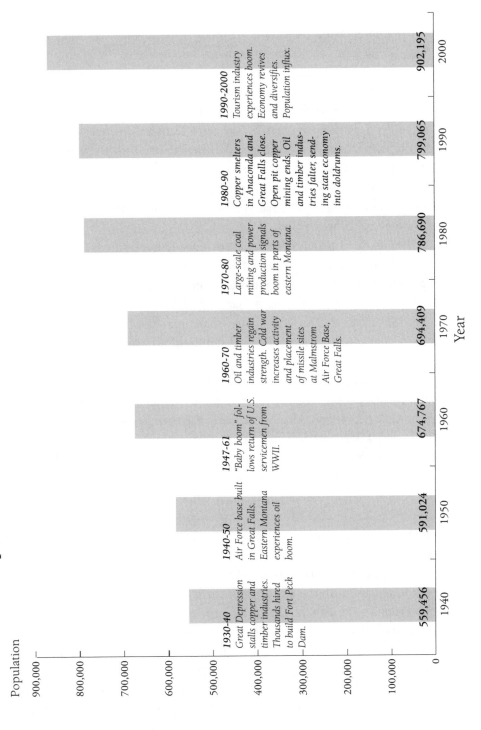

Population

1930-40
Great Depression stalls copper and timber industries. Thousands hired to build Fort Peck Dam.

1940-50
Air Force base built in Great Falls. Eastern Montana experiences oil boom.

1947-61
"Baby boom" follows return of U.S. servicemen from WWII.

1960-70
Oil and timber industries regain strength. Cold war increases activity and placement of missile sites at Malmstrom Air Force Base, Great Falls.

1970-80
Large-scale coal mining and power production signals boom in parts of eastern Montana.

1980-90
Copper smelters in Anaconda and Great Falls close. Open pit copper mining ends. Oil and timber industries falter, sending state economy into doldrums.

1990-2000
Tourism industry experiences boom. Economy revives and diversifies. Population influx.

Year	1940	1950	1960	1970	1980	1990	2000
Population	559,456	591,024	674,767	694,409	786,690	799,065	902,195

people are citizens of their tribe, their state of residence, and the United States.

The Confederated Salish and Kootenai Tribes include the Kootenai, the Salish (in the past, sometimes incorrectly referred to as the Flathead), and the Pend d'Oreille, a Salishan-speaking tribe which includes the band once known as the Kalispel. The origin of the term "Flathead" is obscure. The Salish refer to themselves as Sqélı̆ö, meaning The People. The proper name for the Pend d'Oreille is Qæispé. The term Ktunaxa describes people who identify themselves as Kootenai and "Ksanka" refers to the name of the Ktunaxa band of the Flathead Reservation. The tribes share the 1.2-million-acre Flathead Reservation, which includes the National Bison Range at Moeise, the Ninepipes National Wildlife Refuge, and land along the southern shores of Flathead Lake.

The Gros Ventre and Assiniboine are separate legal entities that share the Fort Belknap Reservation. The Assiniboine were originally of Sioux ancestry. The name derives from the Chippewa, meaning "one who cooks with stone", probably referring to their particular way of using hot stones and boiling water to cook food. The Gros Ventre, sometimes also known as the Atsina, were of Algonquian stock, closely related to the Arapaho at one time. Early French traders, who often misunderstood sign language, named them Gros Ventre, meaning "big bellies," an unfortunate misnomer for people who had quite ordinary stomachs. The Gros Ventre of Montana call themselves "The White Clay People" or "Ahaninin." Today, the Gros Ventre live mainly in the Hayes and Lodgepole area in the southern part of the reservation. The Assiniboine are concentrated in the northern part along the Milk River. While many tribal members engage in farming and ranching on the grassland plains of the reservation, general employment opportunities on the reservation are limited. The tribes are developing tourism to encourage enjoyment of the many annual tribal festivities and the recreational activities available on tribal lands.

The linguistically related Assiniboine and Sioux both reside the Fort Peck Reservation. In the late 16th century, bands of Nakota (Assiniboine) and Dakota and Lakota Sioux all resided in the region between the Mississippi River and Lake Superior. The Fort Peck Reservation in northeastern Montana is the second largest reservation in Montana, located 40 miles west of the North Dakota border and 50 miles south of the Canadian border. A number of towns dot the Missouri rivers north bank, the reservation's southern boundary. The tribal headquarters of Poplar

Susan "Walking Bear" Yellowtail (1903–1981)

After growing up a member of the Crow tribe in Pryor, "Walking Bear" went to western Massachusetts to attend a seminary, then to Boston where she trained as a nurse at Boston General Hospital. When her training ended, she was the first American Indian to become a registered nurse in the United States. She returned to the reservation in 1929, serving her people as a nurse, midwife, and spokesperson. She worked for the Indian Health Service and served on state and federal Indian health councils. Committed to bridging cultures, she also traveled to Europe and North Africa on behalf of the U.S. State Department.

MONTANA HISTORICAL SOCIETY

boosts an industrial park that is one the largest employers in Montana. An electronics manufacturing tribal enterprise and agriculture also play a part in the reservation economy.

The Blackfeet are the largest single tribal group in Montana, with over 15,000 enrolled members. It is commonly thought that they acquired that their name because of the characteristic black color of their moccasins, either intentionally painted or darkened with the ashes of prairie fires and campfires. Today's Blackfeet are descended from tribes known as the Siksika, Kainah (or Bloods), and Piegans, all of Algonquian linguistic stock. These tribes lived in present-day Saskatchewan until the early 1700s, when they began to move south to hunt the abundant buffalo. The 1.5 million acres of the Blackfeet Reservation are bordered on the north by Canada and on the west by Glacier National Park. Tribal economic activities include tourism, grain farming, ranching, oil and gas development, wind generation, and timber harvesting.

Reservation Populations

Names & Reservation Headquarters	Date Est.	Resident Tribes	Indians on Reservation	Enrolled Tribal Members	Non-Indians on Reservation
Blackfeet					
Browning, MT	1851	Blackfeet	8,507	15,118	16%
Crow					
Crow Agency, MT	1851	Crow	5,165	10,333	25%
Flathead		Salish, Pend d'Oreille			
Pablo, MT	1855	Kootenai	6,999	6,961	75%
Fort Belknap		Assiniboine			
Harlem, MT	1888	Gros Ventre	2,790	7,303	6%
Fort Peck		Assiniboine			
Poplar, MT	1888	Sioux	6,391	11,171	38%
Northern Cheyenne					
Lame Deer, MT	1884	Northern Cheyenne	4,029	7,374	10%
Rocky Boy's					
Rocky Boy Agency	1916	Chippewa-Cree	2,578	2,500	4%
Little Shell					
Great Falls, MT	2000	Chippewa	NA	3,850	NA

Source: U.S. Bureau of the Census, 2000.

In the early 1700s, the Cheyenne people farmed along other tribes of the upper Missouri, but once they acquired the horse, they began moving south to hunt buffalo. In 1876, the northern branch of the Cheyenne joined the Sioux to defeat Custer's army at the Battle of the Little Bighorn. In the following years, the Northern Cheyenne were forced to move to Indian Territory in Oklahoma, to live in exile with the Southern Cheyenne. A small band, led by Chief Dull Knife (Morningstar) and Chief Littlewolf, escaped to fight their way back to the homelands of southeastern Montana. In 1884, a tract of land east of the Crow Reservation was set aside for them. The Northern Cheyenne call themselves "the Morning Star people." The Northern Cheyenne Reservation has large coal and methane gas reserves, an electrical power plant, and considerable timber resources.

In the 1600s, the Crow Indians lived in semi-permanent villages of lodges covered with earth, along the Missouri River in the present-day states of South and North Dakota. One group, the Absarokee, migrated westward to live in eastern Montana and northern Wyoming. In the Hidatsa language, the Crow tribe was called Apsaalooké, which means "children of the large-beaked bird." White people later misinterpreted the word as "crow." The tribe numbered over 8,000 members before being devastated by smallpox epidemics in the mid-1800s. In 1851, the Fort Laramie Treat granted these

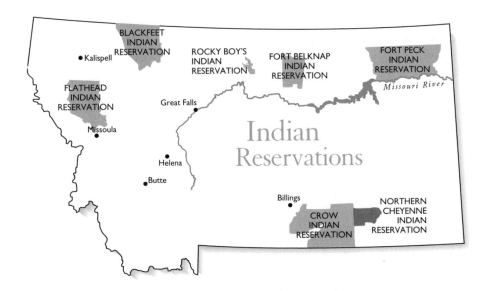

Indian Reservations

Crow Indians nearly 38 million acres of land, an amount that was significantly reduced to 2.4 million acres over the years. The principal economic activities on the Crow Reservation are farming, ranching, tribal services, and coal mining operations. The scenic Big Horn Canyon and the lake behind the Yellowtail Dam offer a bounty of recreational opportunities.

The name of the Rocky Boy's Reservation in north central Montana was derived from an attempt to honor Chief Stone Man, a leader of a band of Chippewa Indians. The chief's name was not translated correctly from Chippewa into English, and "Rocky Boy's" evolved. In the 1890s, bands of Chippewa and Cree Indians, who had often found refuge together, united to find a permanent home. After wandering the state for many years hoping to find acceptance and a suitable location, they were finally offered a tract land south of Havre. In 1935, the Chippewa and Cree people adopted a tribal constitution that officially recognized the coming together of the two tribes, through extensive intermarriage over the years, into the Chippewa-Cree Tribe. One third of Rocky Boy's Reservation is located in the beautiful Bears Paw Mountains, and the remainder is prairie land.

Montana is also home to "The Little Shell Tribe of Chippewa Indians of Montana." Today's members of the Little Shell Tribe trace their ancestry to Chippewa, Cree, and Metis (mixed blood) people who were removed from the reservation roles in the Turtle Mountain area of North Dakota and forced to survive the harsh life of "landless" Indians. Those who came to Montana under the leadership of Chief Little Shell attempted to reestablish their federal recognition as a tribe, to no avail. Finally, after more than one hundred years and the work of many advocates, preliminary recognition was granted in May of 2000. An elected Tribal Council, located at the tribal headquarters in Great Falls, continues to gather records and membership for final recognition. The nearly 4,000 enrolled tribal members live all over Montana and the rest of the United States, but many have remained in the Great Falls area for decades.

According to the 2000 census, the Indian population of Montana was 56,068 persons, approximately 6.2 percent of the state population. While Montana's overall population increased only 1.6 percent from 1980 to 1990, the Indian population increased by 27.9 percent. From 1990 to 2000, the Indian population grew only 6.8 percent, about half that of the state's total percentage growth of 12.9. The extent of Indian heritage in Montana is reflected in the 66,320 respondents to the 2000 census who identified themselves as American Indian or Alaskan Native, alone or in combination with another race. Those who responded to this census question were asked to identify their principal tribal affiliation, resulting in representation of over 80 separate tribes among Montana residents.

Montana ranks fifth in the nation for percentage of Indian population within the total state population.

Recent State Population Trends

In 2000, the U.S. census counted 902,195 people living in Montana, a 12.9 percent increase from the amount counted in 1990. Montana's official population estimate for July 1, 2003, was 917, 621 persons, a 5.2 percent increase in only three years. Researchers attribute the state's recent population growth to three areas: more job development, higher birth to death rates, and migration into the state, or in the demographer's jargon, "in-migration."

The estimated increase has not won us a new place on the national population chart. We're still 44th, the same as in 1980 and 1990. Of the 2003 estimated U.S. population of 290,809,777 people, Montana contributes less than one percent.

Ravalli County, in the Bitterroot Valley south of Missoula, was the fastest growing county between 1990 and 2003.

Since the 1980s, the mountainous areas of Montana, especially counties west of the Continental Divide, have been beckoning a steady flow of newcomers. The prairie counties of northeastern and far eastern Montana have been experiencing a continuous decline in population. From 1990 to 2003,

Fastest Growing Counties

Rank	County	Est. Population Growth 1990-2000	Est. Population Growth 2000-2003
1	Ravalli	35%	21.3
2	Gallatin	31%	23.6%
3	Flathead	25%	20.0%
4	Broadwater	25%	3.1%
5	Jefferson	24%	13.5%
6	Lake	21%	7.9%
7	Missoula	20%	8.9%
8	Stillwater	20%	9.8%
9	Lewis & Clark	17%	7.7%
10	Sanders	17%	6.8%

thirty counties gained population, while twenty-five counties lost population. Blaine County's population remained the same. All but two of the counties reporting losses are located east of the Continental Divide. The two exceptions were Deer Lodge County and Silver Bow County, both in southwestern Montana, reporting a 14 percent and a 2 percent population loss, respectively. During the 1980s, thirty-nine of Montana's fifty-six counties lost population, again, most in eastern Montana.

Two-thirds of Montana's 15,426 population growth from 2000 to 2003 took place in Flathead and Gallatin counties, which grew by 5,014 and 5,412 persons respectively.

Urban Montana, Rural Montana

In 1950, Montana's rural population was 56.3 and the urban population was 43.7.

Montana's urban population is growing. The 2003 estimates show growth in most of the top fifteen urban areas. Missoula, Bozeman, and Kalispell are the fastest growing, both over the past dozen years and since 2000. Some towns with significant population growth since 2000 include Belgrade (19 percent), Polson (11.2 percent), and Whitefish (14.9 percent). During this period, Missoula surpassed Great Falls to become the second largest city. Montana has 129 incorporated cities and towns. Seventy-one of those places have fewer than 1,000 residents. Dozens of the state's smaller towns, especially on the eastern plains, have been losing population over the past decade. Twenty-nine percent of Montanans live in a rural setting that is defined as "not a place" by the U.S. Census.

Montana's Ten Largest Cities

Rank	City	1900 Pop.	1990 Pop.	2000 Pop.	2003 Est. Pop.	% Change 1990-2003
1	Billings	3,221	81,125	89,847	95,220	17.4
2	Missoula	4,366	42,918	57,053	60,722	41.5
3	Great Falls	14,930	55,125	56,690	56,155	1.9
4	Butte-Silver Bow	30,470	33,336	33,892	32,519	-2.5
5	Bozeman	3,419	22,660	27,509	30,753	35.9
6	Helena	10,770	24,609	25,780	26,718	8.6
7	Kalispell	2,526	11,917	14,223	16,391	37.5
8	Havre	1,033	10,102	9,621	9,448	-6.5
9	Anaconda-Deer Lodge County	9,453	10,356	9,417	8,953	-13.5
10	Miles City	1,938	8,461	8,487	8,242	-2.6

*Butte-Silver Bow and Anaconda-Deer Lodge became consolidated city/county governments in the late 1970s.
Source: U.S. Bureau of the Census, Decennial Censuses of Poplation, Montana 2000.

Montana's Ten Smallest Cities

Town	County	Est. Pop. 2003
1. Ismay	Custer	25
2. Outlook	Sheridan	73
3. Bearcreek	Carbon	83
4. Flaxville	Daniels	83
5. Neihart	Cascade	87
6. Opheim	Valley	105
7. Dodson	Phillips	113
8. Virginia City	Madison	130
9. Plevna	Fallon	131
10. Melstone	Musselshell	136

Source: Population Division, U.S. Census Bureau.

Age and Montana's Population

	2003 Est. Pop.	% of Total State Pop in 2003	% in 1990
Under 5	53,510	5.8	7.4
5 to 17	162,264	17.7	20.4
18 to 24	96,129	10.5	8.8
25 to 44	233,247	25.4	31.3
45 to 64	247,311	27.0	18.9
65 and older	125,160	13.6	13.3

Source: Population Division, U.S. Census Bureau Table 2: (SC-EST2003-0230).

Gender

In most counties, females outnumber males. The state ratio is 98 males for every 100 females. In 1890, Montana had about half as many females (44,277) as males (87,882).

According to 2003 population estimates, the median age for males in Montana is 37.8 years old. The median age for females is 40 years old.

Source: US Bureau of the Census, 2000. Population Division, U.S. Census (SC-EST2003-02-30)

Our Age

Montana, like most states, has an aging population. The median age in 1970 was 27 and in 1990, the median age was 33.8. The median age derived from the 2003 population estimates indicates a median age of 39.0.

As of July 1, 2003, 141,000 Montana residents were over 60 years of age. There were 17,489 Montanans 85 years of age or older. The 2000 census showed Montana had 162 people who were 100 years old or older—38 were men and 124 were women. As the Baby Boom generation (those born between 1946 and 1964) reaches retirement age, the growth of the elderly population (65 and over) in Montana and the nation will experience one of the most dramatic demographic transformations in history. More people than ever before will be over age 65 and will be living longer than ever before. Those aged 45 to 64 will represent 44 percent of Montana's population by 2010.

In eight of Montana's counties, at least 20 percent of the population is older than 65 years. Sheridan County has the greatest percentage of people 65 or older (25.4 percent), followed by Daniels (24.1).

The four counties with the most youthful population—Glacier (34.9 percent), Big Horn (35.8 percent), Rosebud (percent) and Roosevelt (34.6 percent)—all contain Indian reservations. The statewide population under age 18 is 25.5 percent of the total population.

Source: U.S. Bureau of the Census, Census 2000.

Montana Population by County

County	1990 Census	2000 Census	7/1/2003 Estimate	% Change 1990 to 2003	Land Area*	People per Sq. Mi., 2003 Est.
Montana	799,065	902,195	917,621	13	145,552	6.3
Yellowstone	113,419	129,352	133,191	15	2,635.2	50.5
Missoula	78,687	95,802	98,616	20	2,597.9	38.0
Cascade	77,691	80,357	79,561	2	2,697.9	29.5
Flathead	59,218	74,471	79,485	25	5,098.3	15.6
Gallatin	50,463	67,831	73,243	31	2,605.8	28.1
Lewis & Clark	47,495	55,716	57,137	17	3,460.9	16.5
Ravalli	25,010	36,070	38,662	35	2,394.2	16.1
Silver Bow	33,941	34,606	33,208	-2	718.3	46.2
Lake	21,041	27,197	26,507	21	1,493.8	17.7
Lincoln	17,481	18,837	18,835	7	3,612.7	5.2
Hill	17,654	16,673	16,350	-7	2,896.4	5.6
Park	14,484	15,694	15,840	9	2,656.2	6.0
Glacier	12,121	13,247	13,250	9	2,994.7	4.4
Big Horn	11,337	12,671	12,894	12	4,994.8	2.6
Fergus	12,083	11,893	11,695	-3	4,339.1	2.7
Custer	11,697	11,696	11,369	-3	3,783.1	3.0
Jefferson	7,939	10,049	10,499	24	1,656.6	6.3
Sanders	8,669	10,227	10,455	17	2,762.2	3.8
Carbon	8,080	9,552	9,770	17	2,048	4.8
Rosebud	10,505	9,383	9,303	-11	5,012.4	1.9
Richland	10,716	9,667	9,155	-15	2,084.1	4.4
Deer Lodge	10,356	9,417	8,953	-14	736.9	12.1
Beaverhead	8,424	9,202	8,919	6	5,542.3	1.6
Dawson	9,505	9,059	8,776	-8	2,373.1	3.7
Stillwater	6,563	8,459	8,195	20	1,795.1	4.6
Valley	8,239	7,675	7,349	-11	4,921.0	1.5
Powell	6,620	7,180	7,006	6	2,325.9	3.0
Madison	5,989	6,851	6,967	14	3,586.5	2.0
Blaine	6,728	7,009	6,729	0	4,226.2	1.6
Teton	6,271	6,445	6,369	2	2,272.6	2.8
Pondera	6,433	6,424	6,166	-4	1,624.7	3.8
Chouteau	5,452	5,970	5,576	2	3,973.3	1.4
Toole	5,046	5,267	5,337	5	1,910.9	2.8
Musselshell	4,106	4,497	4,464	8	1,867.1	2.4
Broadwater	3,318	4,385	4,430	25	1,191.4	3.7
Phillips	5,163	4,601	4,271	-17	5,139.9	0.8
Mineral	3,315	3,884	3,884	15	1,219.8	3.0
Sheridan	4,732	4,105	3,668	-22	1,676.6	2.2
Sweet Grass	3,154	3,609	3,604	12	1,855.1	1.9
Granite	2,548	2,830	2,894	12	1,727.4	1.7

Montana Population by County (cont.)

County	1990 Census	2000 Census	7/1/2003 Estimate	% Change 1990 to 2003	Land Area*	People per Sq. Mi., 2003 Est.
Fallon	3,103	2,837	2,752	-11	1,620.3	1.7
Judith Basin	2,282	2,192	2,329	2	1,869.9	1.2
Wheatland	2,246	2,259	2,106	-6	1,423.1	1.5
Liberty	2,295	2,158	2,055	-10	1,429.8	1.4
Meagher	1,819	1,932	1,967	8	2,391.8	.8
Daniels	2,266	2,017	1,940	-14	1,426.1	1.4
Powder River	2,090	1,858	1,834	-12	3,297.2	0.6
McCone	2,276	1,977	1,818	-20	2,642.5	.7
Carter	1,503	1,360	1,333	-11	3,339.6	.4
Garfield	1,589	1,279	1,233	-22	4,668.1	.3
Prairie	1,383	1,199	1,154	-2	1,736.6	0.7
Golden Valley	912	1,042	1,047	13	1,175.3	.9
Wibaux	1,191	1,068	977	-18	889.3	1.1
Treasure	874	861	735	-2	978.9	0.8
Petroleum	519	493	491	-5	1,653.9	.3
Roosevelt	10,999	10,620	10.451	-5	2,355.6	4.4

* Dry land and land temporarily or partially covered by water in 2000.

Sources: Square miles of land areas in 2000; U.S. Census Bureau, Census 2000 summary File 1; Population Division, U.S. Census Bureau, April 9, 2004.

Our Homes

Quick Housing Facts	1990	2000
Owner-Occupied Houses:	205,899 (67%)	163,397 (69%)
Median Value of Owner-Occupied Housing Units:	$56,600	$99,500
Renter-Occupied Houses:	100,264	105,420
Median Gross Rent (monthly):	$311	$447
Houses Built 1980-March 2000:	17.5%	30.9%
Home Heating: Utility Gas	54.2%	59.1%
Electricity	17.9%	16.1%
Housing Units that are Mobile Homes or Trailers:	34,497	58,957

Source: U.S. Bureau of the Census, Census 2000.

Median Residential Housing Sale Prices

County	2002	2003
Cascade	$94,000	110,000
Flathead	138,000	159,000
Gallatin	160,000	170,000
Jefferson	154,000	161,000
Lake	134,000	154,000
Lewis & Clark	118,000	126,000
Missoula	145,000	160,000
Ravalli	135,000	153,000
Yellowstone	118,000	128,000
Sanders	103,000	120,000
Lincoln	117,000	149,700
Carbon	88,500	115,000

Includes: residential with land, single family, townhomes/condominium, and mobile/modular homes. *Source: Montana Association of Realtors. Home Sales Data, 2004.*

FAMILIAL FACTS

In 2000, there were 358,667 households in Montana. The average household size was 2.45 people. Families made up 65 percent of the households— married-couple families (52 percent) and other families (13 percent). Most of the nonfamily households were people living alone (28 percent), but some were comprised of people living in households in which no one was related to the householder (7 percent).

According to the 2004 Kids Count study, the percentage of single-parent homes in the state increased from 24 percent in 1996 to 31 percent in 2001, compared to the national average of 28 percent, which was up only slightly from 1996.

The 2000 U.S. census counted 237,407 families in Montana. The average size of the families was 2.99 persons. In 1890, there were 27,501 families, whose average size was 4.81 persons.

Source: U.S. Census Bureau. American Community Survey Profile 2003.

Our Work

Annual Civilian Labor Force, 2004	483,043
Annual Unemployed, 2004	4.4%
Annual Per Capita Personal Income, 2004	$26,857
Median Family Income	$40,487
Median Household Income	$34,375
Persons Below Poverty Level	14.0%

Source: www.ourfactsyourfuture.com.

Top Ten Jobs of Montanans, 2003

Official Job Description	No. of Persons Employed
1. Retail Salesperson	15,410
2. General managers, Top-level Executives	10,610
3. Cashiers	10,240
4. Waiters and Waitresses	8,420
5. Janitors and Cleaners (except maids and Housekeeping Cleaners	7,990
6. Registered Nurses	7,760
7. General Office Clerks	7,630
8. Secretaries (except legal, medical and Executive)	7,140
9. K-8 Teachers	6,890
10. Bookkeeping, Accounting, Auditing clerks	6,600

Source: U.S. Department of Labor Bureau of Labor Statistics. May 2003 State Occupational Employment and Wage Estimates.

Household Incomes

Household Income Distribution, 1999	Percent of Households
Less than $10,000	11.3%
$10,000 to $14,999	8.9%
$15,000 to $19,999	8.6%
$20,000 to $24,999	8.5%
$25,000 to $29,999	7.8%
$30,000 to $34,999	7.6%
$35,000 to $39,999	6.8%
$40,000 to $44,999	6.3%
$45,000 to $49,999	5.2%
$50,000 to $59,999	8.7%
$60,000 to $74,999	8.5%
$75,000 to $99,999	6.4%
$100,000 to $124,999	2.5%
$125,000 to $149,999	1.1%
$150,000 to $199,999	0.9%
$200,000 or more	1.0%

Source: U.S. Census Bureau, Census 2000 Summary File 3, Matrices P52, P53, P54, P79, P80, P81, PCT38, PCT40, and PCT41.

Persons Moving Into and Out of Montana By Destination and Origin, 2001

	Persons leaving	Persons Arriving
Montana, All States	34,700	33,000
Washington	4,400	3,900
California	2,900	3,700
Colorado	2,300	2,100
Oregon	2,100	1,600
Idaho	2,400	2,000
Arizona	1,600	1,300
Wyoming	1,600	1,600
Texas	1,500	1,400
Utah	1,100	1,200
North Dakota	1,100	1,000
South Dakota	600	700
All Other States and Abroad	13,100	13,300

Source: Internal Revenue Service.

Who's Moving In

A poll conducted by The University of Montana's Bureau of Business and Economic Research in June 1995 found that many of the newcomers to Montana were actually natives returning to Montana. More than 55 percent of the migrants had at least one member of their household who had previously resided in Montana. The percentage of interstate migration into Montana was approximately 15 percent of the total state population, falling in line with a national average of from 14.5 to 16.5 percent. Most first-time residents were from California and most preferred the scenic, mountainous western and southwestern part of the state and the more urban counties. Gallatin, Yellowstone, and Flathead counties saw the largest percentage of out-of-state people becoming local residents.

Between 1995 and 2000, Montana experienced a net in-migration of around 6,930 people. According to The University of Montana's Bureau of Business and Economic Research, the 111,530 people who moved to Montana were older, wealthier, and more politically conservative than those 104,600 persons who moved out.

Source: Paul E. Polzin, Bureau of Business and Economic Research, University of Montana, 2003.

From the Cradle

There were 11,384 babies born to Montana residents in 2003. While the Montana birth rate exceed the U.S. rate from 1971 to 1985, it began

Montana Births and Deaths

Year	Est. Pop.	Deaths	Rate*	Births	Rate*
1985	826,000	6,725	8.1	13,497	16.3
1990	799,065	6,835	8.6	11,602	14.5
1995	870,280	7,614	8.7	11,136	12.8
2000	902,195	8,071	8.9	10,946	12.1
2001	904,433	8,252	9.1	10,947	12.1
2002	909,453	8,473	9.3	11,045	12.1
2003	917,621	8,445	9.2	11,384	12.4

* Per 1,000 estimated population.
Source: Montana Department of Public Health and Human Services, Office of Vital Statistics. 2003 Montana Vital Statistics. Helena: December 2004.

HUTTERITES, MENNONITES, AND AMISH COMMUNITIES

Approximately forty-eight Hutterite colonies are scattered across north central Montana. Members live communally and adhere to strict religious commitments. They combine their agricultural skills with a dedication to traditional Hutterite qualities of diligence and thrift. Montana Hutterite colonies produce about 60 percent of the state's pork and more than half of the eggs. Membership in the colonies is estimated at 4,800.

Distinguished by their Old World dress and German dialect, the Hutterites are one of three surviving Anabaptist groups in the U.S. that took root in sixteenth-century Europe during the Protestant Reformation. The other two are the Amish and the Mennonites.

The Amish have established communities near Rexford, Whitehall, and St. Ignatius.

Members of various Mennonite congregations live in a number of small Montana towns. Near the town of Lustre, 35 miles northwest of Wolf Point, there are three Mennonite churches and a church-sponsored state accredited high school.

to decline in the early 1980s, fell below the U.S. rate in the mid-1980s, and has been the lower of the two since. Only seven states currently have a lower birth rate than Montana and none of these are west of the Mississippi River.

- In 2003, births to mothers under age 20 accounted for 10.6 percent of all live births by Montana women.
- In 2003, 32.1 percent of the live births were to unmarried women, considerably higher than 1980 (12.5 percent) or 1970 (9.5 percent).
- More males (5,797) were born in 2003 than females (5,587).

Sources: Montana Department of Public Health and Human Services; Office of Vital Statistics. 2003 Montana Vital Statistics, December 2004

To the Grave

Montana's annual mortality rate in 2003 was 9.2 deaths per 1,000 estimated population, or 8,445 deaths.

- The tendency for women to live longer than men is reflected in Montana mortality statistics from 1994 to 2003, when the median age at death was seventy-five for males of all races and eighty-one for women of all races.
- From 1994 to 2003, the median age of death for American Indians was seventeen years less than for non-Indians of the same sex.
- The infant mortality rate for Montana dropped in 2003 to 6.8 after averaging 7.1 per 1,000 live births from 1990 to 2002. The infant mortality rate for both Montana and the nation is dropping, but Montana's rate has been lower than the national average since 1990.

Traffic Deaths, 2004

In 2004, there were 229 traffic fatalities, one fatality every 38 hours, in Montana. There was one traffic-related injury every 57 minutes.

- The hour between 3 and 5 P.M. is when more accidents happened than any other time of day. Friday and January are the day and month when the most accidents occurred.
- More fatal accidents occurred between 4 P.M. and 5 P.M. than any other time of day, and in July and Sepetemeber more than any other month of the year.
- Gallatin, Flathead, and Yellowstone Counties led the state with highway deaths in 2004.

Selected Causes of Death in Montana, 1990–2003 (ranked in order of prevalence in 2003)

Cause of Death	1990 Deaths/Rate*	2003 Deaths/Rate*
Heart disease	1,947/243.7	1,974/215.1
Cancer	1,630/204.0	1,838/200.3
Chronic Lower Resp. Diseases		587/64.0
Cerebrovascular disease		571/62.2
Accidents	398/49.8	515/56.1
Diabetes	154/19.3	263/28.7
Pneumonia & Influenza	213/26.7	257/28.0
Alzheimer's disease	Not available	236/25.7
Suicide	167/20.9	179/19.5
Chronic Liver disease & Cirrhosis	Not available	111/12.1
Nephritis (Kidney Disease)	48/6.0	101/11.0
Homicide	35/4.4	37/4.0

*Rate = deaths per 1,000,000 persons
Source: Montana Department of Public Health and Human Services, Office of Vital Statistics. 2003 Montana Vital Statistics. Helena: December 2004.

Marriages & Divorces in Montana, 1945–2003

Year	Marriages	Rate*	Divorces	Rate*
1945	8,147	14.2	2,380	4.1
1950	7,235	12.2	1,951	3.3
1955	6,514	10.2	1,909	3.0
1960	5,883	8.7	2,003	3.0
1965	4,688	6.6	2,002	2.8
1970	6,919	10.0	3,051	4.4
1975	7,331	9.8	4,286	5.7
1980	8,336	10.6	4,940	6.3
1985	7,178	8.7	4,258	5.2
1990	6,924	8.7	4,049	5.1
1991	6,984	8.6	4,443	5.5
1992	7,189	8.7	4,223	5.1
1993	7,041	8.4	4,311	5.1
1994	7,088	8.3	4,196	4.9
1995	6,818	7.8	4,214	4.8
2000	6,870	7.6	3,694	4.1
2001	6,612	7.3	3,735	4.1
2002	6,514	7.2	3,634	4.0
2003	6,640	7.2	3,255	3.5

* Rate per 1,000 estimated population.
Source: Montana Department of Public Health and Human Services, Office of Vital Statistics. 2003 Montana Vital Statistics. Helena: December 2004.

Church Membership in Montana, 2000

Selected Religious Organizations	No. of Churches	No. of Adherents*	% of MT Population	% of MT Churchgoers
Catholic Church	215	169,250	18.8	41.9
Evangelical Lutheran Church In America	148	50,287	5.6	12.5
Church of Jesus Christ of Latter-Day Saints	117	32,726	3.6	8.1
United Methodist Church	118	17,993	2.0	4.5
Assemblies of God	79	16,365	1.9	4.1
Lutheran Missouri Synod	63	15,441	1.7	3.8
Southern Baptist Convention	105	15,318	1.7	3.8
Presbyterian Church of the USA	53	9,372	1.0	2.3
International Four Square Gospel	24	7,637	0.8	1.9
United Church Of Christ	36	6,713	0.7	1.7
The Episcopal Church	47	6,509	0.7	1.7
Christian & Missionary Alliance	40	5,050	0.6	1.3
Hutterian Brethren*	48	4,800	0.5	1.2
Seventh Day Adventist	46	4,275	0.5	1.1
Christian Churches & Churches of Christ	24	3,522	0.4	0.9
American Baptist Churches in the USA	26	3,105	0.3	0.8
Christian Church (Disciples of Christ)	17	2,933	0.3	0.7
Churches of Christ	52	2,719	0.3	0.7
Church of the Nazarene	21	2,416	0.3	0.6
Salvation Army	8	1,414	0.2	0.4
Judaism	6	850	<0.1	0.2
Mennonite (all denominations)	14	802	<0.1	0.2
Muslim	3	614	<0.1	0.2
Other	233	23,381	2.7	6.0
Total	1,543	403,492	44.70	100

* All members, including full members, their children, and the estimated number of other regular participants who are not considered communicants, confirmed, or full members

Source: Religious Congregations and Membership in the United States 2000. Compiled by the Association of Statisticians of American Religious Bodies (ASARB), as acquired from the American Religious Data Archive at www.thearda.com.

The Rich and/or Famous

A sampling of well-known full-time or part-time residents:

Jeff Ament, Missoula; bass player rock band, Pearl Jam; helping to build a world-class skateboard park in Missoula, where he attended college and played in local bands.

Miller Barber, Rock Creek area; part owner of Streamside Anglers in Missoula; pro golfer who won three U.S. Senior Open titles.

Craig Barrett, ranch near Darby; Chief Executive of computer giant, Intel.

Dirk Benedict, born Dirk Niewaehner, March 1, 1945 in Helena, starred in

ROCKY MOUNTAIN LABORATORIES,
NATIONAL INSTITUTES OF HEALTH

Dr. Robert A. Cooley (1873–1964)

Born in Deerfield, Massachusetts, Cooley became interested in Rocky Mountain Spotted Fever while teaching at Montana State College (Bozeman) at the turn of the century. As head of the state Board of Entomology (1913-1931), he supervised research into the disease at laboratories in the Bitterroot Valley and became the leading authority on RMSF. He worked tirelessly to demonstrate that the mysterious and almost invariably fatal fever was carried by infected wood ticks and that a vaccine could be developed to treat it. Eventually, the federal government joined the battle and a cure was found. Cooley continued to teach at Bozeman until 1957 and authored several textbooks and journal articles. His work earned him national recognition.

George Henry Cowen (?–1924)

The son of a Bitterroot Valley farmer, Cowan never graduated from high school but played a role in the study of Rocky Mountain Spotted Fever. From 1918 to 1924, Cowan gathered ticks and performed other duties in the field and at the Bitterroot laboratories supervised by Dr. Cooley. His hunting and trapping skills and his knowledge of the Valley and its animals proved invaluable to the project. In 1922, he shot a mountain goat covered with more than 1,000 engorged ticks. This particular bounty led

ROCKY MOUNTAIN LABORATORIES,
NATIONAL INSTITUTES OF HEALTH

Cowan and the scientists to realize the ticks needed to ingest blood from their host before they could transmit a virulent strain of the fever. The discovery proved key to developing a vaccine for the disease. During its development in the spring of 1924, Cowan was offered a shot of the unproved vaccine but declined. Sadly, he contracted the fever a few months later and died. He was the fourth of five men who worked at the laboratories and died as a result of their contact with infected ticks.

William Wesley Van Orsdel (1848–1919)

Better known as "Brother Van," Van Orsdel was a minister of the Methodist Episcopal Church and, like frontier judges, rode a circuit on horseback and stagecoach, spreading that old-time religion over approximately 50,000 square miles. He often had to pitch in with the chores before he could get an attentive ear. He carried "the Word" to homes, churches, and camp meetings. He also carried word of the Battle of the Big Hole to a telegraph operator of the stage line that ran from Helena to Salt Lake City. After his riding days were over, he was appointed to administrative church posts in Great Falls and Helena. He was paralyzed by a stroke in the fall of 1919 and died in December.

MONTANA HISTORICAL SOCIETY

Father Anthony Ravalli (1812–1884)

An Italian Jesuit priest, Father Ravalli came to Montana in 1845, lending his considerable talents to the development of St. Mary's Mission in the Bitterroot Valley, where a county is now named for him. He spent the final thirty-nine years of his life in Montana. Missionary, woodcarver, sculptor, architect, physician, scholar: he was all these and then some. He died when he suffered a stroke after lending aid to a half-frozen miner in a blizzard.

MONTANA HISTORICAL SOCIETY

television series *Battlestar Gallactica* and *The A-Team;* wrote *Confessions of a Kamizaze Cowboy,* about his life; lives part-time in Big Fork.

Doug Betters, Whitefish area; former all-pro defensive end for the Miami Dolphins and veteran of two Super Bowls, who sponsors the annual Doug Betters Winter Classic charity event.

Arthur Blank, owns Mountain Sky guest ranch near Emigrant; co-founder of Home Depot chain and owner of the Atlanta Falcons football team.

Jeff Bridges, Livingston area; he made two of his early movies in Montana settings—*Thunderbolt and Lightfoot* in 1974 and *Rancho Deluxe* in 1975. Starred in *The Fisher King* and *The Fabulous Baker Boys.*

Tom and Meredith Auld Brokaw, a ranch on the Boulder River south of Big Timber: He, the retired NBC news anchor; grew up in South Dakota. She, the owner of a toy store chain and author of children's books.

James Lee Burke, Missoula; author more than twenty novels, which have earned him Edgar Awards and a Pulitzer nomination. Some of his detective novels have Montana settings.

Tim Cahill, near Livingston: editor-at-large of Outside magazine; the George Plimpton of the outdoor adventure world; books include *A Wolverine Is Eating My Leg* and *Road Fever.*

Liz Claiborne, and husband Art Ortenberg; Lindbergh Lake and a ranch near Canyon Creek; well-known fashion designer.

Pablo Elvira, Bozeman area: baritone for the New York Metropolitan Opera.

Al Feldstein, Paradise Valley; long-time editor of 1950s favorite, *Mad Magazine,* moved to Montana to pursue career as a Western artist.

Peter Fonda, has owned a ranch in Paradise Valley since the 1970s; actor, director, writer producer; star of *Easy Rider, The Young Lovers, The Wild Angels,* and honored with an Academy Award nomination and Golden Globe Award for Best Actor in *Ulee's Gold.*

John Frohnmayer, Bozeman: former chairman of National Endowment for the Arts; author of *Leaving Town Alive: Confessions of an Arts Warrior* and *Out of Time.*

Jack Hanna, home on Flathead Lake; zookeeper at New York City's Columbus Zoo and animal handler with hundreds of television appearances.

Mary Hart and husband movie producer Burt Sugarman, home near Whitefish; she was the host of television's *Entertainment Tonight* since 1982.

William Hjortsberg, near Big Timber: screenwriter and novelist; his novel *Falling Angel* was made into the movie *Angel Heart* (1987).

Phil Jackson, Whitefish; former coach of the Chicago Bulls and the L.A. Lakers championship basketball teams.

Michael Keaton, ranch near McLeod: actor whose film credits include *Clean and Sober, Mr. Mom, Beetlejuice, Batman,* and *White Noise.*

David Letterman, host of *CBS Late Show with David Letterman* owns a large ranch near Choteau.

Huey Lewis, lives in the Bitterroot Valley, singer, composer, and lead vocalist for Huey Lewis and the News, whose hits include, *Want a New Drug, Small World,* and *Back in Time.*

John Lithgow, two-time Tony award-winning actor, and his wife Mary, a UCLA history professor and native of Conrad, have a vacation home near Lakeside on Flathead Lake, In 1996, Lithgow won a 1996 Emmy nomination and Golden Globe for his role in the hit television series, *Third Rock From the Sun.* Lithgow's other credits include major roles in T*erms of Endearment* and *The World According to Garp.* Lithgow often lends his talents to Montana charitable and musical events.

Christopher Lloyd, ranch north of Darby; actor known for his roles in *Back to the Future* and its sequels and on the television comedy *Taxi.*

Margo Kidder, lives in Livingston with husband Walter Kirn, novelist and columnist for Time magazine. Played Lois Lane in *Superman* and most recently in the NBC TV series *Boston Commons.*

George McGovern, former U.S. Senator from South Dakota, 1972 Democratic presidential candidate and United Nations ambassador, lives part of each year in Stevensville.

Tom McGuane, screenwriter (*Rancho Deluxe* and *The Missouri Breaks)* and writer, lives near McLeod. He is a board of several national environmental organizations.

Brent Musburger, ranch north of Big Timber and at Eagle Bend in Bigfork; this native of Billings became a nationally televised sportscaster for ABC.

Bill Pullman, part owner of a ranch with his brother, a Butte physician; former member of the Montana Shakespeare in the Parks touring group who has starred in dozens of films, including *Sleepless in Seattle, Rocket Gibraltar, A League of their Own,* and *Independent Day.*

Dennis Quaid, part-time resident of the Paradise Valley; actor who has starred in over forty major motion pictures, including *The Right Stuff, The Big Easy,* and *The Alamo;* directed and starred in the Livingston area 1997 television movie, *Everything That Rises.*

Dan Quayle, home at The Yellowstone Club; former vice president elected with President George H. Bush.

Robert Craig "Evel" Knievel (1939–)

The daredevil motorcyclist was born in Butte and became a superhero and popular culture icon for his motorcycle jump stunts. He won notice by jumping over rows of cars, then moved up to rows of school buses, shark tanks, and a fountain at Caesar's Palace in Las Vegas. His ultimate jump was his daring but failed attempt to jump Idaho's Snake River Canyon in 1974. Millions of fans and pay-TV viewers watched as his custom-built rocket bike took him out over the canyon only to crash on the rocks below when his parachute failed. He survived the crash and kept jumping (and crashing) until he put the sport aside in the 1980s to try his hand at painting.

The Smithsonian Institute's Museum of American History in Washington, D.C. displays Evel Knievel's motorcycle and memorabilia, acknowledging him as America's Legendary Daredevil. Three movies have been based on the life of Evel Knieval—a Warner Bros. film staring George Hamilton as Evel, a Viacom Productions made-for-TV movie starring Sam Elliot, and most recently, "Evel Knievel," a made-for-TV on Cable's TNT. In the late 1970s and early 1980s, the Ideal Toy Company produced Evel Knievel action-figure toys.

SELF PORTRAIT IN OIL BY EVEL KNIEVEL

Robbie Knievel—Chip off the Block

"Kaptain" Robbie Knievel, another Butte native, has established himself as his father's successor by breaking all the records held by his father except the Guinness Book of World Records for having broken the most bones. In May 1999, he successfully jumped a 200-foot-wide chasm of the Grand Canyon on an ordinary 500cc motorcycle. In 2005, the A&E TV network premier a reality television series called "Knievel's Wild Ride."

Charles Schwab, home between Stevensville and Hamilton; Chairman of the discount brokerage Charles Schwab & Co. and principal partner in the Bitterroot Valley Stock Farm development and golf course.

Steven Seagal, Ennis area ranch; action movie star shot his 1998 movie *The Patriot* near his ranch.

Ted Turner, four large Montana ranch properties; often considered the nation's largest landowner, Turner also owns over 1.5 million acres of ranchland in the West, much of which is dedicated to raising the nation's largest commercial bison herds; he was president and CEO of Turner Broadcasting Systems and CNN and owns Atlanta Braves.

Hank Williams Jr., ranch near Wisdom: country singer/songwriter; Grammy winner; named Entertainer of the Year, 1987 and 1988, by Country Music Association.

Further Reading

Coleman, Julie. *Golden Opportunities: A Biographical History of Montana's Jewish Communities.* Helena: SkyHouse Publishers, 1994.

Emmons, David M. *The Butte Irish: Class and Ethnicity in an American Mining Town, 1875–1925.* Urbana, Ill.: University of Illinois Press, 1989.

Fritz, Harry W. and Mary Murphy, Robert R. Swartout, Jr., eds. *Montana Legacy, Essays on History, People, and Place.* Helena: Montana Historical Society Press, 2002.

Malone, Michael P., Richard B. Roeder, and William L. Lang. *Montana: A History of Two Centuries,* revised edition. Seattle: University of Washington Press, 1991.

Merriam, H.G. *"Ethnic Settlement of Montana,"* Pacific Historical Review, June 12, 1943, pp. 157–68.

Price, Esther Gaskins. *Fighting Spotted Fever in the Rockies.* Helena: Naegele Printing Co., 1948.

Montana Heritage: An Anthology of Historical Essays. Edited by Robert R. Swartout and Harry W. Fritz. Helena: Montana Historical Society Press, 1990.

Montana Office of Public Instruction, *Montana Indians, Their History and Location,* February 2004.

Religion in Montana: Pathways to the Present. Edited by Lawrence F. Small, vols. I and II. Billings: Rocky Mountain College, 1993–1995.

CHAPTER SIX

Government

For the sixty years prior to establishment of the territory of Montana in 1864, the area's adventurers and settlers showed little interest in establishing organized government. During that time, seven different territories of the western United States governed the area that was to become Montana. After Congress made Montana a territory in May 1864, the delegates to the First Legislative Assembly gathered in December of that year in a dirt-roofed cabin in Bannack City. During the next sixty days, the assembly passed seven hundred pages of laws and chose nearby Virginia City as the new capital of Montana Territory.

Main stairway and barrel vault, with Mike and Maureen Mansfield statues, in rotunda of Montana State Capitol.
PHOTOGRAPH BY
TOM FERRIS

Montana remained a territory for twenty-five years. It was not until the federal government passed the Enabling Act of 1889 and the voters of Montana Territory ratified a new constitution that Montana was admitted into the Union as the forty-first state on November 8, 1889, by presidential proclamation.

State and county governments have evolved since then. By the 1960s, the original 1889 Constitution contained much that was outdated. The document has been amended 36 times over the years. In 1969, at the request of the Legislature, a special commission studied the Constitution, comparing it to those of other states. The council determined that 20 percent of the document needed revision; 30 percent needed outright repeal. Rather than revise a document that had been amended dozens of times over the years, Montana voters called a constitutional convention. The one hundred elected delegates who met from January to March 1972 created one of the most progressive state constitutions in the nation.

Throughout more than a century of Montana statehood, significant government reforms have emerged—initiated by voter-approved changes in the Constitution and the Montana code, decisions of the courts, or acts of the State Legislature. For example, a constitutional amendment gave Montana women the right to vote in 1914, five years before all U.S. women won the

THE 1972 CONSTITUTION

Montana's 1972 Constitution, 33 years old in 2005, added several freedoms to the state's Declaration of Rights:

- the right to participate in governmental decision making
- the right to know about and participate in public processes
- the right of individual privacy
- the right to a clean and healthful environment

The constitution provided for county and municipal governments to review their structure every ten years and for the state to hold a referendum every twenty years to vote on whether or not to hold a new constitutional convention.

The people's right to enact legislation through the initiative and referendum processes was expanded. Citizens may also amend the 1972 Montana Constitution by initiative, a right previously only granted to the legislature.

The 1972 Montana Constitution guaranteed ". . . equality of educational opportunity" to each person in the state and commanded the legislature to provide "a basic system of free quality" pubic schools—two provisions that have prompted several successful school funding lawsuits over the years. In respecting the value of Montana's first residents, another part of the constitution's education clause ". . . recognizes the distinct and unique cultural heritage of American Indians and is committed in its educational goals to the preservation of their cultural integrity."

The size of the legislature was to be decided by statute but must be between 40 and 50 senators and between 80 and 100 representatives. The constitution provided for single member districts and a five-member districting and apportionment panel. The position of state treasurer was eliminated. The terms of supreme court justices and district court judges were extended.

Jeannette Rankin (1880–1973)

Rankin, perhaps Montana's most famous woman, was born near Missoula and attended The University of Montana. She got her start in politics campaigning for woman suffrage in Wash-ington and Montana in 1914. In 1916, she became the first woman ever to be elected to the U.S. Congress, where she served until 1919. She was re-elected in 1940 and served until 1943. She saw politics as the principal avenue to needed social change and was active politically both in and out of

MONTANA HISTORICAL SOCIETY

Congress. Rankin not only fought for women's rights to vote and hold office, she also took a stand against economic injustice and in favor of civil rights. She is the only member of the U.S. Congress to oppose United States entry into both world wars. Her lone vote against our entry into World War II was especially controversial. "As a woman, I can't go to war, and I refuse to send anyone else," she declared as she cast it. Confronted by an angry mob in the Capitol building after the vote, she sneaked into a phone booth and called the Capitol police, who escorted her to her office and stood guard there. She was subjected to intense criticism for weeks after the vote, labelled "stupid," "ignorant," and "a disgrace to Montana." She never regretted her decision and, as an activist against the Vietnam War, she led a march on Washington in January 1968. She died in her sleep in Carmel, California.

MONTANA HISTORICAL SOCIETY

Mike Mansfield (1903–2001)

One of Montana's most respected politicians and highly regarded national leaders, Mansfield grew up in Great Falls and was a Butte miner and college history professor before embarking on his long political career. He was elected as a Democrat to serve in the U.S. House of Representatives in 1942 and the U.S. Senate in 1952. He spent sixteen years, from 1961 to 1977, as the longest serving majority leader in the history of the Senate. He also a member of the Senate Foreign Relations Committee. When he retired from the Senate in 1977 at age 73, Mansfield was appointed ambassador to Japan, a post he held until 1988. Among many accomplishments, he coauthored the Twenty-sixth Amendment to the U.S. Constitution, establishing age 18 as the legal voting age. He was also a steadfast opponent to United States. involvement in the war in Vietnam. Mansfield often credited his wife, Maureen, with all he had accomplished. After 68 years of marriage, she preceded him in death in 2000. He died in Washington, D.C., at age 98.

vote with ratification of the Nineteenth Amendment to the U.S. Constitution. Making good on a campaign promise in 1970, Governor Forrest Anderson encouraged the electorate to approve a constitutional amendment to streamline the executive branch of state government. In 1992, by a vote of almost two to one, Montanans passed a constitutional initiative (CI 64) limiting the terms of statewide elected executive officers and state legislators to eight years in any sixteen-year period. Last but far from least, Montana's electorate frequently exercises their right to amend, reject, or create tax policy in Montana—often rejecting the merest idea of a sales tax.

State Government

The State Capitol

The Montana State Capitol was dedicated on July 4, 1902. The land, much to the east of Helena's bustling Last Chance Gulch at the time, had been purchased for a mere $1. The approximate price tag for the imposing Greek neoclassic style structure was $485,000. The 165-foot dome was faced with copper and topped with a bronze stature of Lady Liberty, holding a torch and a shield. The original three-story structure was made of Montana sandstone. Two wings built of Montana granite were added to the Capitol in 1912. It was one of the first state capitols to boost of electrical lights, indoor plumbing, and electrical elevators. Over the years, artists Charles M. Russell, Edgar S. Paxson, Ralph DeCamp and others have provided wall and ceiling murals that glorify the state's history. Both the interior and the building grounds feature statues of note-worthy Montana political leaders.

The people of Montana celebrated the centennial anniversary of the State Capitol on July 4, 2002. In honor of the occasion, the Capitol was both restored to its 1902 splendor and updated to meet the technological needs of the 21st century. The refurbishing spared no detail. The magnificent barrel vault skylight, removed in the 1960's, was reinstalled as the crown jewel of the $26 million renovation. The exterior of the statehouse was cleaned up with sandblasting, cornices were repaired, and wooden-framed windows replaced aluminum frames added in the 1960s. The Senate chambers were retrofitted with "antique" desks that accommodate laptop computers. Throughout the building, chandeliers now mirror the original light fixtures and doorknobs were cast to feature the state seal.

LEGISLATIVE BRANCH

The Montana Legislature is truly a public forum with many opportunities for citizen involvement. All activities of the Legislature, except caucuses that follow the presession election caucuses, are open to the public and press. Legislators are citizens first and lawmakers second. They are paid only for days actually engaged in legislative session activities or for committee work between sessions. Candidates must be eighteen years old, a resident of the state for one year prior to the general election, and a resident of the candidate's county, or of the legislative district, for six months.

Currently, the Senate is composed of fifty members, each elected for a four-year term from one of the fifty Senate districts in Montana. Half of the Senate membership is elected every two years. The House of Representatives is composed of one hundred members, each elected for a two-year term and each representing one of Montana's one hundred House districts. Since Montana has fifty-six counties, a county with a small population may share a Senate district with other counties.

The 1972 Montana Constitution requires that the House of Representatives have no more than one hundred members and no less than eighty members. The Senate may have no more than fifty and no less than forty members. In order to mitigate the effects of party politics on the designation of legislative districts and to respond to population changes, the Constitution also establishes a five-member Districting and Apportionment Commission that can decide the number of districts and the number of citizens to be represented by each legislative district. The majority and minority leaders of the state Senate and House appoint four members. Those four appoint a fifth, who serves as chairperson.

Both state and federal constitutions require that districts be designed for equal representation. Reapportionment occurs following each decennial U.S. census. The apportionment following the 2000 census designed an optimum House district to represent every 9,022 persons and a Senate district to represent twice that amount, or 18,044 persons. The actual reapportionment came to within five percent larger or smaller.

Legislative Sessions

Legislative sessions occur every odd-numbered year, beginning at noon on the first Monday in January, or the first Wednesday when January 1 falls on a Monday. The length of a regular session is ninety legislative days. Sessions are occasionally extended if required to complete the work of the Legislature. In addition, under special circumstances, the Legislature may be called into special session by the governor or by written request from a majority of members to deal with a specific problem. As of January 2005, governors have called twenty-nine special sessions, ranging in length from one day to several weeks.

When both houses convene in January, joint rules of operation are adopted, along with separate rules for each house.

How a Bill Becomes Law

Each piece of legislation must go through a number of steps to become a law. A bill must be introduced by a legislator or a legislative committee. All bills containing an appropriation must be introduced in the House of Representatives. A bill may not be altered or amended in such a way that it changes the original purpose of the bill.

Bills that pass both houses are called acts and are sent to the governor for signature. The governor then signs the bill, vetoes the bill, or amendatory vetoes the bill. If the governor does not sign or veto the bill within five days after it is delivered, the bill will become law.

Implementation and Publication of Laws

New bills approved by both the Legislature and the governor can become laws at different times. Some bills have clauses that make them laws immediately and others contain clauses that implement the laws in later years. Most appropriation bills are implemented at the beginning of the next fiscal year, always the first of July of the year in which the Legislature has met in regular session. Revenue bills (involving a change in fees or taxes) are implemented January 1 after passage. If no effective date is specified, other bills become effective October 1 of the legislative year.

The complete texts of every bill and resolution that has been passed are published yearly by the Legislative Services Division in The Laws of

AGE AND SERVICE

Senator Bob Brown of Whitefish became the Dean (the longest serving member, at the time) of the Montana Senate in 1991, after having served that body for only sixteen years. At forty-two, Brown was the youngest state senate dean in the United States. He was not the longest serving member ever, though. That honor belongs to Senator Dave Manning of Hysham, who was elected with President Franklin D. Roosevelt in 1932 and served without interruption for fifty-three years. Manning was the senior state legislator in the United States when he left office in 1985.

David Williams, father of Montana's First Lady of Film, Myrna Loy (Myrna Williams) was the youngest person ever elected to the Montana legislature, in 1913. When Paul Richards was elected to the Montana House of Representatives from Helena in 1974, at age 20, he was the youngest person in the United States to be elected to a state legislature.

Alison Conn of Kalispell was elected state representative in 1980, shortly after her nineteenth birthday. She was the youngest woman ever elected to a state legislature. Conn replaced Representative Jack Uhde, who had been elected from the same district four years earlier at the age of eighteen.

Montana. The set is popularly called the "Session Laws." Each bill is assigned a chapter number, with Chapter One being the first bill passed and signed.

The Montana Code Annotated is the systematic arrangement of all permanent state statutes (laws) currently in force in Montana. A fully searchable version of Montana laws and constitution is available at http://leg .state.mt.us/css/mtcode_const/laws.asp The Montana Code Annotated is also available on CD-ROM version.

The Role of Lobbying

Lobbying is a legitimate and valuable function within the legislative process. A lobbyist or spokesperson for an interest or issue can provide information that legislators rarely have time to research on their own. In Montana, any citizen 18 years or older has the right to lobby professionally. An application for a license to lobby can be obtained from the Commissioner of Political Practices. A license is issued upon acceptance of the application and the payment of a fee of one hundred fifty dollars. Lobbyists regularly outnumber the number of legislators during a legislative session. By the end of the 2003 session, 918 lobbyists, or more than six per legislator, had registered with the state's commissioner of political practices.

Any citizen, regardless of age, may testify before the Legislature, write to, or phone a Montana legislator.

EXECUTIVE BRANCH

The executive branch of the state of Montana includes a governor, lieutenant governor, secretary of state, attorney general, auditor, superintendent of public instruction, and five public service commissioners, all of whom are elected to four-year terms by voters at a general election. The term of office for these state leaders begins on the first Monday in January after the November general election in even-numbered years. Each elected official must keep public records of his or her office and perform other duties that are mandated in the 1972 Montana Constitution or in state law. The qualifications for candidates are as follows:

A candidate for the office of governor, lieutenant governor, secretary of state, attorney general, auditor, and superintendent of public instruction must be twenty-five years of age or older at the time of their election. In addition, they must be a citizen of the United States who has resided in the state two years preceding their election.

Legislation passed in 1995 bases the salaries of Montana's judges and executive branch elected officials on the average salary of positions with similar titles in the Idaho, North Dakota, South Dakota, and Wyoming, and of the current salaries of these Montana officials. The Department of Administration is required to conduct a survey of the four contiguous states on these salaries prior to June 30 of even numbered years. The results of the survey become effective July 1 of odd numbered years.

The Governor

The governor is the chief executive officer of Montana, who must see that the laws of the state are faithfully executed. The governor is commander in chief of the militia forces of the state, except when they are in the actual service of the United States. The militia may be called out to protect life and property in natural disasters or to suppress insurrection or repel invasion, should these unlikely events occur. The governor is the official communicator between the government of the state of Montana and the government of any other state or the United States. As the ceremonial head of state, the governor receives official visitors, dedicates public buildings, and has use of the

Access to the Legislature

For people who are in Helena during the regular legislative session (January through April) or a special session, daily agendas of the House and Senate as well as committee hearing schedules and bills are available for a small charge at the Bill Distribution Room (Room 74) in the capitol building. You can also call or visit the Legislative Information Office, located in the first floor lobby in the Capitol, telephone 444-4800, or check on the Internet at http://leg.state.mt.us

- Write your legislator at: Representative
  Montana House of Representatives
  PO Box 200400
  Helena, MT 59620-0400

  Senator
  Montana Senate
  PO Box 200500
  Helena, MT 59620-0500

- The Legislative Information Office, 444-4800, takes phone messages for legislators and provides information on the hearing schedules (between 8 A.M. and 5:00 P.M. Monday through Friday; adjournment on Saturday).

- People can send a fax message to the House of Representatives at 444-4825 and the Senate at 444-4875.

- A telephone device for the deaf (TDD) can be reached by dialing (800) 832-0283.

By computer

The Montana Legislative Branch maintains an information system named LAWS (Legislative Automated Workflow System), which includes an Internet web browser application for accessing legislative session information. Internet users are able to access online bill status information, committee hearing information, agendas, etc., as well as the text of introduced bills, amended bills, enrolled bills, and edited bill drafts. Information for the most current session is at http://leg.state.mt.us/session.htm. Other sessions can be accessed using the links at the left of the resulting page.

Both live and archived legislative proceeding broadcasts are available to the public by the above Internet access. You must have Real Player to listen. During legislative sessions, the House and Senate floor debates are covered in their entirety. Committee Hearings are broadcast on an ad hoc basis.

official governor's mansion as a family residence. The governor appoints, subject to confirmation by the state Senate, all officers provided for in the Constitution or by law whose appointment or election is not otherwise provided for. These appointees hold office until the governor's term ends, or until they are removed from office by the governor. The governor may grant a reprieve or pardon to a person sentenced for a crime. The governor can influence important state policies by serving as a member of the Board of Land Commissioners, the Board of Examiners, and as a nonvoting, ex-officio member of the state Board of Education, the Board of Regents, and the Board of Public Education.

Most bills passed by the Legislature are submitted to the governor for signature. If the governor does not sign or veto the bill within five days after it is delivered, the bill will become law. The governor must return vetoed bills to the Legislature with a statement of reasons for the veto. A vote of two-thirds of the Legislature is required to override a governor's veto. If the Legislature is not in session when the governor vetoes a bill approved by two-thirds of the Legislature, the secretary of state must poll the members of the Legislature by mail and must send each member a copy of the governor's veto message. Legislators must cast a vote and return it within thirty days. The secretary of state tallies the votes. If two-thirds of the legislators vote to override the veto, the bill becomes law.

In 2005, the governor's annual salary was $96,462.

The governor's address and phone number:
Room 204, State Capitol
Helena, MT 59620
444-3111 / (800) 332-2272 (Citizens Advocate Phone)
444-3468 Voice or TDD (Citizens Advocate Phone)
http://governor.mt.gov

Lieutenant Governor

Under the 1972 Montana Constitution, the governor and the lieutenant governor are required to run for office as a team. The previous constitution allowed candidates for the two offices to campaign separately and to be voted on separately. This sometimes resulted in a governor and lieutenant governor at political odds with each other.

The lieutenant governor performs duties assigned by the governor and any duties provided by law. He or she succeeds the governor in the case of a vacancy resulting from the death, resignation, or incapacity of the governor

Montana Territorial Governors

Name	Years in Office	Party Affiliation
Sidney Edgerton	1864-1866	Republican
Thomas Meagher	Acting governor 1865-1866 while Governor Edgerton was in Washington on territorial business.	Union Democrat
Green Clay Smith	1866-1869	Republican
James Monroe Ashley	1869-1870	Republican
Benjamin F. Potts	1870-1883	Republican
John Schuyler Crosby	1883-1884	Democrat
B. Platt Carpenter	1884-1885	Republican
Samuel Thomas Hauser	1885-1887	Democrat
Preston Hopkins Leslie	1887-1889	Democrat
Benjamin F. White	1889-statehood	Republican

State Governors

Name	Years in Office	Party Affiliation
Joseph K. Toole	1889-1893	Democrat
John E. Rickards	1893-1897	Republican
Robert Burns Smith	1897-1901	Democrat-Populist
Joseph K. Toole	1901-1908	Democrat
Edwin L. Norris	1908-1913	Democrat
Sam V. Stewart	1913-1921	Democrat
Joseph Moore Dixon	1921-1925	Republican
John E. Erickson	1925-1933	Democrat
Frank H. Cooney	1933-1935	Democrat
William Elmer Holt	1935-1937	Democrat
Roy Elmer Ayers	1937-1941	Democrat
Samuel C. Ford	1941-1949	Republican
John H. Bonner	1949-1953	Democrat
J. Hugo Aronson	1953-1961	Republican
Donald G. Nutter	1961-1962	Republican
Tim M. Babcock	1962-1969	Republican
Forrest H. Anderson	1969-1973	Democrat
Thomas Lee Judge	1973-1981	Democrat
Ted Schwinden	1981-1989	Democrat
Stan Stephens	1989-1993	Republican
Marc Racicot	1993-2001	Republican
Judy Martz	2001-2005	Republican
Brian Schweitzer	2005-Present	Democrat

to hold the office. The lieutenant governor serves as acting governor when requested to do so in writing by the governor or if the governor has been absent from the state for more than forty-five consecutive days. The lieutenant governor may provide for the administration of an office and hire personnel for the office.

The annual salary for the lieutenant governor in 2005 was $66,724.

The lieutenant governor's address and phone number:
Room 207, State Capitol
Helena, MT 59620
444-3111

Secretary of State

The secretary of state is the chief election officer of the state of Montana and has responsibility for the interpretation, application, and operation of election laws, except those pertaining to campaign finance. The secretary of state is the official record keeper for the state and is responsible for filing, maintaining, storing, and distributing corporate documents, agricultural lien information, official records of the executive branch, and acts of the Legislature. This office publishes the Administrative Rules of Montana, which are developed by state agencies at the statutory direction of the Legislature. The secretary of state administers the state agency records management function, including operation of a central microfilm unit and the state records center. The secretary of state is the official keeper of the Great Seal of the State of Montana. This officeholder serves as a member of the Board of Examiners and the Board of Land Commissioners.

The annual salary for the secretary of state in 2005 was $76,539.

The secretary of state's address and phone number:
Room 260, State Capitol
Helena, MT 59620
444-2034 / 444-9068 (TDD)
(888) 884-8683 (voting information only)

Attorney General

The attorney general is the chief legal officer for the state and as such has the following responsibilities and duties: providing legal services and counsel to state and county agencies and officials; ensuring law enforcement and public safety; prosecuting on behalf of and defending the state, counties, or their officials in cases to which they are a party; assisting local law enforcement agencies and supervising county attorneys; issuing legal opinions when requested by state, county, or local officials; and regulating all gaming activities. The attorney general serves as a member of the Board of Examiners and the State Board of Land Commissioners and performs other duties as required by law.

The annual salary for the state attorney general in 2005 was $85,762.

The attorney general's address and phone number:
Department of Justice
215 North Sanders
Helena, MT 59620
444-2026
http://www.doj.state.mt.us

State Auditor

The state auditor serves as the commissioner of insurance and the commissioner of securities and is a member of the Board of Hail Insurance and Board of Land Commissioners. The auditor has the responsibility to oversee the fiscal duties of the state and to keep an account of all state warrants. The state auditor licenses and regulates insurance companies and agents within the state, adopts insurance rules, administers the Small Employer Health Insurance Availability Act, and regulates and registers securities.

The annual salary for the state auditor in 2005 was $76,579.

The state auditor's address and phone number:
840 Helena Avenue
Helena, MT 59601
444-2040
444-3246 (TDD)
(800) 332-6148
www.state.mt.us/sao/

The Montana Public Service Commission

The Montana Public Service Commission (PSC) has the duty to regulate the state's public utilities, including private, investor-owned natural gas, electric, intrastate telephone, and water companies, and railroads and certain motor carriers hauling regulated commodities. The PSC does not regulate rural electric and telephone cooperatives, cable television companies, propane dealers, or municipal water and sewer services. Each of the five public service commissioners are elected by a regional district to four-year terms.

The annual salary in 2005 for a PSC member was $77,418. The chairperson was paid $78,269.

The commission's address and phone number:
Public Service Commission
1701 Prospect Avenue
P.O. Box 202601
Helena, MT 59620-2601
444-6199 (also TDD)
(800) 646-6150 (utility consumer complaints)
(888) 215-4056 (gas and electric competition questions)
444-6190 (consumer questions regarding transportation)

Superintendent of Public Instruction

The superintendent of public instruction supervises the public schools and districts of the state, as provided by law.

The annual salary for the superintendent in 2005 was $89,472.

The superintendent's address and phone number:
1227 11th Avenue, 2nd floor
P.O. Box 202501
Helena, MT 59620-2501
444-3095 (general information)
444-0169 (TDD)
www.opi.state.mt.us

JUDICIAL BRANCH

Montana has a three-tiered court structure.

I. The Montana Supreme Court

The supreme court has general supervisory control over all other courts in the state. The primary function is to hear and decide appeals on questions of the laws that come to it from the district courts. Since it is not a trial court, arguments before it are presented orally by attorneys or through written briefs.

The seven members of the supreme court—the chief justice and six justices—are elected to eight-year staggered terms in a statewide nonpartisan election. The supreme court may also establish rules governing appeals procedures, the practice and procedure for all other courts, admission to the bar, and the conduct of bar members.

The supreme court must hold four terms each year in Helena, commencing on the first Tuesdays of March, June, October, and December. About six hundred cases per year are filed with the Montana Supreme Court. The court disposes of about 800 cases per year.

The Legislature sets the annual salaries of the supreme court justices: in 2005, $102,466 for the chief justice and $100,884 for the associate justices.

Supreme Court
Room 414, Justice Building
215 North Sanders
P.O. Box 203001
Helena, MT 59620-3001
444–5490

Office of the Court Administrator
Room 315, Justice Building
215 North Sanders
Helena, MT 59620-3002
444–2621

II. District Courts

Montana has twenty-two judicial districts with forty-two district court judges. These judges are elected by a districtwide nonpartisan election. District courts are Montana's trial courts, with jurisdiction, or authority, in civil cases and criminal cases amounting to a felony.

Judicial Districts

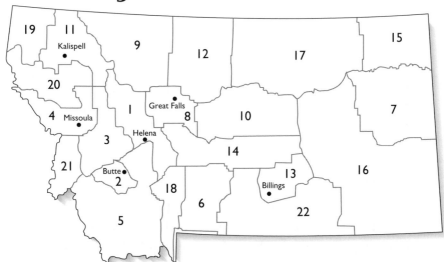

District courts also handle all civil actions against the state for monetary damage, certain misdemeanor cases with penalties more than $500 and more than six months in jail, divorces, annulments, and probate cases. The courts share their authority with city, municipal, and justice of the peace courts in certain misdemeanor cases and civil cases.

The Montana district court system handles over thirty thousand cases a year.

Youth Courts

Each judicial district must operate a youth court and must appoint one of its member district court judges as the judge of the youth court. Youths who are alleged to be delinquent, in need of intervention, or are charged with law violations appear before this court.

III. Courts of Limited Jurisdiction

Justice of the Peace Courts

A Montana justice of the peace wears many hats. This judge usually handles misdemeanor cases, decides small claims cases, issues warrants in most criminal cases, shares jurisdiction in many cases with district courts, and may also act as city judge.

Justice of the peace courts generally have jurisdiction of misdemeanor criminal cases. With certain exceptions, they share jurisdiction with the district courts in civil actions involving claims of $7,000 or less, including all traffic cases.

The small claims cases include civil claims up to $3,000. Nearly any civil case that can be heard in a justice of the peace court may also be filed with the district court.

Justices of the peace are elected in a nonpartisan countywide election during the state general election. Justices serve a four-year term. A candidate for the office must be a U.S. citizen and must have been a resident of the county for at least one year prior to the election. A justice of the peace does not have to be an attorney.

City and Municipal Courts

Each city and incorporated town is required to provide a city court. A justice of the peace or a city judge from another city or town may act as the city judge. These courts have the same jurisdiction as justice of the peace courts but are also given exclusive jurisdiction over city ordinances. Cities with populations of four thousand or more may establish a municipal court instead of a city court. Missoula is the only city that has established a municipal court. These courts have the same jurisdiction as city courts, but a municipal judge must have the same qualifications as a district judge.

City and County Governments

In 1920, there were 110 incorporated towns in Montana. Today, there are 129 incorporated cities and towns, with a variety of governmental management structures.

Town development followed the arrival of white settlers in the late 1800s and early 1900s. The location of towns was based on economic considerations like the existence of mining operations or the proximity of a railway. Most Montana towns remain small. In 2003, only seven had a population over ten thousand, forty-nine had from one thousand to ten thousand people, and seventy-three had a population under one thousand. Of this smallest category, nineteen had fewer than two hundred people.

There is great diversity in the workings and obligations of Montana's municipalities. The larger towns are concerned with issues like zoning, public transportation, and subdivision regulation. Towns of all sizes are engaged in law enforcement, public safety, schools, and certain judicial duties. Municipalities are allowed a charter or noncharter form of government, with various types of management structures. Of the 116 noncharter governments, 100 have a ruling city commission-executive form of government, 4 have a manager form, and 2 are managed by a chairman of the city commission. Six chartered town governments have a manager form of government, and fourteen are governed by a city commission with a chief executive. One chartered town, Pinesdale, operates by town meeting.

Tribal Governments

There are eleven federally recognized tribes in Montana living on seven reservations. The Little Shell tribe of Chippewa-Cree, the "landless" Indian tribe, has been granted recognition from the federal government. Reservations are areas of land "reserved" by or for an Indian band, village, or tribe to live on or use. The jurisdictions are created by treaty, congressional legislation, or by executive order.

The Indian nations of Montana are governed by tribal governments that may engage in a number of activities, including:

- regulating domestic relations of members
- levying taxes
- controlling conduct by ordinance
- administering justice
- conducting elections
- developing health and education programs
- managing tribal economic enterprises and natural resources
- maintaining intergovernmental relations with federal, state, and local authorities.

Citizenship

Each tribal government is legally empowered to determine who is a member of the tribe. All Indians born in the U.S., or born of U.S. citizens who are outside the country at the time of birth, are American citizens, with all the attendant rights and responsibilities. Indians who live in Montana are also citizens of this state. They are also citizens of their quasi-sovereign tribal nation and are recognized as members of an ethnic minority.

Taxes

Indians are subject to most of the same federal tax laws that apply to non-Indians, except for exemptions of federal compensation for takings of property, income from trust allocations, and income from gifts or land exchanges.

Montana cannot tax income earned by a tribal member on his or her own reservation. Indians are also exempt from personal property taxes, such as on an automobile. The state can require, as it sometimes does, that the tribe collect a certain state tax. For example, the state tax on cigarettes is collected on the reservation and passed on to the state. Non-Indians on reservations and

Indians not residing on their own reservation are not exempt from state taxes. The tribes can impose their own taxes on Indians and non-Indians alike.

Hunting and Fishing

A tribe has the power to license hunting and fishing by non-Indians on the reservations. Indians may hunt and fish in Indian country without having to obtain a state permit.

Criminal and Civil Law

Tribes do not have criminal jurisdiction over non-Indians committing a crime in Indian country. Jurisdiction over crimes on all but the Flathead Reservation resides with the federal government; on the Flathead Reservation, that jurisdiction resides with the state. In September 1994, the tribes and jurisdictions on the Flathead Reservation formally agreed that the tribes would have exclusive jurisdiction over misdemeanor crimes committed by Indians and provided for continued concurrent state-tribal jurisdiction over felony crimes committed by Indians. The other reservations do not share jurisdiction with the state.

Tribes have civil authority over the activities of non-Indians on reservations, thus requiring a non-Indian to first exhaust tribal court remedies.

Federal Government Activities in Montana

In 2003, Montana ranked forty-first in the nation for federal taxes paid to Washington, D.C. Federal funds distributed to the state of Montana in 2003 totaled $6.595 billion, which translates to $7,201 for each Montanan. On a per capita basis, only six states and the District of Columbia get more money back from the federal government than did Montana in 2003. Montana received $1.60 per dollar of taxes paid in 2003.

Malmstrom Air Force Base

Montana's relative proximity to Russia became important to national security in the 1950s, when tensions between the United States and Russia developed in "the cold war." As part of the 1947 creation of the United States Air Force, the WWII Army Air Base at Great Falls was modernized to complement the nation's strategic defense system. Another major air base was constructed at Glasgow. By 1954, the Strategic Air Command and its F-84F and F-84G fighters arrived, along with other units, and in June 1956, the Malmstrom Air Force Base was officially dedicated in honor of Col. Einar Axel Malmstrom, the vice-wing commander who died in a plane crash on August 21, 1954.

In July 1961, Malmstrom's mission changed again with the activation of the 341st Strategic Missile wing. Some three hundred of the nation's first Minuteman Intercontinental Ballistic Missiles were placed in underground "silos," spread across 23,000 square miles of nine counties in central Montana. This defense system was dubbed the nation's "Ace in the Hole" during the Cuban missile crisis. On October 26, 1962, the first flights of missiles were placed on alert until the crisis was over. In the 1980s, many Montanans protested the placement of more nuclear warheads in the state. Today, the renamed 341st Space Wing maintains a total strength of two hundred Minuteman III missiles, making it the largest missile complex in the free world. The Glasgow base closed in 1968

Today, Malmstrom Air Force Base contributes at least $250 million annually to the Montana economy in payroll and direct spending in the state. The base has around 8,000 military personnel and dependents, plus another 1,500 civilians who work at or have contracts with the base.

Montana's Congressional Representatives

Senator Max Baucus

(Current term expires Jan. 2, 2009)
511 Hart Senate Office Building
Washington, D.C. 20510-2602
(202) 224-2651 / fax: (202) 224-4700
TDD: (202) 224-1998
e-mail: max@baucus.senate.gov
web site: http://baucus.senate.gov

in Montana:
Empire Block
30 West 14th Street
Helena, MT 59601
449-5480 / fax: 449-5484

1821 South Avenue West, Suite 203
Missoula, MT 59801
329-3123
fax: 728-7610

Silver Bow Center
125 West Granite
Butte, MT 59701
782-8700
fax: 782-6553

113 Third Street North
Great Falls, MT 59401
761-1574
fax: 727-3726

222 North 32nd Street, Suite 100
Billings, MT 59101
(800) 332-6106
657-6790
fax: 657-6793

Federal Building, Room 114
32 East Babcock
P.O. Box 1689
Bozeman, MT 59771
586-6104
fax: 587-9177

75 Claremont, Suite 1
Kalispell, MT 59901
756-1150
fax: 756-1152

Senator Conrad Burns

(Current term expires Jan. 2, 2007)
187 Dirksen Senate Office Building
Washington, D.C. 20510-2603
(202) 224-2644
e-mail: conrad_burns@burns.senate.gov
web site: http://burns.senate.gov

208 North Montana Avenue
Suite 202A
Helena, MT 59601
449-5401
fax: 449-5462

324 West Towne
Glendive, MT 59330
365-2391
fax: 365-8836

1845 Highway 93 South, Suite 210
Kalispell, MT 59901
257-3360
fax: 257-3974

in Montana:
222 North 32nd Street, Suite 400
Billings, MT 59101
252-0550
fax: 252-7768

211 Haggerty Lane
Bozeman, MT 59715
586-4450
fax: 586-7647
116 West Front Street
Missoula, MT 59802
728-3003
fax: 728-2193

321 First Avenue North
Great Falls, MT 59401
452-9585
fax: 452-9586

125 West Granite, Suite 200
Butte, MT 59701
723-3277
fax: 782-4717

Representative Denny Rehberg
(Current term expires January 2, 2007)

Washington, DC Office
516 Cannon House Office
Building
Washington, DC, 20515
202-225-3211
fax: 202-225-5687

in Montana:
950 North Montana Ave.
Helena, MT 59601
(406) 443-7878
fax: (406) 443-8890

105 Smelter Ave. NE, Suite 16
Great Falls, MT 59404
(406) 454-1066
fax: (406) 454-1130

218 East Main, Suite B
Missoula, MT 59802
(406) 543-9550
fax (406) 543-0663

1201 Grand Avenue, Suite 1
Billings, MT 59102
(406) 256-1019
fax: (406) 256-4934

Elections

The first election in Montana was held on October 24, 1864. Approximately 6,500 people voted in this election for the territory's first legislators and a territorial delegate to Congress. In November 2004, with an estimated population of 917,621, Montana counted 638,474 registered voters. Seventy-one percent of those electors turned out to vote in the general election. Based on the census count of all U.S. citizens eligible to vote, Montana has consistently ranked as one of the tops in the nation for voter turnout—the second highest in 1996 and the sixth highest in 2004.

Montana is an open primary state and voters do not need to declare a political party to select party nominations in a primary election. Instead, they choose one party's ballot in the privacy of the voting booth.

The voting public can approve increases in their property taxes through county, city, and school district mill levies. Electors vote on propositions to seek bonding for public buildings under each of those jurisdictions. In addition, all the voters in the state are often asked to approve statewide initiatives and referendums on various constitutional amendments and changes in state statutes concerning taxation and other issues.

Congressional Representatives

Term	Senate	House of Representatives
1889-91	Thomas C. Power, Helena R Wilbur F. Sanders, Helena R	Thomas H. Carter, Helena–R
1891-93	Thomas C. Power Wilbur F. Sanders	William W. Dixon, Butte–D
1893-95	Thomas C. Power Lee Mantle, Butte R	Charles S. Hartman, Bozeman–R
1895-97	Lee Mantle Thomas H. Carter	Charles S. Hartman
1897-99	Lee Mantle Thomas H. Carter	Charles S. Hartman
1899-1901	Thomas H. Carter William A. Clark, Butte D	Albert J. Campbell, Butte–D
1901-03	William A. Clark Paris Gibson, Great Falls D	Caldwell Edwards, Bozeman–D-Pop.
1903-05	William A. Clark Paris Gibson	Joseph M. Dixon, Missoula–R
1905-07	William A. Clark Thomas H. Carter	Joseph M. Dixon
1907-09	Joseph M. Dixon Thomas H. Carter	Charles N. Pray, Fort Benton–R
1909-11	Joseph M. Dixon Thomas H. Carter	Charles N. Pray
1911-13	Joseph M. Dixon Henry L. Myers, Hamilton D	Charles N. Pray
1913-15	Thomas J. Walsh, Helena D Henry L. Myers	John M. Evans, Missoula–D Tom Stout, Lewistown–D
1915-17	Thomas J. Walsh Henry L. Myers	John M. Evans Tom Stout
1917-19	Thomas J. Walsh Henry L. Myers	John M. Evans Jeannette Rankin, Missoula–R
1919-21	Thomas J. Walsh Henry L. Myers	John M. Evans Carl M. Riddick, Lewistown–R
1921-23	Thomas J. Walsh Henry L. Myers	John M. Evans Scott Leavitt, Great Falls–R
1923-25	Thomas J. Walsh, Burton K. Wheeler, Butte D	John M. Evans Scott Leavitt
1925-27	Thomas J. Walsh Burton K. Wheeler	John M. Evans Scott Leavitt
1927-29	Thomas J. Walsh Burton K. Wheeler	John M. Evans Scott Leavitt
1929-31	Thomas J. Walsh Burton K. Wheeler	John M. Evans, Scott Leavitt
1931-33	Thomas J. Walsh Burton K. Wheeler	John M. Evans Scott Leavitt
1933-35	John E. Erickson, Kalispell D *James E. Murray, Butte D Burton K. Wheeler	Joseph P. Monaghan, Butte–D Roy E. Ayers, Lewistown–D
1935-37	James E. Murray Burton K. Wheeler	Joseph P. Monaghan Roy E. Ayers

Congressional Representatives (cont.)

Term	Senate	House of Representatives
1937-39	James E. Murray Burton K. Wheeler	Jerry J. O'Connell, Butte–D J.F. O'Connor, Livingston–D
1939-41	James E. Murray Burton K. Wheeler	Jacob Thorkelson, Butte–R J.F. O'Connor
1941-43	James E. Murray Burton K. Wheeler	Jeannette Rankin J.F. O'Connor
1943-45	James E. Murray Burton K. Wheeler	Mike J. Mansfield, Missoula–D J.F. O'Connor
1945-47	James E. Murray Burton K. Wheeler	Mike J. Mansfield J.F. O'Connor Wesley A. D'Ewart, Wilsall–R
1947-49	James E. Murray Zales N. Ecton, Manhattan R	Mike J. Mansfield Wesley A. D'Ewart
1949-51	James E. Murray Zales N. Ecton	Mike J. Mansfield Wesley A. D'Ewart
1951-53	James E. Murray Zales N. Ecton	Mike J. Mansfield Wesley A. D'Ewart
1953-55	James E. Murray Mike J. Mansfield	Lee Metcalf, Helena–D Wesley A. D'Ewart
1955-57	James E. Murray Mike J. Mansfield	Lee Metcalf Orin B. Fjare, Big Timber–R
1957-59	James E. Murray Mike J. Mansfield	Lee Metcalf Leroy H. Anderson, Conrad–D
1959-61	James E. Murray Mike J. Mansfield	Lee Metcalf Leroy H. Anderson
1961-63	Mike J. Mansfield Lee Metcalf	Arnold Olsen, Helena–D James Battin, Billings–R
1963-65	Mike J. Mansfield Lee Metcalf	Arnold Olsen James Battin
1965-67	Mike J. Mansfield Lee Metcalf	Arnold Olsen James Battin
1967-69	Mike J. Mansfield Lee Metcalf	Arnold Olsen James Battin
1969-71	Mike J. Mansfield Lee Metcalf	Arnold Olsen James Battin John Melcher, Forsyth–D
1971-73	Mike J. Mansfield Lee Metcalf	John Melcher Richard Shoup, Missoula–R
1973-75	Mike J. Mansfield Lee Metcalf	John Melcher Richard Shoup
1975-77	Mike J. Mansfield Lee Metcalf	John Melcher Max S. Baucus, Helena–D
1979-81	John Melcher Lee Metcalf	Max S. Baucus Ron Marlene, Billings–R
1981-83	John Melcher Max S. Baucus	Pat Williams, Butte–D Ron Marlene
1983-85	John Melcher Max S. Baucus	Pat Williams Ron Marlene

*When Walsh died in March 1933, Erickson was appointed to succeed him and was defeated by Murray in a November 1934 election to fill out the term.

Congressional Representatives (cont.)

Term	Senate	House of Representatives
1985-87	John Melcher Max S. Baucus	Pat Williams Ron Marlene
1987-89	John Melcher Max S. Baucus	Pat Williams Ron Marlene
1989-91	Max S. Baucus Conrad Burns, Billings R	Pat Williams Ron Marlene
1991-93	Max S. Baucus Conrad Burns	Pat Williams Ron Marlene
1993-95	Max S. Baucus Conrad Burns	Pat Williams
1995-97	Max S. Baucus Conrad Burns	Pat Williams
1997-99	Max S. Baucus Conrad Burns	Rick Hill, Billings–R
1999-2001	Max S. Baucus Conrad Burns	Denny Rehberg Billings–R
2001-2003	Max S. Baucus Conrad Burns	Denny Rehberg
2003-2005	Max S. Baucus Conrad Burns	Denny Rehberg

Montana Election Calendar

May — first Tuesday after the first Monday; Official school election day; At this election, school trustees are chosen and any school mill levies or bonding propositions are offered for approval. School districts may also hold school district mill levy and bonding elections at any time before August 1 of the school fiscal year beginning on July 1.

June — first Tuesday after the first Monday; Primary nominating election (preceding any general election). Statewide ballot measures can be voted on at this time.

August — last Tuesday, odd-numbered years; Primary nominating election for certain municipal offices.

November — first Tuesday after the first Monday, even-numbered years; General election to select county, state, judicial, and federal offices and to vote on statewide issues offered to the voters. first Tuesday after the first Monday, odd-numbered years; General election to elect certain municipal officers.

The general election for any other political subdivision, such as a fire or irrigation district, is the school election day.

Dolly Smith Cusker Akers (1901–1986)

Akers grew up in Wolf Point and became the first Assini-boine woman to lead the Fort Peck tribal governing board. In 1932, she was the first Indian to be elected to the Montana State Legislature, where she served in the House of Representatives in the 1933 session and in a special session the following year. In 1964, she was elected area vice president of the National Congress of American Indians. From 1969-1979, she served as secretary of the state Inter-Tribal Policy Board.

MONTANA HISTORICAL SOCIETY

MONTANA HISTORICAL SOCIETY

Thomas J. Walsh (1859–1933)

Walsh served as Democratic U.S. senator from 1913 to 1933 and was one of Montana's most distinguished and progressive politicians. He espoused various liberal causes and exposed the Teapot Dome oil scandal in 1923. He was picked by President Franklin D. Roosevelt to become U.S. attorney general but died en route to Washington, D.C. on March 2, 1933, just five days after marrying a Cuban socialite, Señora Nieves Perez Chaumont de Truffin.

Burton Kendall Wheeler (1882–1975)

Wheeler was Montana's controversial, progressive, Democratic U.S. senator from 1923 to 1947. He was nominated as vice president on the Progressive/ Socialist ticket of Robert M. LaFollette in 1924 and nominated on the Socialist ticket in 1928. In his early career as U.S. district attorney for Montana, he was embroiled in controversies surrounding the treatment of liberal opposition to the wartime hysteria of superpatriots in Montana. He served twelve terms.

MONTANA HISTORICAL SOCIETY

QUALIFICATIONS FOR VOTING AND REGISTRATION

Any United States citizen who will be at least eighteen years of age by the time of the next election and who has been a resident of Montana and of the county in which the person wishes to register for thirty days is entitled to register and to vote in Montana. A person may not vote if serving a sentence for a felony in a penal institution, or if the person is of unsound mind, as determined by a court. The elector is assigned a precinct polling location that is nearest to the elector's registration residence.

A qualified individual may register with the county clerk and recorder or the designated election office of a county. A person may also request an official registration form from the county election office, to be returned by mail to the county of the person's residence. Voter registration forms are also available upon application for a driver's license or a hunting license. Perhaps the easiest ways to register are by filling out a registration form found in many Montana phone books or on the website http://sos.state.mt.us and mailing it to the local election office.

Registration is generally permanent unless an elector does not vote in a federal general election (held every November of even numbered years) and does not respond to confirmation mailings. If an elector does not vote in a federal general election and does not respond to mailings, the elector's name will be placed on an inactive voter list. If an elector fails to vote in two federal general elections after the mailings are sent, the elector's name will be removed from the voter rolls. An elector needs to reregister if there is a change of name or a change of address.

In order to vote on election day, a voter must bring to the designated polling place a current photo ID that shows your name (for example, a valid driver's license, school ID, state ID, or tribal ID) or a current utility bill, bank statement, paycheck, voter confirmation notice, government check or other government document that shows your name and current address.

Any registered voter may vote by absentee ballot, even if he or she is able to vote in person on election day.

Absentee ballots may be requested from seventy-five days prior to the primary or general election through noon on the day before election. They must be returned to the local election office by 8 P.M. on election day. Beginning thirty days prior to the election, absentee voters may vote in person at the county courthouse.

For more information about voting, call the local election office or call the Secretary of State's toll-free voter hotline: 1-888-884-VOTE (8683).

Montana Presidential Votes, 1948-2004

Year	State Winner	Democratic % of State Vote	Republican % of State Vote
1948	Truman (D)	53.1	43.2
1952	Eisenhower (R)	40.1	59.4
1956	Eisenhower (R)	42.9	57.1
1960	Nixon (R)	48.6	51.1
1964	Johnson (D)	59.0	40.6
1968	Nixon (R)	41.6	50.6
1972	Nixon (R)	37.9	57.9
1976	Ford (R)	45.4	52.8
1980	Reagan (R)	32.4	56.8
1984	Reagan (R)	38.2	60.5
1988	Bush (R)	47.0	53.0
1992	*Clinton (D)	37.7	35.2
1996	Dole (R)	40.2	43.1
2000	Bush (R)	33.4	58.4
2004	Bush (R)	38.1	58.3

*In the 1992 election, independent candidate Ross Perot garnered 26.2 percent of the state's presidential vote.
Sources: Office of the Montana Secretary of State.

Political Parties in Montana

Elections for county, state, and federal elected offices are partisan elections. District court judges and supreme court judges are elected on a nonpartisan ballot. Cities with an alderman form of government elect their officers on a partisan ballot, while those having commission or commission-manager forms of government hold nonpartisan elections for officials. School trustees and governing bodies of all special districts are also elected on a nonpartisan basis. All candidates are elected by majority vote.

While Montana has shown a preference for Republicans in presidential elections and Democrats in Congressional elections, the two parties are extremely competitive in the internal politics of the state. Since 1949, Republicans have won seven contests for governor, and the Democrats six. From 2004 Montanans have given the Democrats the majority in the state Senate twelve times, the Republicans nine times, and twice elected a Senate equally divided. The Montana House in the same period has had thirteen Republican majorities, nine Democratic majorities, and has been tied once, for the 2005 Legislature.

The result of this narrow partisan balance is that neither party has known any extended period of dominance, and legislators generally don't enjoy long tenure in leadership positions, especially now with term limits. For example,

Marc Racicot (1948–)

Marc Racicot's ancestors came to the Montana Territory in the 1860s. Marc spent his high school years in Libby, where his grandfather has once worked as a logging camp cook in the 1900s. Under the guidance of his father, a teacher and high school basketball and track coach, Marc led the Libby basketball team to its first and only state championship. Marc was also a basketball stand-out for Carroll College, where he was also elected student body president. After receiving his law degree at The University of Montana Law School, he became deputy county attorney for Missoula County. In 1977, Marc became a state Assistant Attorney General, traveling across the state prosecuting scores of cases with a conviction rate of 95 percent.

MONTANA MISTORICAL SOCIETY

Marc was elected Attorney General in 1988 and was sworn in as Montana's twentieth governor on January 4, 1993. When he sought re-election to a second term in 1996, with Judy Martz, a Butte business-woman, as his running mate, they were elected with by the largest winning percentage for a governor in Montana's history and the largest winning percentage for any governor in the nation that year.

In 2002, Marc Racicot was nominated by his long-time friend, President George W. Bush, to serve as the Chairman of the Republican National Committee and then was asked to head the successful 2004 Bush-Cheney re-election campaign. Marc and his wife Theresa have five children.

In August 2005, Racicot became president of the American Insurance Association, a major insurance advocacy group headquartered in Washington, D.C.

Representative John Mercer of Polson became the first person in 108 years of state history to serve as speaker of the House of Representatives three times when he was reelected to that position for the 1997 legislative session.

Initiatives and Referendums

The Montana Constitution grants to the people the right to enact laws through the initiative and the referendum process. Any group or Montana citizen of legal voting age may petition: to enact a law by initiative; to approve or reject an act of the state legislature by referendum; or to amend the state constitution. The first step is to submit the written idea to the Legislative Services Division for review. The legal staff will put the proposal in appropriate legal terminology and review the legal concepts involved. Once completed, the proposal is given to the secretary of state's office, where the staff, along with officials from the attorney general's office, have six weeks to check it over. If the attorney general approves, supporters of the proposal have until June 21 to gather enough signatures to qualify the measure for the November ballot in a general election. It takes 41,020 signatures to get a constitutional amendment on the ballot, including at least 10 percent of the voters in the state, including 10 percent of the voters in 28 counties. Initiatives to change a state law need 20,510 signatures to qualify for the ballot, including at least 5 percent of voters in the state, including 5 percent of the voters in 28 counties.

Taxing and Spending

For state and local revenue, Montana relies on property taxes, income taxes, selected sales taxes, and natural resource taxes, including severance taxes on coal, gas, oil, and metal mining. Montana is one of only five states that have no general sales tax. In a June 1993 election, voters rejected a general sales tax for the second time in twenty-two years.

Montana's selective sales, or excise, taxes include taxes on alcoholic beverages, cigarettes and tobacco products, and motor fuels.

In the past, Montana has depended on the state's vast natural resources for a significant portion of its state revenue. Natural resources taxes include the coal severance tax, coal gross proceeds tax, metal mines gross proceeds tax, metalliferous mines license tax, miscellaneous mines net proceeds tax, oil and natural gas production tax, resource indemnity, groundwater assessment tax, and cement and gypsum taxes. In 1982, the $150 million in rev-

Judy Martz (1943–)

WWW.DISCOVERINGMONTANA.COM

Judy Martz was elected as Montana's first female governor on November 7, 2000. In the four previous years, she served as the state's first female lieutenant governor when she ran with Governor Marc Racicot.

Governor Martz was born in 1943 in Big Timber, where her parents were ranchers. She graduated from Butte High School in 1961 and attended Eastern Montana College. In 1963, Judy was crowned Miss Rodeo Montana. That same year, she represented America in Japan as a member of the 1963 U.S. World Speed Skating Team. She competed in the 1964 Winter Games in Innsbruck, Austria, as a member of the U.S. Olympic Speed Skating Team. She later helped establish the United States. High Altitude Speed Skating Center in Butte and served as the Center's executive director from 1985 to 1989. Governor Martz's interest in politics began in the 1960s, while working for Republican candidates to local, state, and federal positions. For more than thirty years, she and her husband Harry Martz have owned and operated a commercial solid-waste business in Butte. Governor Martz has two grown children.

enue from natural resource taxation made the single largest tax contribution, nearly one-fourth of the state's tax base. The fiscal year 2002 revenues from natural resource taxes declined to about one-third of the collections of two decades before. For example, the annual revenue from the coal severance tax peaked in 1985 at over $91 million. In fiscal year 2002, collections amounted to $31.6 million. Some of the contributing factors to the decline in revenue from natural resource taxation included a reduction of the coal severance tax from 30 percent to 15 percent and the lessening of the "energy crisis" of the 1970s that stimulated production of Montana's oil and gas resources. Collections from the oil and gas production tax have nearly tripled from 2000 to 2004, due to renewed exploration, development, and production.

Actual state tax collections from all sources as a share of total personal income for all residents can reflect the size of the state's tax burden in relation to the size of the economy. Montana's tax revenue as a share of per capita income has steadily fallen from about 12 percent of income in 1970 to 7.55 percent in 2003. For that year, Montana ranked as 46th in the nation.

Corporation Income Tax

Businesses in Montana pay a corporate income (license) tax and property taxes. The corporate income tax rate is a flat 6.75 percent, and is calculated on net income earned in Montana. Montana has thirteen classes of property taxes, and businesses fall into different classes depending on the nature of their business. This is discussed under property taxes. Most of the corporate income tax, is deposited in the general fund of the state.

Property Taxes

Property taxes, paid by both corporate and individual property owners, are the primary source of revenue for local governments in Montana. The Montana Department of Revenue is responsible for ensuring that all classes of property in the state are valued uniformly for tax purposes. It appraises, assesses, and equalizes the value of all property in Montana.

The first half of property taxes is generally due on or before November 30 each year. The second half is due on or before the following May 31.

OF MILLS AND LEVIES

A mill is a tenth of a cent ($0.001), so a levy of 350 mills translates to $350 per $1,000 of taxable value. The following is a sample property tax liability calculation for a home in a Montana town, using a sample mill levy:

Assessed/market value of the home	$80,000
Property tax classification (Class 4 = 3.30 percent)	x.0330
Taxable value	$2,640
Total state, county, school district mill levies (sample 350 mills)	x .350
Property tax liability	$924.00

Classes or Property

Property reappraisal is required every three years. The latest revaluation was completed in December 2002.

Property taxes were first organized into seven property tax classes (types of property) in 1919. The classifications and the rates applied to them have expanded through the years to as many as twenty classes, but recent

Maggie Smith Hathaway
(1867–1955)

Hathaway was a longtime educator in Stevensville and Helena and served several terms as the Lewis and Clark County superintendent of schools between 1894 and 1911. She spent much of her energies on social reform through the Women's Christian Temperance Movement and the suffragettes' crusade for women's voting rights, then became the first woman elected (along with Emma J. Ingalls) to the Montana Legislature in 1917. Later, she served as director of the state's Bureau of Child Welfare. She was a devoted lobbyist, pushing for passage of many social and welfare laws.

MONTANA HISTORICAL SOCIETY

Ella L. Knowles
(1860–1911)

Knowles passed the Montana bar exam in December 1889 to become the first female lawyer in Montana. While practicing law in Butte, she was dedicated to promoting the rights of women in professions, industry, politics, and suffrage. She was the first woman political candidate for an office other than county superintendent of schools. After being defeated as a Populist candidate for the office of attorney general of the state in 1892, she was appointed assistant attorney general and held this position for four years. She had a reputation as a fine orator and was an expert in mining and land law. Knowles was the first woman to represent a state before a governmental authority in Washington, D.C.

MONTANA HISTORICAL SOCIETY

Legislatures, by combining similar property types and tax rates, have reduced the number to eleven.

Montana's Largest Property Owners

Company	Market Value (millions of dollars)	Taxable Value (millions of dollars)
North Western Energy	912.57	102.16
PPL Montana	729.46	43.76
Puget Sound Energy Inc.	437.09	31.49
Burlington Northern Santa Fe Railway	732.00	29.42
Northern Border Pipeline	227.02	27.24
Qwest Corporation	367.84	22.07
Avista Corporation	241.61	18.67
Express Pipeline, LLC	126.90	15.22
Portland General Electric Co.	186.75	13.79
Montana Rail Link Inc.	297.80	11.97

Source: Big Sky Business Journal, *January 19, 2003. Montana Department of Revenue.*

Statewide Taxable Value by Class—Tax Year 2004

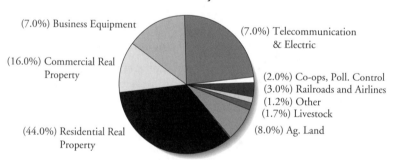

(7.0%) Business Equipment
(16.0%) Commercial Real Property
(44.0%) Residential Real Property
(7.0%) Telecommunication & Electric
(2.0%) Co-ops, Poll. Control
(3.0%) Railroads and Airlines
(1.2%) Other
(1.7%) Livestock
(8.0%) Ag. Land

Source: *Montana Department of Revenue 2003–2004 Biennial Report, 2005.*

Montana's Coal Severance Tax

The earliest taxation on coal mines began in 1921, when a license tax of 5 cents per ton was enacted into law. The most significant change in this tax occurred in 1975, when the Legislature passed legislation to create a 30 percent severance tax on coal extracted from Montana, primarily from strip mining in the southeastern part of the state. The Legislature also approved and submitted to the people a constitutional amendment to deposit a portion of the proceeds of the coal severance tax into a permanent trust fund, with the principal of the trust to remain inviolate unless three-fourths of the members of the Legislature approved a change. The remainder of the coal tax is used for a variety of purposes that have been modified through the years. The Legislature has phased down the tax rate to fifteen percent and established a lower tax rate for coal with a heating quality of less than 7,000 BTU. From 1976 to 2004, the state has collected over $1.525 billion in coal severance tax revenue. The coal tax permanent trust has $526.9 million in 2004.

Other Natural Resource Taxes

Mining operations in which metal or gems are extracted are subject to the metalliferous mines license tax, which is based on the gross value of the product. The first $250,000 of gross value of concentrate shipped to a smelter, mill or reduction work is exempt from taxation and the increment above $250,000 is taxed at 1.81% of gross value. The first $250,000 of gross value of gold, silver or any platinum-group metal that is that is shipped to a refinery is exempt from taxation and the increment above $250,000 is taxed at 1.6% of gross value. In 1998, the ten producers that were subject to this tax paid $3.9 million in revenue. In 2004, four remaining producers, including the Stillwater palladium mine, paid $5.5 million.

Oil and natural gas production in Montana is taxed on royalties and on differing rates for several categories of production. Some rates are linked to the average price of "West Texas Crude Oil." Tax revenues collections from oil and natural gas production vary widely from year to year: in fiscal year 1999, collections were $30 million; in fiscal year 2002, collections were $50.3; and in fiscal year 2004, they were $92.6.

Montana's Motor Fuels Tax

Taxes on motor fuels are levied only on fuels used to propel vehicles on public streets and highways. The tax rate for motor fuels is 27 cents per gallon.

According to the Montana Constitution, a three-fifths vote of the Legislature is required for this revenue to be used for any purpose but the following:
- construction and maintenance of public highways, streets, roads, and bridges
- payment of county, city, and town obligations incurred for streets, roads, and bridges
- enforcement of highway safety
- driver education
- tourist promotion
- administrative collection costs

Lodging Facility Use Tax Collections, 1998–2004

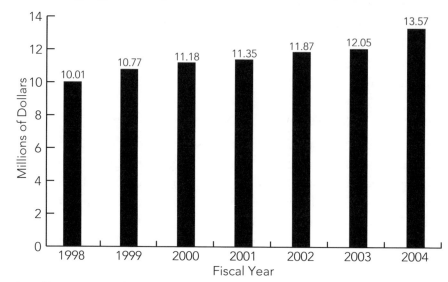

Source: *Montana Department of Revenue.* 2003–2004 Biennial Report.

Montana's "Bed Tax"

Montana enacted a lodging facility use tax of 4 percent in 1987. The 2003 legislature added a 3 percent accommodations sales tax, imposed for the "privilege of using property or services within the state." It is equal to 3 percent of the rate charges on accommodations, to include, a hotel, motel, campground, resort, dormitory, condominium inn, dude ranch, hostel, or bed and breakfast facility. Collections from the 3 percent sales tax are deposited in the state general fund. The lodging facility use tax is dedicated to the promotion of Montana's travel and tourism industries, with the first $400,000 allocated to the Montana Heritage Preservation and Development Fund.

Income Tax

Individual income tax is the largest source of tax revenue for funding state government operations ($605 million in FY 2004). The income tax revenue is deposited to the state general.

The state's income tax system is viewed as being "progressive" because taxpayers with higher incomes are taxed at a higher rate than taxpayers with lower incomes. Montana also allows two-earner married couples to file separate tax returns. This reduces household tax liability when compared to a requirement to file jointly and eliminates any "marriage penalty" at the state level.

Effective January 1, 2005, individual income tax rates, which had ranged from 2 percent to 11 percent, were reduced to range from 1 percent to a top rate of 6.9 percent. Effective at the same time, a single taxpayer who itemizes his/her deductions is limited to a $5,000 deduction for federal income tax paid during the tax year; married couples who file a joint income tax return are allowed to deduct up to $10,000 in federal income taxes paid. Montana is one of a few states in the U.S. to grant any deduction for federal income taxes paid. Other allowable deductions in this state include some charitable contributions, some medical expenses, interest, child care expenses, and some taxes.

Motor Vehicle Taxation

Light motor vehicles are exempt from value-based taxation but are subject to a state registration fee based on the age of the vehicle. The registration rate is determined by subtracting the model year of the vehicle from the calendar year for which the registration fee is due. The registration rate for vehicles 0 to 4 years is $196; 5 to 10 years, $65, and 11 or more years, $6. For example, the age of a 1997 model year Chevrolet passenger car registered in 2004 would be 7 years, resulting in a registration rate of $65.

Counties may impose a county option tax based on the manufacturer's suggested retail price, depreciated according to a schedule established in Montana law. Again, the age of the vehicle is determined by subtracting the model year from the current calendar year. For example, the age of a 2005 model year sport utility vehicle registered in 2004 would be -1 year, resulting in a depreciation multiplier of 100 percent.

Our Vehicles, 2004

Type of Vehicle	Number in State
Licensed Passenger Cars	489,545
Trucks (of all weights)	341,826
Travel Trailers (campers, tent trailers, 5th wheels)	250,975
Boats	58,934
Motorcycles	50,195
Snowmobiles	26,531
Off Highway Vehicles	33,394

Source: Montana Department of Justice Motor Vehicle Division.

Alcohol Taxes

The Department of Revenue collects an excise tax of 16 percent of the retail-selling price on all liquor sold by the state. The excise tax on products sold by companies whose annual sales do not exceed 200,000 proof gallons of liquor nationwide in the preceding year is 13.8 percent. The revenue is deposited in the state general fund. In addition to the liquor excise tax, a license tax equal to 10 percent of the retail selling price of all liquor sold by the state is levied. The liquor license tax on products sold by companies whose annual sales do not exceed 200,000 proof gallons of liquor nation-wide in the preceding year is 8.6 percent. The liquor license tax is deposited 34.5 percent in the state general fund and 65.5 percent to the Department of Public Health and Human Services to fund alcohol treatment programs.

Cigarette and Tobacco Products Tax

The 2003 legislature increased the tax on cigarettes to 70 cents per 20-cigarette package, a 289 percent increase from the previous 18 cent tax. In November 2004, the electorate approved I-149, which raised the tax on packs by $1.00 to $1.70. Beginning January 1, 2005, an increase of 143 percent. The electorate also raised the tax on other tobacco products to 50 percent of the wholesale price and moist snuff to 85 cents per ounce. I-149 adjusted distributions to increase tax revenues for veterans' nursing home operation and to provide revenue to a new state special revenue fund for health and Medicaid initiatives. Montana will now have the third highest tax on cigarettes among all states.

From FY 2000 to FY 2002, cigarette tax collections were $11 million. In FY 2004, collections were $41 million.

Tax Information

Information about state taxes may be obtained from:

> State Department of Revenue
> Sam W. Mitchell Building
> 125 North Roberts, third floor
> Helena, MT 59620
> 444-6900 (customer service center)
> www.discoveringmontana.com/revenue

State General Fund

The state general fund is the primary account that funds a significant portion of the general operations of state government. Expenditures from the account have grown from slightly less than $700 million in fiscal 1990 to nearly $1.3 billion in fiscal 2004, or approximately 5 percent in annual growth.

Fiscal 2004 General Fund Revenues by Revenue Category—$1,381.6 Million

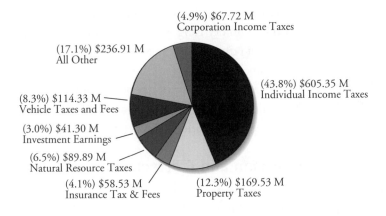

(4.9%) $67.72 M
Corporation Income Taxes

(17.1%) $236.91 M
All Other

(8.3%) $114.33 M
Vehicle Taxes and Fees

(3.0%) $41.30 M
Investment Earnings

(6.5%) $89.89 M
Natural Resource Taxes

(4.1%) $58.53 M
Insurance Tax & Fees

(43.8%) $605.35 M
Individual Income Taxes

(12.3%) $169.53 M
Property Taxes

Fiscal 2004 General Fund Disbursements by Function—$1,282 Million

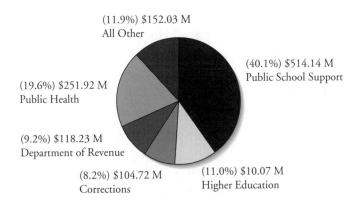

(11.9%) $152.03 M
All Other

(19.6%) $251.92 M
Public Health

(9.2%) $118.23 M
Department of Revenue

(8.2%) $104.72 M
Corrections

(40.1%) $514.14 M
Public School Support

(11.0%) $10.07 M
Higher Education

Sources: Legislative Fiscal Division. Focus on General Fund Fiscal 2004.

Crime and Punishment

Punishment for crimes on Montana's early mining frontier was swift, sure, and cheap. In the mining camps of Virginia City and Bannack, a person who committed a serious crime was often hanged from the nearest tree after a hasty trial by those who could be rounded up in a hurry. In those lawless days, some of the lawmen couldn't even be trusted, as in the case of the infamous Bannack sheriff, Henry Plummer. His outlaw gang had the nerve to call themselves the "Innocents." During their reign of terror, they were reputed to have killed as many as one hundred men on the roads to gold country. Finally, a group of citizens organized for law and order.

Tagged as part of the Plummer gang, George Ives was the first person to die for committing a violent crime in Montana. He was convicted and hanged in Nevada City on December 19, 1863, for the murder of Nicholas Thiebalt. It only took the secret society of "Vigilantes" the first month or so of 1864 to track down the other killers and thieves in the gang. The Vigilantes hanged Plummer and twenty-three others without the benefit of a trial.

Montana State Prison and Correction System

Within seven years of becoming a new territory, Montana built its first prison, which consisted of thirteen cells at Deer Lodge. Upon statehood in 1889, the state instituted a private contract system for the care of prisoners. The firm of Conley and McTague won the bid to run the state prison for 74 cents a day per prisoner. Over the thirty years of Warden Frank Conley's administration, he used prison labor to build not only the new prison but also buildings at Warm Springs and Galen and miles of Montana roads.

In 1957, prisoners took over a cell block and an administration building for 15 hours, relenting when officials promised to improve conditions at the prison. Two years later, when the National Guard was called in to quell a far more violent riot. One of two ringleaders shot and killed a deputy warden. After a successful rescue attempt aided by bazooka and machine-gun fire freed twenty-two hostages, the same ringleader apparently murdered his partner before committing suicide.

In the early 1970s, a new prison was proposed. However, before the new facility was finished in the waning months of that decade, it was determined to be insufficient to house a projected prisoner population of 1,300. A special legislature task force determined that the new prison should be expanded and that a new women's prison should be built on the grounds of Warm

Springs State Hospital. The need for expansion and better separation of prisoners was more than evident after a September 1991 riot in the Maximum Security building resulted in the murder of five protective custody inmates.

Today, the Montana corrections systems holds about 9,000 adults and juveniles accountable for their actions against victims through incarceration in secure facilities and various types of community corrections. These include: Pine Hills Youth Correctional Facility for juvenile males, Riverside Youth Correctional Facility for juvenile females, Montana State Prison, Montana Women's Prison, Treasure State Correctional Training Center (Boot Camp). Crossroads Correctional Center, a private prison in Shelby, houses about 500 males and 80 females.

Source: Philip Kent, Montana State Prison History. Deer Lodge: Powell County Museum and Arts Foundation, 1979.

Montana Crime Statistics

In 2003, there were 3,463 major crimes for every 100,000 persons in Montana. That compares with a crime rate of 4,730 per 100,000 persons in 1994. The crime rate of a given jurisdiction (city police/county sheriff) is defined as the number of major crimes per 100,000 people.

For the most part, the number of offenses committed in Montana has been decreasing over the past five years. However, for the past decade methomphetamine-related crimes have been a huge law enforcement and public safety concern.

Montana ranked 26th for violent crime in the nation in 2003. Over the past decade, Montana has consistently ranked as one of the "safest" states in the nation in comparisons of various crime rates, arrests, and convictions, with ranks of 41st in 2003, 45th in 2000, and 43rd in 1997.

Montana Crime Rate Compared to National Rate 2003		
Major Crime	Montana Crime Rate (per 100,000)	National Crime Rate (per 100,000)
Willful Homicide	3.3	5.7
Forcible Rape	26.8	32.1
Robbery	32.5	142.2
Aggravated Assault	302.6	295.0
Forcible Burglary or Attempts	405.6	740.5
Larceny/Theft	2,484.7	2,414.5
Motor Vehicle Theft	207.7	433.4
TOTAL, VIOLENT CRIME	365.2	475.0
TOTAL, PROPERTY CRIME	3,098.0	3,588.4

Source: Montana Board of Crime Control, Uniform Crime Report Data. Crime in Montana, 2003 Annual Report. Federal Bureau of Investigation, Uniform Crime Report, 2003.

CAPITAL PUNISHMENT

On May 10, 1995, 43-year-old Duncan Peder McKenzie Jr. was put to death by lethal injection at the Montana State Prison. He was the first inmate executed in Montana in nearly fifty-two years. McKenzie was convicted twenty years earlier for the 1974 kidnapping, torture, and murder of schoolteacher Lana Harding, near Conrad.

Prior to McKenzie's death, the last execution in Montana was on September 10, 1943, when Philip "Slim" Coleman was hanged in the Missoula County Jail for murdering a woman in Lothrup, near Missoula. Terry A. Langford, convicted in 1989 for the execution-style murders of Ned and Celene Blackwood at their home near Ovando, was put to death by lethal injection on February 23, 1998.

As of April 2005, there are four people on Montana's death row:

1. David Thomas Dawson, who was convicted of strangling three members of a Billings family, David and Monica Rodstein and their 11-year-old son, in 1986.
2. William Jay Gollehon, convicted of killing a Billings woman in 1985 and beating five fellow prisoners to death in a 1991 prison riot.
3. Ronald Allen Smith, sentenced to two counts of deliberate homicide for his role in the 1982 execution-style murder of two Browning men, Harvey Mad Man and Thomas Running Rabbit.
4. Daniel Martin Johnson, convicted of killing another inmate in 1995.

Further Reading

Bennion, Jon. *Big Sky Politics, Campaigns and Elections in Modern Montana.* Missoula, Mont.: Five Valleys Publishing, 2004.

Burnham, Patricia M., Kirby Lambert, and Susan R. Near. *Montana's State Capitol: The People's House.* Montana Historical Society Press, 2002.

Crime in Montana. Published yearly by Montana Board of Crime Control, 303 North Roberts, Helena, MT 59620.

Kent, Philip, *Montana State Prison History.* Deer Lodge, Mont.: Powell County Museum and Arts Foundation, 1979.

Lopach, James J., Lauren S. McKinsey, Jerry W. Calvert, and Margery Brown. *We the People of Montana: The Workings of a Popular Government.* Missoula: Mountain Press Publishing Company, 1983.

Montana Code Annotated. Helena: Montana State Government Printing Office, 2005.

Montana Counties on the Move. Helena: Montana Association of Counties, 1990.

Montana Office of Public Instruction, *Montana Indians, Their History and Location,* February 2004.

Morrison, John and Catherine Wright Morrison. *Mavericks, The Lives and Battles of Montana's Political Legends.* Helena: Montana Historical Society Press, 1997.

The Tribal Nations of Montana, A Handbook for Legislators. Helena: Montana Legislative Council, 1995.

Waldron, Ellis, and Paul Wilson. *Atlas of Montana Elections, 1889–1976.* Missoula: University of Montana, 1978.

Weaver, Kenneth L. *Governing Montana at the Grass Roots: Local Government Structure, Process and Politics.* Montana State University-Bozeman: Local Government Center, 2002.

CHAPTER SEVEN

Education

*F*or 140 years Montanans have demonstrated a strong commitment to providing accessible, quality educational opportunities for citizens of all ages. The outstanding educational systems that are available in Montana in the twenty-first century are a legacy of the 1972 Montana Constitution:

Article X. Section 1). It is the goal of the people to establish a system of education which will develop the full educational potential of each person. Equality of educational opportunity is guaranteed to each person of the state.

Eva Deem's school in her car roof Homestead House, fall 1914.
MONTANA HISTORICAL
SOCIETY

But education was a priority among Montana citizens for more than a century before passage of the 1972 Constitution. Despite the high costs of establishing and maintaining public schools and universities, Montana voters, when given the choice at the ballot box, have in most cases shown solid support for education.

That support has paid handsome dividends in the form of well-educated students and graduates. An extraordinarily high number of students from the University of Montana-Missoula are selected for Rhodes scholarships. Only seven states have higher percentages of teens completing a high school education. The state's literacy rate for adults is well above the national average.

Montana's exemplary school system includes public and private elementary and high schools, the state university system and its colleges of technology, private and tribal colleges, and community colleges. State and local governments also support an extensive, interconnected public library system. Nearly every large city in Montana can claim an institution of higher education, and most small towns have libraries.

Montana's Indian tribes have developed dynamic tribal colleges, with administrators and teachers who have won renown as some of this country's leading educators. The schools strive to give their students practical knowledge to apply to life on or off the reservation and to be shared in service to the tribes.

From lessons taught amid the bustle of the mining camps and in one-room schoolhouses in the towns and on the prairies to lectures and labs on the modern campuses across the state today, Montana has put stock in its citizens and their need and desire to learn.

K–12 Education

As early as 1861, Fort Owen in the Bitterroot Valley offered schooling to area children. In 1864, the Sisters of Providence of Montreal opened the first missionary school in the Northwest for Indian children, at St. Ignatius. In the pre-territorial mining camps of Bannack, Virginia City, and Nevada City, parents could pay one or two dollars a week to send their children to the local tuition or "subscription" school.

The first territorial legislature, meeting for sixty days in Bannack in the winter of 1864–1865, established a "common school system." In the same year, the federal Organic Act, creating Montana Territory, provided that when the lands of the state were surveyed, sections 16 and 36 of each township would be reserved for school purposes. It was not until many years after statehood that these lands were located and surveyed and the revenue from commercial activities on the lands could be directed to the public schools.

Virginia City organized the first public elementary school in February 1866. Other settlements were quick to follow suit. In the school year of 1867–1868, Montana had fifteen public schools and 1,359 students. By the 1872–1873 school year, the state was spending more than $21,000 on public education.

The pioneer schools were mainly housed in one-room buildings and were open only four or five months of the year. Schools in agricultural areas generally operated during winter, when the students were not required for farm work. In

Total State School Districts

Montana and Selected U.S. States, 2002-2003

Texas	1,224
California	990
New York	701
Montana	**452**
Minnesota	339
Washington	296
North Dakota	217
Oregon	197
Colorado	178
Mississippi	152
Idaho	114
Alaska	53
Wyoming	48
Utah	40
Nevada	17

Rocky Mountain states are shaded. *Note: Source: National Education Association. Estimates of School Statistics 2004.*

other areas, the schools set terms over the summer months to avoid heating the school buildings during severe winter weather.

Today, there are 852 separate schools scattered across Montana's urban and rural landscape. In the 2004–2005 school year, Montana had approximately one hundred schools that could be described as one-room or "ungraded" K–8 schools, with attendance ranging from one student to about twenty.

There are 173 separate high schools, with student populations ranging from twelve students in isolated rural areas to more than 2,000 in Billings West High School, just one of three in that town. Sixty-nine high schools had fewer than seventy-five students in the 2003–2004 school year.

The number of school districts in Montana reached a high of 3,572 in 1930, when transportation was still a challenge in rural locations. Since 1990, some 90 school districts have consolidated. Today, with 450 school districts, Montana has the highest number of districts in the Rocky Mountain and northwestern states.

Each school district in Montana must, by federal and state law, provide appropriate special education programs. Some offer pre-kindergarten programs. In general, school districts commence classes in the week before the Labor Day weekend and operate until the end of the first week in June. Districts are required by law to provide 180 days of pupil instruction.

Public School Enrollments

School Year	K-8	High School	Total *
1989-90	109,579	41,570	151,149
1990-91	111,090	41,789	152,879
1991-92	112,743	42,779	155,799
1992-93	115,233	44,758	160,012
1993-94	116,650	46,370	163,020
1994-95	116,631	47,709	164,340
1995-96	116,337	49,210	165,547
1996-97	114,561	50,031	164,627
1997-98	111,896	50,439	162,335
1998-99	109,450	50,538	159,988
1999-00	107,397	50,159	157,556
2000-01	105,185	49,690	154,875
2001-02	102,671	49,276	151,947
2002-03	101,082	48,913	149,995
2003-04	100,018	48,338	148,356
2004-05	98,490	48,215	146,705

* Totals may include 100-200 students at three state-funded institutions: Pine Hills School, Montana School for the Deaf and Blind after 1991, Mountain View School prior to 1996. *Source: Annual OPI enrollment reports.*

THE OLD SCHOOL

The Trinity School at Canyon Creek in Lewis and Clark County is considered to be the oldest school building still in use in the state. Parts of the 1880s building have been modified over the years, but it has been continually used as an elementary school for over one hundred years.

The granite block Philipsburg elementary school, built in 1893, is the oldest operating two-story stone-construction school building in Montana.

School Enrollment Trends

When the baby boomer generation moved out of its high school years at the end of the 1970s, public school enrollment in Montana declined by nearly 20,000 students from the all-time high of 174,532 in 1971–1972. Enrollment in the 1980s continued to decline to 151,149 students in 1989–1990, the lowest number since the 1962–191963 school year. As the baby boomers added their own babies to the public schools, enrollment increased 9.5 percent (14,398 students) from 1989–1990 to 165,547 for the 1995–1996 school year, the highest enrollment year since 1971–1972.

Estimated Per-Pupil Expenditures for Selected States, 2001–2003

State	Estimated Expenditures Per Enrolled Pupil
New Jersey	$11,793
Connecticut	10,577
Alaska	9,563
Wyoming	8,645
Minnesota	7,736
United States	7734
Oregon	7,642
California	7,434
Montana	7,062
Washington	7,039
Colorado	6,941
North Dakota	6,709
Nevada	6,079
Idaho	6,011
Mississippi	5,354
Utah	4,900

Source: U.S. Department of Education. National Center for Education Statistics, 2004.

School Funding and Spending

In 1958, the total reported cost of operating elementary and high schools in Montana was $59 million. In the 2001–2002 school year, state, federal, and district revenue for all school budgets was $1.96 billion. School general fund budgets, which include personnel salaries, materials, utilities, etc., totaled $1.07 billion. The remainder of the revenue collected was disbursed for spending on new facilities, debt on existing facilities, and other smaller school budgets.

- Montana ranks 36th for the percentage of K-12 funding from state government sources (47.7 percent) and ranks 5th for revenue from federal funding (13.1 percent).
- The state ranks 30th for per pupil revenue from local sources (39.2 percent).

Source: NEA Rankings of the States, 2002.

School Organization and Governance

Board of Public Education

The Montana Constitution charges the Board of Public Education with the general supervision of the public school system. The board:

- adopts and enforces standards of accreditation for schools
- sets teacher certification policies
- performs various other duties

The board also serves as the governing board of the Montana School for the Deaf and Blind.

The Board of Public Education consists of seven voting members, each serving a term of seven years. Members are appointed by the governor and confirmed by the senate. A student representative is also selected annually as a nonvoting member. The governor, the superintendent of public instruction, and the commissioner of higher education serve as ex-officio, nonvoting members.

Board of Public Education
2500 Broadway
Helena, MT 59620
444-6576
www.bpe.state.mt.us

School District Trustees

An elected board of school trustees manages each local school district. The boards:

- select teachers, administrators, and other school personnel
- prepare and adopt budgets
- determine local curricula, in keeping with the Board of Public Education's accreditation standards
- fulfill other responsibilities assigned by the Legislature

An elementary school board may consist of from three to seven members, and a high school board may consist of up to eleven members.

A high school board consists of the trustees of the elementary school district in which the high school buildings are located, plus members elected to represent other areas of the high school district that may encompass other elementary districts.

HUTTERITE HERITAGE

Though many of the schools on the approximately 48 Hutterite colonies in Montana are part of public school districts, the students meet each school day before and/or after their regular day of instruction in English to learn reading and writing in German.

Cornelius Hedges
(1831–1907)

MONTANA HISTORICAL SOCIETY

Hedges made many contributions to the early civic life of Montana but is most remembered as the father of Montana's school system. Armed with degrees from Yale and a law degree from Harvard, he came to Alder Gulch in 1864 with other treasure hunters. But success as a miner was not in his destiny, even after he followed the gold stampede to Helena. In the mining camp that would become the capital, he applied his legal talents and education to a wide variety of professional positions. He was a federal district attorney, Helena city clerk and attorney, and writer for the Helena Herald. After his appointment in 1872 as territorial superintendent of public instruction, he convinced the 1872 Legislature to strengthen the duties of the office in order to help modernize the fledgling school system. He trekked throughout the settled parts of the territory to visit each school each year of his four terms as superintendent. Hedges convinced communities to erect brick school buildings, use standardized tests, and increase attendance requirements. He established a teacher certification system administered by his office. As a delegate to the 1884 Constitutional Convention, he was largely responsible for creating the education article that was later adopted in the 1889 constitution.

Helen Piotopowaka Clarke
(1848–1923)

MONTANA HISTORICAL SOCIETY

The daughter of a West Point graduatae and early day rancher and granddaughter of a Blackfeet chief, Helen Clarke won acclaim in Europe as a classical actress before returning to her home state and taking up teaching in the 1860s. She taught in Fort Benton and Helena, then won election to become the first woman county superintendent of schools—indeed, the first female elected to office in the territory. She served in Lewis and Clark County from 1882 to 1888. Later she worked in Indian affairs as an interpreter and mediator for the Blackfeet and for several tribal groups in Oklahoma. Clarke died at the family cattle ranch in Midvale.

Annual school elections are held in each district on the first Tuesday after the first Monday in May. Any qualified voter who is a legal resident of the district is eligible to vote or to serve as a trustee. School trustees serve without compensation for three-year overlapping terms.

County Superintendent of Schools

In each county, voters elect a county superintendent of schools on a partisan ballot for a four-year term. County commissioners may combine this office with other appropriate county offices or may combine the office with the county superintendent of schools of another county.

In the early days of the state, the county superintendent had a strong role in supervising the teachers and curricula of the many small districts. Today, work of the office has changed as the number of small, teacher-run school districts diminishes. The duties of a county school superintendent now center on assisting districts and other county officials with budgeting and taxation functions.

Teachers

Montana teachers ranked 45th in the nation for average teacher salary, with $36,689 in the 2003-04 school year. This represents $10,137 less than the national average. In the 1983-1984 school year, Montana ranked twenty-fifth in the nation for average teacher salaries. The average teacher's salary in 1883 was sixty dollars per month.

In the 2003-04 school year, there were 10,300 teachers in the public school systems of the state, 145 district superintendents and assistant superintendents, and 504 principals and assistant principals. In that year, 81 percent of elementary teachers and 50 percent of high school teachers were female. Eighty-nine percent of superintendents were male, along with 66 percent of the principals in the state.

Sources: National Education Association. Montana Public School Data, October 2003, Office of Public Instruction.

A LESSON OF LIFE AND DEATH

In 1914, schoolteacher Bertha Rheinhart saved her Poplar area school and her pupils from a raging prairie fire. Miss Rheinhart built a backfire, but some of the pupils ran into the path of the flames. In saving them, this heroine received burns that caused her death.

Student-Teacher Ratios in Montana and Selected States (for School Year 2001–2002)

State	Pupils per Teacher
Utah	21.8
California	20.5
Oregon	19.4
Washington	19.2
Nevada	18.5
Idaho	17.8
Colorado	16.8
Minnesota	16.0
United States	15.9
Mississippi	15.8
Montana	14.6
North Dakota	13.2
Wyoming	12.5

Source: National Center for Education Statistics. Public Elementary and Secondary Education Statistics (Estimated): School Year 2001–2002. Washington: U.S. Department of Education, 2003.

Average Salaries of Public School Teachers, 2003–2004 for Montana and Selected States

California	$58,287 *
Connecticut	$57,000
New York	$53,482
Alaska	$50,697 *
Oregon	$49,169
United States average	$46,829
Washington	$45,429
Minnesota	$45,041 *
Colorado	$43,669
Nevada	$42,254
Idaho	$41,080
Wyoming	$39,130
Utah	$39,156
Montana	$36,689
Mississippi	$35,685
North Dakota	$35,441

* Data estimated by NEA. Source: National Education Association. 2003–2004 Estimates of School Statistics, 2005.

School Rules: Other State Laws Regarding Education

Compulsory Enrollment

- The parents or guardians of a child who is seven years of age or older prior to the first day of school must enroll the child in an accredited school or in a nonpublic or home school that meets certain state requirements.
- Parents or guardians must guarantee a child's school attendance until the child's sixteenth birthday or completion of the work of the eighth grade, whichever occurs later.
- A child must be six years of age by September 1 of the current school year to be enrolled in first grade.

Special Education

In accord with federal and state law, public schools provide free, appropriate education to all children with disabilities, beginning at age three. The schools are required to educate these students with other students, "to the maximum extent possible."

Approximately 12 percent of Montana's public school students receive some form of special education and related services, with the majority of these services provided in regular classes.

Nonpublic Schools

Under Montana law, parents have the authority to instruct their children, stepchildren, or wards in a home school. They are solely responsible for the educational philosophy of the home school; the selection of instructional materials, curriculum, and textbooks; the time, place, and method of instruction; and the evaluation of the home school instruction.

A private or home school must meet the following requirements to qualify for legal enrollment of students under Montana's compulsory attendance laws: maintain records on pupil attendance and disease immunization and make the records available to the county superintendent; provide at least 180

PRIVATE AND HOME SCHOOLS

Approximately 7.3 percent (12,135 students) of Montana's school age population of 177,204 was enrolled in private schools or home schools in the 2004-2005 school year. Private schools enrolled 8,164 students and 3,971 children were schooled at home.

days of pupil instruction; be housed in a building that complies with applicable local health and safety regulations; and provide an organized course of study that includes instruction in the subjects required of public schools for accreditation purposes.

Montana Report Card: The Students

Over recent years, Montana students have scored well above the national average on the ACT (American College Testing) and the SAT (Scholastic Achievement Test) college entrance exams. The 2004 high school graduates who took the ACT ranked fifth among the twenty-five states in which the majority of the state's students elect to take the ACT. About 56 percent of Montana's college-bound high school graduates took the ACT in 2004, while 20 percent took the SAT. Most higher education institutions in the middle of the nation require the ACT test, while the SAT is generally required for schools on either coast.

Montana Report Card: The School System

The accomplishments below are other examples of the long-term excellence of Montana's state and local educational systems.

- The 2002 census shows that 89.7 percent of the persons 25 years and over in Montana had high school degrees or the equivalent, compared to 84.1 percent nationally. About 23.6 percent of Montana's adult population earned a bachelor's degree or higher, compared to 26.7 nationally.
- The 2000 census data show that only 7.9 percent of Montanans ages 16 through 19 were not enrolled in high school and did not have high school degrees, compared to 11.2 percent nationally.
- In the 2003 National Assessment of Educational Progress (NAEP) of eighth-grade math and reading proficiencies, Montana students scored fourth highest nationwide. In the 2003 NAEP fourth-grade reading assessment, Montana students placed ninth highest among the states.
- In 2003, 10,978 students graduated from public school; Montana's graduation rate is 84.9 percent, always one of the highest in the nation.
- The Morgan Quitno Press compiles a variety of education related factors in its Education State Rankings and determined that Montana is the 10th "Smartest state in the Union."
- In the 2004 Adequate Yearly Progress Report required by the federal "No Child Left Behind" Act, 85 percent (732) of Montana schools (857) were able to meet the federal education requirements.

Montana and National Average Scores SAT

| Year | Montana | | National | |
	Verbal	Math	Verbal	Math
1999	545	546	505	511
2000	543	546	505	514
2001	539	539	506	514
2002	541	547	505	516
2003	538	543	507	519
2004	537	539	508	518

Montana and National Average Scores ACT

	Montana	National
1999	21.8	21.0
2000	21.8	21.0
2001	21.7	21.0
2002	21.7	20.8
2003	21.7	20.8
2004	21.7	20.9

Montana 2001–03 Student Statewide Test Scores: Percentage of Students Scoring at Proficient or Above

| | 2001* | 2002* | 2003* | 2001* | 2002* | 2003* | 2001** | 2002** | 2003** |
	Grade 4	Grade 4	Grade 4	Grade 8	Grade 8	Grade 8	Grade 11	Grade 11	Grade 11
Reading	79%	76%	79%	73%	70%	71%	78%	78%	78%
Language Arts	76%	76%	76%	71%	68%	68%	77%	74%	76%
Math	73%	72%	74%	69%	69%	69%	78%	75%	76%
Social Studies	78%	77%	79%	73%	71%	71%	82%	82%	79%
Science	82%	80%	81%	77%	78%	78%	81%	82%	82%

* Grades 4 and 8 took Iowa Tests of Basic Skils
** Grade 11 took Iowa Tests of Educational Development

Colleges and Universities

More than 55 percent of Montana's yearly crop of more than 10,000 high school graduates attend college immediately after high school. As many as 70 percent of those graduates will attend college at some point. Nearly 6,000 degrees are awarded each year by the state's university system.

Montana's University System

Montana's university system is built on a foundation set in place by acts of the U.S. Congress in 1862 and 1881. These acts dedicated sections of public land in Montana, and their potential revenue, to future institutions of higher education. The Enabling Act of 1889, which provided for the organization of the state, added another 340,000 acres of public domain for higher education funding purposes.

The constitution of 1889 established the State Board of Education, and the 1893 Legislature chartered four units of higher education. The 1913 Legislature unified these first four units into The University of Montana and created the position of chancellor to coordinate the work of the higher education components.

Many communities had vied for the location of either the official state capital or a college unit in their area. Paris Gibson, founder of Great Falls, even offered substantial land and money to lure a center of higher education to his growing city, but he failed to attract legislative favor for this idea.

At the end of the nineteenth century and in the first decade of the 1900s, a high school education was luxury enough for many of the state's young people, and few could dream of attending college. The four new campuses vied for students, courses of study, and scarce state finances. Lawmakers and citizens began to wonder if they could afford a multicampus system in a state of small population. However, when the state's voters had the opportunity to approve a 1914 ballot initiative to force consolidation of the higher education system, the idea was rejected. Instead, the Legislature succumbed to pressures to create two new campuses, Eastern Montana College in Billings in 1927 and Northern Montana College in Havre in 1929.

In a 1920 ballot initiative, voters approved the first statewide property tax in support of public higher education. Despite the Great Depression and severe agricultural failures, the 1930 electorate again showed strong support for public education institutions. They renewed the one and one-half mill levy on their property. Voters increased the levy to three and one-half mills in 1940. Every ten years since 1948, voters have renewed this commitment by approving a six-mill property tax levy as one source of funding for higher education. Income for the university system comes from the following sources: appropriations from the six-mill levy, state general fund, student tuition and fees, income and interest from the original land grants, campus sales and services, federal and state grants and contracts, and private gifts, grants, and contracts.

After a series of public and legislative studies throughout the 1980s and 1990s, the Board of Regents in 1994 restructured the six college units and the vocational-technical centers into following affiliations of the Montana university system.

Board of Regents of Higher Education

The 1972 Montana Constitution separated the governance of higher education from that of K-12 public education by creating both the Board of Regents of Higher Education and the Board of Public Education.

The Board of Regents of Higher Education has the full, exclusive power to govern and control the Montana university system. The governor appoints the seven members of the Board of Regents to serve the 7-year overlapping terms of office. The governor and superintendent of public instruction are ex-officio members of the Board of Regents, as is the commissioner of higher education, who is appointed by the regents.

One seat of the appointed members on the Board of Regents is reserved for membership by a student appointed by the governor. The student must be registered as a full-time student at a state unit of higher education. The length of term of the student member is determined by the governor and may range from one to four years.

Regents can be reached at the following address:
Office of the Commissioner of Higher Education
2500 Broadway
Helena, MT 59620
444-6570, 444-1469 fax
www.oche.montana.edu/

Montana's Institutions of Higher Education

The University of Montana-Missoula
32 Campus Drive
Missoula, MT 59812
243-0211, (800) 462-8636
www.umt.edu

The state's leading liberal arts institution comprises the College of Arts and Sciences, Davidson Honors College, and seven professional schools: business administration, education, fine arts, forestry, journalism, law, and pharmacy and allied health sciences. UM-Missoula offers fifty-two undergraduate degrees, fifty-six master's degrees, and thirteen doctoral degrees. In addition to its Missoula campus, UM includes the four affiliated campuses below.

Montana Tech of The University of Montana

1300 West Park Street
Butte, MT 59701
(800) 445-TECH
www.mtech.edu

Programs at this campus focus on the technical sciences: engineering, mineral science, energy and environmental studies, and economic development, but also include a broad range of courses in the humanities, business, and social sciences. Montana's geologic and hydrogeologic research arm, the Bureau of Mines and Geology, is also a department of the school. Montana Tech now includes the College of Technology, offering a wide range of associate's degrees in vocational and technical areas.

Helena College of Technology of The University of Montana

1115 N. Roberts
Helena, MT 59620
444-6800
(800) 241-4882
www.umh.montana.edu

This campus offers two-year programs in business, trades and industry, and technical and health occupations. Other coursework includes mathematics, communications, computer literacy, job preparation, and human relations.

Western Montana College of The University of Montana

710 S. Atlantic
Dillon, MT 59725
683-7011
(800) WMC-MONT
www.umwestern.edu

WMC prepares students for both urban and rural teaching careers, while also offering a liberal arts education. In addition to bachelor's degree programs in elementary or secondary education or liberal studies, a number of associate's degrees are offered in specialties such as business, information processing, tourism and recreation, early childhood education, and advertising design. A complete master's degree program is also available on the Dillon campus through The University of Montana-Missoula.

College of Technology of The University of Montana-Missoula
909 South Avenue West
Missoula, MT 59801
243-7811 or (800) 542-6882
www.cte.umt.edu

The college designs its programs to lead students directly into employment or to prepare them for a licensing examination in their chosen fields. Associate's degrees are offered in business management, food services management, retail management, accounting, medical office technology, nursing, office administration, and computer technology. Certificate programs are offered in surgical technology, respiratory therapy, the culinary arts, business, information processing, sales and marketing, bookkeeping, and paralegal work. Associate's degrees and certificates are available in building maintenance engineering and fashion sales and marketing, diesal technology, and welding.

Montana State University-Bozeman
P.O. Box 172440
Bozeman, MT 59717
994-0211
www.montana.edu

Montana State University-Bozeman is the state's oldest public educational institution. MSU-Bozeman offers bachelor's degrees in forty-eight majors, master's degrees in fifty-one fields, and doctorates in eighteen fields. Disciplines include the natural sciences, social sciences, humanities, engineering, agriculture, education, the creative arts, architecture, business, nursing, medicine, and allied health fields. The Agricultural Experiment Station sponsors agricultural research across seventeen academic departments and laboratories on the campus, in addition to eight research centers located throughout the state and sixty county extension offices. Other campus services to the state include KUSM-Montana Public Television and the Museum of the Rockies. MSU-Bozeman includes four affiliated campuses.

Montana State University-Billings

1500 University Drive

Billings, MT 59101

657-2011 or (800) 585-MSUB

www.msubillings.edu

This campus consists of five colleges: Arts and Sciences, Business, Education and Human Services, Technology, and Professional Studies and Lifelong Learning. Bachelor's and master's programs are offered in business, teacher training, special education, human service, and related areas. Also serving a large portion of the state is the campus-based KEMC-Montana Public Radio.

Montana State University-Northern

P.O. Box 7751

Havre, MT 59501

265-3700 or (800) 662-6132

www.msun.edu

"Northern" offers degree programs in the humanities, sciences, business, nursing, technology, and teacher education. Instruction is maintained at the associate's, bachelor's, and master's levels and includes an extended campus in Great Falls and an extensive interactive distance learning network. The school serves an area that includes four Indian reservations and functions as a cultural resource and continuing education center for north-central Montana.

MSU-Billings College of Technology

3803 Central Ave.

Billings, MT 59102

656-4445 or (800) 565-6782

www.cot.msubillings.edu

MSU Billings COT offers associate's degrees for aspiring legal, medical, and executive secretaries; accountants; automotive technicians; nursing; and computer specialists. Certificate programs are available in information processing, office technologies, accounting, drafting, and welding.

Montana State University College of Technology-Great Falls

2100 16th Ave. South
Great Falls, MT 59405
771-4300

This campus offers certificates and associate of applied science degrees in technical programs such as business, health sciences, such as dental hygiene, EMT paramedic, and practical nursing, and trades/technology. The college also serves as the Montana University System Higher Education Center for Great Falls.

Public Community Colleges

Three public community colleges in Montana provide postsecondary education, including vocational and technical programs, adult and continuing education, and academic and associate's degree programs for students wishing to transfer to a four-year institution for a degree program. The community colleges are funded by a local property tax, state general fund money, student tuition and fees, grants, and other sources.

Dawson Community College (established 1940)

300 College Drive
Glendive, MT 59330
377-3396 or (800) 821-8320
www.dawson.edu

Dawson Community College offers associate's degrees in agri-business, automotive, business and computer sciences, nurses training, human services, law enforcement, outdoor recreation management, and general education. The college also offers coursework at its Sidney extension site via interactive television.

Flathead Valley Community College (established 1967)

777 Grandview Drive
Kalispell, MT 59901
756-3822 or (800) 313-3822
www.fvcc.edu

Flathead Valley Community College offers associate of arts and associate of sciences degrees in business administration, human services, forest technology, and surveying, as well as general studies. The campus offers community outreach educational services in Libby, Eureka, and Troy through its Libby campus and services in Whitefish, Columbia Falls, and Bigfork.

Miles Community College (established 1939)

2715 Dickinson Street

Miles City, MT 59301

874-6100 or (800) 541-9281

www.milescc.edu

Miles Community College offers associate's degree work in business technology, automotive, data processing, electronics, agri-business, nursing, secretarial, health information technology, and photography. The campus coordinates with Dawson Community College via telecommunications to offer the lecture portion of a shared nursing program.

Tribally Controlled Community Colleges

Montana is the only state with a tribally controlled college located on each of its reservations. Both Indian and non-Indian students may pursue two-year associate's degrees in a number of areas. The Salish-Kootenai College recently began offering bachelor's degrees in a limited number of programs.

Blackfeet Community College

P.O. Box 819

Browning, MT 59417

338-5441

www.bfcc.org

Blackfeet Community College offers associate of arts degrees in Blackfeet studies, general studies, human services, and teacher training with emphasis in Blackfeet bilingual education and Blackfeet early childhood and elementary education. Associate of applied science degrees are offered in business management, construction technology, natural resources, health/wellness and counseling, and hospitality management. Some unique course offerings: Blackfeet Drumming and Singing, Positive Indian Parenting, Blackfeet Reservation Environmental Studies, Blackfeet Philosophy.

Chief Dull Knife College

P.O. Box 98

Lame Deer, MT 59043

477-6215

www.cdkc.edu

Dull Knife offers associate of science degrees in alcohol and drug studies, natural resource management, and office management. The college's associate of arts degree areas require credit hours in Cheyenne language, Cheyenne history, Cheyenne oral tradition, or ethnobotany. The associate of arts degree in general studies offers coursework in American Indian art and Cheyenne crafts. Distinctive course offerings include: Plains Indian Sign Language, Foundations in Cheyenne Oral Tradition, Law and the American Indian, Cheyenne Crafts.

Fort Belknap College

P.O. Box 159
Harlem, MT 59526
353-2607
www.fbcc.edu

The college offers associate's degrees in business management and administration, carpentry, chemical dependency counseling, human services technology, data and information processing, and natural resource management.

Fort Peck Community College

P.O. Box 398
Poplar, MT 59255
768-6300
www.fpcc.edu

This college offers associate's degrees in general studies, business administration, and education. The college also offers an associate of science degree in hazardous materials/waste technology. Other unique program areas include tribal administration, foster home parenting, industrial welding and machine shop practice, and truck driving and heavy equipment. Courses include: Fort Peck Tribal Codes, Fetal Alcohol Syndrome, Waste Minimization and Recycling, Dakota Language, Truck Driving Laws.

Little Big Horn Community College

P.O. Box 370
Crow Agency, MT 59022
638-3104
www.lbhc.cc.mt.us

Little Big Horn College offers associate of arts degrees in general science, Crow studies, business administration, mathematics, home economics, data processing, office systems, psychology, and nursing. Course offerings include: Crow Indian Oral Literature, Economics in Indian Country,

Thought and Philosophy of the Crow, Crow Socio-Familial Kinship, History of the Chiefs.

Salish-Kootenai College

P.O. Box 70

Pablo, MT 59855

675-4800

www.skc.edu

The first Indian college in the Northwest to earn regional accreditation (1993), Salish-Kootenai offers fourteen associate degrees in human services/rehabilitation, Native American human services, environmental sciences forestry, nursing, and computer technology. Course offerings include: Holistic Wellness, Job Seeking Skills, Nature and Cultural Tourism, Tepee Construction.

Stone Child College

P.O. Box 1082

Box Elder, MT 59521

395-4875

This college offers associate of arts degrees in general science, Native American studies, liberal arts, mathematics, business administration, computer science, and small business management. Distinctive course offerings include: Chippewa-Cree Art Forms, Story Telling, Contemporary Chippewa-Cree Music, Tribal Uses of Plants.

Private Colleges

Montana's first colleges were privately endowed. In 1878, the Montana Collegiate Institute in Deer Lodge opened its rented facilities to twenty-four students, mostly for college preparatory work. The Presbyterian Church took over this struggling institution in 1883 and renamed it the College of Montana. Copper King William A. Clark helped the school establish a mining, engineering, and metallurgy program, but still the small campus struggled to attract students and find financial backing. It finally closed its doors in 1916. The Montana Wesleyan, located in the Prickly Pear Valley near Helena, was founded in 1890 by the Methodist Church. In 1923, this early college merged with the College of Montana to become the Intermountain Union College. Severe earthquake damage to this Helena campus in 1935 led to the relocation of the institution to the

Billings Polytechnic Institute campus, which had been founded in 1908. After maintaining separate identities on the same campus for several years, the two institutions merged in 1947 to become Rocky Mountain College in Billings.

Montana has two Roman Catholic coeducational colleges. Mount St. Charles College, begun in 1909 by Bishop John P. Carroll as a boys' school, was renamed Carroll College in 1932. In that same year, the Diocese of Eastern Montana opened the Great Falls Junior College as a girls' school. When the school became a four-year accredited institution in 1939, the name was changed to the College of Great Falls. The name was again changed in 1994 to the University of Great Falls.

Carroll College
1601 N. Benton Ave.
Helena, MT 59625
447-4300
www.carroll.edu

University of Great Falls
1301 20th St. S.
Great Falls, MT 59405
761-8210
www.ugf.edu

Rocky Mountain College
1511 Poly Drive
Billings, MT 59102
657-1000 or (800) 877-6259
www.rocky.edu

Montana Bible College
P.O. Box 6070
Bozeman, MT 59771
www.montanabiblecollege.edu
586-3585

Yellowstone Baptist College
1515 South Shiloh Road
Billings, MT 59106
656-9950

Mountain States Baptist College
216 9th Street North
Great Falls, MT 59401
761-0308

John Carroll
(1864–1925)

Born in Dubuque, Iowa, John Patrick Carroll went to St. Joseph's College there and studied for the Roman Catholic priesthood in Montreal. After being ordained, he returned to his alma mater to teach and was later named president of the college. In 1905, Pope Pius X chose him to be the first Roman Catholic bishop of the diocese of Helena after Montana was split into two dioceses. He wasted no time in establishing Catholic education in the capital city. In 1906, he set up St. Aloysius Institute, a school for boys. St. Helena Elementary School opened in 1909. Later that year, President William H. Taft helped Bishop Carroll lay the cornerstone for Mount St. Charles College, soon renamed in Carroll's honor. Besides establishing and staffing other schools throughout the diocese, Carroll managed the building of the Cathedral of St. Helena, the largest house of worship in Montana.

MONTANA HISTORICAL SOCIETY

While on his way to the Vatican in the fall of 1925 to report on the status of the diocese, Carroll suffered a stroke in Switzerland and died.

LEARNING TO WRITE

The University of Montana-Missoula's Master of Fine Arts creative writing program remains one of the premier graduate writing programs in the nation. When renowned author H. G. Merriam initiated the program in 1919, the only other similar program was available at Harvard University. Writers Leslie Fiedler, A. B. Guthrie, Jr., Madeline DeFrees, Walter van Tilburg Clark, Richard Hugo, Deirdre McNamer, and William Kittredge, among others, have influenced the program's fine reputation.

UM's program in creative writing tied to 10th place in *U.S. News and World Report*'s list of America's best graduate programs.

Enrollment in Montana's Colleges and Universities

Each year, fewer than 1,800 of Montana's high school graduates go out of state for their post-secondary education, while generally more than 6,500 nonresidents come to school in Montana.

Montana University System Enrollment

	1990	1995	2000	2004
UNIVERSITY SYSTEM				
The University of Montana-Missoula	8,852	9,910	10,514	11,119
Montana State University	9,501	10,285	10,402	10,665
Montana Tech of the UM	1,612	1,679	1,683	1,797
Western Montana College of the UM	915	1,082	1,009	1,006
Montana State University-Billings	3,408	3,276	3,371	3,503
Montana State University -Northern	1,765	1,495	1,418	1,431
TOTAL UNIVERSITIES	**26,053**	**27,727**	**30,971**	**28,430**
COLLEGES OF TECHNOLOGY				
MSU College of Technology–Billings	280	436	510	666
MT Tech College of Technology–Butte	248	329	310	260
MSU College of Technology–Great Falls	479	727	766	1,09
UM College of Technology–Helena	418	468	704	749
College of Technology of UM—Missoula	454	629	776	895
Total Colleges of Technology	1,879	2,589	3,098	3,668

Note: The University System and Colleges of Technology enrollment is based on fiscal year full-time equivalent enrollment. Source: Montana Office of Commissioner of Higher Education.

Fall 2003 Enrollment for Other Colleges

	Total Students
Community Colleges	
Dawson Community College	376
Flathead Community College	1,533
Miles City Community College	458
Tribal Colleges	
Salish Kootenai College	810
Fort Belknap College	147
Chief Dull Knife College	214
Fort Peck Community College	315
Stone Child College	275
Blackfeet Community College	491
Little Big Horn Community College	309
Private Colleges	
Carroll College	1,301
University of Great Falls	622
Rocky Mountain College	902
Total	**7,753**

Source: Montana Office of Commissioner of Higher Education Fall 2003 IPEDS data.

NOTABLE

Joseph F. "Joe" McDonald (1933–)

McDonald was born and raised in St. Ignatius on the Flathead Reservation, a great-grandson of Catherine, a Nez Perce woman, and Angus McDonald, a Scottish Highlander. Joe McDonald earned an athletic scholarship to Western Montana College and competed in football, basketball, and track. He earned a bachelor's degree in education and a master's in health and physical education from The University of Montana. After working as a smokejumper, driving a school bus, and coaching basketball in Hamilton and at both his alma maters, McDonald returned to the reservation as a high school principal in Ronan. He left that post to work at Flathead Valley Community College, where he developed branches of the college on the Blackfeet and Flathead reservations and spearheaded the creation of Salish-Kootenai College. As the only president the college has ever had, McDonald has won acclaim and honors as a great educator. McDonald helped the creation of the American Indian Higher Education Consortium and developed the American Indian College Fund, which has raised $11 million in scholar-ships for the nation's thirty-one tribal colleges. He also served two terms on the Confederated Salish and Kootenai tribal council.

MONTANANS

HONORS

Selected marks of distinction for Montana's higher education system:

✴ The University of Montana-Missoula ranks fourth in the nation for the per capita number of students selected as Rhodes Scholars over the years (twenty-eight). UM has also produced thirty-one International Fulbright Scholars and ten Truman Scholars.

✴ MSU-Bozeman is one of the top ten schools nationwide in terms of consistent student success on the National Association of State Boards of Accounting exam. Engineering graduates who take the Fundamentals of Engineering exam have a pass rate of over 95 percent. The average pass rate for nursing graduates taking the professional licensing exam has been 96 percent (national rate is 86 percent). Graduates of MSU's architecture program consistently score above the national average on the Architectural Registration Examination.

✴ MSU ranks eighth in the nation for universities with the most students (41) who have received the prestigious Goldwater Scholarship, given for excellence in math and science.

✴ MSU offers an interdisciplinary Master of Arts in Native American Studies, one of only a handful in the nation.

✴ The MSU film school is one of the top film schools in the nation and the only one to offer a Master's degree in filmmaking that is partially funded through the Discovery Channel.

✴ Entrepreneur Magazine named MSU's College of Business as one of the top 10 programs in the nation for teaching entrepreurship in 2004.

✴ The UM School of Law's moot court team won the 2000 national championship.

✴ UM journalism graduates have won eight Pulitzer Prizes.

✴ The UM School of Business Administration had the highest first-time pass rate in the nation in the 2000 Uniform Certified Public Accountant Examination.

✴ Montana Tech College of the University of Montana and UM were named as two of the nation's 77 "best value" undergraduate colleges, according to Princeton Review's 2004 America's Best Value Colleges.

✴ On the average, ninety percent of the graduates of Montana's colleges of technology find employment in the state.

✴ The Carroll College Talking Saints Forensics team won the 1999 National Parliamentary Debate Association Season Sweepstakes Award. The Talking Saints are consistently near the top among hundreds of colleges in parliamentary debate.

CHAPTER EIGHT

Communications

*O*n scattered slabs of sandstone and other rock in Montana, one can find ancient images painted or carved by early inhabitants. The prehistoric native people told stories and related news by applying plant resins, charcoal, animal oils, and other substances to the rock or by scraping the sandstone with sharpened implements. Some drawings are easily understandable—the hunters and the animals they pursued. Others seem abstract and unfathomable. No words accompany the images.

Phone on the range.

Eons later, Montana's news was carried by horseback, by stagecoach, and over telegraph wire. It took all three methods to bring news of the Battle of the Big Hole in 1877 to the wider world. On the first leg of this relay, the traveling Methodist minister William Wesley Van Orsdel (Brother Van), who carried the word of God to isolated homesteads and churches, carried the news on horseback to a stagecoach route east of Bannack.

Though we like to point out to guests how uncommon the Big Sky state can be, our means of communication are as modern as in most other places around the world. For over 140 years, Montana newspapers have been an essential communication tool. Montanans have access to over twenty television stations, cable television connections, and satellite dishes that broadcast

MONTANA HISTORICAL SOCIETY

Joseph Kinsey Howard (1906–1951)

Born in Iowa, Howard spent part of his youth in Alberta before moving with his mother to Great Falls, where he graduated from high school in 1923. He then started on a distinguished career path which won him acclaim as a journalist, regional historian, and social and political critic. Whenever "favorite Montana books" are discussed, Howard's *Montana: High, Wide, and Handsome* (1943) inevitably appears at or near the top of the list. His view of the first eighty years of Montana has endured as one of the most insightful and courageous commentaries on the state's social, economic, and political history. While the work was acclaimed by other historians, Howard's criticism of Montana's establishment was considered so shocking that the book was at first sold only "under the counter."

After high school, Howard worked as a reporter for the *Leader*, a local daily (Great Falls). He became the news editor of that paper three years later, a job he held for the next eighteen years. After publishing *High, Wide, and Handsome*, Howard worked from 1944 to 1946 on the Montana Study, a project sponsored by the Rockefeller Foundation and The University of Montana and designed to study and improve the quality of life in small-town and rural communities. As a by-product of this work, Howard edited *Montana Margins: A State Anthology* (1946), a collection of literary and historical topics on the Montana experience.

Much of Howard's later writing was done under two fellowships granted by the Guggenheim Memorial Foundation in 1947 and 1948. His articles were published in the *Saturday Evening Post, Harper's, Yale Review,* the *Nation, Esquire,* and other magazines and journals. He was Montana correspondent for *Time* and *Life*. In addition to lecturing and promoting the development of regional history and literature, Howard wrote *Strange Empire: A Narrative of the Northwest* (published posthumously in 1952), a sympathetic history of the struggles of Louis Riel and the Métis people of Canada.

Howard died of a heart attack at his summer home in Choteau. Friends rode horses up Flattop Mountain and scattered his ashes to the winds. A. B. Guthrie called him "Montana's conscience. . . the greatest Montanan of our time, perhaps of any time."

PETROGLYPHS AND PICTOGRAPHS

Pictographs are images painted onto stone by ancient peoples with materials derived from plants, soils, or animal products. Petroglyphs are similar images that were etched or carved into soft rock with a sharpened tool.

Over 600 sites in Montana have evidence of the artistic talents of early people. You can see cave paintings at Pictograph Cave State Park, southeast of Billings on the south side of the Yellowstone River. Researchers believe the members of prehistoric, or paleo-Indian, cultures used these caves for about 5,000 years. This is considered one of the most important archaeological sites on the Northern Plains.

Boaters can see pictographs on steep rocks along the east side of the Missouri River, near the Gates of the Mountains, outside Helena and along the Smith River.

images and words from all over the earth to the Big Sky. Radio stations have been broadcasting over the Big Sky's airwaves for more than eighty years. High-speed internet connections are available in most populated areas of the state.

Since the dawn of the Information Age, Montana has remained wide awake to the possibilities the telecommunications superhighways offer: to bring citizens together in government, education, recreation, business, and innumerable other fields. Montana has more than ten local exchange companies and numerous other telecommunications service providers that offer advanced voice, data, and video telecommunications services to business and residential consumers throughout the state. More than 5,000 miles of fiber optics link Montana's rural communities and urban centers with high-speed, broadband on-ramps to the Internet. Web-based companies with a need for international exposure are successfully growing in communities throughout Montana. With our advanced telecommunications infrastructure, these businesses are able to locate wherever they choose, even in our most rural communities. The state and these telecommunications entities continue daily to upgrade the telecommunications infrastructure for the benefit of its citizens and those who wish to communicate with us.

Newspapers

Wilbur Fisk Sanders, the man who was to become one of Montana's first U.S. senators, was the editor of Montana's first news sheet, published in Virginia City in February 1864. Assisting in the venture was John A.

Creighton, who later founded Creighton University in Omaha, Nebraska. By the spring of 1864, merchant Francis M. Thompson was printing commercial items and local news in his *Beaverhead News Letter* in Bannack. The *Montana Post,* Montana's first real newspaper, began publication in Virginia City on August 27, 1864. It sold for fifty cents an issue, the cost of most daily newspapers today. Under the editorial leadership of Thomas J. Dimsdale, this paper was unrelenting in its call for law and order in the rather lawless territory.

A sample of other early newspapers includes the *Helena Radiator* (1865); the first daily and staunchly Republican paper, the *Helena Daily Herald* (1867); the Deer Lodge *New North-West* (1868); Bozeman's *The Pick and Plow* (1869); the Missoula and Cedar Creek *Pioneer* (1870); the *Helena Daily Independent* (1874); the Diamond City *Rocky Mountain Husbandman* (1875—later moved to White Sulphur Springs); Fort Benton's *The Benton Record* (1875); and the Miles City *Yellowstone Journal* (1879).

In 1885, a group of editors and publishers formed the Montana Press Association. It still exists today, though the name has been changed to the Montana Newspaper Association.

The so-called War of the Copper Kings had a profound and long-lasting effect on Montana journalism. Each of the copper kings owned a newspaper with which he could incite the populace to his advantage. Marcus Daly owned the *Anaconda Standard,* and William Clark owned the *Butte Miner.* Despite its parochial interests, the *Anaconda Standard* was not only considered the best newspaper in the state, but could also be found on newsstands in major cities around the nation. The Reveille was owned by another copper magnate, F. Augustus Heinze, and specialized in attacking Daly and the formation of the Standard Oil-Amalgamated Copper Company (later called the Anaconda Copper Mining Company). Perhaps stirred by these attacks, that oil and copper conglomerate formed the Fairmont Company and began buying up the state's major newspapers in Montana.

By 1929, the Anaconda Copper Mining Company owned the *Anaconda Standard;* the *Daily Post* and *Montana Standard* in Butte; the *Daily Missoulian* and the *Sentinel* in Missoula; the *Billings Gazette;* the *Helena Independent Record;* and the *Livingston Enterprise.* These eight newspapers accounted for half the coverage in the entire state. Even the Great Falls Tribune was sold to Clark interests at the turn of the century but was bought back by O. S. Warden and William M. Bole in 1905.

From the early 1900s into the 1930s, the Anaconda Company papers

Chet Huntley (1911–1974)

For nearly fifteen years, Chester Robert Huntley, born in Cardwell, was a face familiar to millions of Americans. He joined CBS as a radio newscaster in 1939, moved to ABC in 1951, and was hired by NBC in 1955. In 1956 Huntley was teamed up with co-anchor David Brinkley for *The Huntley-Brinkley Report*, the nightly NBC television newscast. Huntley retired from NBC in 1970 to return to Montana to oversee the development of the Big Sky Inc.,

MONTANA HISTORICAL SOCIETY a ski and recreation resort in the Gallatin Canyon south of Bozeman. He died just months before Big Sky opened. Up to the time of his death, Huntley continued to broadcast radio commentaries five times weekly.

Mel Ruder (1915–2000)

Born in North Dakota, Ruder came to Columbia Falls in 1946 to pursue his love of photography in nearby Glacier National Park. With his wife, Ruth, he founded the *Hungry Horse News* that year. He was editor, publisher, reporter, photographer, and more.

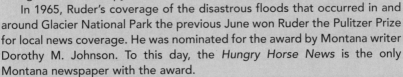

In 1947, the *News* moved into a log building Ruder had erected with the help of a GI loan. He lived upstairs. For years, the *News* was said to be the only newspaper in the country whose offices were housed in a "log cabin." The copy desk was a slice of an enormous larch tree.

In 1965, Ruder's coverage of the disastrous floods that occurred in and around Glacier National Park the previous June won Ruder the Pulitzer Prize for local news coverage. He was nominated for the award by Montana writer Dorothy M. Johnson. To this day, the *Hungry Horse News* is the only Montana newspaper with the award.

Ruder School, an elementary school building in Columbia Falls, was named for the Ruders' longtime support of local schools. Ruder and his wife sold the newspaper and retired in 1978.

Arthur L. Stone (1865–1945)

Arthur Stone founded the University of Montana School of Journalism in 1914, after 23 years as a newspaperman and educator. He nurtured the journalism school as it grew from humble beginnings in a tent, bicycle shed, and tarpaper Army barracks. Finally, more than 20 years later, in 1937, Dean Stone was able to see his dream of a permanent campus building come to fruition. His passion for journalism was equaled only by his love for the traditions of the University and chroni-

UNIVERSITY OF MONTANA ARCHIVES cling western life. He was considered an authority on Montana history and Indian lore.

Major Daily Newspapers

Newspaper	Date Established	2004 Circulation	
Billings Gazette* (800) 543-2505 657-1200, 657-1208 fax	1885	a.m. daily Sunday	47,899 52,274
Bozeman Daily Chronicle 587-4491, 587-7995 fax	1883, weekly 1911, daily	a.m. daily Sunday	13,545 15,992
Montana Standard (Butte) * 496-5500 496-5551 fax	1928 - merger of Anaconda Standard (1889) and Butte Miner (1876)	a.m. daily Sunday	14,091 14,091
Great Falls Tribune 791-1444, 791-1431 fax	1884	a.m. daily Sunday	34,401 40,874
Havre Daily News 265-6795, 265-6798 fax	1928	p.m. daily	4,362
Helena Independent Record* 447-4000, 447-4052 fax	1943	a.m. daily Sunday	13,980 14,440
The Daily Inter Lake (Kalispell) 755-7000, 752-6114 fax	1889	a.m. daily Sunday	16,500 18,006
Livingston Enterprise 222-2000 222-8580 fax	1883	p.m. daily	3,300
Miles City Star 232-0450, 232-6687 fax	1903, weekly 1911, daily	p.m. daily	3,673
The Missoulian* 523-5210, 532-5221 fax	1870	a.m. daily Sunday	29,779 34,504
Ravalli Republic (Hamilton) 363-3300, 363-1767 fax	1889	a.m. daily	4,675
* Owned by Lee Newspapers.			

Other Newspapers

Newspaper	Phone	Date Established
Anaconda Leader	563-5283	1970
(Baker) Fallon County Times	778-3344	1914
(Belgrade) High Country Independent Press	388-6762	1979
(Belt) The Eagle	277-4473	
(Big Sandy) Mountaineer	378-2176	1911
(Big Sky) Lone Peak Lookout	995-4133	
Big Timber Pioneer	932-5298	1889
An early owner, Jean P. Decker, had previously been a stagecoach guard in the Black Hills.		
Bigfork Eagle	837-5131	1976
The Billings Outpost	247-5020	1891
Boulder Monitor	225-3821	
(Bozeman-MSU) The Exponent	994-2611	1895
Managed independently of the university by students.		
(Broadus) Powder River Examiner	436-2244	1919

Other Newspapers (cont.)

Newspaper	Phone	Date Established
(Browning) *Glacier Reporter*	338-2090	1930
Many readers still call it by its old name, the *Browning Chief*.		
Butte Weekly	782-3820	
Cascade Courier	468-9231	1910
(Chester) *Liberty County Times*	759-5355	1905
(Chinook) *The Journal News-Opinion*	357-3573	1889
One of the oldest weeklies in the state; the oldest surviving business in Chinook.		
Choteau Acantha	466-2403	late 1800s
A.B. Guthrie's father was an editor. Acantha is the name of a Greek thornbush.		
Circle Banner	485-2330	1914
(Columbia Falls) *Hungry Horse News*	892-2151	1946
Won a Pulitzer in 1965.		
(Columbus) *Stillwater Country News*	322-5212	
(Conrad) *Independent-Observer*	278-5561	1905
(Culbertson) *The Searchlight*	787-5821	1902
The oldest continuously published newspaper in eastern Montana.		
Cut Bank Pioneer Press	873-2201	1909
An article in the first issue was "based on reliable rumour."		
(Cut Bank) *Western Breeze*	873-4128	1953
(Deer Lodge) *Silver State Post*	846-2424	1889
Dillon Tribune	683-2331	1881
Ekalaka Eagle	775-6245	1909
Founded by a 21-year-old printer, Oscar Dahl, from South Dakota.		
(Eureka) *Tobacco Valley News*	296-2514	1960
(Fairfield) *Sun Times*	467-2334	1941
(Forsyth) *Independent-Enterprise*	356-2149	1916
(Fort Benton) *River Press*	622-3311	1882
Glasgow Courier	228-9301	1912
(Glendive) *Ranger-Review*	365-3303	*1880s
(Hardin) *Big Horn County News*	665-1009	
Harlem News	353-2441	circa 1908
(Harlowton) *Times Clarion*	632-5633	1917
(Helena) *Montana Catholic*	442-5820	
(Jordan) *Tradewind*	557-2337	1913
Laurel Outlook	628-4412	1909
Lewistown News-Argus	538-3401	1883
An early editor, Tom Stout, went on to serve two terms as U.S. congressman, 1913–1919.		
(Libby) *Montanian*	293-8202	
(Libby) *Western News*	293-4124	1898
(Malta) *Phillips County News*	654-2020	1898
Missoula Independent	543-6609	
Montana's largest weekly, with 20,000 circulation		
(Missoula-UM) *Montana Kaimin*	243-4310	1909
Was a literary magazine from 1899 to 1909.		

Other Newspapers (cont.)

Newspaper	Phone	Date Established
(Pablo) *Char-Koosta News*	675-3000	
Philipsburg Mail	859-3223	1887
Originally published from a cowshed.		
(Plains) *Clark Fork Valley Press*	826-3402	
(Plentywood) *Sheridan County News*	765-2190	1908
(Polson) *Lake County Leader*	883-4343	
(Poplar) *Wowatin Wowapi Fort Peck Tribal News*	768-5387	
(Red Lodge) *Carbon County News*	446-2222	1924
Published front-page obituaries of miners for four weeks after explosion of Smith Coal Mine killed seventy-four in 1943.		
Roundup Record-Tribune & Winnett Times	323-1105	1908
Ownership has remained in one family since its founding.		
(Scobey) *Daniels County Leader*	487-5303	*1924
Seeley Swan Pathfinder	677-2022	
Shelby Promoter	434-5171	1912
Sidney Herald	482-2403	1908
(Stanford) *Judith Basin Press*	566-2471	1905
(Stevensville) *Bitterroot Star*	777-3928	
(Superior) *Mineral Independent*	826-3402	1915
Terry Tribune	637-5513	1907
(Thompson Falls) *Sanders County Ledger*	827-3421	unknown
Three Forks Herald	285-3414	1908
First issue printed in a tent on Main Street when the only buildings in the town were the offices of two lumber yards.		
Townsend Star	266-3333	1897
The second publisher was a carpenter who published the paper in his spare time.		
(Valier) *Prairie Star*	279-3722	
The Valierian	279-3719	1952
(Virginia City) *Madisonian*	682-7755	1873
Montana's oldest weekly. Presses were run by steam engine until 1911.		
West Yellowstone News	646-9719	
Whitefish Pilot	862-3505	1904
(White Sulphur Springs) *Meagher County News*	547-3831	1889
Whitehall Ledger	287-5301	1984
Wibaux Pioneer-Gazette	795-2218	1907
(Wolf Point) *Herald-News*	653-2222	1912

* Dates are approximate due to mergers, consolidations, name changes, or otherwise less-than-precise histories.

Montana Television Stations

Billings	KULR	NBC	Max Media of Montana	656-8000
Billings	KSVI	ABC	Nexstar	652-4743
Billings	KHMT	FOX	Big Horn Communication, Inc.	652-7366
Billings	KTVQ	CBS	Cordillera Communications	252-5611
Great Falls	KFBB	ABC	Max Media of Montana	453-4377
Great Falls	KTGF	FOX	Destiny Communications	761-8816
Great Falls	KRTV	CBS	Cordillera Communications	791-5400
Butte	KWYB	ABC	Max Media of Montana	782-7185
Butte	KXLF	CBS	Cordillera Communications	782-0444
Helena	KTVH	NBC	Sunbelt Communications	457-1212
Helena	KHBB	ABC	Max Media of Montana	457-1860
Bozeman	KBZK	CBS	Cordillera Communications	585-3444
Missoula	KMMF	FOX	Max Media of Montana	542-8900
Missoula	KPAX	CBS	Cordillera Communications	542-4400
Missoula	KTMF	ABC	Max Media of Montana	542-8900
Missoula	KECI	NBC	Lamco Communications	721-2063
Kalispell	KCFW	NBC	Lamco Communications	755-5239
Kalispell	KAJ	CBS	Cordillera Communications	756-5888

launched seething editorial attacks on certain politicians and others who battled the mining giants. While denying any direct corporate control of the press, the newspapers in the 1930s switched from outright attacks on politicians and unions to disregard of opposing news and local views. During these years, even the Tribune was challenged to remain an independent daily newspaper.

In 1959, the Anaconda Copper Mining Company sold the Fairmont Company to Lee Newspapers, a midwestern chain that consolidated, professionalized, and modernized the state's press output. In 1965, the Warden family sold the *Great Falls Tribune* to the Minneapolis Star and Tribune Company. In the late 1980s, that daily Great Falls newspaper was sold to the Gannett chain.

Today, Montana has eleven major daily newspapers. Many local communities rely on the more than seventy-five weekly and semiweekly newspapers for local information.

Broadcast and Electronic Media

Montana joined the radio age when the first station, KDYS, began broadcasting in 1922 from Great Falls. The first permanent station began in Havre as KFBB in late 1922. After broadcasting for a time from the basement of a

Buttrey store in Havre, the station moved to Great Falls in 1929, where it would eventually spawn present-day KFBB-TV.

By the 1930s, all of the state's larger cities supported radio stations. One of the region's first radio networks, the XL Radio Network, was established by Ed Craney of Butte.

It was Craney who also pioneered Montana's first television station in 1953, broadcasting as KXLF-TV in Butte. That same year a now-defunct station went on the air in Butte, and KOOK-TV began broadcasting from Billings. Today, commercial television stations are supplemented by extensive cable and satellite-dish television service, as well as public television programming from KUSM/ KUFM -TV in Bozeman and numerous local access television stations.

Tapping Into Everything You Need to Know About Montana

The official website of the State of Montana is http://discoveringmontana.com. It offers an extensive array of content and services for citizens, businesses, and on-line visitors. Some of the major citizen services include:

- **General information:** Corporate Records; Montana Laws; Labor Market Information; State Bids and Proposals; State Telephone Directory; Online Voter File; State Agency Reports and Rulemaking; Agricultural and Drought Information; Legislative Activities and Bills; Supreme Court Opinions; Press Releases

- **Filing Services:** Business Entity Annual Reports; Business Tax Express; Wage-automated Reporting Program; Self-issuing Truck Permits; Professional License Renewal

- **Search Services:** Vehicle Search; Driving Record Search; Registered Principal Search (cross match individuals names with business entities); Correctional Offender Search; Employment Opportunities; Recreational Opportunities

The state also sponsors a wonderful site just for its youngest citizens. Aimed at school-aged children, it is also attractive to adults who want to learn fascinating facts about Montana geography, history, climate, government, recreations, wildlife, and numerous other topics. http://montanakids.com/.

The official tourism site for the state is http://visitmt.com/, where citizens and visitors alike can use the handy search tools to most of what one needs to know about our cities and towns, attractions, events, recreational opportunities, accommodations and reservations services, conference planning, weather, maps, and a myriad of other fun and interesting details about the year around vacation opportunities under the Big Sky. The site even offers electronic postcards. You can also access the same information by calling 1-800-VISITMT, to speak first hand with friendly travel counselors.

The State METNET System

In 1989, the Montana legislature was a leader in the nation's public telecommunications development when it created the Montana Educational Telecommunication Network. The Montana Educational Telecommunications Network (METNET) Interactive Video System consists of a number of locations having two-way interactive compressed digital video facilities. It is owned and operated by the State of Montana. METNET is available for use by state agencies, higher education, K-12 schools, and approved nonprofit corporations where usage qualifies under state statute. The Montana Educational Telecommunications Network Interactive Video System consists of 20 video conference room sites. The sites are at university, community college, or state agency or state/private alliance locations in Montana. The METNET system allows customers to hold interactive video classes, training, and hearings among METNET sites. Participants can hold interactive conferences with sites not on the state network, including national and international locations using video capabilities offered by Sprint and AT&T.

METNET site locations include: Billings, Boulder, Bozeman, Butte, Deer Lodge, Dillon, Great Falls, Havre, Helena, Kalispell, Miles City, Missoula, and Warm Springs State Hospital. Additional sites accessible by METNET include Montana tribal colleges; Eastern Montana Telemedicine Network (at 10 mainly eastern Montana sites, 657-4870); VideoLink of St. Peter's Hospital (447-2800); REACH Montana Telemedicine Network (at 10 central Montana sites, 455-5588); Montana Partners in Health Telemedicine Network (at 10 mainly southeastern Montana sites, 237-4527).

For information on video conferencing on the METNET: Montana Department of Administration, Information Technology Services Division, 444-6788 or 1-800-628-4917.

METNET System Keeps Montana Education World in Touch

The METNET System is also a statewide network for educators and students, which today has over 10,000 users. Teachers and administrators can use the system for e-mail, daily educational news, school finance and curricula information, and access to the Internet. Students use it for a variety of school projects. Most of Montana's schools now have their own web site and through that mechanism, offer an information hub for their local community.

For more information on the METNET system for educators, contact:
Montana Office of Public Instruction
Information/Technology Services Division
444-3563

SummitNet

SummitNet, another statewide telecommunications network, is the state's data communications network. It links cities in all of Montana's 56 counties, including the entire university system and all seven tribal colleges. SummitNet provides voice, data, and video communications to state and local government, law enforcement agencies, and educational institutions throughout the state.

For further information, contact:
Department of Administration
Information Technology Services Division
444-2700
fax 444-2701
http://www.discoveringmontana.com/itsd/

Further Reading

Ashby, Norma Beatty. *Movie Stars & Rattlesnakes: The Heyday of Montana Live Television.* Helena: Farcountry Press, 2004. Norma Beatty Ashby, one of Montana's pioneer live television personalities, recalls her twenty-six years at the helm of Today in Montana.

Brier, Warren J., and Nathan Blumberg. *A Century of Montana Journalism.* Missoula: Mountain Press Publishing, 1971. It may be thirty-five years old and once was used as a textbook at the University's School of Journalism, but this still makes good reading for anyone interested in newspapers in the state.

Gilluly, Sam. *The Press Gang: A Century of Montana Newspapers, 1885–1985.* Helena: Montana Press Association, 1985.

Lawrence, Tom. *Pictures, A Park, and a Pulitzer: Mel Ruder and the Hungry Horse News.* Helena: Farcountry Press, 2004.

CHAPTER NINE

Agriculture and Natural Resources

"Montana need not call on the outside world for a single necessity."

— FROM A BOOK RELEASED IN 1914
BY THE STATE DEPARTMENT OF AGRICULTURE AND PUBLICITY

*I*n the early years of statehood, it would have been fair for Montanans to think that if they were cut off from the rest of the world, they could do just fine with what was here. They would lack for nothing but a few luxuries like coffee, tea, and bananas. The same cannot be said today. As diversified and blessed with natural resources as Montana is in the first decade of the new millennium, our ideas of what are essentials and what are luxuries have changed. Montanans trade their labor and resources in the global marketplace—for cars and tractors built in Japan, for fruits and vegetables grown in kinder climates, and for clothing made in countries new to the world map.

Mich-hay-lin-man — a creation of the annual "What the Hay" contest.
CRAIG AND LIZ LARCUM

The uses of the state's bountiful natural resources have changed too. Today, the cattle grown on Montana's rich native and cultivated grasslands may end up on the table of a restaurant in Japan. The state's vast coal deposits transform into power for the cities of the Pacific Coast. Our

BEAVERSLIDES

The beaverslide haystacker revolutionized haying when it was invented and patented almost a century ago by Big Hole Valley ranchers David J. Stephens and Herbert S. Armitage. The inexpensive implement caught on with haystackers in many western states and Canadian provinces because it saved stacking time and created compact, wind-proof haystacks.

Today it remains one of Montana's agricultural landmarks. Ranchers and farmers in the Beaverhead, Big Hole, Flint Creek, Deer Lodge, and Avon valleys of southwestern Montana still use the ingenious derrick-like beaver-slide to make those tall, tidy haystacks that dot the lush hayfields of mountain valleys.

The beaverslide may look like a catapult, but it doesn't work that way. After the large haybasket is loaded, a cable and pulley system pulls the basket up the sloping arms of the slanting glide surface. At the top, the hay falls onto the stack through an opening in the frame. The side gates allow for a tall, compact pile.

Originally, horse teams moved at right angles to the beaverslide, pulling cables that muscled the hay up the slide. Today the power is more likely to come from a tractor, truck, or car axle. Some new Montana-made beaver-slides are made of steel, but many hayers prefer the original type, made of lodgepole timbers and slippery spruce boards.

timber is used in construction of houses across America, and Montana's gold becomes circuitry in mainframe computers and has many uses in the space program and satellites.

Agriculture

One of Montana's nicknames, the Treasure State, may bring to mind mainly extractable resources like minerals and timber, but it also celebrates the state's immeasurable wealth of natural resources like soil and water, the basis of agriculture.

Agriculture has been Montana's number one industry for the past century, and farming and ranching have played a big role in the development, economy, and culture of Montana. The promise of practicing agriculture has lured a great number of people to Montana over the years, especially during the homestead boom of the early part of the past century. The farmers and ranchers of today practice sound land and water stewardship and tap into the global marketplace in order to remain competitive.

Agriculture replaced mining as the state's leading industry in the first decade of the 20th century, and between 1909 and 1919, tens of thousands of eager homesteaders rushed to farm the rich prairie soils. In those ten years, the land seemed as productive as promised and the rains were plentiful. Cultivated land increased from 258,000 acres to more than 3.4 million acres. At first, the drought that began in 1917 only affected parts of Montana, and farmers were encouraged to work as much land as possible for the food production needed to sustain the war effort. By 1919, the drought was widespread. By 1925, half of Montana's farmers had lost their farms because they could not repay the banks for their investments. Montanans also suffered the droughts and economic bad times of the rest of the nation in the 1930s.

Since those difficult decades, farming in Montana has seen more prosperous times. Since the 1990s, agriculture has added over $2 billion in cash receipts each year to the state economy. Wheat and cattle lead Montana's agricultural economy. Wheat accounted for almost 23.6 percent of the cash received for agricultural commodities in 2003; cattle accounted for 50.5 percent.

Montana exported $400.3 million in agricultural products in 2003. Almost 78 percent of Montana's agricultural exports in 2003 were wheat

Cash Receipts — 2003

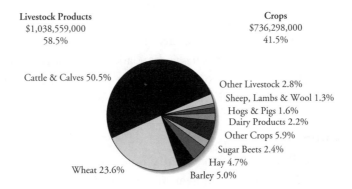

Livestock Products
$1,038,559,000
58.5%

Crops
$736,298,000
41.5%

Cattle & Calves 50.5%

Other Livestock 2.8%
Sheep, Lambs & Wool 1.3%
Hogs & Pigs 1.6%
Dairy Products 2.2%
Other Crops 5.9%
Sugar Beets 2.4%
Hay 4.7%
Barley 5.0%

Wheat 23.6%

and wheat products. Montana ranked 32nd in the United States. for export of all agricultural products. It ranked fourth for export of wheat and wheat products.

Agricultural Production in Montana

Cattle, wheat, and barley account for 80 percent of the state's agricultural receipts. Other top commodities include hay, sugar beets, dairy products, hogs and pigs, sheep and lambs, potatoes, and honey. Other crops and livestock grown or raised in Montana include llamas, horses, apples, buckwheat, canola, dry beans, cherries, flax, mustard, lentils, sunflowers, rapeseed, mint, kabocha squash, and Christmas trees. The value-added sector is a growing segment of Montana's agriculture industry. A few of the products that are produced through value-added processing include bread and cereal, processed meat and fish, pasta, jams and syrups, and soup mixes.

A Prophetic Vision

After studying the climate and geology of the arid lands of the West, John Wesley Powell, in a report to Congress in 1878, made a number of suggestions regarding the region. He warned that stockmen must have a large area to support stock. He suggested 2,560 acres or more per family for a pasture farm with as many farms as possible having waterfront on the state's rivers and streams. He concluded that homes would need to be widely scattered, and the land should not be fenced, but instead should allow for cooperative commingling of herds. He suggested legislation be enacted allowing nine or more persons to organize an irrigation district.

Though most of his recommendations were ignored, part of his report reflects the history of agriculture in Montana. The trend from 1920 to the present has been fewer and larger farms. In the 1970s and 1980s, the average ranged very close to Powell's recommendation of 2,560 acres. The trend into the 21st Century is again to smaller average size. Irrigation districts are, of course, very much a part of Montana farming and ranching.

Farmlands

In 2000, some 32,000 Montanans were employed in agricultural activities. That is nearly 200,000 fewer Montanans than those who worked the land during the heyday of homesteading. Nonetheless, the hope of owning enough acreage to raise some animals or crops is still a draw today to life-

Top Ten Montana Agricultural Commodities, 2003

Product	Cash receipts	%Total Receipts for all Agricultural Commodities
Cattle and calves	954,930,000	50.5
Wheat	446,418,000	23.6
Barley	94,297,000	5.0
Hay	89,054,000	4.7
Sugar beets	44,936,000	2.4
Dairy products	42,160,000	2.2
Hog and pigs	30,135,000	1.6
Potatoes	24,230,000	1.3
Sheep and lambs	22,456,000	1.2
Honey	14,164,000	0.7

Montana's Place in U.S. Agriculture, 2003

Crops	Amount Produced	Rank in U.S.
All wheat	142,330,000 bushels	4
Barley	34,000,000 bushels	3
Oats	1,980,000 bushels	16
Dry beans	233,000 cwt.	12
Potatoes-fall	3,339,000 cwt.	14
Sugar beets	1,308,000 tons	6
Corn-grain	2,380,000 bushels	40
Corn-silage	1,128,000 tons	23
Livestock		
All cattle & calves	2,400,000 head	10
All cows	1,490,000 head	8
Beef cows	1,472,000 head	7
Milk cows	18,000 head	39
Cattle on feed	70,000 head	22
Hogs & pigs	170,000 head	26
Sheep & lambs	300,000 head	6
Wool production	2,597,000 lbs.	5
All chickens	485,000 birds	38
Egg production	107,000,000 eggs	38
Honey production	9,570,000 lbs.	6

cwt. is abbreviation for hundred weight.

Montana Farms and Farmlands, 1910–2003

Year	Number of Farms*	Land in Farms (Millions of Acres)	Average Size of All Farms (in Acres)
1910	28,800	N/A	N/A
1920	57,700	N/A	N/A
1930	55,000	N/A	N/A
1940	44,500	N/A	N/A
1950	37,200	65.0	1,747
1955	34,800	66.1	1,899
1960	31,700	66.7	2,104
1965	28,400	66.7	2,349
1970	26,400	64.2	2,432
1975	23,400	62.2	2,658
1980	23,800	61.9	2,601
1985	24,300	61.0	2,510
1990	24,700	60.5	2,449
1995	26,000	59.4	2,285
2000	27,800	59.3	2,133
2001	27,800	59.6	2,144
2002	27,900	59.8	2,143
2003	28,000	60.1	2,146

N/A - Figures not available.
The U.S. Census of Agriculture defines farms as places with annual sales of agricultural products of $1,000 or more.
Source: Montana Agricultural Statistics—State Historical Series, 1996, and Montana Agricultural Statistics, 2004.

long residents and newcomers alike. Many wealthy newcomers who have been buying up ranch properties in the state's recreational paradises in the past decade intend to keep a working ranch alive in some capacity.

- Over two-thirds (64.0 percent) of Montana's 93.1 million acres is in farm and ranch land.

- Of the total acreage, 64.2 percent is range and pastureland, 3.7 percent is woodland, and 30.7 percent is cropland; only 14.7 percent was harvested cropland in 2002, with the remainder in cultivated summerfallow (5.8 percent) and other uses (10.2 percent).

- Montana ranks second in the nation, behind Texas, in acres of land in farms and ranches.

- In 2002, the state's leading agricultural county in total cash receipts from crops, livestock, and livestock products was Yellowstone County, followed by Chouteau and Fergus Counties.

- The county with the most land in farms in 2002 was Big Horn County (2.81 million acres), followed by Rosebud County (2.54 million acres) and Choteau County (2.30 million acres).

In 2002, total farm and ranch assets (excluding farm operators' household assets and debts) amounted to $25.8 billion. The average value per farm or ranch was $924,236, with an average real estate value of $734,292. That amounts to an average value of $390 per acre for land and buildings on January 1, 2003. The average farm and ranch debt per operation was $102,160.

Farm Real Estate Values (Land and Buildings)

Year	Value in Dollars/Acre
1870	$ 4
1880	8
1890	13
1900	5
1910	19
1920	22
1930	12
1940	8
1950	17
1960	35
1970	60
1980	235
1990	222
2000	330
2003	390

Crop Production

Montana's major grain crop is wheat, which in 2003 accounted for about 57 percent of cash receipts from crops. Montana's wheat crop in 2003 was valued at about $527.4 million. The 1995 wheat crop was the most valuable ever, reaching a record $897.4 million, due to unusually high prices and the second-largest volume ever. The 2003 average price per bushel for winter, spring, and durum wheat was $3.73, compared with $4.04 for 2002. Wheat prices remained high in the 1990s due to a strong export demand.

Dry Land Farming, Strip Farming, and Summer Fallowing

When you're traveling by air over Montana, you see a patchwork of strips below you, at times stretching as far as you can see. This is the landscape of strip farming, an essential part of dry land farming, where irrigating crops is impossible or impractical.

The broad strips of grain crops are green in the spring and golden at harvest time. Alternating with them are strips of summer fallow. These strips aren't planted in grain until the following year. In order to keep enough land

In 1895, this Northern Pacific Railroad car extolled the virtues of homesteading the unsettled land of the Midwest and West. MONTANA HISTORICAL SOCIETY

ATTRACTING A TIDE

During the homestead era, the 1913 Legislature and other power-brokers of the day were so determined to "attract a tide of desirable immigration" that they created a new Department of Agriculture and Publicity. The department's 1914 "fact" book is full of the kind of "glittering generalities encompassed in superlatives" that it claimed to be dead-set against when it came to bragging about Montana's opportunities. The publication wanted to lure ". . . high class, energetic and upright men and women who, with reward assured, are not afraid of honest endeavor." The following are some samples of the dramatic boasts about the state highlighted on each page of the book.

- Literally hundreds of Montana's beautiful streams flow over beds of gold.

- Earthquakes, cyclones, tornadoes, and dangerous floods are unknown in Montana.

- Montana winters are mild.

- Heat prostrations are unknown in Montana.

- Montana is destined to be the greatest dairying state in the Union.

- God made Montana with a smile.

- Montana is a gentle and generous mistress.

- Opportunity wears brass knuckles in Montana.

- There is room for millions of prosperous, contented people in Montana.

- There is no place in Montana for the loafer.

Source: Department of Agriculture and Publicity. The Resources and Opportunities of Montana. Helena, Mont.: Independent Publishing Company, 1914.

Wheat Production in Montana, 1880–2003

Year	Acres Harvested	Yield per Acre in Bushels	Total Bushels	Value of Production
1880	19,000	23.5	446,000	$379,000
1920	3,608,000	12.4	44,768,000	$71,629,000
1950	4,953,000	18.5	91,434,000	$173,499,000
2000	4,920,000	27.5	135,210,000	409,007,000
2001	4,215,000	22.9	96,570,000	304,487,000
2002	4,795,000	23.1	110,735,000	449,483,000
2003	5,200,000	27.4	142,330,000	527,394,000

Source: Montana Agricultural Statistics—State Historical Series, 1996 and Montana Agricultural Statistics, 2004.

Top 5 Crop-Producing Counties, 2003

Winter Wheat		Spring Wheat (excluding durum)	
County	Bushels	County	Bushels
1. Chouteau	15,958,000	1. Roosevelt	6,675,000
2. Hill	9,275,000	2. Valley	6,412,000
3. Fergus	4,620,000	3. McCone	4,557,000
4. Liberty	4,216,000	4. Hill	4,046,000
5. Big Horn	4,108,000	5. Daniels	3,877,000

Durum		Alfalfa	
County	Bushels	County	Bushels
1. Sheridan	7,459,000	1. Gallatin	187,900
2. Roosevelt	2,335,000	2. Teton	168,500
3. Daniels	1,766,000	3. Fergus	159,400
4. Richland	630,000	4. Beaverhead	141,000
5. Valley	453,000	5. Madison	130,800

Barley		Oats	
County	Bushels	County	Bushels
1. Teton	5,282,000	1. Richland	200,000
2. Pondera	5,212,000	2. Lake	115,000
3. Glacier	3,216,000	3. Dawson	91,000
4. Toole	2,073,000	4. Roosevelt	88,000
5. Yellowstone	1,544,000	5. Wibaux	86,000

JUST DOUGH IT

In September 1995, Wheat Montana Farms & Bakery of Three Forks claimed a new world record for cutting wheat from the field, milling it, mixing a recipe, and turning it into a loaf of bread. The feat was accomplished in 8 minutes, 13 seconds by Wheat Montana employees wearing jackets that said "Just Dough It." A loaf of the record-setting bread was shipped to President Bill Clinton.

In 2003, Wheat Montana Farms & Bakery was named the Top Agricultural Operation in the nation by *Top Producer* Magazine.

Source: Guinness Book of World Records, 1995, Bantam Books.

in fallow, then, a dry land farmer needs twice as much land as the acreage he will plant and harvest in a season. Reduced tillage is the most effective way yet found to get a crop in the plains country, where the annual rainfall may be only 10 inches.

Years ago farmers burned the huge heaps of straw that remained after the grain was threshed. In central Montana's "breadbasket" country, the skies glowed at night with the light of straw fires. Now, however, they make use of the decaying leftovers. Increasingly since the early 1980s, reduced tillage practices have come to be widely accepted. Rather than turning the stubble under the soil, the stubble is left on the surface, where it helps protect the soil and preserves moisture from rain and snow. Some farmers apply chemicals to the fallow to kill weeds that sprout among the stubble.

Special Contributions to the Nation's Market Basket— Past and Present

Before the advent of frozen foods, imported foods, and reliable refrigerated transportation, Montana was one of the nation's largest producers of certain vegetable crops. In 1918, the Bozeman Canning Company opened to take advantage of the satisfactory climate for growing peas and green beans. It produced some 326,000 cases of vegetables in the 1920s. In the late 1930s and early 1940s, canneries operated in Billings, Red Lodge, Stevensville, and Hamilton.

Following World War II, a series of hailstorms caused crops to fail and the factories to decline. Montana's first frozen-food plant opened in Glendive in 1945. In 1947, this plant shipped five carloads of frozen corn on the cob, which represented 20 percent of the nation's production of that commodity.

Most of these canneries and plants folded by the 1950s.

Montana's sugar beet industry also got a boost during World War II. Even before those profitable years, more than 4,000 farmers were growing more than 900,000 tons of sugar beets, mainly in the Yellowstone Valley. Wartime labor shortages encouraged hundreds of migrant workers from Mexico to help bring in the sugar beet crop. In some locations, the work was done by captured German and Italian soldiers and Japanese-Americans who were interned in "relocation" camps.

Montana was also known as a primary apple-raising state. The first apple trees were planted in the Bitterroot Valley in 1866. About 1870, the Bass brothers of Stevensville planted the first commercial orchard. Once that valley could boast of irrigation, agents were sent to the Midwest to lure farmers onto 10-acre orchard tracts with promises of prosperity. In the 1910s, Montana's delicious Macintosh apple became a market favorite and production was high. Crops during those years sometimes yielded 900,000 bushels per year. Apples were a viable state crop through the 1930s but have gradually tapered off since that time. With the high price of farm land and Montana's unpredictable weather patterns, it became too risky to count on a crop that might be wiped out in one frosty spring night.

Cherries

Montana was once a strong producer of both sour, or pie cherries, and sweet cherries. The famous Flathead sweet cherry industry got started at the turn of the century when late-maturing Lambert cherry trees were planted. These cherries came on the market later in the season than those

Sweet Cherry Production and Value, 1950–2003		
Year	Total Tons	Avg. Price per Ton
1950	320	$340
1990	280	$1,670
2000	1,100	1,490
2001	1,850	1,130
2002	2,220	1,840
2003	1,730	1,600

Source: Montana Agricultural Statistics, 2004.

from other U.S. areas, affording those growers lucky enough to survive a spring frost some good prices in the nation's market basket. Today growing commercial sour cherries is limited to several large orchards in Ravalli County. Flathead sweet cherries remain a coveted summer treat both for Montanans and the national marketplace. The best year in recent times was 1987, when some 3,800 tons plumped up for the picking. After some severe frost years in the early 1990s required the replanting of many orchards, production and prices have been promising in the 2000s.

Montana Cattle Inventory, 1870–2004

Year	Number of Head	Average Price per Head
1870	117,000	$26.40
1900	910,000	$27.70
1950	1,726,000	$128.00
1990	2,250,000	$675.00
2000	2,600,000	$800.00
2004	2,400,000	$950.00

Source: Montana Agricultural Statistics—State Historical Series, 1996 and Montana Agricultural Statistics, 2004.

HOLY COW

In 1995, cattle outnumbered people in Montana by better than three to one, but a decade later the human population has gained a bit of an advantage. The ratio is still two and one-half cows to one person.

Ranching and Livestock Production

The livestock industry accounted for about half of the nearly $2 billion annual agricultural production of the state in recent years.

Sheep and Wool

A number of early immigrants brought small herds of sheep to the first mining areas and agricultural valleys, the Beaverhead establishing itself by 1870 as a major center. Conrad Kohrs, who was to become one of Montana's premier cattlemen, is credited with bringing 400 head of sheep to Montana in 1864. He discovered that mutton was not so popular with the miners, but they appreciated the wool for mattresses. Major C. C. Kimball brought the first sizable herd to Virginia City from Red Bluff, California, in 1865. In 1867, Jesuit missionaries of the St. Peter's Mission west of Cascade brought sheep into Montana from Oregon. They hoped to interest the Indians in the sheep business. But Indians were less interested than the coyotes who gobbled up this new, easy prey. The first permanent sheep ranch in Montana started in the Beaverhead Valley near Dillon in 1869, with 1,500 sheep brought from Oregon.

By 1880, there were 385,000 sheep in the state. Montana's peak for the

Montana Sheep Inventory, 1870–2004

Year	Number of Head	Average Price per Head
1870	11,000	$2.60
1900	4,504,000	2.85
1950	1,464,000	19.40
1990	640,000	85.00
2000	370,000	91.00
2004	300,000	120.00

Wool Production, 1910–2003

Year	Sheep Shorn	Lbs. of Wool	Price per lb.
1910	5,008,000	38,061,000	$0.21
1950	1,347,000	12,796,000	$0.63
1990	627,000	6,204,000	$0.91
2000	347,000	3,315,000	$0.37
2003	272,000	2,597,000	$1.03

sheep industry came in the first years of the twentieth century, with somewhere between 5 and 6 million head.

The industry declined as the rich grasslands were carved up and fenced by homesteaders. More damaging were predation of the sheep by coyotes, increased competition after World War II from other sheep-producing nations (Australia, New Zealand, and Argentina), and termination in the early 1990s of a federal wool incentive program initiated by President Dwight D. Eisenhower.

Hogs and Pigs

Montana's pork industry was one of the state's earliest agricultural industries. Many of the first permanent settlers and homesteaders here raised hogs as a reliable meat source for the family and for the essential commodity of lard for cooking and baking. Pigs proved to be adaptable to the sometimes harsh Montana climate. They could be fed grain grown on the farm, along with other family food scraps. Over the years, hog production grew from two or three sows serving the family to larger herds intended for market. From the time of earliest settlement, small local slaughter plants, or the farmers themselves, processed the hogs for butcher shops and grocery stores. One large pork packing plant in Billings bought many of the hogs raised in Montana until it went out of business in 1980.

Today, producer marketing cooperatives collect the hogs for shipment to packing plants in South Dakota, Idaho, Oregon, and California. Many farms still have a few sows or feeder pigs for home use or youth agricultural projects. For large-scale producers, hog production is now a high-technology agribusiness. Thousands of sows can be raised in confinement buildings, where temperature, cleanliness, and feed are monitored and controlled. These producers often use artificial insemination for breeding and employ strict disease control measures. In recent years, producers have bred hogs for leanness, reducing the fat and calorie content to address the concerns of health-conscious Americans. Montana's Hutterite colonies now produce most of the hogs raised.

Montana Hog and Pig Inventory, 1870–2004

Year	Number of Head	Average Price per Head
1870	4,000	$6.40
1900	43,000	$6.60
1950	145,000	$33.90
1990	185,000	$89.00
2000	155,000	$80.00
2003	120,000	$69.00

Source: Montana Agricultural Statistics, 2004.

NOTABLE

MONTANA HISTORICAL SOCIETY

Charles M. Bair (1857–1943)

Bair began ranching in 1893 after coming to Montana as a railroad conductor. By the turn of the century, Bair's sheep herd was reputed to be the largest in North America. At one time 300,000 animals belonged to him. In 1905, he filled forty-four freight cars with his wool clip. He made a fortune in the Alaskan gold rush and multiplied his assets with investments in several other interests, including cattle, coal, mines, metals, oil, banking, and irrigation projects on the Crow Reservation. He lived in a 26-room mansion in Martinsdale with his wife, Mary, and daughters Alberta and Marguerite. The home and the ranch headquarters opened as a public museum in 1996, but was closed in 2004.

MONTANANS

Water Resource Gives Rise to Dams and Reservoirs

The building of dams for hydroelectric power and irrigation has been beneficial to both Montana and states along the great rivers that rise in the mountains here. Montana is part of the Pacific Northwest Electric Power, Conservation, and Planning Commission and other consortia that manage adequate flood control, power sources, irrigation, recreation, and habitat of the West's water resources.

The largest body of water in the state is the 134-mile-long artificial Fort Peck Lake on the Missouri River. The 379-square-mile lake is formed behind Fort Peck Dam. As the fifth largest manmade reservoir in the United States, Fort Peck Lake holds 17.9 million acre-feet* of Missouri River water. The dam is a source of power and flood control for the Mississippi River downstream. Fort Peck Dam was begun in 1933 and was operational by 1940.

Libby Dam on Lake Koocanusa was built in 1973 to hold 5.8 million acre-feet of water. **Hungry Horse Dam,** 564 feet high, on the South Fork of the Flathead River, is the 10th highest dam in the nation.

For comparison, Hoover Dam in Nevada is 725 feet high and holds 28.3 million acre-feet of the Colorado River.

* The water that will cover one acre to the depth of one foot.

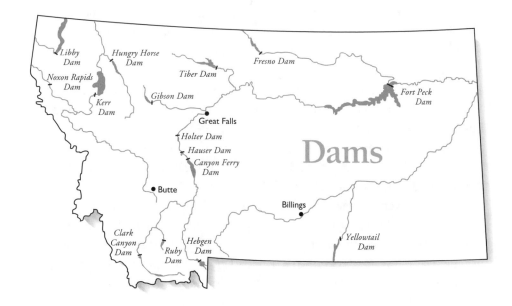

Forest Products

Twenty-four percent of Montana's land area, approximately 22.4 million acres, is forested. Some 64 percent of Montana's forests is owned by the federal government, with nearly 11.4 million acres administered by the USDA Forest Service and the remainder under the Bureau of Land Management. Some 3.4 million acres of forested land are reserved in wilderness areas, national parks, and national monuments.

The State of Montana owns 4 percent of the state's forested timberlands. The forest industry owns 8 percent (1.6 million acres), and the remaining 24 percent (4.4 million acres) is in private, nonindustrial ownership. Most nonindustrial private timberland is owned by individual farmers and ranchers. More than 600,000 acres are under the control of Indian tribes.

The estimated volume of wood on all timberlands totals almost 31.6 billion cubic feet. About 95 percent of what was forest in the early part of the century is still forested today.

The two most prevalent trees of this growing stock are lodgepole pine (30 percent) and Douglas-fir (29 percent). The other major species in this growing stock are ponderosa pine, western larch, Engelmann spruce, and subalpine fir.

Early Days of the Timber Industry

The first sawmill of record in Montana was constructed in 1845 near St. Mary's Mission in the Bitterroot Valley by the Jesuit missionary Father Anthony Ravalli. In the early 1860s, mills opened in Virginia City, Bannack, and Helena, and dozens followed suit in the western part of the state. Two grades of lumber were produced in the Virginia City mill, sluice lumber selling for $140 per thousand board feet and building lumber that sold for $125 per thousand board feet.

Lumber mills sprang up around the gold mines. In 1869 a number of small sawmills produced about 13 million board feet of lumber. The mills were abandoned, though, as the gold strikes played out in the 1870s and 1880s. Two events turned the faltering lumber industry around. The hard rock mining industry, especially copper, began to flourish, and the transcontinental railroads came into the state, requiring wood for rail ties, trestles, tunnels, and fuel. By 1888, the Anaconda Copper Company was spending more than a million dollars a year on timber for its smelter in Anaconda.

The Forest Products Industry in the 20th Century

After World War II, Montana's lumber production grew steadily. Harvests increased dramatically, driven by a strong market for homes and other uses. Some of the timber was processed into lumber for use within the state or in nearby states. In 1957, the Hoerner-Waldorf Company built a pulp and paper mill west of Missoula, near Frenchtown. At this plant, wood chips from Montana sawmills and other sources were made into linerboard for corrugated boxes. As the plant expanded, Missoula became the boomtown of the 1960s. Now owned by Smurfit-Stone Container Corporation, the plant is still the state's largest wood products facility.

During the 1960s and 1970s, the wood products industry of western Montana continued to expand and diversify, with the addition of several large plywood and particleboard manufacturing plants. While there began a reduction in the supply of timber from national forest lands, more harvesting from private and industrial timberland owners increased.

From 1987 to 1993, Montana's total timber harvest fell by 25 percent and lumber production experienced a sharp decline, mainly due to reduced offerings from the national forests. Reasons for the decline in timber offerings included increased appeals and litigation regarding timber sales and interest in protection of threatened and endangered species. Montana's 1993 timber harvest was 1 billion board feet, down 27 percent from the record harvest of 1.376 billion board feet in 1987. High prices and high demand kept employment in the wood products industry at around 11,100 workers in 1994, not much less than in the late 1980s.

Through the 1990s, despite sharply decreasing timber supplies, lumber prices and the general economy remained strong and global markets for Montana wood products increased. High prices made it economically feasible to harvest timber in more socially desirable ways and to use lower quality timber. These trends kept industry employment on a par with the 1980s. The labor-intensive log home industry expanded, as did the secondary processing of other primary wood products.

Even though sixteen lumber mills closed down between 1990 and 2000, the forest products industry held steady as the third largest basic industry sector in Montana, as measured in terms of labor income, exceeded only by federal government employment and agricultural activities. The forest products industry contributed just under 14 percent of the state's economic base as measured by labor income and 10 percent of the state's economic base as measured by employment. In 2000, some 10,000 logging and production workers remained employed, producing 1.2 billion board feet of lumber products.

The Forest Products Industry Today

The first year of the 21st century turned out to be one of the most challenging years in decades for the forest products industry. Not only did products prices fall, due to a number of globally influenced reasons, but also it was the one of worst fire seasons on record in Montana. Timber harvesting was called to a halt because of fire threat and lumber mills were forced to curtail activities. To add fuel to the flames, the deregulation of the national and local electricity market led to sky-high fuel costs and further curtailments at many lumber mills, the Smurfit-Stone Container Plant, and the Louisiana Pacific particleboard plant in Missoula. Through 2004, the forest products industry continued to endure a dwindling timber supply, low prices, and other tough fire seasons, fueled by the state's recent drought cycle. Employment in the industry has fallen as several of the larger mills closed their doors, resulting in a decline to 9,400 workers. The number of production workers, which account for 40 to 50 percent of all workers in the forest products industry, fell by a thousand workers, from 4,556 at the begin-

HOMEMADE LOG HOMES

Montana is one of the nation's major producers of log homes. Three types of house logs are made here—hand-hewn, sawn, and machine-lathed. Sales of log homes increased 50 percent between 1993 and 1998, to nearly a $100 million business. Twenty percent of the log houses produced here stay in Montana. Four percent are exported to other countries.

ning of 2000. Even the log home industry, a sector that had been growing consistently since the 1970s, experienced years of weaker sales.

Nine contiguous counties in western Montana account for over 80 percent of the industry's labor income in the state, but the number of timber operations and mills in eastern Montana counties has increased in recent decades. The state's leading timber-processing counties are still Flathead County, followed by Lincoln County and Missoula County.

Most of the lunber produce by Montana's forest industry is shipped out of state for construction or further processing. The products that remain in Montana are used by the construction industry or businesses that manufacture secondary wood products such as cabinets, log and prefabricated homes, mobile homes, and furniture. The mills in Montana ship throughout the world, but three-quarters of these products are shipped to the north-central and western states.

Mining and Energy Resources

Western, central, and eastern Montana differ in the minerals they contain. The differences are related to the geology and structure of the rock formations found in each region.

The mountainous parts of the state contains numerous deposits of metallic ore. The deposits consist mostly of gold, silver, copper, lead, zinc, palladium, platinum, and tungsten. Sedimentary rocks are sources of phosphate

MAD ABOUT SAPPHIRES

Early prospectors sometimes cursed the sapphires that clogged the gold sluices. Even those miners willing to speculate on the sapphire's potential had a hard time rounding up local financial backing for gemstone mining during the 1860s epidemic of gold fever. However, a few decades later, far-sighted European and Eastern interests invested in the sapphire discovery areas and, for the most part, held on to many successful sites over the years. In the 1890s the rush was on to find sapphires in Quartz and Rock creeks west of Philipsburg, in Brown's Gulch and Dry Cottonwood Creek near Anaconda, and along the Missouri River north of Helena. In many of these locations, you'll still find tourists and natives alike picking through buckets of gravel at various commercial operations, with the hope of finding a valuable keepsake. The biggest bonanza occurred in 1894 at Yogo Gulch, near Utica, in the central Montana county of Judith Basin. The U.S. Geological Survey once termed the Yogo sapphire mines "America's most important gem locality."

rock, limestone, silica, crushed and dimension stone, clays, and other industrial minerals. Some bentonite has been found in beds of volcanic ash. In the southwestern part of the state, deposits of talc, corundum, iron ore, graphite, sillimanite, and kyanite are found.

Central Montana is best known for the production of petroleum and natural gas. Metallic ore deposits have been found in the Little Rocky Mountains, the Judith Mountains, the Little Belt Mountains, and other isolated ranges. Some clay in this region has been found suitable for brick and tiles.

Eastern Montana has mostly sedimentary rocks. This region contains over 90 percent of the coal reserves in the state. No metallic ore deposits have been found in this region.

In addition to the above, Montana has been mined at various times for dozens of minerals and metals.

The Mining Industry Today

The mining industry includes coal, oil and gas extraction, and nonfuel mineral production. The latter includes: precious metals like gold, copper and platinum; and industrial minerals like cement, gemstones, talc, and crushed stone.

Montana ranked twenty-sixth in the nation in nonfuel mineral production in 2003. The estimated value for that year was $492 million. The mineral production in Montana accounted for about one percent of the total of U.S. production.

Only two major gold mines remain in operation in 2005: Apollo Gold Corp.'s Montana Tunnels Mine, a gold, lead, silver, and zinc mine in Jefferson County; and Placer Dome Inc.'s Golden Sunlight Mine near Whitehall. Three large gold mines once owned by Pegasus Gold, Inc. are no longer in production—Beal Mountain Mine in Silver Bow County, Zortman Mine in Phillips County, and Basin Creek Mine southwest of Helena. Spurred on by high gold, silver, and copper prices in recent years, numerous mines are in exploration and development stages across the state. Some companies are reworking sites near Montana's legendary goldfields of Butte, Virginia City, Alder Gulch, and Elkhorn. In November 2004, voters upheld the ban on cyanide heap-leach gold mining by rejecting a repeal of Initiative-147.

In 2003, Montana Resources Inc. resumed mining of copper and molybdenum from the Continental Pit near Butte, after being shut down for more than three years, largely due to high electrical costs. The Stillwater Mining Company, partly owned by a Russian company, continues to mine the only known source of palladium and platinum in the Western Hemisphere. Stillwater has over 1,500 employees and operates two underground mines, the Nye mine and the newer East Boulder location. A company smelter and base metals refinery is located at Columbus, Montana. There is currently strong interest in building stone quarried at a number of Montana sites. There are over 2,000 open-pit sites for mining sand, clay, gravel, bentonite, and phosphate.

The Bull Mountain Coal Mine near Roundup is the first full-scale underground coal mine to operate in Montana since the 1970s. The owners hope to create a billion dollar energy complex of coal mines, a railroad, and a power plant.

Montana's Rank in the Nation's Nonfuel Mineral Production

    1st—palladium and platinum
    4th—gold
    2nd—bentonite
    4th—zinc and lead
    7th—silver
    8th—gemstones

Current Principal Mineral-Producing Counties

    Broadwater—gemstones, lime plant
    Carter—bentonite
    Flathead—aluminum plant, sand and gravel, peat
    Gallatin—cement plant, stone and gravel
    Granite—gemstones

Jefferson—cement plant, zinc, gold, silver, lead

Judith Basin—gemstones

Lewis and Clark—gold, gemstones

Lincoln—copper, silver, dimension marble

Madison—talc, garnets

Meagher—iron

Missoula—sand and gravel

Park—dimension marble, gold

Petroleum—stone and gravel

Ravalli—stone and gravel

Rosebud—stone and gravel, gypsum

Sanders—dimension marble

Silver Bow—copper, molybdenum, gold, stone and gravel

Stillwater—platinum group metals

Yellowstone—stone and gravel, sulfur

Source: Montana Bureau of Mines and Geology/U.S. Geological Survey (2003).

Coal

Coal underlies 35 percent of Montana's surface area, forming the base of Montana's major mining industry. This coal is part of the Fort Union formation, probably the largest coal basin on earth. It extends under parts of Montana, Wyoming, North Dakota, and Saskatchewan. The power grid that reaps the benefits of this mother lode extends even farther. Electrical power generated at the huge coal power plants in our state's southeastern corner flows all the way to the West Coast, where it helps to meet the high energy demands of that region.

THE COAL SEVERANCE TAX

Montanans remembered the past economic disruptions from the ups and downs of the state's mining industry and realized coal is irreplaceable. In 1975, the Montana Legislature approved the Coal Severance Tax, meant to protect the state and its citizens from hard times in the case of a shutdown of the mines. The tax, paid by mining companies on the coal they extract, was a bitter pill for the companies to swallow but was upheld by the courts in 1981. Part of the tax proceeds are distributed in grants to towns and counties where coal has been extracted. The remainder of the proceeds is placed in a variety of state funds for highways, the arts, libraries, parks, agriculture, conservation, and more.

Montana has coal reserves estimated at 120 billion tons, the largest reserve base in the nation. The Energy Information Administration estimates that as many as 1.4 billion tons of this reserve are recoverable from currently producing coal mines. If all of Montana's coal reserves were capable of being mined, and were mined at the current rate, mining of this resource could be sustained for 3,000 years.

Eastern Montana coal is both lignite and subbituminous grades. It is remarkably free from impurities and easy to extract by stripping. The overburden, the earth and rock above the coal seam, is loosened by blasting. Then the coal is loaded onto trains with huge mechanical shovels. There's nothing to cave in, so about 95 percent of the coal can be taken out.

Since 1975, Montana has produced an annual average of 32.6 million tons of taxable coal. Coal companies predict production will remain at that level well into the new century.

Oil and Natural Gas

Before the turn of the century, oil was found in and around Glacier National Park but the finds were not developed. It was not until the 1910s and 1920s, when the use of automobiles increased dramatically, that Montana's oil and natural gas industry came into being.

In 1915, the first major oil field was opened at Elk Basin, along the Wyoming-Montana border in Carbon County. Next came the Cat Creek field on the lower Musselshell River and the Devil's Basin near Roundup in 1919. The Kevin-Sunburst oil discoveries in the early 1920s made the north-central towns of Shelby and Cut Bank boomtowns. The Cut Bank and Pondera fields yielded high-quality crude oil and natural gas and convinced several large companies to get into the refinery business.

Montana's oil production remained relatively small in scale until after World War II, when national prosperity brought increased demand for petroleum. Major oil companies encouraged exploration across the state, and two refineries were built at Billings. Major discoveries in Montana's portion of the oil-rich Williston Basin sparked a leasing frenzy in eastern Montana. The basin also underlies western North Dakota and southern Saskatchewan. In the 1950s, Billings became the center of the state's petroleum industry as lucrative oil strikes were made near Wibaux, Sidney, Baker, and throughout northeastern Montana. The Yellowstone Pipeline was completed from Billings to Spokane in 1954.

Montana's oil business was somewhat quiet during the first half of the

1960s, but big oil discoveries at Bell Creek in Powder River County and a natural gas bonanza at Tiger Ridge in Blaine County sent hopes soaring again. The state's peak year for oil production was 1968, with 48 million barrels. The height of natural gas production came later, in 1973, at nearly 59 billion cubic feet. The top money year for petroleum was 1981, with $1.45 billion, largely the result of increased exploration and high prices brought on by the world energy shortage in the late 1970s. Those good times were dampened by conservation measures and overseas oil development. Many wells were capped at that time to await the next boom cycle. Only 1,400 persons were employed in oil and gas related operations in 1995, significantly less than the peak of 4,700 workers in 1980.

As of 2004, Montana's natural gas industry was experiencing healthy growth, with production of 79 million cubic feet from 4,500 wells. It is estimated that at least six trillion cubic feet of natural gas reserves remain untapped in the state.

Montana Superfund Sites

The Environmental Protection Agency's Superfund was created by Congress in 1980 to discover and clean up, if possible, areas where hazardous substances might harm human health and the environment.

Montana's Upper Clark Fork Basin is the largest Superfund area in the nation. It extends 140 miles from the headwaters of Silver Bow Creek north of Butte to the Milltown Dam near Missoula. It is the legacy of more than one hundred years of mining and smelting in the Butte-Anaconda area at the headwaters of the Columbia River Basin.

The initial investigations in this area by the EPA began in 1982. In 1983, three sites—Silver Bow Creek, the Anaconda Smelter, and the Milltown Reservoir—were put on the Superfund priority list. The Montana Pole site was added to the priority list in 1987.

The Silver Bow Creek/Butte Area

This site consists of about 450 acres of soil and water that contain heavy metals from the years of mining that took place here. The site is in Butte and Walkerville and runs from Silver Bow Creek to the Warm Springs Ponds. One of the most well-known sites of contamination is the Berkeley Pit. Water was pumped from surface and underground mines in Butte for about 100 years until 1982, when the Anaconda Minerals Company, a subsidiary of Atlantic Richfield Company (ARCO), ceased mining operations in the area and shut down the pumps. Since then, water has been filling the Berkeley Pit at about 5 million gallons a day. The water is highly acidic and contains a wide variety of heavy metals. Monitoring of the water in the Berkeley Pit began in 1990 and continues today. The water in the Berkeley Pit rises roughly a foot per month. In fall 2004, the funnel-shaped pit lake was over 800 feet deep, at an elevation of over 5,248 feet above sea level. The water will only be allowed to rise to 5,419 feet above sea level before a water treatment facility will begin to clean the water. Since February 2004, Montana Resources mine has pumped 13 million gallon of water per day out of "Lake Berkeley" in order to reclaim some of the copper still in the water. The copper-laden water flows into cells filled with recycled scrap iron, where the iron in the cells and the copper in the water trade places. The iron-rich water is returned to the Pit. The copper product is dried through filter press and sent to an off-site smelter.

SELECTED AGRICULTURE AND RESOURCE INDUSTRY EVENTS

Ag Days and Trade Show, Sidney, January, 433-1206.
Agri-Trade Exposition, Glendive, February, 377-5601.
Central Montana Horse Show, Fair, and Rodeo, Lewistown, July, 538-8841.
Governor's Cup All Breed Horse Show (longest running horse show in
    Montana), Helena, August, 458-6165.
Libby Logger Days, Libby, July, 293-1881.
Macintosh Apple Day, Ravalli County Museum, Hamilton, October, 363-3338.
Manhattan Potato Festival, Manhattan, third Sunday in August, 284-4162.
Milk River Wagon Train, Malta, September, 654-1100.
Montana Agricultural Industrial Exhibit, Great Falls, January, 761-7600.
Montana Mule Days, Drummond, June, 777-2331.
Montana Agri-Trade Exposition, Billings, February, 651-0440.
Montana Winter Fair, Bozeman, Gallatin County Fairgrounds,
    January, 585-1397.
Northern International Livestock Exposition and Rodeo (NILE), Billings
    MetraPark arena, October, 256-2495.
Pioneer Power Day Threshing Bee, Lewistown, September, 538-5236.
Roundup Cattle Drive, Roundup, mid-August, 358-2454.
"Running of the Sheep" (Sheep Drive), Reedpoint, Sunday of Labor Day
    weekend, 326-2325.
Threshing Bee and Antique Show, Culbertson, September, 787-5265.
Threshing Bee, Choteau, September, (800) 823-3866.
Threshing Bee, Huntley, August, 976-6687.
Western Heritage Days, Grant-Kohrs Ranch National Historic Site,
    Deer Lodge, July, 846-2070.

The Anaconda Smelter

Operated for nearly 100 years, the Anaconda Company smelter accumulated waste materials that cover about 4,000 acres. The waste materials consist mainly of tailings and flue dust and are located in and around the city of Anaconda. The Old Works/East Anaconda Development Area contained the first copper smelting facilities built in Anaconda to process the ore being mined in Butte. The Upper Works began in 1884 and the Lower Works in 1888. A silver refinery was located between the two smelters. They operated until 1902. In 1994, the land was transferred to the County of Anaconda/Deer Lodge. Smelting wastes have been covered with limestone and topsoil, and The Old Works, a Jack Nicklaus–designed golf course, now occupies the site.

Milltown Reservoir

Located just above the Milltown Dam near Missoula, this site contains pollutants from the reservoir sediments that have seeped into the groundwater, which at one time served as the source for Milltown's water supply. In 2004, the federal Environmental Protection Agency and state officials approved the final plan for the cleanup and restoration of the Clark Fork River Basin Superfund site, including removal of the aging Milltown Dam near Missoula.

Further Reading

Feldman, Robert. *Rockhounding Montana*. Helena: Falcon Press, 1985, revised 1996.

Fletcher, Robert H. *Free Grass to Fences: The Montana Cattle Range Story*. New York: University Publishers Incorporated, 1960.

Fritz, Harry W. *Montana, Land of Contrasts, An Illustrated History*. Sun Valley, Calif.: American Historical Press. 2001.

Gilles, T. J. *When Tillage Begins: A History of Agriculture in Montana*. Laurel, Mont.: UMP Publishing, 1977.

Grosskopf, Linda, with Rick Newby. *On Flatwillow Creek: The Story of Montana's N Bar Ranch*. Los Alamos, N.M.: Exceptional Books, Ltd., 1991.

Gustafson, Rib. *Under the Chinook Arch: Tales of a Montana Veterinarian*. Helena: SkyHouse Publishers, 1993.

_____. *Room to Roam: More Tales of a Montana Veterinarian*. Helena: SkyHouse Publishers, 1996.

Howard, Joseph Kinsey. *Montana: High, Wide, and Handsome*. Lincoln: University of Nebraska Press, 1943.

Keegan, Charles E., III, et al. *Montana's Forest Products Industry: A Descriptive Analysis, 1969–2000*. Missoula: University of Montana Bureau of Business and Economic Research, 2001.

Malone, Michael P. *Montana: A Contemporary Profile*. Helena: *Montana Magazine*, 1996.

Toole, K. Ross. *The Rape of the Great Plains.* Boston: Little, Brown, 1976.

Vichorek, Daniel N. *Montana's Homestead Era.* Montana Geographic Series, No.15. Helena: *Montana Magazine,* 1987.

Voynick, Stephen M. *Yogo: The Great American Sapphire.* Missoula: Mountain Press Publishing, 1985.

Writers Project of Montana. *Copper Camp, Stories of the World's Greatest Mining Camp, Butte, Montana.* First published in 1943. Reissued by Riverbend Publishing, Helena, Mont., 2002.

Sources

Unless otherwise noted, the source for all tabular information in this chapter is *Montana Agricultural Statistics,* the 2004 edition, compiled by Montana Agricultural Statistics Service.

CHAPTER TEN

Business

$\mathcal{J}$n the first decade of the twenty-first century, agriculture remains Montana's largest basic industry, having dethroned mining from that distinction in the first decade of the last century. The state continues to move away from an economy built primarily on other natural resource-based industries and toward a more diversified economy. Behind agriculture, which accounts for about 30 percent of economic activity in Montana, tourism and other non-goods producing businesses are growing.

Elkhorn Mine—sorting ore in 1908.
MONTANA HISTORICAL SOCIETY

The service industry, which includes private health and social services, business services, and hotels and other lodging, is the fastest-growing source of employment. When economists try to predict economic growth in terms of jobs, they foresee personal and business services as Montana's fastest-growing industries, followed by wholesale and retail trade.

Montana's economic markets have expanded in recent years to include increased trade relations with the Pacific Rim nations and beyond. This expansion, together with the state's close proximity to Canada and beyond Canadian markets, have enhanced Montana's international trade opportunities. New technology, advanced telecommunication, and improved transportation continue to make Montana's somewhat remote location more accessible to expanded trade opportunities in the United States and abroad.

The U.S. Bureau of Economic Analysis prepares annual estimates of the nation's Gross State Product, which measures Montana's contribution to the Gross Domestic Product by measuring the output or production of the state, sometimes referred to as "value added." This is a dollar figure that is equal to gross sales or receipts minus goods and services purchased.

Gross State Product in Current Dollars 2000–2003 (Millions of dollars)

Montana	1999	2000	2001	2002	2003	2004	% change 2003-04
GSP	$20,589	$21,535	$22,495	$23,773	$25,510	$27,701	8.6%

Sources: Montana Department of Labor and Industry, Montana Annual Planning Information, June, 1996; Job Projections for Montana's Industries and Occupations,1994-2000, January 1996. Montana Business Quarterly, Winter 1996.

Employment and Labor

Recent Job Growth

Montana gained about 10,000 payroll jobs in 2004, for an increase of about 2.5 percent from 2003 to 2004.

Natural Resources and Mining

This sector includes employment in oil and gas drilling, logging, and mining. During the 1990s, jobs in mining experienced around a 20 percent decline, but the trend is turning upward again in the new century. In 2004, this sector added over 1,100 jobs. Between 2003 and 2004, this sector saw the largest percentage increase in employment, with a 23 percent increase. The increase can be attributed to the reopening of Montana Resources metal mining in Butte and high worldwide prices for oil, which have encouraged oil and gas exploration in Montana. Jobs in this sector are generally high paying.

Construction

During the 1990s, construction saw more than a 90 percent increase for the decade, from 10,000 to 20,000 jobs. The construction industry provided

Marcus Daly (1841–1900)

Daly immigrated to America from Ireland in 1856, and worked in New York, California, and Nevada. A mining company sent him to Montana to investigate the potential of Butte's Alice Mine. He recommended its purchase, invested $5,000 of his own money in the mine, and managed the mine for the company. In the early 1880s, he bought the Anaconda Mine, also in Butte, from the man who originally developed the mine. After buying out neighboring mines and building a smelter, Daly amassed one of the world's most powerful monopolies. He founded the city of Anaconda and developed it into an up-to-date center of smelting and processing. Bluff and genial, he remained more popular with the working miners than his rivals, William Clark and Augustus Heinze. He later established a thoroughbred ranch in the Bitterroot Valley and involved himself in irrigation projects and other development that helped settle the region.

MONTANA HISTORICAL SOCIETY

F. Augustus Heinze (1869–1914)

WORLD MUSEUM OF MINING

Fritz Augustus Heinze, the son of German immigrants, came to Butte around 1890 as a young mining engineer. With his persuasive manner and backing from his wealthy family, Heinze soon owned mines and a smelter. After first allying himself with Daly, Heinze joined forces with Clark in a battle against the Amalgamated Copper Company, formerly Daly's Anaconda Company, which had been bought by Standard Oil.

After Daly died in 1900 and Clark had gone to Washington as a senator, Heinze continued to wage war with Amalgamated. In the Butte Reveille, the paper he owned, he portrayed himself as the miner's friend—the little guy out to slay the corporate giant. In the end, the giant had its way: Heinze sold out to Amalgamated in 1906. He was paid more than $10 million for his properties, on the promise that he leave Butte and stay out of the copper business. He moved to New York and to Wall Street, where he soon broke his promise and tried to corner the copper market. This bid was his last and meant his financial ruin, supposedly at the hands of his old nemesis, Standard Oil. He died at the age of forty-five.

robust growth in the Montana economy between 2003 and 2004. With 1,600 added jobs, that represented an over 7 percent increase. Many of the new construction jobs were found among the high paying specialty trade contractors.

Manufacturing

The manufacturing sector of Montana's economy includes lumber, wood, and paper products (not logging); printing and publishing; food processing and production of food products; machinery, equipment, and instruments; primary metals processing; production of chemicals, petroleum, cement, and glass, and miscellaneous manufacturing. With 19,000 generally high paying jobs, it accounts for about 20 percent of Montana's economic base. This sector saw steady growth in the 1990s with a high point of over 22,000 jobs in 1999 but the sector started to decline in 2001. About one-third (around 4,800 jobs) of the jobs in this sector are in the wood products industry. Even with a number of sawmill closures, this portion of manufacturing experienced no overall loss of jobs from 2003.

Trade, Transportation and Utilities

The sector represents the largest employment sector in the Montana economy, with around 85,000 jobs in trucking, railroads, energy companies, and wholesale and retail trade (general merchandise and apparel, food stores, auto dealers and service stations, building materials and garden supply stores, and eating and drinking establishments). Retail trade continues strong growth mostly in cities, partly due to the influx of discount and franchise stores into the state.

Finance, Insurance, and Real Estate

This segment of the economy has shown a relatively steady increase from 1990 to the present. During the 1990s the sector grew by 33 percent. Another 800 jobs were added to this healthy economic sector between 2003 and 2004. The real estate markets show no real signs of slowing in some of the high-growth areas, even with higher interest rates and home prices.

Information

Employment in this sector include jobs in publishing, motion pictures, broadcasting, Internet publishing, telecommunications, and Internet service

Annual Average Nonagricultural Employment by Selected Industries (Not Seasonally Adjusted) (thousands of persons)

Industry	1995	1996	1997	1998	1999	2000	2001	2002	2003	2004
Natural Resources & Mining	6.4	6.4	6.3	6.1	6.1	6.0	6.2	6.2	6.2	7.2
Construction	16.4	17.6	18.3	19.3	20.0	20.4	21.2	21.7	23.1	24.9
Manufacturing	21.2	21.9	22.1	21.0	22.5	22.4	21.4	20.0	19.0	19.1
Transportation & Utilities	16.7	16.4	16.4	16.7	16.8	16.8	16.2	15.9	15.4	15.4
Wholesale & Retail Trade	64.7	66.3	66.9	68.4	69.0	69.4	68.9	68.9	69.1	70.7
Information	6.5	6.7	7.1	7.4	7.8	7.9	7.9	7.8	7.7	7.8
Financial Activities	16.1	16.6	17.1	17.6	18.1	18.5	18.8	19.3	20.3	21.1
Professional & Busniess Services	23.3	25.3	25.7	26.7	28.6	30.8	31.8	32.3	32.5	33.2
Educational & Health Services	42.6	44.0	44.9	46.1	47.7	49.0	49.7	52.0	53.1	54.2
Leisure & Hospitality	46.0	47.8	47.9	48.7	49.1	50.1	49.4	51.0	52.3	54.6
Other Services	13.3	13.9	14.2	14.7	15.1	15.3	16.0	16.1	16.3	17.0
Federal Government	13.2	12.8	12.6	12.7	12.7	13.4	13.4	13.8	13.8	13.8
State Government	22.3	22.7	23.1	23.4	23.8	24.2	23.9	24.3	24.7	25.1
Local Government	41.2	41.3	41.6	42.3	42.2	42.6	46.8	46.8	47.3	48.1
Total Employment	349.9	359.7	364.2	372.1	379.5	386.8	391.7	396.0	400.7	412.0

Note: Effective in 2002, industry categories have been changed due to reporting changes by the U.S. Department of Labor. Data for prior years has been revised. *Source: U.S. Department of Labor, Bureau of Labor Statistics* providers. The peak years in the past decade for this sector were in 2000 and 2001, years in which there were approximately 7,900 jobs. In 2004, this sector still employ 7,800 workers.

Professional and Business Services

This fast-growing component of Montana's economy continues steady growth, adding over 10,000 jobs in the past ten years. Job activities in this sector include: legal advice and representation; accounting, bookkeeping, and payroll services; architectural, engineering, design services; computer services; consulting services; research services; advertising services; photographic services; translation and interpretation services; veterinary services; and other professional, scientific, and technical services.

Education and Health Services

This sector includes only private sector education jobs, which provide instruction and training at specialized establishments, such as private schools, colleges, universities, and training centers (3,500 jobs in 2003). It also included private health care and social assistance jobs, such as jobs in nursing homes and hospitals (48,700 jobs in 2004).

Leisure and Hospitality

This sector represents the second largest employment component of the Montana economy, with over 54,000 jobs in 2004. It includes jobs in the arts, entertainment, recreation, and the accommodation and food services sector, with many of the jobs directly related to the states tourism industry.

Government

The two largest Montana employers are public employers. The U.S. government, both civilian and military, employed nearly 14,000 people in 2004. The Montana state government employed approximately 25,000 residents in 2004 and includes state government workers and those employed at the state's units of higher education. Local government is the largest in the government sector, with over 48,000 workers who keep the day-to-day workings of our communities running smoothly—law enforcement officers, road workers, K–12 educators, and other city and county employees.

Source: Montana Department of Labor and Industry.

Montana's Major Employers, 2000

Employer	Activity	Number of Jobs in Montana
Montana State government (includes educational institutions)	Government Services	24,000
United States government (civilian and military)	Government Services	22,000
Providence Services (hospitals and education services)	Hospital Services	3,900
Wal-Mart	Retail Trade	2,700
Sisters of Charity of Leavenworth Health Services (St. Patrick Hospital, Missoula)	Hospital Services	2,600
Deaconess Billings Clinic Health System	Hospital Services	2,300
Burlington Northern Santa Fe Railway	Transportation Services	2,300
Albertson's	Hospital Services	2,300
Billings School District	Education	2,000
NorthWestern Energy	Utility, Mining	1,800

Source: U.S. Bureau of Economic Analysis.

Small is Beautiful

Small businesses are a vital part of the state's business climate. About 54 percent of wage-and-salary jobs in Montana are with businesses of fewer than 50 employees. About 34 percent of Montana's small businesses employ fewer than 20 people. Only about 4 percent of Montana businesses have more than 50 employees. Most of our work sites (54.5 percent) employ four or fewer persons.

Unemployment Trends

Since 2001, Montana's unemployment rate has remained well below the national average and is also low compared to the state's historical levels.

Licensed Professionals

The following numbers indicate only the number of people granted licenses to practice the listed professions in 2004 and should not be interpreted as a measure of how many are actually practicing.

Unemployment Rates for Montana and the U.S.

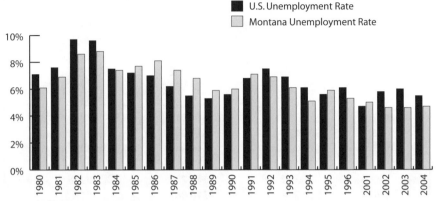

- U.S. Unemployment Rate
- Montana Unemployment Rate

Sources: U.S. Department of Labor, Bureau of Labor, Statistics, January 2005. Montana forecast by Montana Department of Labor and Industry, January 2005.

Top Jobs, Projected to 2010

Estimated Jobs to Be Gained Annually
Due to Growth and Replacements

Salespersons, Retail	933
Waiters and Waitresses	533
General and Operation Managers	441
Cashiers	627
Child Care Workers	443
Registered Nurses	322
Carpenters	404
Food Preparation Workers and Fast Food Workers	364

Source: Montana Department of Labor and Industry, Research and Analysis Bureau 2004.

Per Capita Personal Income

Montana's per capita personal income was $26,857 in 2004, a 4.2 percent increase over 2003. Montana's per capita personal income ranked 45th among the 50 states.

Personal income includes the following:

- wage and salary income
- self-employment income
- employer contribution for benefits
- personal dividends and interest
- property income
- government and business transfer payments

Per Capita Personal Income

Year	U.S.	Montana	% of U.S. Average
2003	$31,459	$25,775	82%
2002	$30,795	$24,744	80%
2001	$30,580	$24,594	80%
2000	$29,847	$22,932	77%
1999	$27,939	$21,585	77%
1998	$26,883	$21,130	79%
1997	$25,334	$19,877	78%
1996	$24,175	$19,047	79%
1995	$23,076	$18,349	80%
1994	$22,172	$17,861	81%
1993	$21,346	$17,770	83%
1992	$20,854	$16,867	81%
1991	$19,892	$16,318	82%
1990	$19,477	$15,448	79%
1980	$10,183	$9,143	90%
1970	$4,095	$3,625	89%

Source: U.S. Department of Commerce Bureau of Economic Analysis, Regional Economic Information System, released September 2004.

The Travel Industry

Even since its earliest days, the state has attracted tourists to its many splendors and attractions. The long-standing prediction has come to pass that preserving the state's natural resources would sustain tourism and assure economic prosperity.

In 2003, tourism brought about $1.87 billion to the state from nonresident visitors. Hundreds of businesses benefited from the 9.67 million persons who visited Montana that year, more than ten times the population of the state.

Visitors to Montana have increased 13.6 percent since 1993, Glacier National Park suffered a slight decrease in visitors from 2002 to 2003, due to August forest fires near and inside the park. Yellowstone National Park, though, had its best season ever: more than 3.1 million people visited.

Tourism Regions

The Montana Department of Commerce, Travel Division, divides Montana into six tourist regions. Contact these offices for information on the various recreational activities and attractions of each area. Call (800) 847-4868 (outside Montana) or 444-2654 (in Montana).

Tourism Regions

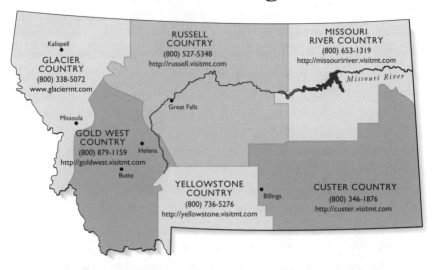

Montana's Most Popular Attractions		
Destination	2002	2003
1. Glacier National Park	1,905,689	1,664,046
2. Yellowstone National Park	1,516,575	1,539,881
3. Little Bighorn Battlefield	425,995	422,566
4. Fort Peck Lake	222,353	209,634
5. National Bison Range	114,900	105,700
6. Museum of the Rockies	74,900	70,293
7. Lewis & Clark Interpretive Center	61,197	59,618
8. Lewis & Clark Caverns State Park	49,396	50,113
9. Big Hole Battlefield	61,142	56,146
10. Pompey's Pillar	36,000	38,500

Sources: Bureau of Land Management; National Park Service; Travel Montana

Utility Infrastructure

History of Power to the People

When electricity was first demonstrated to Montanans in 1882, it was steam-generated. The early mining industry and other entrepreneurs foresaw the need and demand for more electrical energy and looked to the large rivers of Montana as power sources for the generation of electric power. The mining and ore-processing industries invested in the development of hydroelectric power, and by the late 1890s, the Missouri River was harnessed at Great Falls and at Canyon Ferry, near Helena. Most of the transmission lines headed over the hills to the copper mines of Butte. Other dams were built on that river, as well as on the Madison, Big Hole, and the Clark Fork rivers.

These power sources helped the copper mining, lumber, and other industries grow throughout most of the 20th century. In turn, these large consumers of electricity helped justify the creation of expensive hydroelectrical projects that could also provide economical heating and lighting to households and small businesses.

All the early hydroelectrical projects started as private business ventures, but from the Great Depression onward, the federal government became involved in the development of electrical power distribution and water power facilities. In the 1930s, the federal Rural Electrification Administration brought electric service to the more remote single dwellings in Montana. The U.S. Army Corps of Engineers and other federal reclamation projects have built some of the state's largest dams. As a Depression Era public works project, Fort Peck Dam was fully operational by 1943. Fort Peck Dam is the fifth largest dam in the U.S. It holds 17.9 million acre-feet of Missouri River water in Fort Peck Lake. Both Hungry Horse Dam and a new Canyon Ferry Dam were government built by 1954. Libby Dam on Lake Koocanusa (a combination of the words Kootenai, Canada, and the USA) was built in 1973. It holds 5.8 million acre-feet of water. Hungry Horse Dam on the South Fork of the Flathead River is the 10th highest dam in the United States.

In 1902, Big Timber's power supply was disrupted by a touring 3-ton circus elephant whose sitz bath blocked up the 3-mile ditch from the Boulder River used for power generation.

Dennis R. Washington (1934–)

Founder of Washington Corporation in Missoula and the Boise-based Washington Group International, Inc., this Montana industrialist has been on the Forbes magazine list of the 400 richest Americans since 1989. He ranked 103rd in 1996 and 124th in 2004, with an estimated wealth of $1.8 billion. In 2004, Forbes magazine also listed Washington as the 310th richest person in the world.

In 1995, Washington was a recipient of the Horatio Alger

MONTANA HISTORICAL SOCIETY

Award, which is given to ten distinguished Americans who have overcome adversity to achieve success. He was bedridden with polio at age eight. Having recovered from the disease, he worked heavy construction as a young adult and, and at age 23, managed the largest highway construction project in the state for his uncle, Bud King, of King-McLaughlin Construction. In 1964, with a $30,000 loan, he started his own highway construction business, Washington Construction Company, and became the largest contractor in Montana. His Washington Corporation bought the Anaconda Company copper mine in Butte and other holdings from Atlantic Richfield in 1986, which now operates as Montana Resources.

Washington Corporation bought Burlington Northern Railroad's southern Montana system in 1988 and revitalized it as Montana Rail Link. He also reopened the Livingston Rebuild Center, a facility that repairs locomotives and railroad cars from all over the country. Another Montana venture, Envirocon, specializes in environmental cleanup. In 1992, his Washington Contractors Group acquired a near monopoly on the towing business in the Port of Vancouver, B.C. and later bought other Canadian tugboat companies and shipping lines.

Dennis and Phyllis Washington have homes in Missoula, California, and at an island lodge, complete with golf course, off the coast of British Columbia. He and his wife support many charitable causes in Montana. The Washington-Grizzly football stadium was so-named in honor of his contributions to The University of Montana. Dennis Washington celebrated his 70th birthday at a number of venues, and his big bash in Missoula in July 2004 included many of America's rich and famous.

The Demise of Montana's Largest Corporation

For nearly 90 years, the Montana Power Company provided cheap, reliable electricity for the people of Montana, employed thousands of people, and delivered reliable dividends to its stockholders. Montanans had some of the lowest electricity bills in the country, as the rates were regulated by the state, in exchange for Montana Power Company's monopoly. However, in the late 1990's, following federal and state deregulation of the power industry, the Montana Power Company begin to withdraw from the utility business. In 1999, MPC sold hydroelectric dams and its share of power plants to Pennsylvania Power and Light (PPL Montana) and in 2000, its coal business was sold to Westmoreland Coal Co. By 2002, NorthWestern Corp. had purchased MPC's transmission and distribution systems for electricity and natural gas, and MPC officially became Touch America, a company proposing to make it big in the expanding world of telecommunications. Touch America had begun as a small telecommunications subsidiary of Montana Power. With nearly $3 billion dollars from the sale of Montana Power's assets, Touch America hoped to lay a 26,000-mile fiber optic network that would carry voice video and data transmission across a dozen western states.

The unraveling of Montana's largest corporation did not work out well for Montana in general. Deregulation caused electricity prices to shoot through the roof and PPL Montana could sell Montana's once cheap electricity out of state to the highest bidder. Sky rocketing electricity prices in Montana caused refineries, lumber mills, and the last working copper mine in Butte to suspend operations. Touch America failed to make it in the over-expanded fiber optic cable business and its stock plummeted, causing further layoffs of its Montana employees. In June 2003, Touch America filed for bankruptcy.

Utilities

Today, various public and private utilities provide the state with electrical and natural gas service. Private utilities include PPL Montana; NorthWestern Energy; and Montana-Dakota Utilities, which provides electrical power and natural gas to eastern Montana. PPL Montana, a subsidiary of PPL Corporation, provides about 60 percent of the electricity used in Montana. It operates eleven former Montana Power Company hydroelectric stations along the Clark Fork, Flathead, Madison rivers and Rosebud Creek and generates power at two coal-fired plants—the Colstrip facility and the

Elouise C. Cobell (1946-)

Elouise Cobell, a member of the Blackfeet Indian Tribe, helped launch the first Indian-owned financial institution in the United States, the Blackfeet National Bank in Browning. She now serves on the boards of the Native American Bank Corp. and First Interstate Bancsystem. Elouise also served for thirteen years as the Treasurer for the Blackfeet Indian Nation in Montana. In 1996, she filed a class action lawsuit against the federal government for the mismanagement of over $13 billion in Individual Indian Trust Funds.

MICHAEL GALLACHER

Elouise Cobell graduated from the Great Falls Business College and attended Montana State University where she recently received an Honorary Doctorate Degree. In addition to operating a working ranch with her husband, she is active in local agriculture and environmental issues. Ms. Cobell received the 2002 International Women's Award for Women Who Make a Difference and is a recipient of the 1997 "Genius Grant" from the John D. and Catherine T. MacArthur Foundation's Fellowship Program. She was appointed to the Montana Board of Investments in 2005.

J. E. Corette facility near Billings. PPL Montana employs about 500 people. The four generating units at Colstrip are operated by a variety of companies, including PPL Montana, AVISTA Corporation, NorthWestern Energy, PacifiCorp, Portland General Electric Company, and Puget Sound Energy.

Consumer-operated cooperatives provide power to nearly 300,000 rural and small-town residences in the state. Twenty-six rural electrical co-ops, twenty-four from Montana and two from Idaho, serve all 56 counties and maintain 50,000 miles of cooperative power lines in Montana.

Railroads

Railroads were, and still are, vital in the development of mining, agriculture, tourism, and other commerce in Montana. Farmers and ranchers needed the railroads to enable them to reach their markets—and still do. Mining corporations utilized the railroads to transport heavy equipment to their operations in Montana, to move their ore to smelters, and to export metal products to the world.

John D. Ryan (1864–1933)

MONTANA HISTORICAL SOCIETY

John D. Ryan was the most important person in the history of Montana's power industry. In 1912, Ryan formed the Montana Power Company from the merger of forty-four regional electric companies. At that time, he was head of the gigantic Anaconda Copper Company and a director of the Milwaukee Railroad. He envisioned selling power to both the copper industry and the Milwaukee, which had plans to electrify its rail lines across Montana. The Montana Power Company soon controlled most of Montana's hydroelectric power and secured the rights to additional power sites. John D. Ryan was president of both the ever-expanding new power company and the Anaconda Copper Mining Company. The Montana Power Company was not technically part of the Anaconda Company. However, through Ryan's leadership both companies began a very profitable and interdependent relationship. Montanans usually referred to both as "The Company." Hand in hand, these two industries ruled Montana's economic and political history through almost all the twentieth century.

Thomas C. Power (1839–1923)

MONTANA HISTORICAL SOCIETY

Born in Dubuque, Iowa, Power rode up the Missouri to Fort Benton on a riverboat in 1867 with a shipment of dry goods. He stored the goods in a large tent, which was loaned to him from his soon-to-be rival, I. G. Baker. By the following year, Power and his brother John had entered the freighting business, transshipping goods from Fort Benton by wagons and teams of draft animals. Power invested his fortune in scores of businesses. Evidence suggests he founded or had interest in almost one hundred firms, most of them involved with cattle, sheep, mining, and freight. He formed several stagecoach lines and was a founding partner of the Judith Cattle Company in the late 1870s. He moved to Helena in 1878, where he had established a store and where he would enter politics. In 1889, he lost the new state's first election for governor by a slim margin but was chosen by Republicans for a seat in the U.S. Senate later that year.

The Utah and Northern, a branch of the Union Pacific Railroad, came north from Ogden, Utah, to the site of Dillon in 1880, and marched on to the promising mining town of Butte by December of 1881. In September of 1883, the Northern Pacific celebrated the connection of its east-west, transcontinental route with a "golden spike" ceremony near Gold Creek (between present-day Garrison and Drummond).

In 1887, James J. Hill made railroad history when his crew of 9,000 men finished the 550-mile line of the St. Paul, Minneapolis, & Manitoba Railroad from Minot, North Dakota, to Great Falls in less than eight months. Helena's Col. Charles Broadwater completed Hill's Montana Central line from Great Falls to Butte, via Helena, in 1889. This hard-won route provided Hill and the copper kings with a direct shipping route to the Great Lakes.

That same year, Hill and his associates consolidated their holdings to form the Great Northern Railway Company. This company expanded westward from Havre over Marias Pass through Columbia Falls and Kalispell and into Idaho. It reached Seattle in 1893. The well-managed Great Northern Railway Company not only survived the nationwide depression of 1893-94, but Hill and associates acquired controlling shares of the troubled Northern Pacific. The Great Northern and Northern Pacific were known as the "Hill Lines," and Hill was crowned the "Empire Builder."

The Chicago, Burlington & Quincy Railroad reached the Montana site of Huntley in 1894, with an agreement to use Northern Pacific track into Billings. In 1901 Hill and the other owners of Great Northern and Northern Pacific purchased control of the Burlington, which had a direct connection to Chicago. In 1969 these holdings became the Burlington Northern. The Chicago, Milwaukee, St. Paul and Pacific Railroad, "the Milwaukee Road," completed a line through central Montana and along the Clark Fork River to Seattle in 1909. This railroad was the last main line construction in Montana but made history as the first long-distance electrified rail span in America.

During the 1980s, almost 1,400 miles of track were abandoned in Montana, yet the volume of freight shipped by rail has remained relatively steady. Today, there remain 3,344 train route miles in Montana, for the seven freight railroads and four passenger and tour railways that operate within and through here. Forty eight percent of freight traffic in Montana is just passing through from one state to another. Forty-seven percent originates in Montana, bound for another state, while only four percent that originates in another state is destined for Montana. From 1978 to 1999, there was a 58 percent increase in freight carried within Montana. By far the largest carrier, Burlington Northern Santa Fe, moved 370,533 carloads of freight, weighing 39 million tons in 1999. Over 90 percent of Montana's agricultural products are shipped out of state by rail.

Three passenger and tour railways operate in Montana. Amtrak, along the; the BNSF's northern route through Montana from Wolf Point, around Glacier National Park and on to Sandpoint Idaho; the Charlie Russell Chew-Choo, and the Alder Gulch Shortline (Virginia City tour train). In October 1979, Amtrak discontinued its east-west service across southern Montana, from Glendive, through Billings, Butte, and Missoula, thus cutting rail passenger service in half. Several legislative and public efforts have not been successful, as yet, in restoring some level of service through this population area, with its strong tourism potential.

Source: R. L. Banks & Associates. 2000 Montana State Rail Plan Update, submitted December 2000 to the Montana Department of Transportation.

Freight Railroads

Class I

more than $259.4 million in annual gross operating revenues

Burlington Northern and Santa Fe Railway Company (BNSF)
235 Main Street, Havre, MT 59501
265-0416
Burlington Northern and Santa Fe Railway Company merged in 1996 to form the second largest rail company in the U.S. The new railroad system spans the western two-thirds of the United States, from Pacific Northwest ports to the Great Lakes and from two Canadian provinces (Manitoba and British Columbia) to the Gulf of Mexico. It operates 2,135 miles of track in Montana, about 66 percent of Montana's rail system. Two of its twenty-two operating divisions are located in the state—the Montana Division, based in Havre, and the Yellowstone Division, based in Glendive. Coal, wheat and other farm products, lumber, stone, clay, ore, container freight, automotive goods, and general merchandise are the main commodities that it carries. Approximately thirty-five trains move across the northern line in a day; about twenty across the southern route.

Union Pacific (UP)
1400 Douglas
Omaha, NE 68179
(402) 271-5777

Josephine "Chicago Joe" Hensley (1844-1899)

She was born in Ireland as Mary Welch and immigrated to the United States at the age of 14. She worked in Chicago's red-light district in her twenties, during the Civil War. She moved to Helena near the end of the war. On the western frontier in the late 1800s, prostitution was the most common mode of employment for women outside the home. Hensley rose to the top of this business class with a shrewd sense for buying real estate and an excellent record of repaying loans and mortgages.

MONTANA HISTORICAL SOCIETY

By 1880, Hensley had become known as "Chicago Joe" and controlled most of Helena's prostitution district. She acquired unimproved lots, a farm, a warehouse, small saloons (or "hurdy-gurdies"), and the Coliseum, a theater where prostitutes plied their trade in the curtained boxes. When legal, moral, and political pressures threatened to close down her Red Star Saloon, she upgraded the venue to a vaudeville house with great success. The same pressures, however, changed the economic face of prostitution during the 1880s and Chicago Joe met with financial ruin in the 1890s. She died in her Helena home of pneumonia. Her death and those of the other Helena madams who held the purse strings of the city's prostitution business opened the way for men to take control of the business.

William Andrews Clark (1839-1925)

A native of Pennsylvania and a former schoolteacher, Clark came to Bannack in 1863 with other gold seekers but moved on to Deer Lodge and became a banker. He invested in several mines in nearby "Butte City"; by 1885, he owned at least a part of forty-six mines, most producing silver or copper. The Clark-Daly feud that went down in history as "the War of the Copper Kings" boils down to petty jealousy. It is believed to have begun with a remark by Clark that slighted Daly. The conflict escalated when Clark set his sights on a seat in the U.S.

MONTANA HISTORICAL SOCIETY

Senate. He won the nomination for territorial delegate but failed to be elected for the seat by the Montana Legislature. When he tried again in 1899, he won election to the Senate but was never seated due to accusations, raised by Daly, that Clark bribed his way to victory. After Daly's death in 1900, Clark finally won election and served in the Senate from 1901–1907.

This railroad operates 125.8 miles of track from Butte south through Dillon into the state of Idaho, and accounts for 3.7 percent of the rail in the state. It provides access to the Pacific Northwest, the Southwest, and California. The primary products it carries are grain, talc, metallic ores, stone, lumber, wood, and farm products.

Class II

$20.8 million to $259.4 million in annual gross revenues

Montana Rail Link (MRL)

101 International Way

Missoula, MT 59808

523-1500

MRL extends from Huntley, Montana, to Sandpoint, Idaho, to serve southwest Montana. It operates 812 miles in Montana, 24 percent of the rail system in the state. Grain, petroleum, coal, lumber, farm products, and wood products are the main goods it carries.

Class III

less than $20.8 million in annual gross revenues. These lines deliver loaded rail cars to the Class I and II railroads:

Montana Western Railway (MWRR)

700 Railroad Avenue Butte, MT 59701

782-1249

This line was created in 1986 from a section of BN line between Montana Rail Link at Garrison and the Union Pacific and RARUS railroads at Silver Bow. It has 58.1 miles of track. This is considered essentially a "bridge" carrier, which is a railroad that primarily handles traffic between two other railroads. MWRR's largest on-line customer is Louisiana Pacific at Deer Lodge. It also carries talc, fertilizer, lumber, grain, and other commodities to and from the Port of Montana in Butte.

Rarus (RARW)

300 West Commercial, P.O. Box 1070

Anaconda, MT 59711-1070

563-7121

This is a segment of the old Butte, Anaconda and Pacific Railroad that was donated to the State of Montana in 1985 by ARCO, which operated the Butte copper mines. This short line was formed and leased from the state in 1985 and operates 25.29 miles or 0.8 percent of the Montana rail, between Butte and Anaconda. It transports copper concentrate from Montana Resources and slag from Anaconda to Silver Bow for interchange with the UP or MWRR.

Central Montana Rail (CMR)

P.O. Box 868

Denton, MT 59430-0868

567-2223

CMR operates 87 miles of track out of the Lewistown area. This line was formed in 1984 from a branch that was abandoned by the Burlington Northern Railroad, obtained by the state, and turned over to a nonprofit corporation to manage in order to preserve service on this short line. Its main products are grain and fertilizer.

Dakota, Missouri Valley and Western Railroad (DMVW)

1131 South 22nd Street

Bismarck, ND 58504

(701) 223-9282

With headquarters in Bismarck, North Dakota, this railroad leases miles of rail line from Whitetail to the border in the northeast corner of the state. It carries area wheat bound for the West Coast and durum wheat bound for eastern mills. It primarily ships wheat from Montana to North Dakota.

The Gambling Industry

Gambling, legal or otherwise, has been a part of Montana as long as people have gathered here. Indian culture has a long history of taking pleasure in games of chance. The arrival of non-Indian culture into Montana included many new forms of gambling, like cards, dice, and lotteries. For example, the Chinese who emigrated to Butte in the heyday of mining, introduced Butte, Montana, and the nation, to the game of keno. The Montana Territorial Constitution in 1889, made all forms of gambling illegal, but the declaration did little to discourage almost 100 years of various forms of illegal gambling, some underground and some right out in the open. Slot machines and "pull tab" games were a common site in the state's saloons and few questioned the weekly bingo games in the church basements across Montana.

Over the years, various law enforcement authorities tried periodically to "crack down" on the many forms of gambling, usually with short-lived success. The 1972 Montana Constitution allowed the legislature to determine which forms of gambling might be legal, and by 1986, the state had an official lottery and video gaming machines were legalized.

Amounts Wagered on Gambling Activities

Fiscal Year	1994	2000	2001	2002	2003	2004
Live Horse Racing**	$4.8	$2.3	$2.1	$1.8	$1.8	$2.2
Simulcast Racing***	4.2	8.2	6.5	7.8	9.5	7.5
Commercial Live Keno	5.5	3.5	3.8	3.8	3.5	2.9
Commercial Live Bingo	8.5	6.8	6.7	6.3	5.2	4.8
Lottery	37.5	29.9	30.4	33.6	34.7	36.7
Video Gambling Machines+	444.5	658.0	672.9	708.1	750.1	814.2
Total Amounts Wagered	$505.0	$708.7	$722.4	$761.4	$804.8	$868.3

* Dollar amounts given in millions.
** Live season covers May through September of each year.
*** Covers winter season (October-May).
+ Figures for amounts wagered on video gaming machines include credits played and may not translate to cash paid out to players.
Source: Montana Department of Justice, Gambling Control Division. Biennial Report (FY 2003 and 2004). Gaming Advisory Council, Helena, November 2004.

Today, the Montana Department of Justice Gambling Control Division regulates the following types of legal gambling in Montana: Video gambling machines offering poker, keno, or bingo; ten live card games, including bridge, cribbage, hearts, panguingue, pinochle, pitch, poker, rummy, solo, and whist (blackjack is prohibited); live bingo; live keno; sports pools; sports tab games; raffles; casino nights; Calcutta pools; shake-a-day; shaking for drinks or music; fantasy sports pools; fishing derbies; and wagering on natural occurrences (betting on predictions of the date and time of an event related to weather or climate).

On an ever increasing level, the gaming industry, especially video gaming machines, plays a significant part in Montana's economy. In 1988, there were about 8,000 video gaming machines in Montana, producing about $70 million in income reported for tax purposes and earning the state $10.5 million in tax revenue. By 2004, $333 million in income on some 20,510 machines was reported, with a tax revenue of $50 million. Most of the $50 million in video gambling revenue goes into the state general fund, to be disbursed back to municipalities according to a negotiated formula.

In 2004, live horse racing was held at six sites in the state from mid-May to the third week in September. There were eleven establishments around the state offering simulcast horse racing. The Montana Board of Horse Racing, under the Montana Department of Livestock, regulates both live horse racing and simulcast horse racing. The Montana Lottery, discussed in the next section, is under the jurisdiction of the Montana Lottery Commission.

Gaming taxes have been growing in the 4-7 percent range annually since the mid-1990s. The last time the issue was studied (1998), gaming revenues were providing an average of 14.4 percent of city government revenues. Some cities were realizing as much as 24 percent of their budgets from gaming machine taxes.

The Montana Lottery

The 1985 Legislature approved a referendum to allow for a state lottery. The referendum was sent to the voters on the November 1986 ballot and won approval by almost 70 percent of the voters. The first scratch or "instant win" game was "Pot of Gold," which went on sale in June 1987. These games are changed frequently; a new game is introduced every six weeks. Tickets are sold at 550 locations around the state. Drawings for the lotteries are held on Wednesday and Saturday nights.

Montana Cash was established in May 1991 with a minimum jackpot of $20,000. The odds of winning some prize are 1 in 43. Fifteen jackpot tickets worth from $30,000 to $170,000 were sold in fiscal year 2004.

Powerball is a 28-state drawing partnership that was established in April of 1992, with nine prize levels. The odds are about 1 in 121 million for winning the jackpot and 1 in 36 of winning some prize. Four tickets worth $100,000 were sold in Montana in fiscal year 2004.

Wild Card 2 is a lottery among the states of Montana, Idaho, North Dakota, and South Dakota. The tickets are two plays for a minimum of $1. The guaranteed jackpot is $1,000,000, which grows each time the jackpot is not won. The over-all odds of winning a prize are 1 in 6. Wild Card 2 prizes paid out $1.2 million in fiscal year 2004.

Hot Lotto is a multi-state, multi-level lottery among the states of Montana, Iowa, Minnesota, New Hampshire, North Dakota, South Dakota, West Virginia, and the District of Columbia. Overall odds of winning a prize are 1 in 6. One jackpot ticket worth $3.68 million was sold in Montana in October 2003.

In 2004, the Montana Lottery introduced Qwik Tix, an innovation in the lottery industry. Unlike typical lotto games, Qwik Tix are instant–win games but players can get their Qwik Tix tickets printed at the lotto terminal like they do lotto tickets. However, upon playing any of the four games, they know immediately if their tickets are winners or not. Also unlike typical lotto games, each ticket is $2 and provides two plays. In the first year of play, $62,000 in $500 prizes were awarded instantly.

The Montana Lottery has an assortment of Scratch Tickets, or instant win games, ranging in ticket prices from $1 to $5. Top prizes vary but can be as much as $12,000.

The Montana Lottery is governed by a five-member commission, appointed by the governor, that sets policies and oversees the operation of the lottery. The governor also appoints the lottery director, who supervises the security, operations, and marketing divisions. The lottery is administratively affiliated with the state Department of Commerce.

For news on winning numbers, how to play, and other lottery information, see **www.montanalottery.com.**

Where the Lottery Money Goes

Until July 1, 1995, most of the net lottery revenue (90.9 percent of net) was dedicated to the State Equalization Aid Account, a source of funding for Montana's elementary and secondary public schools. To that date, the lottery transferred over $49 million to Montana's public schools. In July 1991, the Board of Crime Control began receiving a small portion of the lottery's net revenue to help fund the operation of juvenile detention centers. The Board of Crime Control received a total of more than $2.6 million.

Beginning July 1, 1995, the Legislature redirected all lottery net revenue to the State General Fund. Since the Montana Lottery sold its first ticket in 1987, it has transferred more than $113 million to the state of Montana.

The Number of Montana Problem Gamblers

The 1997 legislature commissioned a study of various aspects of gambling in Montana. Findings indicated that about 23,400, or 3.6 percent, of Montanans were probable problem or pathological gamblers. Of those, about 10,400 were pathological gamblers, as determined by various indicators. Roughly 13,000 were in a less severe classification of problem gambler. Montana problem gambler rates rose between a similar 1992 study and the 1998 study. However, Montana's overall problem gambling rate was similar to other states, as was the increase. Problem and pathological gamblers wager a disproportionate amount of the total wagered: 37 percent of video gambling machine revenue, 29 percent of live keno, 18 percent of scratch tickets, 17 percent of other lottery games, and 13 percent of live bingo.

Further Reading and Resources

Malone, Michael P. Montana: *A Contemporary Profile.* Helena: *Montana Magazine,* 1996.

Montana Business Quarterly. Published by the Bureau of Business and Economic Research, The University of Montana, Missoula. http://www.bber.umt.edu/.

Montana Department of Commerce, Census and Economic Information Center http://ceic
.commerce.state.mt.us/publications.

Montana Department of Labor & Industry, Research & Analysis Bureau http://www
.ourfactsyourfuture.org/.

Montana Labor Employment and Labor Force Trends. Published periodically by the Montana
Department of Labor and Industry.

CHAPTER ELEVEN

Sports

$\mathcal{M}$any Montanans are active sports participants. Some compete in amateur leagues. Others either make an appearance or lend a hand at their favorite seasonal or annual events. The list of activities is long. It includes sports and events you'd find almost anywhere in the U.S.—fast- and slow-pitch softball, baseball, basketball, football, soccer, volleyball, tennis, golf, track and field, sailing, ice and roller hockey, bowling, fishing, motocross races, figure skating, equestrian events, swimming, distance running, and road and mountain biking races. Other popular pastimes and passions pursued here include archery, target and clay shooting, snowmobiling, downhill and cross-country skiing, snowboarding, and dog sledding.

A cowgirl leans her horse into a turn during a barrel race.
G. WUNDERWALD/
TRAVEL MONTANA

A hearty few of us are called to participate in rodeo; thousands more of us choose to stay glued to our seats in the stands, content to just watch.

Almost each week during the school year, tens of thousands of fans gather in gymnasiums and beside playing fields to cheer on Montana's high school and college teams. Even the smallest high schools field teams for basketball, football, volleyball, and track and field. At the other end of the scale, The University of Montana's Washington-Grizzly

Dave McNally
(1942-2002)

He pitched his way from Billings, where he played brilliantly in American Legion ball, to the World Series, where, playing for the Baltimore Orioles in the 1970 series, he hit a grand slam in the third game. The homer helped the Orioles beat Cincinnati, 9-3, and they went on to win the series, 4-1. McNally helped the team to 184 victories during the 1960s and 1970s. From 1968 to 1971, he recorded at least twenty wins each year. His 21-5 record in 1971 amounted to a .808 winning percentage, the best in the American League that season. McNally was selected to the American League All-Star team in 1969, 1970, and 1972. *Sports Illustrated* magazine named him Montana's Athlete of the Century (1900–2000). He retired to Billings, where he owned a car dealership.

MONTANA HISTORICAL SOCIETY

Alice Greenough
Orr (1902-1995)

She was born in Red Lodge into the Greenough family of rodeo performers and was one of five siblings known as the Riding Greenoughs. Later in her life, the rodeo world crowned her "Queen of the Bronc Riders." She won four world saddle bronc championships in the 1930s and 1940s, had tea with the Queen of England, and rubbed shoulders with the likes of Will Rogers and Ernest Hemingway. She thrilled crowds around the world as a performer in Wild West shows and international rodeos. In 1975, she was the first inductee into the Cowgirl Hall of Fame and was named to the National Cowboy Hall of Fame in 1983. She died in her sleep in Tucson, Arizona, at the age of 93.

RING OF GOLD

Montana's first professional sports event, a boxing match between Virginia City saloonkeeper Con Orem and local miner Hugh O'Neil, was staged outdoors on January 2, 1865. The fight ended in a draw, with each fighter receiving $1,000 and various sacks of gold tossed into the ring by enthusiastic fans.

When the rich Kevin-Sunburst oil field was discovered in 1922, the nearby town of Shelby came alive like boomtowns of the gold mining era. Money was plentiful and some local entrepreneurs concocted a plan to host a world boxing championship in their "wild and woolly" town. On July 5, 1923, world heavyweight champion Jack Dempsey held his title against Tommy Gibbons in a 15 round decision. Local promoters and bankers "lost their shirts" when the expected crowd of 40,000 failed to travel to such a remote location.

Stadium can accommodate more than 23,500 fans and all the noise they can muster. On any given "Game Day" an equivalent to 2.5 percent of the Montana population gathers to cheer on the Montana Grizzly football team.

Montana has a rich history of professional baseball and today the "national pastime" continues to draw fans to ball parks in Billings, Great Falls, Missoula, and Helena to watch minor league games. A junior hockey league operating teams in three Montana cities has developed a similar following. These leagues may not be the majors but Montanans get the chance to watch contests in comparably intimate settings and pay a fraction of the cost to sit in a cavernous big league stadium.

Under the Big Sky, competitors strive for big wins and grand achievements. In the following pages, we recognize some of their feats.

High School Sports

The Teams and Their Mascots

You learned your ABCs a long time ago, but do you know your As, double As, Bs, and Cs? Montana's thirteen largest high schools compete as Class AA schools. There are 25 Class A high school teams, 43 Class B teams (from 57 high schools), and 45 Class C teams (from 59 schools). In Class B and Class

Girls basketball team at Old Fort Shaw Indian School, ca. 1902–1903. PHOTOGRAPH BY G.M. EDDIES, GREAT FALLS, MT. COURTESY OF MONTANA HISTORICAL SOCIETY, HELENA

SHOOT, MINNIE, SHOOT!

"Shoot, Minnie, Shoot!" was the cheer that often went up to encourage a scoring basketball shot by Minnie Burton, star Shoshone forward on the famous champion girls' basketball team from the Fort Shaw Government Indian Boarding School located in the Sun River Valley, north of Great Falls. Between 1892 and 1910, Indian children of many Montana and Idaho tribes were sent to live and learn at this once-grand frontier military fort. In 1902, the school's superintendent, Fred Campbell, began training a group of young women in the fledging sport of "basket ball." The team began traveling the state, where they defeated all high school and college challengers to become the undisputed state champions. In 1904, they were invited to the St. Louis World's Fair, where they lived at the Model Indian School on the grounds of the fair and defeated all the teams who came to challenge their virtuosity on the basketball court. They were declared the "Champions of the 1904 World's Fair," and came back to Fort Shaw with a silver trophy. The young women had also impressed the large fair-going crowds with their abilities in dance, music, and recitation. Many of the women went on to become teachers or nurses.

C, some high schools join together to sponsor an area wide football team. Ten teams from nonpublic high schools also compete with the public school teams.

You also may know your big league Dolphins from your Marlins and your Pirates from your Buccaneers, but Montana's high school team names or mascots cover a wide variety of species and icons. There are:

9 Bulldogs Bainville, Butte, Choteau, Ekalaka, Hardin, Moore, St. Ignatius, Townsend, and Whitefish high schools

7 Panthers Alberton, Belgrade, Boulder, Park City, Peerless, Roundup, and Saco.

9 Eagles Blue Sky, Fairfield, Lewistown, Manhattan Christian, Missoula, Big Sky, Mount Ellis Academy, Northern Cheyenne, Sidney, and Two Eagle River.

Understandably, we have Warriors (at Brockton, Fairview, Savage, and Heart Butte), Cowboys (at Conrad, Culbertson, and Miles City), Wranglers (at Geyser and Rosebud), Rustlers (at Great Falls C. M. Russell), Horsemen (at Plains), Sheepherders (at Big Timber), 7 Broncs at Billings Senior, Brady, Frenchtown, Hamilton, Melstone, Sheridan, and Willow Creek, Mustangs (at Ennis, Jordan, the Montana School for the Deaf and Blind, Malta, and Shepherd), and Colts (at Colstrip). The Longhorns (at Fort Benton and Wibaux) are accompanied by the Dogies (at Forsyth).

Harder to figure in this landlocked state are our eight Pirates (at Broadview, Hysham, Polson, Power, Reedpoint, Roy, Valier, and Victor) and the Vikings (at Big Fork, Charlo, and Opheim). We have no Vigilantes.

We do have Bats (in our Belfry), Penguins (at Whitewater), Copperheads (in the former copper smelting center of Anaconda), Locomotives (at Laurel, a railroad town), Engineers (at Harlowton, another railroad town), Miners (at the former coal mining town, Centerville), Wardens (at Deer Lodge, the town with the state prison), and Refiners (in Sunburst, where oil was discovered in 1923).

We have Red Devils (at Glendive, Noxon, and Huntley Project), Blue Devils (at Corvallis), Red Raiders (at Winifred), Bluejays (at Outlook), Blue Ponies (at Havre), Bluehawks (at Thompson Falls), Blackhawks (at Seeley-Swan), Golden Bears (at Billings West), Golden Eagles (at Fergus), and Yellowjackets (at Stevensville).

We run the gamut from Demons (at Ryegate) to Royals (at Richey). Perhaps the team that has garnered us the most attention though, is the Sugarbeeters of Chinook High School, recognized nationwide on Late Night with David Letterman for having the strangest mascot that could be found.

College Sports

"Brawl of the Wild," the rivalry between the Montana State University Bobcats and The University of Montana Grizzlies began in 1897 and is one of the

Grizzlies vs. Bobcats—Men's Football

	The Grizzlies	The Bobcats
Victories in Rivalry	65	35
Overall Record	457-442-23	395-425-33
Big Sky Conference Championships	13 (1969, 70, 82, 93, 95, 96, 98, 99, 2000, 2001, 2002*, 2003*, 2004*)	7 (1964, 66, 77, 72, 76, 79, 84, 2002*, 2003*)
Longest Field Goal	57 Chris Snyder, 2002	59 Yards Jan Stenerud, 1965
Most Yards Gained in a Game	574 Dave Dickenson, 1995	298 Don Hass, 1967
Most Yards Rushing in a Career	4, 040 Yohance Humphery, 1998-01	3,646 Ryan Johnson, 2002
Most Yards Passing in a Career	11,080 Dave Dickenson, 1992-95	8,152 Kelly Bradley, 1983-86
Best Completion % in a Career	67.3% Dave Dickenson	57.770 Kelly Bradley

Grizzlies vs. Bobcats—Men's Basketball

	The Grizzlies	The Bobcats
Victories in Rivalry	142	127
Overall Record	1,955-2,001	1,253-1,051
Big Sky Conference Championships	5 (1974-75, 77-78, 90-91, 91-92, 94-95*)	4 (1963-64, 66-67,** 86-87, 95-96, 2000-2001)
Most Points Scored in a Career	2,017 Larry Krystkowiak, 1982-86	2,034 Larry Chaney, 1956-60
Highest Scoring Average (per game in a season)	24.2 Michael Ray Richardson, 1977-78	23.7 Larry Chaney, 1959-60
Most Rebounds in a Career	1,105 Larry Krystkowiak, 1982-86	1,011 Jack Gillespie, 1966-69
Highest Rebound Average	15.1 Ray Howard, 1954-55	15.3 Jack Gillespie, 1968-69
Most Assists in a Career	435 Travis DeCuire 1991-94	608 Scott Hatler, 1992-96

Shared title with Weber State. ** *Shared title with Gonzaga.*

Grizzlies vs. Bobcats—Women's Basketball

	The Grizzlies	the Bobcats
Victories in Rivalry	68	12
Overall Record	634-221	412-380
Most Points Scored in a Career	2,172 Shannon Cate, 1988-92	1,176 Kathleen McLaughlin, 1982-86
Highest Scoring Average	23.3 Shannon Cate, 1991-92	18.4 Lynne Andrew, 1987-88
Most Rebounds in a Career	886 Ann Lake, 1990-94	990 Kathleen McLaughlin, 1982-86
Highest Rebound Average	9.8 Jill Greenfield, 1979-81	9.4 Kathleen McLaughlin, 1985-86
Most Assists in a Career	701 Brooklyn Lorenzen, 2000-2004	443 Vicki Heebner, 1980-84

TODD GOODRICH, UNIVERSITY OF MONTANA

Monte, the Grizzly Mascot Scores Twice

The wickedly funny UM grizzly bear mascot, Monte, has twice been named the national collegiate "Capital One" and ESPN mascot of the year—in 2002 and 2004. Barry Anderson, the UM theater student from Terry who revealed his long-held secret identity as the award-winning Monte, is now Benny the Bull, the official mascot for the NBA's Chicago Bulls. Barry helped to train two other UM students to take over his lovable antics at UM games and charitable events.

TODD GOODRICH, UNIVERSITY OF MONTANA

Larry Krystkowiak (1965–)

In 2004, one of The University of Montana's basketball greats returned to his alma mater as the new head men's hoop coach. He holds the record as Montana's all-time leading scorer and rebounder with 2,017 points and 1,105 rebounds. Those accomplishments rank him as third in Big Sky conference history. He set another Montana record by scoring 709 points in the 1985-86 season. During his four-year career from 1983-86 he was honored three times as the Big Sky Conference Most Valuable Player.

Krystkowiak played 11 years of professional basketball, including his rookie season with the San Antonio Spurs. He then played five seasons (1988-92) as the starting forward for the Milwaukee Bucks. After a season with the Utah Jazz, he moved on to starting jobs with the Orlando Magic, the Chicago Bulls, and the Los Angeles Lakers. In recent years, he held a number of coaching jobs before coming back home to the town where he first earned accolades as the Montana "AA" state MVP as a senior at Big Sky High School.

Dave Dickenson (1973–)

This Great Falls native has been called the greatest quarterback in University of Montana history. He broke thirteen school records and led the Grizzlies to the 1995 NCAA Division I-AA football championship over the Marshall University Thundering Herd, from West Virginia.

Dickenson was given the 1995 Walter Peyton Award for being the best player in Division I-AA. He was also named to the Associated Press I-AA All-American first team that year. His accomplishments include the following single season records:

most touchdowns rushing	14, 1993	most total offense	4,209, 1995
most pass completions	309, 1995	most points scored	84, 1993
most passing yards	4,176, 1995	most touchdown passes	38, 1995
highest completion rate 68.2%, 1994		most passing yards per game	379.6, 1995

Other records set by Dickenson include longest touchdown pass (90 yards, 1995), highest career completion percentage (67.3 percent), and most career passing yards (11,080).

Dickenson is now a member of the British Columbia Lions, where he was selected as the Western Division's Most Outstanding Player in 2003. A number of Montana newspapers selected Dave as the Montana athlete of the century (1900–2000).

Ryan Johnson (1980–)

Ryan was a Montana State University record-setting running back. He was named the 2001 Verizon Academic All-American of the year for football in Division 1-A and I-AA. He was also selected as a 2003 NCAA Top VIII Award, an honor awarded to the top eight student athletes in the NCAA. The award is based on academic and athletic achievement as well as community involvement. Ryan holds the MSU Bobcat career rushing record with 3,646 yards and single-season record with 1,537. For that and other accomplishments, Ryan was a finalist for the Walter Payton Trophy, the award given to the top player in Division I-AA football and named third-team All-America by Football Gazette. Named the Roland Renne award winner as the outstanding senior at Montana State.

Robin Selvig (1952-)

One of eight children born into an Outlook family, Selvig went to The University of Montana and played freshman and varsity basketball. In his senior year, 1973-74, he was the top defensive player on the team, an all-conference guard, and won the Grizzly Cup, recognizing him as the top athlete on campus. He has far surpassed his achievements as a player, though, in the years since he stepped off the court to coach the Lady Grizzly basketball team.

TODD GOODRICH

He took over the team in 1978 and by the following season, the team went 19-10 and earned a berth in its first national tournament.

As the coach with the most wins in Big Sky Conference history, Selvig has directed his alma mater to 19 national tournament appearances, 18 conference championships, and 15 postseason conference championships. In twenty-six of Selvig's UM coaching years, twenty-four have been winning seasons. When Montana defeated Portland State in March 2004, Selvig reached 600 career wins, doing so in just 772 games.

In 2005, the Montana Lady Griz basketball program was ranked the seventh best all-time women's programs in the nation by Street and Smith's magazine.

longest-running competitions west of the Mississippi. In the early years, the annual football game was held in Butte, with enthusiastic fans arriving from Missoula and Bozeman in railroad cars for the statewide party of the year. Today, the annual football and basketball contests between the two teams still draw sellout crowds of students and alumni from across the state.

Generally, the sports accomplishments of the smaller public and private colleges in Montana are overshadowed by MSU and UM team events, but it was a different story in 1931 when the Mount St. Charles (now Helena's Carroll College) football team became the Montana State Collegiate Football Champs.

Baseball

Baseball has been a popular sport here since the earliest days of the Montana Territory. Historical records tell us that games took place in the mining camps of Virginia City in 1866 and Helena in 1867. In 1892, a statewide

THOSE CHAMPIONSHIP SEASONS

The 1931 Mount St. Charles (now Carroll College) football team was named Montana State Collegiate Football Champs when, against all odds, they shut out all six opponents from much larger schools and one private team of miners and professional players. Carroll College's Fighting Saints won three National Association of Intercollegiate Athletics football championships in a row in 2002, 2003 and 2004. The Helena is the only Catholic college in the United States to win the NAIA title, much less triple the win in the small college division.

In the 1995 championship season, University of Montana coach Don Read was named Division I-AA coach of the year by American Football Quarterly. Read is the winningest coach in UM history with a 75-35 record. He retired in April 1996. Since 1993, the UM Grizzlies have been the Division I-AA Big Sky Conference Football Champions seven times and the conference Co-Champions in 2002, 2003, and 2004. The Griz have reached the NCAA Division I-AA finals five times in the past decade and won the national championship in 1995 and 2001.

The 1995 University of Montana-Boise State football game at Washington-Grizzly Stadium had the highest attendance (18,505) of any Montana sporting event since the Jack Dempsey-Tommy Gibbons fight in Shelby in 1923. Since the completion of additional seating, the stadium regularly accommodates over 25,000 on a Game Day.

The Montana State University Bobcats won the NCAA Division I-AA championship in 1984 against Louisiana Tech (19-6) in Charleston, South Carolina.

league was established. In 1948, a Great Falls team, the Selectrics, and the Billings Mustangs joined the fledgling Pioneer Baseball League, with teams from Utah, Idaho, and Canada. The Helena Phillies and the Butte Copper Kings joined in 1978. The Copper Kings' last season in Butte was 2000. The Missoula Timberjacks played in the Pioneer League from 1956 to 1960. The Missoula Osprey joined the league in 1999.

Montana's Pioneer League teams, which play at the Rookie Advanced level, have sent many talented players on to major league teams over the years. George Brett, who played for Billings in 1971, went on to the Kansas City Royals, where he won the American League's batting championship in 1976 (.333) and 1990 (.329). George Bell, who played in Helena in 1978, was the American League's Most Valuable Player in 1987 as a member of the Toronto Blue Jays. And of course, there is country music star, Charlie Pride, who played briefly for the Pioneer League Missoula Timberjacks in 1960. He moved his young family to Helena, worked at the East Helena Smelter, and

LEGION LEGENDS

Between 1950–1971, the Billings American Legion Post 4 baseball team won twenty-four state championships and played in four American Legion World Series playoffs.

Dave McNally pitched in the 1960 American Legion World Series game, but the team lost 9-3. When Billings began to host two American Legion teams, the Billings Royals won four state championships since 1974 and the Billings Scarlets have won eight state championships since 1976.

Jeff Ballard, who also played American Legion baseball in Billings and earned a scholarship to Stanford University, set three baseball records while playing for the St. Louis Cardinals. He also pitched for the Orioles and Pirates from 1987 to 1994.

In 2004, Billings Scarlets pitcher Nolan Gallagher was named the American Legion Baseball National Player of the Year.

Teams of the 2004 Pioneer League

Team	Box office numbers
Helena Brewers	495-0500
Great Falls White Sox	452-5311
Billings Mustangs	252-1241
Missoula Osprey	543-3300
Ogden Raptors	(801) 393-2400
Idaho Falls Chukars	(208) 522-8363
Casper Rockies	(307) 232-1111
Orem Owlz	(801) 377-2255

played ball for the smelter team, right before he got his first big break as a promising country western singer. In the late 1950s, Charlie had played professional baseball with Memphis teams in the Negro American League.

Hockey

Three Montana hockey teams are in the North American Hockey League, West Division. The Billings Bulls, Bozeman Ice Dogs, and Helena Bighorns (formerly Ice Pirates) are joined by the Bismarck Bobcats and Fargo-Moorhead Jets. The NAHL is a Junior A hockey league affiliated with USA Hockey, with the primary goal of enhancing the development of players under the age of 20. Prior to 2003, the Montana teams, including the Great Falls Americans, were part of the American Frontier Hockey League, which merged with the North American Hockey League. Montana's "Junior "A" teams are well-supported in their communities, with some of the highest attendance among Junior "A" clubs in the nation. In addition, Montana teams have represented their league at the National Junior "A" Championship Tournament the past six years.

Team	Box office numbers
Helena Bighorns	451-2817
Billings Bulls	256-2451/256-2422
Bozeman Ice Dogs	585-1415

The Montana Amateur Hockey Association (MAHA) sanctions programs in Billings, Butte, Bozeman, Glasgow, Great Falls, Havre, Helena, Miles City, Missoula, Helena, and Whitefish. Each of these cities offer hockey for boys and girls according to age, much like little league baseball.

World-class Athletes & Olympians from Montana

Jim Barrier went from Kalispell in 1960 to the Winter Olympics at Squaw Valley, California, to race in the slalom and giant slalom competitions. He now lives in Southern California.

David Berkoff, a Missoula lawyer with a law degree from UM law school, was a member of the US swimming team at the 1988 Seoul Olympics where he earned a silver medal in the 100-meter back stroke ad a gold as a member of the world-record Medley relay. In the 1992 Barcelona Olympics, won a bronze medal in the men's 100-meter backstroke and a gold medal in the men's 400-meter relay.

Terry Casey of Great Falls was named captain of the 1968 U.S. Olympic hockey team but was killed in an automobile accident in July 1967 before he was to report to training. The Great Falls Hockey Association named an annual tournament in his honor. The Terry Casey Memorial Cup tournament is held in late winter.

Lindsay Burns of Big Timber won a silver medal in the women's lightweight double sculls at the 1996 Summer Olympic Games in Atlanta.

Gene Davis, a four-time state wrestling champion from Missoula County High School, won four national freestyle championships and a bronze medal in the 1976 Montreal Olympics. He also coached the U.S. team in the 1988 Olympics in Seoul, South Korea.

Scott Davis of Great Falls represented the U.S. at the World Figure Skating

Championships from 1992 to 1995. He finished seventh in 1994 and 1995 and sixth in 1993. Davis took fourth place at the 1996 U.S. Figure Skating Championships, just out of contention to skate in the world championships. He was a U.S. champion in 1993 and 1994, and a runner-up in 1995. At the 1996 Centennial on Ice, a world-class competition in St. Petersburg, Russia, celebrating the 100th anniversary of the world championships, he placed fourth, the top effort by an American.

Todd Foster of Great Falls represented the U.S. as a boxer at the 1988 Olympics in Seoul, South Korea. He won the National Golden Gloves championship and the National Olympic Festival championship in 1987. When he turned professional in 1989, he was a contender for the World Lightweight Boxing Championship. By September 1996, Foster had recorded thirty-six victories in forty professional fights, including thirty-two knockouts.

Alex Lowe of Bozeman lost his life in October 1999, in an avalanche on Shishapangma in Tibet, the world's 14th highest mountain. That year, Lowe had been acclaimed in an *Outside* magazine cover story as the best mountain climber in the world. Lowe's climbing career spanned 25 years, including challenging mountains in six countries, Antarctica, and two assents on Mount Everest. He was a member of The North Face clothing company's "Dream Team," which included the best-known climbers in the country.

John Misha Petkevich, a Great Falls native, won both the National and the North American Figure Skating Championships in 1971. He finished fifth at the 1972 Sapporo Olympics. After a successful career in skating, he earned a doctorate in cellular biology from Oxford as a Rhodes Scholar. He then went on to study music, becoming a composer in residence at Harvard in 1980. He is author of The Skater's Handbook, a respected reference work for figure skaters.

David Silk, a Butte native, won the 5,000-meter World Cup Speed Skating Championship in 1986 and competed on the 1984 U.S. Olympic speed skating team.

Lones Wigger, Jr., a native of Carter, has won more Olympic medals than any other Montanan. At the 1964 Tokyo Olympics, he won a gold medal in the three-position small-bore shooting event and a silver in the standing small-bore event. At Munich in 1972, he won the gold medal in the three-position free-rifle event. In addition, he has won over 80 national championships, held 29 world records and 32 U.S. records, and has managed U.S. Olympic shooting teams.

B. J. Worth of Whitefish is a three-time World Parachuting Champion, and has earned ten World Records in parachuting. He received the World Air Sports Federation Bronze Medal for organizing the skydiving exhibition for the Opening Ceremonies of the 1988 Seoul Olympics. Since 1975, he has been a movie stunt skydiver for movies and television, including a number of "James Bond" movies. He, Blaine Wright of Whitefish, and Gary Sanders of Missoula were among 357 skydivers on the World Team that established a world record for the largest freefall formation above Takhli, Thailand in 2004.

Dr. A. R. "Bud" Little of Helena is a member of the United States Ski Association's Ski Hall of Fame. Little was a top administrator of ski events for the USSA and the International Ski Federation. He officiated at events, managed the U.S. ski alpine team (1960–68), and attended the Winter Olympics in 1960, '64, '68, '72, '76, and '80.

Rogers Little, Dr. Little's son, Helena, was a two-time NCAA All-American who made the U.S. World Cup downhill ski team for the 1972 Winter Olympics in Sapporo, Japan.

N O T A B L E

ARLAN BERGOUST

Eric Bergoust (1969–)

Eric Bergoust won the freestyle aerial skiing gold medal at the 1998 Olympics in Nagano, Japan. "Air Bergy" went on to win the World Championship in 1999. His career includes seven World Cup victories and two U.S. championships. Eric grew up on ranch near Stevensville, where he practiced flips off the roof of his house onto mattresses and learned to soar off hand-made jumps at Lost Trail Ski Area. He was considered the favorite at the 2002 Olympics at Salt Lake City but was not able collect a medal. Despite that disappointment, Bergoust's contributions to this exciting sport have won him the title of the "best freestyle aerial skier who ever lived."

M O N T A N A N S

Rodeo and Horse Events

Rodeo is truly the definitive Western sport. Some say it is the roughest of all sports. The rodeo events you see today derived from the activities of the day-to-day work of early cowboys, who held informal contests and wagers to see who was the best hand.

Early public exhibitions of bronc riding, steer roping and wrestling, and bull riding grew in popularity as an athletic event and spectator sport across the West. Here in Montana, they qualify strongly as both. Each summer, in addition to over fifty sanctioned National Rodeo Association and Pro National Rodeo Association events across the state, there are dozens of ranch rodeos, old-timer rodeos, youth rodeos, and team roping contests. Most participants are no longer working cowboys, but are trained professional athletes who get their start on the high school and college rodeo circuit.

In addition to the exhilarating and often dangerous contests between man and beast, rodeos often feature novelty events like greased pig chases, children's "Little Britches" events, and wild-cow milking contests. Rodeo clowns are not there for laughs alone, but to help keep cowboys, cowgirls, and the rodeo stock out of danger.

N O T A B L E

Dan Mortensen (1968–)

BOB TRENT

Dan Mortensen, world champion saddle bronc rider, grew up in Billings, won his sixth world title in 2003, tying the record set by the legendary cowboy Casey Tibbs. He won saddle bronc titles in 1993, 1994, 1995, 1997, and 1998. In order to qualify as the World's Top Cowboy of 1997, Dan had to compete successfully in more than one event so he also rode bulls in several rodeos. He was the first Montana cowboy to win the all-around championship since the legendary Benny Reynolds in 1961. Dan became the first roughstock cowboy in PRCA history to go over the $2 million mark in career earnings in the fall of 2003. A larger-than-life bronze of Dan Mortensen, by well-known artist Ron Raines of Park City, Montana, graces the grounds of MetraPark in Billings.

M O N T A N A N S

Rodeo Events

Augusta American Legion Rodeo, Augusta, June, 562-3477. *Largest one-day rodeo, annual for nearly seventy years.*

Beaverhead County Fair and Jaycee Rodeo, Dillon, Labor Day weekend, 683-5511.

Big Timber Rodeo, Big Timber, May, 932-5311.

Broadwater County Fair & Rodeo, Townsend, August 1–4, 266-9242.

Bronco Days Rodeo, Baker, March, 862-2537. *Events take place in an indoor arena.*

C. M. Russell Stampede Rodeo, Stanford, July 12-21, 566-2422. *Famous for its wild cow milking contest.*

Central Montana Horseshow Fair and Rodeo, Lewistown, July, 538-8841.

Days of '85 Rodeo, Ekalaka, mid-August, 775-8714.

Drummond PRCA Rodeo, Drummond, July 7, 288-3479.

East Helena Rodeo, East Helena, July, 227-6677. *Four days of rodeo, annually for more than 45 years.*

Ennis Rodeo, Ennis, July, 682-4700. *NRA sanctioned event.*

Harlowton Rodeo, Harlowton, July 4th, 632-4694.

Home of Champions Rodeo, Red Lodge, July 4th weekend, 888-261-0625. *Celebrating more than 75 years of rodeos.*

Jefferson County Rodeo, Boulder, late August, 225-4385.

Last Chance Stampede and Rodeo, Helena, third week of July, 442-1098.

Lincoln Rodeo and Parade, Lincoln, July 5-6, 362-4231.

Livingston Roundup Rodeo, July 4th weekend, 222-3199. *More than 80 years of the largest pro rodeo in Montana*

Mineral County Fair and Rodeo, Superior, August 1–4, 822-3096.

BATTLE CRY

One of the world's most recognizable slogans during World War I, the battle cry "Powder River, let 'er buck!" originated in the Powder River country of southeastern Montana. The yell greets a bronc rider as he comes out of the chute on some fishtailing horseflesh. You can still hear this challenging, sometimes admiring, term from the stands at rodeos and other Montana sporting events today.

Montana Women Honored at the National Cowgirl Hall of Fame & Western Heritage Center, Fort Worth, Texas

Name/Hometown	Year Inducted	Accomplishments
Alice Greenough Orr, Red Lodge (1902-1995)	1975	Very first cowgirl honoree Four-time World Champion Bronc Rider
Margie Greenough Hensen, Red Lodge (1908-)	1978	Another of the "Riding Greenoughs" Bronc rider in King's Wild West Show of 1930s
Fanny Sperry Steele, Helena (1887-1983)	1978	1912 World Champion Bronc Rider
Lynn "Jonnie" Jonckowski, Billings (1956-)	1991	1986 and 1988 World Champion Bull Rider
Evelyn Cameron	2001	frontier photographer

Miles City Bucking Horse Sale. Miles City, May, 232-7700. *The world-famous Miles City Bucking Horse Sale is mainly a bucking horse auction, but features bareback and saddle bronc riding for top prizes, along with bull riding, wild horse races, street dances, and a parade.*

Montana State University Spring Rodeo, Bozeman, March, 994-2403.

Montana Pro Rodeo Circuit Association Finals, mid-January, Great Falls, 727-8900. *Big purse event, with Montana's best PRCA pro rodeo contestants and stock. Includes Miss Rodeo Montana Pageant.*

Montana High School Rodeo, May, Three Forks, 285-4677.

NILE Stock Show, Pro Rodeo, Horse Extravaganza, Billings Metrapark, October, 256-2495. *Big money at stake and one of the last chances to qualify for the National Rodeo Finals in Las Vegas; features three commercial trade shows.*

Northern Rodeo Association Finals, Billings Metrapark, February 252-1122. *One of the largest regional rodeo associations in the United States. Event features top ten money winners in eight rodeo events.*

Harlowton Rodeo, Harlowton, July 4th weekend, 632-4694. *NRA sanctioned.*

Roundup Rodeo, Livingston, July 4th weekend, 222-3199.

Three Forks Rodeo and Parade, Three Forks, July, 285-3198.

Tobacco Valley Rodeo, Eureka, July 27-28, 296-3477.

State High School Rodeo Finals, Helena, June, 800-7HELENA (743-5362). *Puts the best 350 young participants against top stock for an action-packed rodeo.*

Vigilante Rodeo, Butte, July, 494-3002.

Montanans Honored at the National Cowgirl Hall of Rodeo Fame in Oklahoma City, Oklahoma

Name/Hometown	Year Inducted	Accomplishments
Bob Askin (1900-1973)	1978	1925 World Champion Bronc Rider
Turk Greenough, Red Lodge (1905-1995)	1983	1928 World Champion Saddle Bronc Rider
Margie Greenough Hensen, Red Lodge (1908-)	1983	Bronc rider in the wild west shows in the 1930s
Alice Greenough Orr, Red Lodge (1902-1995)	1983	Four-time World Champion Bronc Rider in the 1920s and 1930s
Bill Linderman, Red Lodge (1920-1965)	1955	1945, 1950, 1953 All-Around Cowboy, 1945 and 1950 World Champion Saddle Bronc Rider; 1950 World Steer Wrestling Champion
Bud Linderman, Red Lodge (1922-1961)	1987	1945 World Champion Bareback Rider
Benny Reynolds, Melrose (1936-)	1961	1961 All-Around Cowboy
Raddy Ryan, Ismay (1896-1980)	1978	1924 World Champion Bronc Rider
Fanny Sperry Steele, Helena (1887-1983)	1975	1912 World Champion Bronc Rider
Oral Sumwalt, Missoula (1903-1962)	1963	Bronc rider and rodeo stock producer who died in the arena
C. R. Boucher (1931- 2001)	2001	1964 Steer Wrestling Champion
Cy Taillon (1907-1980)	1986	MT Rodeo Announcer
Bill Smith (1941-)	2000	1969, 1971 & 1973 World Saddle Bronc Riding Champion
Dan Mortensen (1968-)	1997	1997 World All-Around Champion; 1993,1994,1995, 1997, and 1998 World Saddle Bronc Riding Champion
Pete Logan (1917-1993)	1991	Rodeo Announcer

White Sulphur Springs Ranch Rodeo, 4th of July 2, 547-2209. *Roping, branding, pasture doctoring, hide race, bareback rescue race, barrel racing, and ribbon roping*

Wolf Point Wild Horse Stampede, Wolf Point, July, 653-2012. *With more than 85 years of rodeo fun, this is Montana's oldest pro rodeo.*

Horse Racing

Copper King Marcus Daly started his Bitterroot Stock Farm in 1887 near Hamilton because he believed that a mountain climate would produce horses with a greater lung capacity and superiority over horses from England or the East Coast. After building barns for six hundred harness and thoroughbred horses, Daly erected the brick show barn called Tammany Castle to house his famous stallions. He also built a three-quarter-mile covered track and a cov-

Tammany

In the 1890s, Marcus Daly's horse farm turned out big winners on racetracks around the country—Bathhampton, Scottish Chieftain, Montana, and others. Only one, however, was memorialized on the floor of the Montana Hotel in Anaconda. It was there, after Tammany's death, that Daly would remove his

MONTANA HISTORICAL SOCIETY

hat and pause in reverence over a replica of his beloved horse's head, carved from colored hardwoods and inlaid on the floor.

Tammany won many of the great races of the day, becoming a legend among the people of Butte and Anaconda. The horse's stable at the farm was said to contain carpeted floors, brass rails, and modern plumbing. After he'd won the Withers, Lorillard, Lawrence Realization, and the Jerome stakes, Tammany was beaten by Charade in the Tidal Stakes at Coney Island. His trainer devoted the next month to eliminating whatever weakness caused the defeat. In their next meeting, four weeks after the Coney Island race, Tammany beat Charade by three lengths.

The horse died after that season.

ered straightaway three-eighths of a mile long. The farm's tree-lined lanes made it the equine showplace of the West, and Daly's copper-and-green racing colors became familiar around the world as the winnings poured in from his most famous horses: Tammany, Ogden, Hamburg, Sysonby, and Prodigal. These horses and the direct offspring of their bloodlines resulted in four Kentucky Derby winners: Regret, Paul Jones, Zev, and Flying Ebony.

Another Montana horse, Spokane, owned by Noah D. Armstrong of the Alaska Ranch at Twin Bridges, won the 1889 Kentucky Derby at 6-to-1 odds.

Today, Montana's racing season begins in May in Miles City. There is horse racing at the Flathead County Fair and Race Meet in August, at MetraPark in Billings throughout the summer, and at Missoula's Western Montana Fair in mid-August.

Sled Dog Racing

The men and women who compete in the intrepid sport of sled dog racing must be tough and shrewd to end up the winners, but they are, in truth, only the "coaches" in this event. The true athletes are the sled dogs.

Sports Illustrated's Top Ten Montana Athletes of the Century

Dave McNally, Billings, four-time, 20-game winner with the Baltimore orioles.

Dan Mortensen, Billings, rodeo all-around world champion in 1997; saddle bronc winner in 1993, 1994, 1995, 1997, 1998 (and 2003).

Lones Wigger, Jr., Great Falls, 1972 Olympic gold medal in 300-meter three-position rifle shooting. Olympic silver medal in free-rifle prone, 1964.

Pat Donovan, Helena, four-time Pro Bowl offensive lineman for the Dallas Cowboys from 1975 to 1983.

Corey Widmer, Bozeman, two-time All-Big sky conference at Montana State University and starting linebacker for Giants.

Jeff Ballard, Billings, set three baseball records while playing for the St. Louis Cardinals; pitched for the Orioles and Pirates from 1987 to 1994.

Ryan Leaf, Great Falls, led CM. Russell High to state championship; took Washington State to the 1997 Rose Bowl; second pick by San Diego Chargers in 1998 (last played for Dallas Cowboys, 2001).

Greg Rice, Missoula, Sullivan Ward winner in 1940; two-time NCAA two-mile champion for Notre Dame.

Gene Davis, Missoula, NCAA 137-pound wrestling champion in 1966; Olympic bronze medallist in 1976.

Scott Davis, Great Falls, 1993 and 1994 U.S. figure skating championship.

Source: Sports Illustrated, December 27, 1999.

Among the most successful Montana mushers are Doug Swingley and his brother Greg, of Simms; Dave Armstrong of Helena, who started mushing dog teams in 1936 and was still racing in 1995 at the age of 74; and Terry Adkins of Sand Coulee, who has run Alaska's Iditarod Trail Sled Dog Race twenty times, more than any other Montanan.

Race to the Sky

From 1986 to 1996, a 500-mile test of endurance, speed, and survival teamed men or women ("mushers") with dogs and pitted them against other such teams in the February cold along the west slope of Montana's Continental Divide. The Race to the Sky was the longest sled dog race in the lower 48 states.

In 1997, organizers shortened the race to 350 miles to eliminate parts of the course where the snow cover was often insufficient, consolidating the 500-miler with a shorter race that has shared the bill since 1991.

THE U.S. HIGH ALTITUDE SPORTS CENTER, BUTTE

The speed skating oval at the sports center (elevation: 5,528 feet) is the highest in the world and, among skaters who compete there, is known for its fast surface. The High Altitude Center has produced some of the fastest outdoor times in the world. Besides having hosted a world championship, American and World Cup meets, and national and  Canadian-American championships, it is a national training site for the U.S. speed skating team.

In keeping with Butte's history of a varied ethnic mix, flags of many nations fly during world competitions at the oval. In March 1997, the center hosted the World Junior Speed Skating Championships. Skaters came from the Netherlands, Russia, Italy, Sweden, Japan, South Korea, and other countries for the event.

For Montana residents who don't feel ready to skate in international competitions, the oval is occasionally open to the public. The Montana Amateur Speed Skating Association supervises a "Learn to Skate" program at the center. Call 494-3406 for information.

Further Reading

"The Bobcats and the Grizzlies," *The New Yorker,* December 13, 1969, pp. 152–67.

Kearney, Pat. *The Divide War: Montana's Golden Treasure.* Butte, Mont.: Skyhigh Communications, 2004. Recounts in great detail the century-plus Bobcat-Grizzly football competition, fondly called the Brawl of the Wild.

"Montana Town's Boys Are Its Last Gasp of Hope," *Washington Post,* November 17, 2004, p. A01. Article about six-man football in small-town Montana high schools.

CHAPTER TWELVE

Travel

*D*ecades ago the following words were etched onto large wooden signs posted at the state line on all arterial highways leading into Montana:

You are coming into the heart of the West where you will cut a lot of mighty interesting old time trails. Just turn your fancy loose to range the coulees, gulches, prairie and mountains and if your imagination isn't hobbled you can people them with picturesque phantoms of the past.

Virgelle Ferry across the Missouri River.
CRAIG AND LIZ LARCUM

We have marked and explained many of the most interesting historical and scenic spots along the highways. Watch for them and help us to preserve these markers.

Here is wishing you lots of luck and many pleasant miles in Montana.

More recently, these border greetings have been replaced with modern signs whose message of welcome is far briefer. Montana roads and roadsides have changed a lot since visitors read the old signs. Automobiles are faster. Travelers seem in more of a hurry to get someplace. The wood of the signs may have turned to splinters and dust by now, but its message is still very true and scores of wooden signs still point out interesting parts of the state's history, geography, and people. Despite all that has changed, Montana still offers incomparable opportunities to the traveler, the explorer, the student of regional and local histories.

On the following pages, we offer "roadside assistance," help in getting around. Make plans. Pack provisions. Hit the road.

Our Roadways

Many parts of Montana's modern highway system follow the travel routes used by Indian tribes and the migrating bison. These trails were most often the best way through the lowest mountain passes and around rivers and other obstacles, while providing good trailside food sources and protection from the elements. The Mullan Road, a military supply route, was the first engineered road in the Northwest. With the completion of the Mullan Road from Fort Walla Walla in the Oregon Territory to Fort Benton in 1862, Montana was linked to a natural highway from the Pacific to the Atlantic.

Today, Montana's highway system consists of over 11,000 miles of interstate highways, primary highways, and secondary roads, and 2,100 bridges. In total, there are about 70,000 miles of public highways and roads in Montana—that's more than all the interstate miles in the entire United States.

Road Type	Miles
• National highway system	3,874
• Primary highways	2,815
• Secondary roads	4,709
• State highways	1,174

Montana's portion of the nation's interstate system was completed in 1988. The system includes Interstate I-90, I-94, and I-15. It cost over $1.2 billion to create Montana's interstates, a sum paid mainly by the federal government with a $100 million investment by the state.

On Our Plates

There were only six thousand "horseless carriages" in Montana in 1913, the year the state first required registration of motor vehicles. The rationale for the system of assigning each county a prefix number for license plates remains one of Montana's unsolved mysteries.

The legislated numbering system was purportedly based on a county census in 1930—though politics and local pride also may have played a role in number assignments. Silver Bow County, home of Butte and the most powerful politicians of the day, was awarded the number "1," even though sev-

Montana Mileage Chart

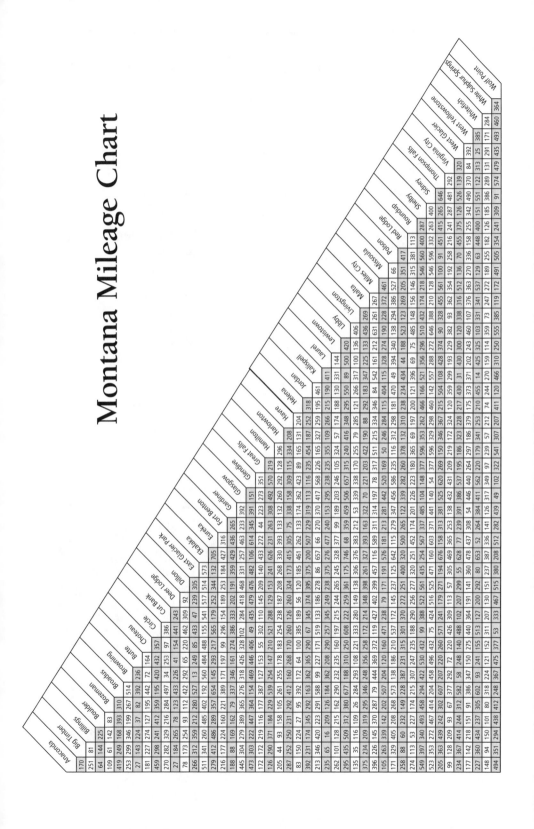

THE MONTANA LICENSE PLATE NUMBERING SYSTEM

1. Silver Bow
2. Cascade
3. Yellowstone
4. Missoula
5. Lewis and Clark
6. Gallatin
7. Flathead
8. Fergus
9. Powder River
10. Carbon
11. Phillips
12. Hill
13. Ravalli
14. Custer
15. Lake
16. Dawson
17. Roosevelt
18. Beaverhead
19. Chouteau
20. Valley
21. Toole
22. Big Horn
23. Musselshell
24. Blaine
25. Madison
26. Pondera
27. Richland
28. Powell

29. Rosebud
30. Deer Lodge
31. Teton
32. Stillwater
33. Treasure
34. Sheridan
35. Sanders
36. Judith Basin
37. Daniels
38. Glacier
39. Fallon
40. Sweet Grass
41. McCone
42. Carter

43. Broadwater
44. Wheatland
45. Prairie
46. Granite
47. Meagher
48. Liberty
49. Park
50. Garfield
51. Jefferson
52. Wibaux
53. Golden Valley
54. Mineral
55. Petroleum
56. Lincoln

eral other counties had larger populations. Every once in a while, the Montana Legislature considers matching the prevailing county population to a new numbering system, but rarely does such a radical idea get off the ground.

As part of the World War II war effort, in 1944 Montana's steel license plates were replaced by a tag made of soybean composition fiberboard. It wasn't unusual to have the corners nibbled off by the family goat.

Montana's license plates are still made at the men's prison at Deer Lodge.

Specialty License Plates

Over eighty non-profit organizations, government entities, and schools work with the State of Montana to sell specialty license plates as a fund-raising mechanism. The most popular of the specialty license plates are those featuring explorers Meriwether Lewis and William Clark. In 2004, Montanans paid the extra $20 each to purchase 27,000 specialty plates. www.doj.state.mt.us/driving/plates/organizationsspecialtyplates.asp

Gateway Visitor Information Centers

At gateways to Montana, these community-based visitor centers are open seven days a week, May through September, except for the Hardin and West Yellowstone centers, which are open year-round. In addition to these centers, there are locally operated information centers in other communities throughout the state.

Broadus Visitor Information Center
119 East Wilson
436-2992

Culbertson Visitor Information Center
1 mile east of Culbertson on U.S. Highway 2
787-6320

Dillon Visitor Information Center
125 S. Montana
683-5511

Hardin Visitor Information Center
Exit 497, Interstate 90
665-1671

Shelby Visitor Information Cener
100 2nd Avenue South
434-9151

St. Regis Visitors Information Center
Exit 33 on Interstate 90
649-2290

West Yellowstone Visitors Information Center
20 Yellowstone Avenue
646-7701

Wilbaux Visitor Information Center
500 North 2nd Avenue East
796-2253

Travel Information

Travel Montana is the state's travel and tour information bureau. It can provide maps and vacation guides to help plan a trip in any season. Call Travel Montana at (800) 847-4868 or 841-2870. The bureau's TDD number is 444-2978. Montana visitor information is available http://travel montana.state.mt.us or www.visitmt.com.

Scenic and Back Country Byways

The USDA Forest Service and the Bureau of Land Management have given official designation to certain routes in the U.S., both paved and unpaved, for their outstanding scenic value. Five routes in Montana have earned the Scenic Byway designation from the USDA Forest Service. An equal number carry the BLM's title of Back Country Byway.

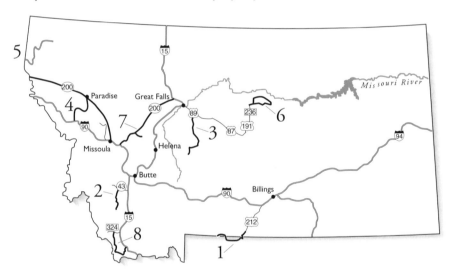

Scenic Byways

1. Beartooth Highway

60 miles over alpine plateaus, past lakes, magnificent vistas, and access points to rugged expanses of wilderness. Open Memorial Day to about mid-October, depending on the weather. The road, U.S. Highway 212, climbs to 10,946 feet and features 10 campgrounds and travel services at Cooke City and Red Lodge. Be prepared for high altitude and variable weather.

2. Pioneer Mountains Scenic Byway

27 miles bisecting the East and West Pioneer Mountains southwest of Butte;

paved and gravel. Open from mid-May through Thanksgiving; then closed by winter snows between Elkhorn Hot Springs and Sheep Creek. Features of the route include six campgrounds, limited travel services in Wise River, lodging at Elkhorn Hot Springs, hiking, trout streams, and rockhounding.

3. Kings Hill Scenic Byway
70 miles of road among the coulees, buttes, ranchland, limestone canyons and wooded peaks of the Little Belt Mountains in central Montana; route follows U.S. Highway 89; four campgrounds in Lewis and Clark National Forest. Attractions include historic mines and buildings, fishing, hunting, camping, and downhill and cross-country skiing. Traveler services in White Sulphur Springs.

4. St. Regis-Paradise Scenic Byway
30 miles along a winding section of the Clark Fork River within the Lolo National Forest; paved highway is an alternate route off Interstate 90 to reach Flathead Lake, Glacier National Park, or the National Bison Range off U.S. Highway 200. Motorists will enjoy spectacular scenery, bountiful wildlife, and a variety of recreational opportunities. Herds of mountain sheep are often found grazing along the road.

5. Lake Koocanusa Scenic Byway
67 miles, via State Highway 37, follow the Kootenai River and Lake Koocanusa within the Kootenai National Forest. The route also connects the towns of Libby and Eureka. The byway also includes a side loop (Forest Development Road No. 228) around the west side of Lake Koocanusa and is open in all but the winter season.

6. Missouri Breaks
73 miles of central Montana landscape that contains farms, ranches, and badlands; part of this byway follows the southern rim of the Upper Missouri River. Spur roads lead to the river bottom, overlooks, the north edge of the Missouri Breaks, and more.

7. Garnet
12 miles of winter recreation byway near Missoula, maintained for snowmobiling and ski touring; leads to the well-preserved ghost town of Garnet. Deer, elk, and moose winter in the area.

8. Big Sheep Creek

50 miles of gravel road through remote country near the Idaho border; generally passable from May through October, but some stretches can pose problems during wet periods. Attractions include camping, hiking, fishing, and scenic views.

International Border Crossings

Port of	Location	Hours of Season	Operation*
1. Roosville 889-3865	MT 93, north of Eureka	all year	24 hours a day
2. Chief Mountain (403) 653-3317	MT 17, northeast of Glacier National Park	May 20–31 June 1–Labor Day To Sept. 30	9:00AM–6:00PM 7:00AM–10:00PM 9:00AM–6:00PM
3. Piegan 732-5572	MT 89, 16 miles north of Babb	all year	7:00AM–11:00PM
4. Del Bonita 336-2130	Hwy 213, northwest of Cut Bank	Sept 16–May 31 June 1–Labor Day	9:00AM–6:00PM 8:00AM–9:00PM
5. Sweetgrass 335-9610	I-15, north of Shelby	all year	24 hours a day
6. Whitlash 432-5522	northwest of Chester	all year	9:00AM–5:00PM
7. Wild Horse 394-2371	Hwy 232, northwest of Havre	Oct 1–May 14 May 15–Sept 30	8:00AM–5:00PM 8:00AM–9:00PM
8. Willow Creek 398-5512	north of Havre	all year	9:00AM–5:00PM
9. Turner 379-2651	Hwy 241, northeast of Harlem	Sept 16–May 31 June 1–Sept 15	9:00AM–6:00PM 8:00AM–9:00PM
10. Morgan 674-5248	Hwy 242, north of Malta	Sept 16–May 31 June 1–Sept 15	9:00AM–6:00PM 8:00AM–9:00PM
11. Opheim 724-3212	MT 24, north of Glasgow	Sept 16–May 31 June 1–Sept 15	9:00AM–6:00PM 8:00AM–9:00PM
12. Scobey 783-5375	Hwy 13, north of Scobey	Sept 16–May 31 June 1–Sept 15	9:00AM–6:00PM 8:00AM–9:00PM
13. Whitetail 779-3531	Hwy 511, northeast of Scobey	Sept 16–May 31 June 1–Sept 15	9:00AM–6:00PM 8:00AM–9:00PM
14. Raymond 895-2664	Hwy 16, north of Plentywood	all year	24 hours a day

*Note: These seasons and hours of operation were in effect in 2004. Call to be sure they haven't changed.

Ports of Entry

There are fourteen ports of entry on the 454-mile border between Montana and three Canadian provinces, including two on the edges of Glacier

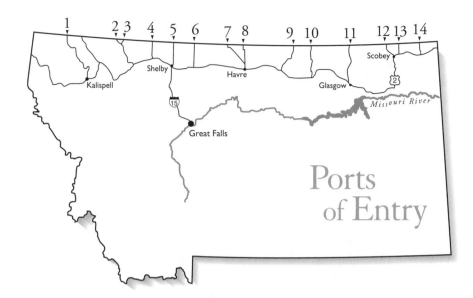

Ports of Entry

National Park that are open during the summer only. The border crossings at Roosville (on U.S. Highway 93 north of Eureka), Sweetgrass (Interstate 15 north of Shelby), and Raymond (Montana 16 north of Plentywood) are open 24 hours a day. U.S. citizens need to show a driver's license or proof of citizenship to cross back and forth over the international border. Citizens of other nations should be prepared to show a passport or the appropriate visas.

The port of entry north of Scobey on Montana 13 became the world's first voice-activated port of entry in 1996. Carefully screened local residents on both sides of the border are able to open the border barrier by punching in an identification number and speaking a predetermined phrase. If the computer recognizes all three—number, voice, and phrase—the barricade opens.

Customs information is available at five airports: Great Falls, 453-0861; Butte, 494-3492; Kalispell, 257-7034; Helena, 495-2145, and Cut Bank, 873-4352.

There are twenty-two highway ports of entry on the Montana borders where highways cross from Wyoming, Idaho, and the Dakotas. There are numerous unnumbered or unpaved local or logging roads that enter the state along these borders.

Ferries 'cross the Missouri

Three ferries cross the Missouri River in north-central Montana. In 2004, new ferries replaced the ones in operation for over 60 years. They are open from various dates from spring through October, depending on river conditions, to vehicles weighing not more than 30,000 pounds. The three ferries together make about 4,000 crossings a year. Call ahead to schedule a ride at times other than listed. The crossings are indicated on the map below.

Carter Ferry   14 miles west of Fort Benton and 20 miles northeast of Great Falls off U.S. Highway 87, then a 5-mile drive on gravel road from Carter to the ferry; 734-5335. Open March–October, Mon.–Sat., 7 A.M.–7 P.M.; Sunday, 9 A.M.–5 P.M. Free. A toll is charged for unscheduled crossings.

Virgelle Ferry 30 miles northeast of Fort Benton off U.S. Highway 87, then 8 miles on gravel road from highway to the ferry; 378-3194. Open May–October, Mon.–Sat., 7 A.M.–7 P.M.; Sun 9 A.M.–5 P.M. Free. A toll is charged for unscheduled crossings.

McClelland-Stafford Ferry At mouth of Missouri River's White Cliff area, 50 miles north of Lewistown; 462-5513. Open April–October, 7 A.M.–7 P.M. Free.

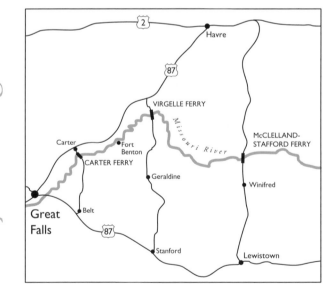

Road Conditions

Due to the wide-ranging and quick-changing weather conditions of the Big Sky, it's always advisable to check on travel conditions before hitting the road. If the wind is picking up or the sky is darkening, pick up the phone before getting behind the wheel.

Statewide	(800) 226-ROAD (7623)
	444-6339, or dial "511"
	cell phone users *ROAD
	(800) 335-7592 (TTY)
Highway patrol emergency	(800) 525-5555
Billings	657-0209
Butte	494-9646
Great Falls	453-1605
Havre	265-1416
Kalispell	751-2037
Lewistown	538-1358
Miles City	233-3638
Missoula	728-8553
Wolf Point	653-1692

Internet access: www.mdt.state.mt.us/travinfo/

Roadside History Lessons

Since 1935, Montanans and tourists have enjoyed reading the state's colorful history on historical markers along the state's highways. These history lessons were the first such markers in the country. The now-famous signs were created by Bob Fletcher, a traffic engineer for the Montana Highway Department. His survey work around the state had brought him into contact with many of the people who participated in or collected stories about Montana's early years. Fletcher's charming, colloquial renditions of Montana history tell much about local landmarks and events across Montana. Unfortunately, many of the markers along the state's main routes had to be removed because of rules governing interstate signboards. However, 170 still remain along roads and at various rest areas, including many to highlight new attractions and Indian history.

Source: Glenda Clay Bradshaw, ed. Montana's Historical Highway Markers. *Helena: Montana Historical Society, revised edition, 1994.*

Montana Speed Limits

Montana earned national attention from December 1995 to May 1999 for not having a specific daytime speed limit to replace the standard 55 or 65 mph when the government lifted speed limit mandates. Even when the federal limits were in place, though, the state had a certain fame for issuing tickets as low as $5 for "the offense of unnecessary waste of a resource." The $5 speeding violation was not recorded on a person's driving record.

Visions of the state's highways turning into the "Montanabahn" did not materialize. Though traffic fatalities climbed to 265 in 1997—the highest number in 15 years—studies showed that most drivers cruised along the interstates at rates under 75 mph. However, on a July day in 1996, a convoy of fifteen cars driven by test drivers for the German automaker Mercedes-Benz was pulled over on Interstate 90 near Park City and ticketed for speeding. The Montana Highway Patrol fined each driver $70 for failing to drive "at a speed no greater than is reasonable and proper under existing conditions," the state's "basic rule" at the time. A newspaper account said the cars were clocked "at a speed in excess of 95 mph."

The 1999 legislature approved a numerical daytime speed limit, which went into effect May 28, 1999. For cars and light trucks traveling interstate highways, the speed limit is 75 mph for both daytime and nighttime. Heavy trucks must limit speed to 65 mph. On the state's two-lane highways, the

NOTABLE

MONTANA HISTORICAL SOCIETY

Robert H. Fletcher (1885–1972)

Born in Iowa, Fletcher traveled all over Montana as a surveyor before going to work for the state Highway Department in Helena. He managed promotional campaigns that urged tourists to visit, then authored the highway markers that cause so many travelers to pause along the roadway and learn some Montana history. He also wrote a historical account of Montana's cattle industry, "From Free Grass to Fences," and poetry. His best-known verse became the basis of the Cole Porter song, "Don't Fence Me In."

MONTANANS

daytime speed limit for cars and light trucks is 65 mph, and the limit for heavy trucks is 60 mph. The speed limit is 65 mph on Interstate 93 in Western Montana, one of the most traveled, yet most dangerous, roadways in the state.

Other Motor Vehicle Laws

- Newcomers to the state must apply for a Montana driver's license within 120 days of residence and must register their motor vehicles immediately upon establishment of residence, acceptance of employment, or placement of children in public school.
- The minimum driving age is 16, or age 15 if the applicant has passed an approved driver's education course.
- Required registration of motor vehicles may be for a 12-month or 24-month period. The owner of a vehicle 11 years old or older may choose to permanently register the vehicle. Fees are based on the age of the vehicle. A copy of registration must be carried in all vehicles.
- All occupants of a vehicle must wear a seatbelt; children under six years of age or weighting less than 60 pounds must wear a child safety restraint.
- Littering upon or near a highway is prohibited. Punishable by fine, imprisonment, or both.
- Driving under the influence (DUI) of alcohol, drugs or both is more than illegal—it can be deadly. The maximum blood-alcohol concentration level for drivers is 0.08; the maximum blood-alcohol level for drivers under 21 years of age is 0.02
- It is unlawful for anyone to operate a motor vehicle (excluding motorcycles) in Montana without a valid policy of liability insurance. Owner must sign a statement stating that they have liability insurance when registering a motor vehicle.

For further information about vehicle registration, contact the County Treasurer in the county of residence or:

Montana Department of Justice
Motor Vehicle Division
303 North Roberts
Helena, MT 59620-1419
444-1773

Montana Department of Justice
Title and Registration Bureau,
Motor Vehicle Division
1032 Buckskin Drive
Deer Lodge, MT 59722
846-6000
www.doj.state.mt.us

The Montana Highway Patrol

In 1933 and 1934, Montana led the nation with a 74 percent increase in highway fatalities. In the year following the creation of the Montana Highway Patrol in 1935, traffic fatalities decreased 25 percent.

In addition to enforcing the highway safety laws of the state, the approximately 200 highway patrol officers enforce state drunken driving laws, assist in drug interdiction, and perform various records management duties.

In 1978, women joined the force for the first time. Since 1935, four Montana Highway Patrol officers have died in the line of duty.

Highway Patrol activity, 2003

violators stopped	93,510
"driving under the influence" arrests	2,312
seat belt citations	14,590
speed, over legal limit	37,113
accidents investigated	10,459
assist public	12,733
Total arrest tickets	80,012

Flying the Big Sky

If you think airfare is expensive, remember that in 1868, Wells, Fargo, and Company charged passengers $120 to ride a stagecoach from Helena to Salt Lake City and $25 to ride from Helena to Virginia City or Fort Benton.

Here are Montana's air carriers, today's fastest transportation providers:

American West	(800) 235-9292, www.americanwest.com
Big Sky Airlines	(800) 237-7788, www.bigskyair.com
Delta and	
The Delta Connection	(800) 221-1212, www.delta.com
Horizon Air	(800) 547-9308, www.horizonair.com
Northwest Airlines	(800) 225-2525, www.nwa.com
SkyWest Airlines	(800) 453-9417, www.skywest.com
United Airlines	(800) 241-6522, www.ual.com

Montana has 118 additional public use airports and over 350 private use airports. Montana has twice the number of private pilots as the national average and nearly five times the number of general aviation aircraft. 1,309,811 passengers deboarded from air carriers at Montana's eight major airports in 2003.

Montana's Commercial Airports

Airport/Location	Carriers
Gallatin Field Airport Bozeman/Belgrade, MT 388-6632	Delta, Horizon, Big Sky Northwest, SkyWest, United
Logan International Airport Billings, MT 59101 657-8495	Horizon, Big Sky, Northwest, SkyWest, United, American West Frontier
Bert Mooney Airport 101 Airport Road Butte, MT 59701 494-3771	Horizon, SkyWest
Great Falls International Airport 2800 Terminal Drive Great Falls, MT 59404 727-3404	Delta, Horizon, Big Sky, Northwest
Helena Regional Airport 2850 Skyway Drive Helena, MT 59601 442-2821	Horizon, Big Sky, Comair SkyWest, Northwest,
Glacier Park International Airport 4170 Highway 2 East Kalispell, MT 59901 257-5994	Delta, Horizon, Northwest, Big Sky, American West
Missoula International Airport 5225 Highway 10 West Missoula, MT 59801 728-4381	Delta, Horizon, United, Northwest, SkyWest, Big Sky, Allegiant Air

Montana's Smaller Airports

Airport/Location	Telephone
Glasgow International Airport	228-4023
Dawson Community Airport/Glendive	359-2054/Mobile 365-5528
Havre City County Airport	265-4671
Lewistown Airport	538-3264
Frank Wiley Field/Miles City	232-1296
Sidney-Richland Airport	482-2415
Wolf Point Airport	653-1740
West Yellowstone Airport*	646-7631/Winter 444-2506

*West Yellowstone provides commericial service on a seasonal basis. This airport is open from June 1 to September 30. The airport is owned by the State of Montana.

Robert R. "Bob" Johnson, (1893–1980)

Bob Johnson has often been called the father of "mountain flying." In 1927, Johnson bought his first open-cockpit airplane and began flying the mountainous areas of Western Montana to spot forest fires for the Forest Service. During the 1930s, he delivered mail and Forest Service supplies to remote locations. In winter, he flew food and supplies to snowbound residents in a plane that landed on skis rather than wheels. In the early 1940s, his Johnson Flying Service trained over 4,000 pilots for the U.S. war effort. Bob is credited with development of special equipment to bombard fires with chemical retardant, to spray pesticides, and to reseed burned over areas. By the 1970s, Johnson Flying Service had a fleet of 37 planes and 10 helicopters. Business had expanded to delivering sportsmen to remote lakes and hunting areas, dropping feed to snowbound cattle, delivering equipment and supplies to mining, oil, and timber operations, evacuating the injured, the transplanting of fish and wild game and the annual big game count for the Montana Department of Fish, Wildlife, and Parks. The 1953 book, *Tall Timber Pilots*, recounts the incredible exploits of Bob Johnson and his brother Dick, who died in 1945, in a plane crash while counting elk in the rugged Teton Mountains of Wyoming. Steve Smith's, *Fly the Biggest Piece Back*, traces the history of Johnson Flying Service.

M O N T A N A N S

On the Bus

Because passenger trains cover little more than the northern tier of the state, Montanans depend on buses to get them to other points.

Greyhound Lines Serves the following cities and towns along Interstate
(800) 231-2222 90: St. Regis, Superior, Alberton, Missoula, Drummond, Deer Lodge, Warm Springs,

"SHEP, ED SHIELDS AND A.V. SCHANCHE

MONTANA HISTORICAL SOCIETY

Shep (?-1942)

Epitome of the faithful dog, Shep was a half-breed collie who had followed the body of his now-unknown sheepherder master to where it was placed on a train at Fort Benton in 1936. From then up to January 1942, Shep lived at the depot and went out to meet every incoming train to see if his master had returned, until the morning that he slipped crossing the tracks and was crushed by the train he had come to meet. A booklet celebrating Shep was sold to Great Northern passengers and helped raise funds for the Montana School for the Deaf and Blind. Shep's story made it into a Ripley's Believe It or Not strip, into a Gold Medal paperback story for children, and into the periodicals *Farm Journal* and *Reader's Digest*.

Butte, Whitehall, Three Forks, Manhattan, Belgrade, Bozeman, Livingston, Big Timber, Columbus, Park City, Laurel, Billings.

Rimrock Trailways
(800) 255-7655
www.rimrocktrail.com

Serves over 60 Montana communities, including Butte, Great Falls, Missoula, Billings, Havre, Whitefish, Big Timber, St. Ignatius, Simms, Belt, Moccasin, Big Sandy, Worden, Custer, Hysham, Forsyth, Miles City, Terry, Glendive, and Wibaux. Also connects to points serve by Greyhound.

Powder River
Trailways
(800) 442-3682

Serves Billings, Laurel, Bridger, and Hardin; also travels south to Cody and Gillette, Wyo., and Denver.

Most cities, including Billings, Butte, Great Falls, Helena, and Missoula, provide mass transit services. Local transportation services can also be found in Fergus, Flathead, Garfield, Liberty, McCone, Powder River, and Valley counties and on the Fort Peck and Blackfeet Indian Reservations.

Call-A-Ride services are available in several communities—mostly small, rural ones. The services do not follow a designated route. Most require passengers to call 24 hours ahead to arrange to be picked up and delivered to the destination of their choice. www.mdt.state.mt.us/transit/tranguide.shtml

Riding the Rails

The National Railroad Passenger Service (AMTRAK) provides east and west passenger service across northern Montana, making stops in Libby, Whitefish, West Glacier, Essex, Browning, Cut Bank, Shelby, Havre, Malta, Glasgow, and Wolf Point. The train services Chicago and Minneapolis/St. Paul to the east; Portland and Seattle to the west. This train, known as the "Empire Builder," has both coach and sleeper accommodations. Most boardings and deboardings occur in Whitefish. AMTRAK also provides delivery services of everything from cut flowers to medical supplies along its route. This service is vital to the northern part of the state, especially in severe weather when other modes of transportation may be halted.

AMTRAK
Washington Union Station
60 Massachusetts Avenue
Washington, D.C. 20022
(800) 872-7245
www.amtrak.com

Further Reading

Alt, David, and Donald W. Hyndman. *Roadside Geology of Montana.* Missoula: Mountain Press Publishing Company, 2003.

Bradshaw, Glenda Clay. *Montana's Historical Highway Markers.* Helena: Montana Historical Society, 1989.

Dougherty, Michael, and Heide Pfeil Dougherty. *The Ultimate Montana Atlas and Travel Encyclopedia,* second edition. Bozeman, Mont.: Ultimate Press, 2002.

Fanselow, Julie. *Traveler's Guide to the Lewis and Clark Trail.* Helena: Falcon Press, 1995.

Federal Writers' Project of the Work Projects Administration. *Montana: A State Guide Book.* New York: Hastings House, 1949. A paperback edition has been published by University of Arizona Press (1994), making this wonderful traveling companion available again. The reissue includes a foreword by Missoula writer William Kittredge.

Green, Stewart. *Back Country Byways.* Helena: Falcon Press, 1991.

James, H. L. *The Beartooth Highway.* Butte: Montana Bureau of Mines and Geology, 1995.

_____. *Scenic Driving the Beartooth Highway.* Helena: Falcon Publishing Co., 1997.

Johanek, Durrae and John. *Montana Behind the Scenes.* Helena: The Globe Pequot Press, 2000.

McRae, W. C., and Judy Jewell. *Montana Handbook,* fifth edition. Chico, Calif.: Moon Publications, Inc., 2002.

Magley, Beverly. *National Forest Scenic Byways.* Helena: Falcon Press, 1990.

_____. *National Forest Scenic Byways, Vol. II.* Helena: Falcon Press, 1992.

McCoy, Michael. *Montana Off the Beaten Path, A Guide to Unique Places,* sixth edition, Guilford, Conn., The Globe Pequot Press, 2005

Montana: The Last Best Place. Helena: Falcon Press, 1993.

Montana Atlas and Gazetteer. Freeport, Maine: DeLorme Mapping Co. Fourth edition, 2001. Indispensable for finding your way under the Big Sky.

Snyder, S. A. *Scenic Driving Montana.* Helena: Falcon Press, 1996. From the Anaconda-Pintler Scenic Route to Yaak River country, here are twenty-four drives along some of the state's most cherished roadways.

Spritzer, Donald. *Roadside History of Montana.* Missoula: Mountain Press Publishing Company, 1999.

Van West, Carroll. *Traveler's Companion to Montana History.* Helena: Montana Historical Society Press, 1990.

Willard, John. *Adventure Trails in Montana.* (out of print).

Wyss, Marilyn. *Road to Romance: The Origins and Development of the Road and Trail System in Montana.* Helena: Montana Department of Transportation, 1992.

CHAPTER THIRTEEN

Outdoor Recreation

*M*ontana is a four-season outdoor recreation playground, with over 30 million acres of public lands including more than 6 million acres of state lands with forests, parks, and fishing access sites. The state contains more than 3 million acres of designated wilderness areas with more than 4,000 miles of trails. There is plenty of space and soul-satisfying solitude for hikers,

Iceboat on Canyon Ferry Reservoir.
CRAIG AND LIZ LARCUM

campers, skiers, bikers, rock climbers, rockhounds, water skiers, boaters, snowmobilers, and more. Hunting and fishing are part of the traditional Montana lifestyle; both began as a way to survive on the frontier. Today, hundreds of thousands of hunters and anglers carry on that way of life through the recreational pursuit of Montana's varied and plentiful game and fish.

One of the best things about living in Montana is the possibility of being at a favorite trout stream, ski slope, hiking trail, or other outdoor adventure within a few minutes of leaving home or work. On sunny summer days, it's easy to find a restful campsite, an inviting body of water, or a trail with a view of heaven. Even on a starry winter night, you can be skiing or ice fishing close to home.

The abundance and variety of Montana's outdoor recreation opportunities attract a large number of visitors each year; those visitors pump millions of dollars into local economies. And many Montana residents choose to live here in large part for the chance to get outdoors and have fun. Today, there are more people on Montana's hiking trails, fishing streams, ski slopes, and snowmobile routes than ever. So it has become more important than ever to use our natural resources for recreation wisely and share those resources courteously with other users. After all, there are plenty of outdoor treasures in the Treasure State to go around.

Hiking and Backpacking

Backpacking and hiking opportunities in Montana are nearly unlimited. There are 22,000 miles of designated non-motorized trails and about 9,700 miles of designed motorized trails in Montana.

Many of these trails meander along rivers and streams, touch the shores of alpine lakes full of trout, and scale lofty summits with endless views. Eighteen trails are listed as National Recreation or Scenic Trails, including more than 900 miles of the Continental Divide National Scenic Trail within Montana. Glacier Park has over 1,000 miles of trails.

National Recreation Trails

National Recreation Trail	Distance	National Forest	Trailhead
Basin Lakes	4.8 miles	Custer	FR 71
Bear Trap	9 miles	Beaverhead-Deer Lodge	3 miles south of Red Mountain Campground
Big Hole Battlefield	3.8 miles	Bitterroot	Indian Trees Campground
Crystal Lake Shoreline	1.7-mile loop	Lewis and Clark	Crystal Lake Campground
Danny On Memorial	6.4-mile network	Flathead	Big Mountain Ski Resort
Easthouse	23 miles	Bitterroot	Skalkaho Pass
Hanging Valley	6 miles	Helena	Vigilante Campground
Holland Falls	1.5 miles	Flathead	end of FR 44, Holland Lake
Louise Lake	1.75 miles	Deerlodge	FR 107
Morrell Falls	2.3 miles	Lolo	FR 4364, near Seeley Lake
Mortimer Gulch	5 miles	Lewis and Clark	Mortimer Gulch Campground
Mount Helena Ridge	5.7 miles	Helena	Various Mount Helena trailheads
Palisade Falls	0.6 miles	Gallatin	East Fork Road
Pioneer Loop	35-mile loop	Beaverhead-Deerlodge	Lacy Creek Road
Skyline	13-mile loop	Kootenai	end of FR 399
Stateline-CC Divide	5.5 miles	Lolo	FR 7 at state border

Many sections of state and national trails are accessible to persons with disabilities. For example, in the Sheepshead Recreation Area near Butte, there is a 5-mile paved trail around Maney Lake. For the urban hiker, many Montana towns provide maps of walking tours through designated historic districts and nature areas within the city limits. A brief sampling includes: Mount Helena City Park and historic district; the river walks in Missoula, Great Falls, Billings, and Fort Benton; the historic district walks in Livingston, Butte, Deer Lodge, and Philipsburg; and the Pattee Canyon Recreation Area and Rattlesnake Wilderness Area walks just a few miles outside Missoula. The Gallatin Valley Land Trust has a trail system around Bozeman called Main Street to the Mountains.

Camping

Even in Montana's busy summer tourist season, you can generally find a campsite. Camping opportunities range from campgrounds with swimming pools and stores to primitive areas with limited facilities. There are about 120 campgrounds on lakes that are accessible by car and some 170 campsites along the rivers and streams of the state. There are also many hundreds of locations in the backcountry where camping is allowed, but the facilities may be primitive. Campers are required to pack their garbage out of most areas.

Most state parks and forest service campsites are available on a first-come, first-served basis. Some forest service campgrounds require reservations. While services vary among individual parks, most sites have a picnic table, a fire ring or grill, and parking for one vehicle and a recreational vehicle. For those requiring camping with more creature comforts, there are more than 120 private campgrounds along the byways and highways. Fees for private campgrounds vary widely depending on the area and services.

USDA Forest Service reservations: (877) 444-6777 or www.reserveusa.com

For information on private campgrounds, contact Montana Campground Owners Association, www.campingmontana.com.

Cabin Rentals

The USDA Forest Service offers rustic cabins and fire lookouts for rent on a first-come, first-served basis at 48 locations within the state's nine national forests. Some of the cabins can even be rented in the winter months. Cabins are furnished with the bare basics, like table, chairs, a wood stove, and bunks. Cooking utensils, electricity, and indoor plumbing may also be available but not at all rental cabins. For rates ranging from $15 to $50, you can enjoy scenic splendors and the life of early rangers for up to five consecutive nights. Most of these cabins were built in the 1920s and 1930s to house forest rangers and their crews. Most of the rentable former fire lookouts are in the northwestern corner of the state. For more information, contact local ranger stations. For a directory of all cabin rentals, write Regional Office of the USDA Forest Service, Federal Building, P.O. Box 7669, Missoula, MT 59807; 329-3511.

Montana Fish, Wildlife & Parks also rents rustic cabins at Lewis and Clark Caverns State Park, tipis at Beavertail Hill State Park and Bannack State Park, and a yurt at the Big Arm unit of Flathead State Park.

Cycling

The advent of the mountain bike has tremendously increased the number of people pedaling wherever the pavement, dirt roads, and single-track trails will take them. There are dozens of designated cycling routes in

Montana. Mountain bike races, often with several amateur categories open to the public, are held in the mountains near Missoula, Helena, Kalispell, and Bozeman. Check with area bicycle shops for dates and details. Mountain bike guidebooks from Falcon Publishing offer detailed information on local rides around Bozeman and Helena.

Road races, sanctioned by the United States Cycling Federation, are held throughout spring and summer near Missoula, Helena, and Billings. The annual Tour of the Swan River Valley offers "roadies" two days and more than 200 miles of scenic pedaling between Missoula and Bigfork. Each fall the Double Divide Ride draws hardy cyclists to Helena for a two-day 170-mile loop that twice climbs over the Continental Divide at 6,320-foot MacDonald Pass and 6,131-foot Flesher Pass.

The Adventure Cycling Association has additional information on road routes and bike trails throughout western Montana. Founded in 1973 as

Bikecentennial, Adventure Cycling Association is America's premier nonprofit organization dedicated to bicycle travel, with 41,100 members nationwide. This Missoula-based cycling organization offers many programs for cyclists, including a national network of bicycle touring routes and organized trips.

www.adventurecycling.org

Adventure Cycling Association
P.O. Box 8308
Missoula, MT 59802
721-1776, (800) 755-2453, 721-8754 fax

Climbing

The Rocky Mountains have special meaning to Montana's technical climbers and mountaineers. Numerous world-class mountaineers and rock climbers have trained here. The exposed cliffs of steep, compact rock along with dramatic glacier-carved mountains are a geologic wonderland and a climber's paradise. Moreover, Montana's easily accessible climbing areas are relatively uncrowded and unknown, while the remote backcountry still holds first-ascent adventures for the intrepid.

Often tucked away in idyllic settings, the sweeping expanses of granite and gneiss, craggy limestone fins and faces, and steep quartzite cliffs are gymnastic playgrounds for the vertically inclined. The high peaks of Glacier National Park, and the Mission, Bitterroot, Madison, Absaroka, and Beartooth mountains tantalize those with a desire to visit high and remote summits. The Humbug Spires area south of Butte offers some of the best rock climbing in the region.

Prospecting & Rockhounding

Folks have been hunting for gold for at least 150 years in Montana, and there is still some left for those who know where to look (and those who just get lucky). Montana also offers numerous opportunities to hunt for agates, quartz crystals, and semiprecious stones like sapphires. Sapphire mines offer the opportunity to dig for this sought-after stone or to buy buckets of dirt for sorting through. At a sapphire mine in Philipsburg, you can sift through your bucket of treasures indoors in a comfortable setting. You can hunt for gold in Confederate Gulch, sapphires at Gem Mountain near Philipsburg, quartz crystals at Crystal Park in the Pioneer Mountains, and moss agates along the Yellowstone River near Forsyth.

The best spot to find the Montana agate is in alluvial gravels along the lower 200 miles of the Yellowstone River, from Custer, 50 miles east of Billings, to the Missouri River. Petrified wood, colored jasper, and fossils are also common in the area. It takes a trained eye to find top grade rough Montana agate, but if you do, it may be worth as much as $40 a pound. The low water times of early spring and late fall are best for hunting along the bars and banks where virgin gravel has been exposed. To help overcome the challenges of hunting for agates on a river of unpredictable waters and limited access, the Glendive Chamber of Commerce offers the combination of a guided float trip on the Yellowstone and an agate hunt. The Agate Stop in Savage is home to the Montana Agate Museum.

Water Sports

Montana has over 120 lakes and dozens of rivers that are accessible by motor vehicle so you can launch a boat, personal watercraft, raft, or canoe. Montana Fish, Wildlife & Parks maintains dozens of boat launching sites at various state parks and fishing access sites. High-powered motorboats are not allowed on all lakes and rivers. Some waters, like Flathead Lake, Georgetown Lake, Lake Mary Ronan, or Fort Peck Reservoir, are many miles long, offering hours of scenic cruising and sailing.

For those seeking nonmotorized water adventures, the choices include rafting, canoeing, or kayaking on Montana's many lakes and rivers. More

GATES OF THE MOUNTAINS

One of Montana's favorite tourist attractions for the past half-century is the boat trips through the Gates of the Mountains in the Holter Lake Recreation Area of the Missouri River. This area was named by Lewis and Clark for its magnificent cliffs that seem to open and close like a gate as one floats upriver. The boat ride can include a picnic at the Meriwether Picnic Area or a hike through the Gates of the Mountains Wilderness Area. The boat rides are available from Memorial Day to the middle of September. (Contact Gates of the Mountains Boat Club, 458-5241). The boat ride cruises by the entrance to Mann Gulch, where a devastating forest fire killed thirteen men in 1949. The fire is immortalized in Norman Maclean's book, *Young Men and Fire*. More than 35,000 visitors enjoy the Gates of the Mountains tour boats in each summer season. For more information, visit www.gatesofthemountains.com.

than twenty-five of Montana's wildlife viewing areas can be enjoyed from canoes or rafts. The Blackfoot River corridor and the Clearwater River Canoe Trail are two such developed river access areas.

If you're crazy enough to want to float some of the whitewater sections of Montana's rivers, you can go it alone or engage the services of dozens of white-water rafting outfitters. There are great whitewater floats on the Sun River, the Alberton Gorge of the Clark Fork River, the Dearborn, the Beartrap Canyon of the Madison River in the Lee Metcalf Wilderness Area, the Yankee Jim Canyon of the Yellowstone River, and the Flathead National Wild and Scenic River. For a lazy and lovely float, try the 149-mile Wild and Scenic portion of the Missouri River, from Fort Benton to the Fred Robinson Bridge.

Hard Water Sailing

Montana is a natural place for two of the state's newest sports—ice surfing and ice sailing. Canyon Ferry Reservoir near Helena has been called one of the best spots in the U.S. to engage in these fast growing winter activities. The lakes of the Seeley Swan Valley, the bays of Flathead Lake, and Fort Peck Lake are other possible destinations.

Hot Springs

There are over a dozen commercial hot springs in Montana, ranging from the completely low-key and funky to full-scale resorts. There are also numerous noncommercial hot springs around Montana, but you usually have to bribe someone to tell you where they are.

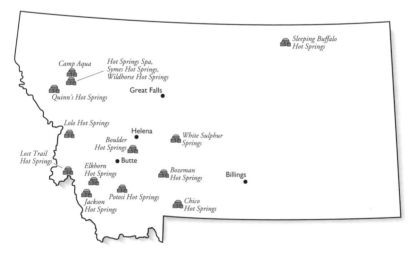

Hot Springs

Area Name	Location	For Information	Decription
Lost Trail Hot Springs	6 mi south of Lost Trail Pass	821-3574	Outdoor hot swimming pool, indoor soaking pool, sauna, lodging, RV park, picnic ground, restaurant
Hot Springs Spa	Hot Springs	741-2283	The springs in this town are noted for their exceptionally high mineral content.
Camp Aqua	East of Hwy 28, 2.5 mi north of Hot Springs	741-3480	Indoor hot pools, steam baths, saunas, lodging, RV park, picnic ground
Quinn's Hot Springs	At the junction of Hwys 200 and 135	826-3150	Outdoor swimming pool and soaking pool, lodging, RV park, picnic ground, restaurant, bar.
Spa Hot Springs	202 W Main, White Sulphur Springs	547-3366	The town grew up around this natural hot spring. Two pools are open year-round to the public.
Bozeman Hot Springs	81123 Gallatin Road, Bozeman	586-6492	Indoor hot swimming pool, four soaking pools, cold pool, campground, RV park, picnic ground, grocery store.
Chico Hot Springs	South of Livingston off US 89	333-4933	Indoor and outdoor hot swimming and soaking pools, massage, lodging, restaurant, bar.
Sleeping Buffalo Hot Springs	10 mi west of Saco	527-3370	Two indoor pools and one outdoor pool. Bar, cafe, steakhouse, casino, lodging, golf course, rodeo grounds, RV camp ground, waterslide, hunting, fishing.
Elkhorn Hot Springs	North of Polaris on Pioneer Mountains Scenic Drive	834-3434	Surrounded by Beaverhead National Forest at 7,500 feet in elevation. Outdoor soaking pool, indoor wet saunas, rustic cabins, restaurant, camping, cross-country skiing.
Jackson Hot Springs	in Jackson	834-3151	Indoor-outdoor swimming pool free of chemicals or sulphur odor. RV park, camping, cabins, restaurant.
Boulder Hot Springs	1 mi south of Boulder on MT 69	225-4339	Separate men's and women's indoor soaking pools and steam baths, outdoor heated pool, lodging, restaurant.
Fairmont Hot Springs	1500 Fairmont Rd. Anaconda	800-332-3272	4 hot spring pools, golf course, water slide, lodging restaurant.
Lolo Hot Springs Resort	37 miles southwest of Missoula on Hwy. 12 W.	800-273-2290	Outdoor swinning pool, indoor soaking pool, RV park, bumper cars, picnic area, restaurant, snowmobile trails
Wildhorse Hot Springs	Near Hot Springs off Hwy. 28	741-3777	Private rooms with plunges, saunas
Symes Hotel and Mineral Baths	Hot Springs	741-2361	Outdoor mineral pool, private indoor baths, health spa services, lodging
Potosi Hot Springs	Beyond Pony on Hwy. 293, south of Three Forks	888-685-1695	Outdoor swimming pool, indoor soaking pool restaurant, cabin rentals

Downhill Skiing

It may not have as many ski resorts as Colorado and Utah, or the angle of repose of other western slopes, but Montana has several resorts with "major league" skiing and much shorter lift lines than you'll find at Vail, Park City, and other famous slopes. In addition, Montana's big skies drop snow on about dozens of smaller ski areas.

Skiing has been a popular family sport in Montana since the 1930s. Local ski clubs cleared promising hillsides and started volunteer-run ski hills in Anaconda, Helena, Butte, Bozeman, Townsend, Whitefish, and a few other towns and ranching communities. In the late 1940s, the sport really took off. Big Mountain opened in 1947, complete with a T-bar. In 1967, Snowbowl was the site of the U.S. National Alpine Championships. In 1995, Big Sky Resort completed a $3 million project to expand the lifts and runs. Big Sky now has the most vertical feet of skiing (4,350 feet) in the nation.

Contact Montana Promotions Division (Travel Montana), the state tourism office, for a Montana Winter Guide, which provides further details on Montana's ski opportunities: (800) 847-4868 for out-of-state callers; in Montana, call 841-2870 or http://travelmontana.state.mt.com.

For Skiers with Special Needs

Several Montana ski areas make it possible for skiers with disabilities or special needs to make use of the slopes. The Dream Ski program at Big Mountain offers individualized one-on-one ski instruction and free use of adaptive ski equipment from December 1 through March.

Eagle Mount Ski Montana is a similar program available at Bridger Bowl, Red Lodge Mountain, and Showdown. At each of these areas, downhill and cross-country skiing are taught to skiers with special needs. For more information, visit www.eaglemount.org.

Cross-Country Skiing

Wherever there is adequate snowfall to cover rocks and roots, the hardy species of cross-country skier can practice the sport as it was meant to

Montana Downhill Ski Areas

Ski Area	Map No.	2003-2004 Vertical Drop (in feet)	Single-day Adult Lift Ticket Price	Description
Bear Paw Ski Bowl Havre, 265-8404	1	900	$15	Day-use area 29 miles S of Havre, along Amtrak route on Rocky Boy's Indian Reservation; full services in Havre
Big Mountain Whitefish, 862-2900 800-858-3913	2	2,500	$49	Full service destination resort in NW Montana, on Amtrak route & served by Delta, Northwest, and Horizon airlines; near Glacier National Park
Big Sky Big Sky (800) 548-4486	3	4,350	$59	Full service destination & conference resort between Bozeman & Yellowstone National Park; open summer & winter
Blacktail Mountain Lakeside, 844-0999	4	1,440	$30	Day-use area near Flathead Lake, restaurant, rentals, cross-country trails
Bridger Bowl Bozeman (800) 223-9609	5	2,000	$36	Destination area with plenty of skiing & full services in Bozeman
Discovery Basin Anaconda 563-2184	6	1,680	$28	Day-use area near Anaconda; cafeteria, lounge sales, rentals, and cross-country trails, Fairmont Hot Springs Resort 30 miles east
Great Divide Marysville 449-3746	7	1,510	$29	Day-use area about 20 miles NW of Helena; cafeteria, bar, restaurant, night skiing, groomed cross-country skiing; full services in Helena
Lost Trail Powder Mt. Connor 821-3211	8	1,800	$22	Day-use area S of Missoula on the Montana-Idaho border; lodging nearby; 6 miles to Lost Trail Hot Springs
Maverick Mountain Dillon 834-3454	9	2,120	$23	Day-use area W of Dillon; open Thurs.-Sun.; half-price lift tickets Thurs. & Fri.; nursery available/reservations required
Montana Snowbowl Missoula, 549-9777	10	2,600	$32	Day-use area outside of Missoula; expert slopes attract extreme skiers, but there's plenty of terrain for other skill levels
Moonlight Basin Big Sky, 800-845-4428	11	3,050	$40	Full service destination near Big Sky Resort
Red Lodge Mountain Red Lodge, 446-2610	12	2,400	$39	Destination area with plenty of skiing & full services in Red Lodge
Teton Pass Fairfield 467-3664	13	1,010	$22	Day-use area on the Rocky Mountain Front; rentals, lessons, lounge, and concessions; services in Choteau
Showdown Ski Area Neihart 236-5522	14	1,400	$29	Day-use area S of Great Falls; cross-country & snowmobile trails nearby; services in Neihart, Monarch, White Sulphur Springs, and Great Falls
Turner Mountain Libby 293-4317	15	2,110	$23	Day-use area 22 miles N of Libby in Montana's NW corner; warming hut and snack bar; services in Libby

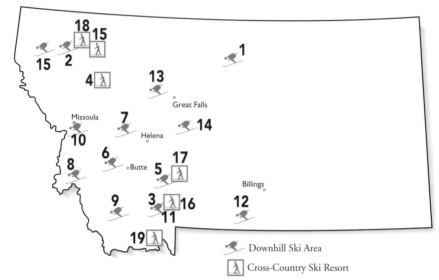

Great Falls

Missoula

Helena

Butte

Billings

🎿 Downhill Ski Area

🎿 Cross-Country Ski Resort

be—by simply heading out and making fresh tracks. Many Montanans choose to telemark off-trail on public lands—in times of low avalanche danger.

Montana has twenty-seven designated cross-country ski areas at various locations within seven national forests. Some are groomed and some require skiers to break their own trails on accessible public lands and logging roads throughout the state. Sixteen wildlife viewing areas offer cross-country skiing trails. The Mount Haggin Nordic Ski Area, off Highway 274 between Anaconda and Wise River, is within a state wildlife management area. The trails of this area lead skiers along the remnants of an 18-mile-long flume that once carried logs along a zigzag route over creeks and the Continental Divide to provide timber and boiler fuel for the Anaconda Smelter.

There are over fifteen destination ski centers offering groomed trails, lodging, meals, and other amenities. Most of Montana's downhill ski areas have some groomed trails for the cross-country crowd. Many Montana towns allow cross-country skiing on local golf courses or river walks.

Snowmobiling

Montana boasts 4,100 miles of groomed snowmobile trails and nearly 20 million acres of public lands accessible to snow machines. In the snowiest parts of Montana the snowmobile season can be as long as six months, running from as early as the end of October to as late as May.

Selected Cross-Country Ski Resorts

Name Address	Map No.	Location	Trail Distance	Amenities
Izaak Walton Inn Box 653 Essex, MT 59916 888-5700	15	Halfway between West and East Glacier, Hwy 2	33 km + w/ set track, and skating lane	guided ski tours, rentals, sauna, lessons, historic railroad setting
Lone Mtn. Ranch Box 160069 Big Sky, MT 59716 (800) 514-4644, 995-4644	16	Hwy 64, Big Sky Road, between village and Big Sky ski resort	65 km groomed w/ set track and skating lane	7-night stays include backcountry ski tours of Yellowstone N.P., sleigh ride, dinners, trail fees
Bohart Ranch 16621 Bridger Canyon Rd. Bozeman, MT 59714 586-9070	17	Hwy 86 in Bridger Canyon	25 km groomed w/ set track and skating lane	biathlon range, rentals, lessons, warming cabin
Mountain Timbers Wilderness Lodge Box 94 W. Glacier, MT 59936 (800) 841-3835, 387-5830	18	Rabe Rd., between N. Fork Rd. and U.S. 2	15 km of groomed trails	secluded lodge w/ library, pool table, views, hot tub, country breakfasts
Wade Lake Resort Box 107 Cameron, MT 59720 682-7560	19	40 miles south of Ennis; west of Hebgen Lake in Beaverhead N.F.	30 km track-set trails	Wade Lake is a wildlife viewing area; ski in or ride a shuttle from Hwy 287; hot tub

SKIING FOR SPAM

West Yellowstone can almost always be counted on for plentiful snow weeks before the first day of winter. Recreational and competitive skiers alike converge on the town for the Thanksgiving holiday, when U.S. Olympic cross-country skiers are hitting the trails and working on speed and form. Recreational skiers who visit around Thanksgiving can learn the latest techniques during multi-day clinics and a week-long camp. The instructors are experts, some of them world-class.

Races are also part of the community's winter scene. Hundreds of competitors have taken part in the Rendezvous Ski Race (usually held in early March), and a "Spam Cup" citizens' race is held each month, with a can of the legendary meat going to the winner.

For information on cross-country skiing in West Yellowstone, call 646-9427.

No wonder, then, that during the winter of 2003 nearly 23,240 residents registered snowmobiles for use on public lands within Montana (and an untold number of unregistered snowmobilers use their machines only on private land). Dozens of local snowmobile associations throughout the state promote the sport, hold competitions, groom trails, and offer trail maps. In recent years, snowmobiling directly contributed $163 million to the state's economy.

AVALANCHE DANGER

Since 1985, there have been 43 avalanche related deaths in Montana—most have occurred while snowmobiling. Avalanches may occur at any time during the winter. Advice on avalanche conditions is available at local USDA Forest Service offices, and these are avalanche advisory numbers in your area.

Glacier Country Avalanche Center, (800) 526-5329 or 257-8402
Cooke City, 838-2341
Southwest Montana, 587-6981
West Yellowstone, 646-7912
Missoula Regional Avalanche Advisory, 549-4488 or (800) 281-1030
Gallatin National Forest Avalanche Center, 587-6984

State Parks

Montana's natural, cultural, and recreational resources are greatly enhanced by its fine state park system. In turn, at least one of the state's natural resources helps support the system. The interest on 1.27 percent of the state's coal severance tax is dedicated to a trust fund for the acquisition and maintenance of park sites. Each year, the state park system has over 4 million visitors.

In 1936, Lewis and Clark Caverns became Montana's first state park when the site was transferred to the state from the federal government. Makoshika State Park in southeastern Montana is the largest state park, with 8,834 acres of land, much of it containing unique geologic formations.

State parks and other state recreational lands offer a variety of landscapes, natural features, historical significance, and recreational opportunities in areas all across Montana. Some parks feature a wide range of visitor facilities

National Forest Contacts

Area Name	Location	Miles Groomed	Contacts
Cut Bank	Between Cut Bank and Kalispell on U.S. 2	45	Lewis & Clark National Forest, 791-7700; Rocky Mountain Ranger District, 466-5341
The Flathead	Columbia Falls, Whitefish Big Fork and Kalispell	220	Flathead National Forest, 755-5401
Haugan	On the Montana-Idaho border in Northwest Montana	120	Superior Ranger District, 822-4233
Libby/Ten Lakes Scenic Area/Yaak	Northwest Montana	153	Libby Ranger District, 293-7773 Three Rivers Ranger District, 295-4693
Lolo Pass	On U.S. 12 at the Montana-Idaho border	250	Missoula Ranger District, 329-3750; Powell Ranger District, 942-3113
Seeley Lake	15 miles north of the junction of MT 83 and 200 in western Montana	230	Seeley Lake Ranger District, 677-2233
Skalkaho	15 miles east of Hamilton on Skalkaho Hwy. 38	56	Bitterroot National Forest, 363-7100; Darby Ranger District, 821-3913
Deer Lodge	8 miles southwest of city center	51	Pintler Ranger District, 846-1770
Dillon/Polaris	33 miles northwest of Dillon	200	Dillon Ranger District, 683-3900
Garnet	30 miles east of Missoula on MT 200	100	Garnet Resource Area, BLM, 329-3914; Garnet Preservation Assoc., 329-1031
Georgetown Lake	MT 1 between Drummond and Anaconda	140	Philipsburg Ranger District, 859-3211
Helena	At the junction of I-15, U.S. 12, and U.S. 287	245	Helena Ranger District, 449-5490
Lincoln	Between Great Falls and Missoula on MT 200	250	Lincoln Ranger District, 369-4140
Virginia City/Ennis	In southwest Montana along U.S. 287	130	Madison Ranger District, 682-4253
Wisdom/Jackson	Junction of MT 43 and 287 in southwest Montana	150	Wisdom Ranger District, 689-3243
Wise River	12 miles west of I-15, between Butte and Dillon	150	Wise River Ranger District, 832-3178
Big Timber	I-90 between Bozeman and Billings	34	Big Timber Ranger District, 932-5155
Bozeman/Big Sky	!-90 between Billings and Butte	200	Bozeman Ranger District, 522-2520
Cooke City/ Silver Gate	South-central Montana on U.S. 212	60	Gardiner Ranger District, 848-7375; Yellowstone National Park, 307-344-7381 ext. 2206;
Livingston	Junction of I-90 at U.S. 89 in southwest Montana	44	Livingston Ranger District, 222-1892
West Yellowstone/ Gardiner	West and north entrances to Yellowstone National Park	580	Hebgen Lake Ranger District, 823-6961; Yellowstone National Park, 307-344-7381 ext. 2206
Kings Hill/Little Belts	U.S. 89 between Great Falls and White Sulphur Springs	325	Kings Hill Ranger District, 547-3361

Source: http://wintermt.com/snomoareas/www.snotana.com.

such as camping, boat launch sites, and concessions. Other sites are less developed but, depending on rules established for each park, visitors may still camp, picnic, observe wildlife, and enjoy other recreational activities.

All of Montana's state parks are open for day use. Many offer camping facilities. Others prohibit overnight stays. When camping is allowed, fees vary according to the services provided. Some parks close some or all of their facilities during the winter months.

As of 2004, Montanans have free access to the state's forty-four State Parks. Having a Montana license plate on your car will serve as the pass to some of the most desirable vacation and cultural destinations in the state. Residents have this privilege through an optional $4 annual fee on Montana vehicle registrations. Nonresident park visitors will continue to pay $2-5 for daily use of state parks or may purchase a nonresident State Parks Passport on the FWP web site. Residents and nonresidents will continue to pay camping fees, which range from $12 to $15.

For more information contact Montana Fish, Wildlife & Parks, 1420 East 6th Avenue, Helena MT 59620, 444-3750.

Hunting

Hunting is very much a part of Montana's past. The early Indian tribes depended on the bison herds and other game animals for food, shelter, and clothing. The early fur trappers were lured to Montana by the abundance of fur-bearing animals. The early prospectors and homesteaders depended on wild game to supplement their diets.

The first big game season in Montana in 1895, allowed each hunter to bag eight deer, eight mountain sheep, eight mountain goat, eight antelope, two moose, and two elk.

Today hunting in Montana offers a large selection of big game, waterfowl, and game birds in a wide variety of habitats. Upland game birds include sharp-tailed grouse, sage grouse, Hungarian partridge, chukar partridge, ruffed grouse, blue grouse, spruce (or Franklin's) grouse, ring-necked pheasants, and Merriam's turkeys. Willow ptarmigans also occur in some parts of Montana, but they cannot be legally hunted. Waterfowl that may be hunted include geese, ducks, swans, cranes, mourning doves, coots, and snipes. Whooping cranes are protected by law and may not be hunted.

Montana is known to have the best big game selection in the lower 48 states including mule deer, white-tailed deer, elk, antelope, bighorn sheep,

Hunter Harvests, 2003

Game	Number of Licenses Issued to Residents & Nonresidents	Total Harvest
Deer	175,759	140,553
Elk	129,914	28,916
Moose	660	525
Antelope	55,150	30,540
Bighorn Sheep	325	159
Mountain Goat	319	229

Greatest Weights Harvested for Montana Big Game

Species	Whole lbs.	Dressed lbs.
Black Bear	505	NA
Grizzly Bear	1,102	NA
Mountain Lion	176	NA
American Elk	1,010	810
Mule Deer	453	340
Whitetailed Deer	375	275
Shiras Moose	1,117	840
Pronghorn	160	121
Bison	1,555	NA
Rocky Mountain Goat	310	212
Bighorn Sheep	302	222

mountain goats, Shiras moose, black bears, mountain lions, and bison. Many big game populations have been increasing since the 1930s and are now at record levels. But management problems persist as civilization encroaches on plains and lowlands where game species like to feed. This has required the development of some winter ranges for big game.

Nearly 44 percent of the adult males and 13 percent of the adult females in the state purchase a Montana hunting license annually. Though out-of-state hunters may take home some of our wildlife, they generally spend over $50 million every year on outfitter services and equipment.

The week beginning on the third Monday in September is an official week of observance in Montana to commemorate this state's valued heritage of hunting.

Fishing

Montanans love to fish, and the state boasts an impressive number of places for anglers to go—1,900 cold-water lakes totaling 400,000 acres, 15,000 miles of cold-water streams, and 6,100 miles of warm-water rivers and streams. Warm-water lakes cover approximately 350,000 acres and include bodies of water as large as Fork Peck Reservoir and as small as stock and farm ponds. There are 320 offical fishing access sites.

Thirty-four percent of all adult Montanans purchase a fishing license annually. In 2001, anglers cumulatively spent over 4 million days fishing Montana waters. In the lake-rich areas of Montana, 25 to 30 percent of the fishing action takes place during the winter months.

Montana's climate and geography, along with a strong commitment to natural resources conservation and fisheries management, contribute to the state's reputation as a fishing paradise. As early as 1963, the state enacted the nation's first stream preservation legislation. In the 1970s, the state curtailed the stocking of hatchery trout in the rivers and streams of the state to increase populations of wild trout. Hatchery trout are still stocked in many lakes and reservoirs. In 2002, nearly 43 million fish, including rainbow trout, kokanee salmon, walleye, and largemouth bass, were stocked in waters throughout Montana.

DUD LUTTON

Bud Lilly (1925–)

Bud Lilly, born in Manhattan, Montana, began fishing as soon as he could hold a fishing rod. Though his first career was as a science teacher, his lasting love was the art and science of fly-fishing. The tackle shop he opened in West Yellowstone in 1952 became the world famous, Bud Lilly's Trout Shop. Bud encouraged the growing sport of fly-fishing by publishing promotional materials, creating catalogues, and offering seminars and angling instructions. He became known as "the Dean of Fly-fishing." His love of the sport led to promotion of responsible environmental practices. He was founding president of Montana Trout Unlimited, first chairperson of the International Fly Fishing Center, and a director of the Greater Yellowstone Coalition.

Montana's Record Fish (as of March 2005)

Fish	Record Weight	Year	Area
Arctic grayling	3.63 lb.	2003	Washtub Lake
Bigmouth buffalo	57.75 lb.	1994	Nelson Reservoir
Brook trout	9.06 lb.	1940	Lower Two Medicine Lake
Brown trout	29.00 lb.	1966	Wade Lake
Bull trout (Dolly Varden)	25.63 lb.	1916	Unknown
Chinook (king salmon)	31.13 lb.	1991	Fort Peck Reservoir
Cutthroat trout	16.00 lb.	1955	Red Eagle Lake
Golden trout	5.43 lb.	2000	Cave Lake
Kokanee Salmon	7.85 lb.	2003	Hauser Lake
Lake trout	42.69 oz.	2004	Flathead Lake
Largemouth bass	8.29 lb.	1999	Many Lakes
Mountain whitefish	5.09 lb.	1987	Kootenai River
Northern pike	37.50 lb.	1972	Tongue River Reservoir
Paddlefish	142.50 lb.	1973	Missouri River
Rainbow trout	33.10 lb.	1997	Kootenai River
Smallmouth bass	6.66 lb.	2002	Fort Peck Reservoir
Walleye	16.63 lb.	2001	Fort Peck Reservoir
Yellow Perch	2.37 lb.	1988	Ashley Lake

Source: http://fwp.state.mt.us/fishing/fishingmontana/fishrecords.html.

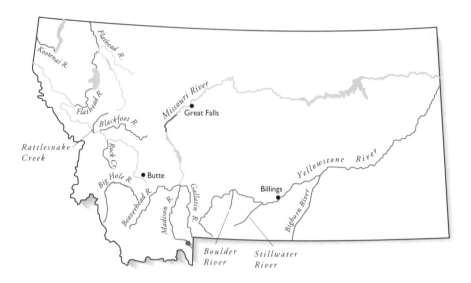

Blue-Ribbon Streams

The following bodies of water, totaling 1,139 miles, are classified as Blue-Ribbon Streams because of their productivity, number of game fish present, use by anglers, accessibility, and aesthetics.

Beaverhead River

Big Hole River

Bighorn River

Blackfoot River

Boulder River

Flathead River (main stem)

Flathead River (South Fork)

Gallatin River

Kootenai River below Libby Dam

Madison River

Missouri River from Holter Dam
to Cascade

Rattlesnake Creek

Rock Creek

Stillwater River

Yellowstone River

The net economic value of fishing in Montana is estimated in excess of $292 million a year. In 1997, the rivers receiving the heaviest fishing pressure were the Madison River above Ennis and the Missouri River below Holter. Those lakes receiving the heaviest fishing pressure in 1993 were Canyon Ferry Reservoir, Hauser Reservoir, and Holter Lake.

Golfing

Montana has over ninety scenic, reasonably priced, and enjoyable golf courses. Seventy-two are public courses and the rest are part of semi-public "country clubs" or destination resorts. The Old Works Golf Course in Anaconda is a

Selected Fishing Events

- Annual Federation of Fly Fishing Conclave and Show, August, 585-7592
- Governors Cup Walleye Tournament, Glasgow, July, 228-2222
- Hell Creek/Jordan Ladies Walleye Tournament, Hell Creek State Park, July, 232-4365 or 557-2995
- Montana Walleye Unlimited Fall Classic, Fort Peck Marina, August, 392-5558
- Canyon Ferry Walleye Festival, June, 266-5279
- Ennis on the Madison Fly Fishing Festival, September, 682-4388
- Cooke City Fish Fry and Big Fish Tournament, Cooke City, 838-2495

Whirling Disease

In the past, Montana's rainbow trout populations have been locally decimated by whirling disease, a waterborne infection that disturbs the equilibrium of these fish. The Madison River near Ennis is the epicenter of whirling disease in Montana. The following tips may help you prevent the spread of whirling disease to your own favorite stream:

- Remove all mud and aquatic plants from your vehicle, boat, anchor, trailer and axles, waders, boots, and fishing gear before departing the fishing access site or boat dock.
- Drain all water from your boat and equipment—including coolers, buckets, and live wells—before departing the fishing access site or boat dock.
- Dry your boat and equipment between river trips.
- Don't transport fish from one body of water to another.
- Don't dispose of fish entrails, skeletal parts, or other by-products in any body of water.
- Don't collect sculpins (also known as bullheads) or use sculpins as bait. www.whirlingdisease.org

unique golf venue. It is one of only two public courses in the nation designed by Jack Nicklaus. It sits on what was once a nineteenth century smelter and twentieth century EPA Superfund site. *Golf Digest* has ranked Old Works as the top-ranked public course in Montana. *Golf Digest* also rated the Flathead Valley, with its nine championship courses, as one of the 50 greatest golf destinations in the world.

Further Reading:

Cold Smoke, Skiers Remembers Montana Bear Canyon and Bridger Bowl. Missoula, Mont.: Mountain Press Publishing, 1996.

Cunningham, Bill. *Wild Montana.* Helena: Falcon Press, 1995. A guide to 55 roadless recreation areas.

Feldman, Robert. *The Rockhound's Guide to Montana.* Helena: Falcon Press, 1985.

Green, Randall, ed. *Rock Climber's Guide to Montana.* Helena: Falcon Press, 1995.

Harmon, Will. *Fat/Trax Bozeman.* Helena: Falcon Press, 1996.

Holton, G. D. *A Field Guide to Montana Fishes.* Montana Department of Fish, Wildlife & Parks, 2003.

Montana Hunting Almanac. Annual publication of the *Missoulian*, P.O. Box 8029, Missoula, MT 59807.

Montana Outdoors. The official bi-monthly publication of the Montana Department of Fish, Wildlife & Parks, 1420 East 6th Avenue, Helena, MT 59620.

Posewitz, Jim. *Beyond Fair Chase: The Ethic and Tradition of Hunting.* Helena: The Globe Pequot Press, 2001.

_____. *Inherit the Hunt: A Journey into the Heart of Hunting.* Helena: The Globe Pequot Press, 2001.

_____. *Rifle in Hand, How Wild America Was Saved.* Riverbend Publishing, 2004

Sample, Michael S. *Fishing Montana.* Helena: Falcon Publishing, Co., 1997.

Schneider, Bill. *Bear Aware: Hiking and Camping in Bear Country.* Helena: Falcon Press, 1996.

_____. *Hiking Montana.* Helena: Falcon Press, 1995.

CHAPTER FOURTEEN

Arts and Culture

Montanans cherish a robust tradition of public and private support for the arts of all kinds. This nurturing atmosphere has produced an astonishing number of successful folk artists and craftspersons, visual artists, writers, and performers—many of whom are just plain folks with day jobs and remarkable talents.

Folk and traditional arts have long been part of the picture. Across the state, most towns have at least one

Solitude on the Missouri.
MONTE DOLACK

annual community event celebrating local heritage and folklife, including such varied arts as chainsaw sculpture, quilting, cowboy poetry, and old-time fiddle music. Woven, sculpted, or somehow blended into these traditional arts are pieces of Montana's many heritages. The colorful decorative arts of the state's many Plains Indian tribes are but one example.

Montanans love to explore art in all its forms. Visit a few of our more than 200 galleries, museum shops, and arts markets, and you will see for yourself that our state continues to inspire and nurture artists whose works tell of their love of this special place. Painters, photographers, sculptors, ceramists, and fiber artists create unique visions of our surrounding landscapes—and the landscapes of the mind.

For a state of small population, Montana boasts an impressive number of museum collections, community art centers, and art auctions that have gained widespread fame: the Montana Historical Society Museum in Helena, the Yellowstone Art Center in Billings, and the Museum of the Rockies in Bozeman, to name a few. The tremendous attendance at the world-famous C. M. Russell Art Auction in Great Falls each spring indicates continued interest in the realistic style of contemporary artists who portray the wildlife, landscapes, native peoples, and historical life of the region.

Perhaps our area is best known as a literary haven. Writers are an abundant species in Montana, and most have something interesting to say. Some of our homegrown novelists, poets, and essayists write about life here in the Big Sky state; others write adventures, mysteries, and life in other places.

Montana's performing arts shine equally as bright. Theater and dance companies entertain us regularly and garner grants and awards in the process. Hundreds of musicians meet weekly to play music together and to share their gifts with their neighbors. Nine cities support symphony orchestras, many of which have been active for a half-century or more. Homegrown blue grass, country, and rock bands play nightly in all corners of the state. Local jazz scenes bubble up with sound, just another instance of the artistic ferment around us.

And, as most folks around the nation know, Montana is one of the last, best places for making films—both homegrown filmmakers and major industry productions have used the state as either set or inspiration.

The arts have not only intrinsic value to Montanans but also important

Arts Festivals

Event	Location, Date, or Season	For Information
Art in the Park	Anaconda, July	563-2422
Artists and Craftsmen of the Flathead	Kalispell, April	881-4288
Bigfork Festival of the Arts	Bigfork, August	881-4636
CM Russell Auction of	Great Falls, March	800-803-3351 or
Original Western Art		761-6453
Daly Days	Hamilton, July	363-2400
High Plains Bookfest	Billings, May	294-5059
Indian Arts Showcase	Sidney, August	443-1916
Montana Festival of the Book	Missoula, September	243-6022 or
Mountain Heritage Artists Rendezvous	Livingston, September	974-6464
Outdoor Art Fair	Polson, August	849-5242
Sunrise Festival of the Arts	Sidney, July	482-1916
Sweet Pea, A Festival of the Arts	Bozeman, August	586-4003
Western Rendezvous of Art	Helena, August	442-4263
Western Art Roundup	Miles City, May	232-0635
Whitefish Annual Arts Festival	Whitefish, July	862-5875
		800-624-6001

economic benefits for the state. Montana's arts advocacy groups, the Montana Arts Council, and the state tourism office work hand in hand with local governments, businesses, and individuals to create vibrant cultural offerings that stimulate Montana commerce as well as the creativity of its citizens and visitors.

Montana nonprofit arts institutions have a total economic impact of $85 million on the Montana economy. This includes nearly 2,000 full-time jobs paying an average annual salary of $18, 275.

According to the 2000 U.S. census, a total of 5,840 artists made their living through the arts, or one in every 78 people in Montana's labor market. This represents a greater employment impact than Montana's mining industry (4,800) or the wood products manufacturing industry (5,700).

Source: State of the Arts, July/August, November/December, 2003. The Economic Impact of Mantana Artists. Center for the Applied Economic Research. Montana State University-Billings, March 2005.

Traditional and Folk Arts

Folk artists are people working in traditional forms that are passed from generation to generation through the family, ethnic, or occupational group. Their work serves to give identity to the groups from which they arise. Folk arts might be divided into three major categories:

- Occupational arts, such as folk architecture, basketmaking, leather working, whittling, blacksmithing, or weaving. Montana is home to many quilters, furniture makers, and other craftspersons who use traditional methods or elaborations on these to create beautiful and functional objects.
- Ethnic arts, such as decorative work, music, dance, or costume. Montana's many Indian tribes continue to pass on their cultural legacy to younger generations by means of native arts. Other Montana ethnic

RED LODGE FESTIVAL OF NATIONS

For nine days in early August, a visit to Red Lodge is a trip around the world as this small Montana town, once a mining center, celebrates the many ethnic groups who migrated to it. The town's kaleidoscopic heritage includes Scottish, Finnish, German, Italian, Irish, English, Welsh, Scandinavian, and Slavic cultures. Each day of the festival is dedicated to a different ethnic heritage and culminates with the All Nations Parade on the final Sunday.

The festival, held since 1950, attracts more than 15,000 visitors each year. Events include arts and crafts exhibits, ethnic foods, music, and dancing.

groups, such as those celebrated in Red Lodge's Festival of Nations, also share their heritage through song, dance, artwork, and other creations.

- Verbal and musical arts, such as stories, poetry, legend, song, humor, or family narratives. Among Montana's treasures are its oral and aural traditions, including folk music and cowboy poetry. From singers to storytellers, Montana is an earful.

Selected Cultural and Heritage Calendar

Event	Location	For Information
Billings Hispanic Fiesta	Billings, August	259-0191 or
		248-8492
Festival of Cultures	Billings, June	800-877-6259
Festival of Nations	Red Lodge, August	888-281-0625
Herbsfest	Laurel, Sept	628-7852
Heritage Days and Victorian Ball	Virginia City/August	843-5833
Heritage Days	Columbia Falls, June	892-PLAY
Libby Nordicfest	Libby, September	800-785-6541
Mining Heritage Days	Butte, September	723-7211
Montana Cowboy Poetry Gathering	Lewistown,	
	3rd weekend in August	538-8278
Townsend Cowboy Entertainer Gathering	Townsend, June	266-3946
Trout Creek Huckleberry Festival	Trout Creek, August	
The Virginia City Gathering (cowboy Poetry)	Virginia City, August	843-5455

CROW FAIR

On the third weekend of every August, Crow Agency is host to the Crow Fair and Rodeo Celebration, billed as the "tepee capital of the world" and the biggest all-Indian rodeo in the state. Indians from all over the western states and Canada converge to camp along the Little Bighorn River and to participate in competitive Indian dancing, pari-mutuel horse racing and betting, wild horse races, and other Indian games. Each morning visitors wake to camp criers on horseback and Crow language wake-up calls on the loudspeaker, followed by a spectacular parade to herald the day's colorful events. There are Giveaways and Specials, in which family, friends, lost loved ones, and other deserving persons are honored with gifts like blankets or branches tied with dollar bills.

Considered one of the premier powwows of the Plains Indians, Crow Fair is part family reunion, part party, part sporting event, part tourist attraction, and a cornucopia of visual delights, tasty foods, hypnotic music—a spiritual and intercultural renewal for all.

Powwow Calendar

Event	Location, Date or Season	For Information
Arlee 4th of July Powwow	Arlee, July	745-4984
Badlands Celebration	Brockton, June	768-5155
Bitterroot Valley All Nations Powwow	Hamilton, July	363-5383
Crow Fair	Crow Agency, August	638-3793
North American Indian Days	Browning, July	338-7276
North American Indian Alliance Powwow	Butte, September	728-0461
4th of July Powwow	Lame Deer, July	477-6284
Red Bottom Celebration	Frazer, June	768-5155
Rocky Boy's Powwow	Box Elder, August	800-823-4478
Standing Arrow Powwow	Elmo, July	849-5541
Valley of the Chiefs Powwow and Rodeo	Lodge Grass, July	638-3774
White River Cheyenne Powwow	Busby, August	477-6284

Visual Arts

Talented artists, with a sensitive eye focused on the amazing natural canvases and the diverse faces of our Big Sky, were part of the stream of people who followed the first explorers or accompanied the early settlers to Montana.

A century and a half later, Montana continues to be an inspirational working environment for hundreds of visual artists of all mediums. The Archie Bray Foundation for the Ceramic Arts in Helena, for example, attracts renowned ceramic artsits from the world over.

Many Montana photographers, sculptors, painters, and other media artists have worked on the advance edge of their chosen fields. Contemporary artists who have enjoyed a world wide reputation include Rudy Autio, the Finnish-American painter and ceramist from Missoula known for his colorful, swirling designs with human and animal figures; Floyd Tennison DeWitt, who sculpts bronze horses and historical scenes with a nod to the European tradition; David Shaner, the Bigfork ceramic artist who sculpted highly textured works in metal; Peter Voulho, considered the leading ceramic sculptor of the 1960s; Deborah Butterfield, the Bozeman-based sculptor, perhaps the best-known Montana artist on the national contemporary art scene, noted for her horses made of bronze and other materials; Dana Boussard creates glass art, painted fiber murals, paintings, and large-scale art that graces numerous public and corporate spaces around the country.

John L. Clarke (1881–1970)

This beloved Montana sculptor, painter, and carver was also known as Cutapuis (Man-Who-Talks-Not), his Blackfeet name. He was born in Highwood and as a toddler, he became deaf from scarlet fever. Clarke studied the wild animals of his home region near Glacier National Park and made figures of them in clay, later turning to carving. He attended the Montana and North Dakota Schools for the Deaf and studied woodcarving at the St. Francis Academy in Milwaukee. He later had his own shop in the northwest corner of East Glacier, where John D. Rockefeller was one of his customers. His carvings of the wildlife and paintings of the landscapes of the Glacier region gained him national recognition. He was included in the recently published *Deaf Heritage: A Narrative History of Deaf America*, released by the National Association of the Deaf. The Museum of the Plains Indian at Browning and the School for the Deaf and Blind in Great Falls display Clarke's large-scale murals of Blackfeet life.

James Welch (1940–2003)

Born in Browning to a Blackfeet father and Gros Ventre mother, Welch went to schools on the Blackfeet and Fort Belknap Reservations. After studying under Richard Hugo at the University of Montana in the 1960s, Welch began telling the world about life on Montana's Hi-Line and in Indian country. His books have been translated and published in France, Italy, Sweden, Japan, Germany, and other countries and read widely here in the United States.

Welch's first book of poetry *Riding the Earthboy 40* was published in 1971, the beginning of an impressive body of poetry and fiction. His novels include *Winter in the Blood* (1974), *The Death of Jim Loney* (1979), *The Indian Lawyer* (1990), and *Fools Crow* (1986), for which Welch won an American Book Award and the *Los Angeles Times* Book Prize. His 1994 "Killing Custer" was an examination of the famous Last Stand at Little Bighorn from the Indian point of view. Welch's last work was *The Heartsong of Charging Elk* (2000).

Among his most prized honors is the Lifetime Achievement Award from the Native Writers' Circle of the Americas. In 1995, Welch was knighted by the French government for his contribution to arts and letters. Jim Welch died in Missoula of a heart attack at age 62.

William D'Arcy McNickle (1904–1977)

Born in St. Ignatius to a Métis mother and an Anglo father, McNickle became an honored novelist and writer-editor on American Indian cultural heritage. He graduated from The University of Montana in 1925 and went on to study at Oxford University (1925-26) and the University of Grenoble (1931). Following his degree work, McNickle wrote for the Federal Writers' Project in Washington, D.C. and was the director of tribal relations for the Bureau of Indian Affairs.

McNickle's three novels were released over a period of some four decades. The first, The Surrounded (1936), was inspired by his own Montana background. The second, Runner in the Sun, was released in 1954. His third, the highly acclaimed Wind from an Enemy Sky, was published following his death in 1977. McNickle wrote or edited numerous histories of Indian culture in America.

In later life, he taught anthropology at the University of Saskatchewan and became program director of the Center for American Indian History at The Newberry Library in Chicago, later renamed the D'Arcy McNickle Center for the History of the American Indian in his honor.

A. B. Guthrie Jr. (1901–1991)

His richly detailed novels of life in Montana and the Old West won him wide acclaim, including the Pulitzer Prize for The Way West in 1950, and made him one of the state's most beloved writers. Alfred Bertram Guthrie Jr. was born in 1901 in Indiana, but grew up in Chinook and Great Falls and graduated from The University of Montana in 1923. He worked as a writing teacher, a journalist, and an editor in Kentucky before turning to writing novels.

MONTANA HISTORICAL SOCIETY

From his home near Choteau, he wrote stories that matched the scope of the land around him and the sky above him. He wrote of Indians, fur trappers, mountain men, and other inhabitants of Montana and of their relationship to the land, the waters. Later in his life, in lectures and essays, he spoke just as eloquently, but more directly, for the defense and stewardship of that land, those waters. In addition to the Pulitzer winner, his books include The Big Sky, These Thousand Hills, The Last Valley, and an autobiography called The Blue Hen's Chick.

From early modernists to the many Montana artists who represent the state of the arts today, our state sustains those who actively seek new visions.

Visual Artists

In 1832, the painter George Catlin (1796–1872) rode up the Missouri River on the steamboat *Yellowstone* and spent a summer soaking up details of the Indian culture of Montana and the Upper Missouri country. The paintings inspired by his time here contributed to our historical understanding of this land.

Karl Bodmer, a young Swiss artist who had been studying in Paris, came up the river on the same steamboat the following year, accompanying a wealthy Prussian prince who was collecting specimens of the area's natural history. Bodmer gave us some of the first drawings and paintings of the river and its valley. They show us what the land looked like before settlements sprang up.

Later, resident artists gave us their renditions of our landscape and people. Among them was Charlie Russell. Russell may not have expected his illustrated letters to friends near and far to bring him fame, but Montana has come to claim the man whose later oil paintings and watercolors captured its essence as its own painter king. His canvases of the Montana sky may appear romantic or impressionistic, but anyone who spends a few days here knows he got it right.

Other artists include Olaf C. Seltzer (1878–1957), who immigrated from Denmark, befriended Russell, and became known for portraits of early Montanans; Edgar S. Paxson (1852–1919), whose murals can still be seen today in the Missoula County Courthouse; and Winold Reiss (1888–1953), noted for depicting the art and costumes of the Blackfeet.

Western and landscape art is still one of Montana's favorite representations. Gary Carter, a painter and sculptor from West Yellowstone, specializes in mountain men and Indian scenes from the nineteenth century. Russell Chatham is a cultural guru and Renaissance man of the Paradise Valley. He produces fine oils and lithographs of impressionistic landscapes, particularly of the Paradise. He owns galleries, an art center, and a restaurant. He has

LINDERMAN COLLECTION/K.ROSS TOOLE ARCHIVES

Frank Bird Linderman (1869–1938)

The Indians called him "Sign-Talker with a Straight Tongue." He lived several lives—trapper, cow hand, miner, woodsman, newspaper editor, merchant, and politician—but we remember him best for his books on Indians and Montana.

He moved to the Flathead Valley at the age of sixteen from Cleveland, Ohio. In 1917, he moved to the west shore of Flathead Lake and assumed the life of a writer, publishing five volumes on traditional Indian lore, two novels, a book of poetry, and more. His books were the end-product of exhaustive, meticulous research. He interviewed Indian elders, confirming his interpreter's translation with his thorough knowledge of sign language. His efforts to get the facts straight may have been part of the reason he was adopted into the Blackfeet, Cree, and Crow tribes. His best known works are Indian Why Stories; The American, a biography of Chief Plenty Coups; Pretty Shield; and Old Man Coyote. After Linderman finished The American, Plenty Coups said "I am glad I have told you these things, Sign-Talker. You have felt my heart, and I have felt yours."

Grace Stone Coates (1881–1976)

Coates gained national fame in the 1920s and 1930s for poetry and her critically acclaimed first novel, Black Cherries. Coates's work appeared in the Christian Science Monitor, New York Times, and other publications. She lived and wrote in Martinsdale, where she also served as Meagher County Superintendent of Schools from 1918 to 1921. In the early 1960s, neighbors managed to have Coates, who was losing her memory, committed to a nursing home. A book dealer got Coates's collection of books, and many of her journals and papers were destroyed. She died in the nursing home.

The life of Grace Coates is told in Honey Wine and Hunger Root, by Martinsdale writer Lee Rostad.

also delved into publishing as the owner of Clark City Press. Jessica Zemsky, a watercolor and pastel artist from Big Timber, is known for her pictures of western children, especially Indian children, and nineteenth-century homestead scenes. Dale Livesey of Helena paints impressionistic landscapes, bolder in color than Chatham's hazy or snowy scenes. The images of Jay R. Rummell, Missoula ceramist, painter, print-maker provide insight on Montana's past, present, and future.

Much current art shows a sense of humor, too. Monte Dolack, Nancy Erickson, and Parks Reece, with their pun-intended animal prints, are just a few of the many artists here who keep us looking and laughing. Many homes and businesses display at least one of Dolack's engaging, often humorous, poster depictions of the West and its animal icons.

Photographers

Montana's open spaces have inspired photographers, too. F. J. Haynes rode the rails of the Northern Pacific, shooting the landscapes he passed through and the people he met. He processed and printed some of his work in a customized railroad car. Haynes was also an early documenter of the wonders of Yellowstone National Park. Many of his works can be seen in an exhibit at the Montana Historical Society Museum. L. A. Huffman of Miles City captured cowboys and the Plains Indians in his photographs.

In the early years of this century, Lady Evelyn Cameron, an Englishwoman who came to the U.S. with her husband in 1889, worked her ranch in Terry while creating some of the most poignant pictures of eastern Montana's dry land settlers. Later photographers saw some of the same beauty in sparse country. On the contemporary scene, Joanne Berghold, based in Wilsall, shoots landscapes and still lifes in black and white. Many of her photographs are marked by glossy, shiny surfaces—wet roads and such. As founder of *Montana Magazine,* Rick Graetz filled that publication and many books on the regions and features of the state with stunning images of backcountry and other sights that others may never be privileged to view on their own. He and his wife Susie continue to document through photography nearly every scenic vista in the state.

Literary Arts

In an attempt to capture the pageant of life here, numerous Montana writers have made significant contributions to the literary wealth of America. The

Mary MacLane (1881-1929)

MONTANA HISTORICAL SOCIETY

MacLane came to Butte from Winnipeg as a 10-year-old with her family. Nine years later she wrote a book that became a national sensation overnight. In *The Story of Mary MacLane*, the teenager detailed her life in Butte, her longings, her reverence for the Devil, and her "good odd philosophy." Her candor shocked the average reader. After her early success, she left Butte, living in bohemian New York and later in Chicago. She wrote two other autobiographical books and the script for a silent film, *Men Who Have Made Love to Me*, which she also starred in, but never regained the attention she had when she was 19. She died in a Chicago rooming house at the age of 48.

Evelyn Cameron (1868-1928)

She was born in England and came to eastern Montana as a 21-year-old bride in 1889. She and her husband Ewen S. Cameron, the son of Lord Cameron, fell in love with eastern Montana after their honeymoon hunting trip and returned to establish a ranch near Terry. They later moved to the Marsh area, between Miles City and Wibaux.

MONTANA HISTORICAL SOCIETY

Evelyn bought her first camera in 1894 and began to document frontier life in rich, black-and-white detail. Her camera captured people of all economic and ethnic classes at work and at play, recorded the lonesome landscapes on which she ranged, and above all, reflected her own intelligence and wit. In the accompanying photo, she poses with a kestrel, gaining its attention with a grasshopper.

Her diaries add to the legacy she left. Cameron's extensive photographic gift was nearly lost to posterity. Her photographs sat in a friend's cellar for half a century before being rediscovered by writer Donna Lucey, who compiled Cameron's work in *Photographing Montana, 1894–1928*.

Lady Cameron managed the ranch for thirteen years after her husband died, until her own death in 1928.

Norman Maclean
(1902–1990)

Maclean was born in Iowa but grew up in Missoula. When he was seventy years old, he began writing about his beloved Montana. He made a significant contribution to the state's literature with only two books—his memoir, *A River Runs Through It and Other Stories* (1976) and *Young Men and Fire* (1992), an account of the 1949 Mann Gulch fire and its aftermath. As revealed in *A River Runs Through It*, he attended Dartmouth College, accepted a job with the University of Chicago's English Department, and earned a doctorate there. Though most of his life was spent in a rigorous academic environment, his writing reflects his upbringing as the son of a Presbyterian minister, his work as an adolescent for the Forest Service, and his love of Montana, especially its rivers and wild land. His family owned a place on Seeley Lake and, as his much-loved memoir showed, he spent innumerable hours fishing the Blackfoot River.

number and quality of contributions to *The Last Best Place: A Montana Anthology*, compiled in the mid-1980s by William Kittredge, Annick Smith, and a distinguished editorial board, speak volumes on this point.

The book's 1,160 pages encompass the state's literary traditions: myths and stories, handed down orally and in great writing, by Native Americans; observations taken from journals of early explorers; writings by pioneers and Indians; stories inspired by life on the farm and ranch; poems, stories, and recollections of Butte; modern literature; and contemporary poetry and fiction.

Before Indian writers had gained a wide audience, non-Indians such as James Willard Schultz and Frank Bird Linderman portrayed with respectful voices the lives and legends of the first Montanans.

In the intervening years, the voices have risen and grown, producing novels and short stories out of our cities, small towns, and wilderness. We have heard from an abundance of fiction writers—B. M. Bower, Dan Cushman, Dorothy Johnson, A. B. Guthrie (Montana's only Pulitzer Prize winner, in 1950, for The Way West), and Norman Maclean, as members of earlier generations; Thomas McGuane, Ivan Doig, Mary Clearman Blew, William Kittredge, Pete Fromm, Rick deMarinis, David Long, Deirdre McNamer, Debra Magpie Earling, Judy Blunt, Rick Bass, Greg Keeler, Maile Meloy, William Hjortsberg, and Lise McClendon, among others today.

Poetry lives here, too, in new work produced by writers such as Sheryl Noethe, Rick Newby, Dave Thomas, Lowell Jaeger, Ed Lahey, Wilbur Wood, Roger Dunsmore, Patricia Goedicke, Sandra Alcosser, and others, and in a cult of nearly mythic proportions—a "dead poets society" of sorts—around such disparate late poets as Richard Hugo and Richard Brautigan.

The 2005 legislature created the post of Montana Poet Laureate. The first person named was Sandra Alcosser, a widely acclaimed poet, editor, and professor, who has a masters of fine arts from the University of Montana.

Cowboy poets address a wide range of subjects, some traditional, some modern, with free-spirited voices. Wally McRae, Paul Zarzyski, Mike Logan, and Gwen Petersen are a few that ride our literary fence line.

Montana continues to serve as a grounding point for an impressive number of modern essayists and magazine writers who portray Montana and the West—or American culture in general—with fresh observations. The works of David Quammen, Tim Cahill, and Peter Stark first came to us through *Outside* magazine. Between them, these men have since published a number of books. Before finding a niche at *Outside,* Cahill was a top-flight journalist for *Rolling Stone,* the magazine that spawned *Outside.*

Gary Ferguson, Richard Manning, Rick Bass, and Annick Smith are others who have won acclaim with their essays, articles, and books of nonfiction.

Montana is also blessed with a number of publishing houses committed to promoting Montana to a world that can't seem to get enough of it.

The Best Montana Books

With all that has been written about Montana or by Montanans, who can say which authors or books are the best? Everyone has a favorite or a list of favorites.

In 2001, Harry W. Fritz, the much respected University of Montana history professor and former legislator, and the Montana Historical Society distributed 14,000 questionnaires, asking respondents to name the "five best books about Montana." The resulting list of seventy-five books appeared in the Autumn 2002 edition of the Montana Historical Society's *Montana, The Magazine of Western History,* as "The Best Books About Montana—Twenty-first Century Edition," by Harry W. Fritz. Professor Fritz had conducted a

Monte Dolack (1950–)

Dolack was born in Great Falls, where he worked for a short time in the refinery of the Anaconda Copper Company and played in local rock bands. The money he earned at these jobs helped him get started in the study of art, first at Montana State University, later at The University of Montana, Missoula and at the California College of Arts and Crafts. Along the way, Dolack developed the whimsical style he brings to the making of his posters, paintings, and prints. He borrowed traditional watercolor methods for use in his acrylic painting, also

COURTESY OF MONTE DOLACK

using an airbrush. His work, especially the posters that comment slyly on the coexistence of humanity and nature, is seen in galleries and museums, but perhaps most pervasively in Montana's living rooms, kitchens, bedrooms, and bathrooms. In recent years, Montana's most famous graphic artist has concentrated on acrylic oil and water color painting. He is still much sought after for commissioned pieces portraying events and attractions in his home state. His gallery is on West Front Street in Missoula.

Robert (Bob) M. Scriver (1914 –1999)

Born in Browning, Bob's first creative talents were teaching, music and taxidermy. At age 42, he picked up a sculptor's knife and began a passionate and prolific career as one of the West's most revered sculptors. Until the day of his death at age 84, Bob worked in his Browning museum and workshop to create more than 400 bronze casts, depicting figures, wildlife, and scenes from the Old West

MONTANA HISTORICAL SOCIETY

he hoped to capture before it disappeared. He was internationally recognized for the many mediums in which he excelled and was the recipient of many awards, including gold and silver medals from the Cowboy Artists of America and the National Academy of Western Arts. He is the author of *Blackfeet: Artists of the Northern Plains* and other books. Many of his works and much of his extensive collection of Old West memorabilia, once displayed at his studio and Museum of Montana Wildlife in Browning, have been donated to the Montana Historical Society, for use by various Montana and Canadian museums.

previous survey in 1981, the results of which were published in the winter 1982 edition of Montana, *The Magazine of Western History.*

We have listed the first twenty-five Best Books About Montana

1. Doig, Ivan. *This House of Sky: Landscapes of a Western Mind.* New York: Harcourt Brace Jovanovich, 1978.
2. Howard, Joseph Kinsey. *Montana: High, Wide, and Handsome.* New Haven, Conn.: Yale University Press, 1943.
3. Guthrie, A. B., Jr. *The Big Sky.* New York: William Sloane Associates, 1947.
4. Kittredge, William, and Annick Smith, Eds. *The Last Best Place: A Montana Anthology.* Seattle, Wash.: University of Washington Press, 5th Printing, 2000.
5. Maclean, Norman. *A River Runs Through It, and Other Stories.* Chicago: University of Chicago Press, 1976.
6. Malone, Michael P., Richard B. Roeder, and William L. Lang. *Montana: A History of Two Centuries.* (2nd ed.) Seattle: University of Washington Press, 1991.
7. Toole, K. Ross. *Montana: An Uncommon Land.* Norman: University of Oklahoma Press, 1959.
8. Garcia, Andrew. *Tough Trip Through Paradise, 1878-1879.* Ed. by Bennet H. Stein. Boston: Houghton Mifflin Co., 1967.
9. Welch, James. *Fools Crow.* New York: Viking, 1986.
10. Walker, Mildred. *Winter Wheat.* New York: Harcourt, Brace and Co., 1944.
11. Doig, Ivan. *English Creek.* New York: Atheneum, 1984.
12. Doig, Ivan. *Dancing at the Rascal Fair.* New York: Atheneum, 1987.
13. Russell, Charles M. *Trails Plowed Under.* Garden City, N.Y.: Doubleday, Page & Co., 1927
14. Moulton, Gary E., ed. *The Journals of the Lewis and Clark Expedition.* 13 vol. Lincoln: University of Nebraska Press, 1989.
15. Glasscock, Carl B. *The War of the Copper Kings: Builders of Butte and Wolves of Wall Street.* Indianapolis: Bobbs-Merrill, 1935.
16. Lucey, Donna M. *Photographing Montana 1894-1928. The Life and Work of Evelyn Cameron.* Missoula, Montana: Mountain Press Publishing Company.
17. Raban, Jonathan. *Bad Land: An American Romance.* New York: Pantheon Books, 1996.
18. Ambrose, Stephen E. *Undaunted Courage, Meriwether Lewis, Thomas Jefferson, and the Opening of the American West.* New York: Simon & Schuster, 1996.

19. Blew, Mary Clearman. *All but the Waltz: A Memoir of Five Generations in the Life of A Montana Family.* New York: Penguin, 1991.
20. Malone, Michael P. *The Battle for Butte: Mining and Politics on the Northern Frontier, 1864-1906.* Seattle: University of Washington Press, 1981
21. Maclean, Norman. *Young Men and Fire.* Chicago: University of Chicago Press, 1992.
22. Cushman, Dan. *Stay Away, Joe, a Novel.* New York: Viking Press, 1953.
23. Johnson, Dorothy M. *The Bloody Bozeman.* New York: McGraw-Hill, 1971.
24. Welch, James. *Winter in the Blood.* New York: Harper and Row. 1974
25. Brown, Mark Herbert and W. R Felton. *Before Barbed Wire: L.A. Huffman, Photographer on Horseback.* New York: Holt, 1955.

Montana Festival of the Book

Since 2000, Montanans have celebrated the written word with a three-day Montana Festival of the Book in Missoula. The Festival takes place in late September with most events scheduled for the Holiday Inn Parkside and multiple downtown Missoula venues. There are sixty or more sessions of readings, panels, exhibits, performances, an artists reception and silent auction, book appraisals, gala readings, and more. Over the years, the event has attracted audiences of 4,000 to 5,000 persons, many from outside the region.

Some of the most important voices of the West have appeared at the Festival, including Richard Ford, Annie Proulx, James Lee Burke, David James Duncan, Mary Clearman Blew, William Kittredge, Rick Bass, Annick Smith, James Welch, David Quammen, Tim Cahill, Nicholas Evans, Judy Blunt, Pete Fromm, Richard Manning, Jeff Shaara, Diane Smith, Melanie Thon, Greg Keeler, Sandra Alcosser, Deirdre McNamer, James Crumley, Larry Watson, Richard Wheeler, Debra Magpie Earling, Robert Wrigley, Kevin Canty, Kim Barnes, Jon A. Jackson, Mark Spragg, Peter Stark, Kat Martin, C. J. Box, and many others.

Festival sponsors include the Montana Committee for the Humanities and its Montana Center for the Book, National Endowment for the Humanities, the National Endowment for the Arts, and the Montana Arts Council.

243-6022 (in Montana) 800-624-6001

www.bookfest-mt.org/

Several other Montana cities host book festivals:

Great Falls Festival of the Book, April

High Plains Bookfest, Billings, July
Helena Festival of the Book, October

The One Book Montana Program

The Montana Center for the Book, in partnership with Montana Public Radio, Yellowstone Public Radio, Penguin Group USA, and other organizations, selected *Fools Crow* by James Welch as the 2004 One Book Montana selection. The 2003 One Book Montana selection was Mildred Walker's *Winter Wheat*. A Program of the Montana Committee for the Humanities and its Montana Center for the Book, an Affiliate of the Center for the Book in the Library of Congress.

The One Book Montana program offers an invitation to all Montanans to read Fools Crow over the spring, summer, and fall. Montana Center for the Book provides reading and discussion guides, suggestions for library, school and book group projects, and opportunities for reader comments and other tools on its website, www.montanabook.org/onebook.htm.

Performing Arts

Music

Montana is home to several classical music organizations, including large symphony orchestras with regular seasons. The Missoula Civic Symphony began in 1903. The Great Falls Symphony came into being in 1947. Butte, Billings, Helena, and Kalispell initiated symphony orchestras in the 1950s, and Bozeman followed in 1986. The Scobey-based Prairie Symphonette is music to the ears of eastern Montanans.

Many of the musicians receive their training in the fine musical programs supported by the community through the public schools and the institutions of higher education in the state. Some young people become accomplished members of a local orchestra well before they can vote.

Symphony performances are often accompanied by outstanding local choral groups or are presented in conjunction with the state's several ballet and dance companies.

In summer, the Montana hills are alive with the sound of music, from bluegrass and jazz festivals to week-long music festivals at Red Lodge, Kalispell, Bigfork, and Big Sky, which feature a vast array of musical offerings.

Many talented musicians often return from national recording and performing schedules to play for appreciative audiences in the state they once

William Kittredge (1932-)

Kittredge grew up on a ranch in southeastern Oregon, but a love for books led him to the prestigious University of Iowa Writers' Workshop. After earning an MFA there, he came to Missoula to teach in the creative writing program at the university. His works include a memoir, *Hole in the Sky* (1992); the short story collections *We Are Not in This Together* (1984) and *The Van Gogh Field* (1978); and a collection of autobiographical essays, *Owning It All* (1987). He also contributes short stories and essays to periodicals such as *Harper's* and *Outside* magazine.

He has also made significant contributions to Montana literature as an editor. With his partner, Annick Smith, he edited (and is credited with naming) the massive anthology of the state's literature, *The Last Best Place*. He also edited a book of essays, *Montana Spaces: Essays in Celebration of Montana*, with contributions by Thomas McGuane, Wallace Stegner, Gretel Ehrlich, and Tim Cahill, among others.

Richard Hugo (1923–1982)

Dick Hugo was born in Seattle, served in the Army, Air Corps as a bombardier, and received a master's degree from the University of Washington, where he studied under the poet Theodore Roethke. After working as a technical writer for the Boeing Company, Hugo accepted a job with The University of Montana's English department, where he would direct and cultivate the creative writing program. His poetry is the most beloved form he left, but he also wrote autobiographical essays, a book about writing, and one detective novel set in western Montana, *Death and the Good Life*.

Hugo was a member of a literary family. Works by his wife, poet Ripley Schemm; his mother-in-law, novelist Mildred Walker Schemm; and his stepson, Matthew Hansen, appear in the anthology of Montana literature, *The Last Best Place*.

Nina Russell (1911–2003)

She played jazz and blues at nightclubs in Las Vegas, Chicago, and Los Angeles, where she entertained Judy Garland, Lana Turner, John Wayne, and other Hollywood stars. Al Capone's brother threatened to burn her family's house down if she didn't play at his Chicago nightclub, but she showed him the error of his ways. Until a few years before her death at age 91, she played in a piano bar on the west shore of Flathead Lake, and in a Bigfork bookstore on Sunday afternoons, passing out song sheets so her audience could sing along.

Russell was born in South Carolina to a "buffalo soldier," a member of the 25th Infantry under Colonel Nelson Miles, with a heritage which includes Cherokee Indian, Jewish, Irish, Scot, and "Negro" bloodlines. (She preferred this term.)

Russell heard her father's stories of Montana and came here to fish on vacations. She and her husband bought property in Hungry Horse in 1950. Russell moved there in 1971, after her husband died. "Montana's Queen of Jazz" also played organ at a church in Coram for more than seventeen. In March 2000, the Montana Arts Council honored Nina as a "Montana Living Legend."

Music Festivals of Note

Event	Town/Season	Information
An Ri Ra Butte Irish Festival	Butte	498-3812
Bitterroot Valley Bluegrass Festival	Hamilton/July	363-1250
Buddy DeFranco Jazz Festival	Missoula/April	243-5071
Country Music Campout	Troy/July	295-4358
Dixieland Jazz Festival	Great Falls/August	(800) 851-9980
Flathead Music Festival	Whitefish/mid-July to mid-August	257-0787
Glacier Jazz Stampede	Kalispell/October	862-3814
International Choral Festival	Missoula/July	721-7985
Lincoln Fiddlers Contest	Lincoln/August	362-9200
Madison River Music Festival	Ennis/May	682-4053
Montana State Old-Time Fiddlers Contest	Red Lodge/July	236-5385
Montana Urban Music Festival	Billings/July	670-2329
Mount Helena Music Festival	Helena/July	(800) 851-9980
Red Lodge Music Festival	Red Lodge/June	446-1905
Sleeping Giant Swing 'n Jazz Jubilee	Helena/June	227-9711

called home. George Winston, the pianist who records for the Windham Hill record label, grew up in Miles City and Billings. He has described his compositions as "rural folk piano" pieces and returns to Montana often to share his wide-ranging talents.

Montanans are jazzed up, too. Jazz in its traditional forms—Dixieland, ragtime, and big band/swing—collects audiences from all over the country and Canada in Helena in the third week of June, in Missoula in April, and in Kalispell in October. Perhaps this present-day enthusiasm for jazz festivals hearkens back to the ragtime music of the mining camp hurdy-gurdies and saloons of the 1890s, or to the dozens of dance bands in the 1920s to 1950s that had folks "dancin' 'til after milking time" in the urban clubs and rural roadhouses of the state.

Here in the 1990s, the Big Sky still has plenty of homegrown talent and plenty of dance clubs and roadhouses. On any Saturday night, we've got plenty of local musical talent to fit your mood or preferences. Groups that can lively up our musical life include: Bob Wire and the Fencemenders, Too Slim and the Taildraggers, the Volumen, Cash for Junkers, Little Elmo and the Mambo Kings, the Clintons, Big Sky Mudflaps, Shane Clause and Stomping Ground, and the Tropical Montana Marimba Ensemble. Rob Quist and his Great Northern band perform throughout the West and even venture eastward with old and new Montana favorites like "In Without Knockin'" and "Take a Whiff." Quist originally performed with the Montana Band, whose national fame ended in 1987 when ten people, including band members, died in the state's worst air disaster near Flathead Lake.

A Billings songwriter who goes by only one name, Kostas, left Montana to find fame as a key Nashville songwriter. Kostas has written dozens of songs that have made the country and western charts. He appeared with Jimmy Buffett playing "Livingston Saturday Night" in the movie *Rancho Deluxe*. That song is among several of Buffett's Montana-based tunes, which also include "Come Monday Morning," and "Ringling, Ringling."

Those who don't require a dance floor can often find a venue with a balladeer like Browning's Jack Gladstone, troubadours like Bozeman's Greg Keeler, or a music and humor troupe like the Ringling Five or the Montana Logging and Ballet Company. Some acts are harder to define. The Drum Brothers, from Arlee, beat out ancient and New Age rhythms. Walkin' Jim Stoltz treks hundreds of miles through Montana wilderness, then hits the road for a few months with his guitar, slide shows, and songs.

Eden Atwood (1969 –)

Eden Atwood hails from a family long respected for its patronage of and contributions to the arts in Montana. She was born in Memphis but moved to Montana at the age of five with her mother, Gus Guthrie Miller of Butte. Miller is a longtime advocate of the arts and the daughter of A. B. Guthrie Jr. Eden's father, Hub Atwood, was a well-known composer and arranger who worked for Frank Sinatra and Harry James.

CONCORD JAXX, INC.

Both her parents encouraged Atwood's talents as a pianist and singer, and throughout her youth, she visited her father's Memphis musical world for training and inspiration. She studied drama and musical theater at the University of Montana, and performed with a Missoula jazz combo, but left Montana at the age of 19 for Chicago's lively jazz scene. There, she attended the American Conservatory of Music and later headlined at the legendary Gold Star Sardine Bar.

For a brief time, Atwood was a television actress in New York and a model in Paris, but she returned to music, performing at New York's Algonquin Hotel and other top jazz venues. She has released six CDs of jazz standards, ballads, and her own compositions on the Concord and Groove Note labels, in addition to tracks on major jazz compilations.

MONTANA HISTORICAL SOCIETY

Taylor Gordon
(1893-1971)

From his hometown of White Sulphur Springs to Harlem in its heyday, this black concert singer trod the vaudeville stages of the U.S., later touring European concert halls. He even appeared in a number of motion pictures in the 1930s. Gordon's singing talents were first encouraged in 1915 while he was working on the private railway car of financier and circus impresario John Ringling. Ringling had befriended the young black man on a visit to the White Sulphur Springs area, where Ringling owned property.

In 1915, Gordon, who worked as Ringling's chauffeur, cook, and attendant, was singing along with an Enrico Caruso recording in the railroad car when a passerby complimented him on his voice and gave him the name of a New York voice teacher. Thus Gordon began a long, sometimes frustrating effort to sing professionally. He did not meet with success until the mid-1920s. Gordon's autobiography, *Born to Be* (1929), tells of his life in Montana and features some impressions of the Harlem Renaissance he was a part of in the 1920s. In the winter of 1935–1936, Gordon returned to Montana to write a utopian novel, Doanda. He met with bitter disappointment when he was unable to find a publisher for the book, but he did find modest success with a mechanical toy he had invented during his 1935 retreat to a cabin near his hometown. After several hospitalizations for mental illness in New York, he returned to White Sulphur Springs in 1959 where he found solace and a respected place in the community.

Theater

A summer without theater in Montana is like a winter without snow. Each summer season, Montanans and visitors enjoy theatrical offerings in communities across the state, including offerings by the Port Polson Players, the Badland Players in Havre, the Fort Peck Summer Theater, and the Bigfork

Summer Playhouse, celebrating its forty-fourth season in 2004. The oldest theatrical company in Montana, the Virginia City Players, has played to packed audiences since it first offered melodramas in 1949. Folks all across the state mark their calendars to catch the summer tour of the Shakespeare in the Parks troupe, celebrating over thirty-four years of bringing to dozens of Montana communities some creative interpretations of the works of Shakespeare and his contemporaries.

Dozens of theater groups in the state also have winter performance seasons, the mainstays of the Montana stage. The Montana Repertory Theatre, the Vigilante Theater Company, and Missoula Children's Theatre are a few of the professional theater organizations in the state. Some of the most vibrant shows are presented by college students or talented local children and adults, including the shows at the Grandstreet Theater in Helena, Montana's oldest year-round community playhouse.

Montana in the Movies

The Montana Film Office was created in 1974 as a central information source for filmmakers who seek locations in Montana. It is part of the Department of Commerce and is funded entirely by the state's 7 percent tax on accommodations. The primary role of the Montana Film Office is to bring productions (feature films, commercials, television, still shoots, and documentaries) into Montana for the overall economic benefit of the state.

Statewide Arts Organizations

Montana Arts Council

The 1967 Legislature created the Montana Arts Council to provide citizens of all economic and geographic circumstances with an equal opportunity to have the best of arts in their lives. The governor appoints the Montana Arts Council's fifteen members from the various geographical areas of the state and from those who have a keen interest in one or more of the arts and a willingness to devote time and effort in the public interest. The council's duties are to encourage the presentation of and participation in the arts—including music, theater, dance, painting, sculpture, architecture, and allied arts and crafts—and to foster public interest in and expansion of the state's cultural heritage and resources. Since 1970, the Artists in Schools program has provided thousands of public school children in even the most remote communities of the state the opportunity to learn about all aspects of the arts.

Feature Films & TV Productions, Scenes Filmed in Montana

Year	Film	Company	Location
1920	Devils Horse		Hardin area
1920	Where the Rivers Rise		Columbia Falls
1950	Red Skies Over Montana	20th Century Fox	Missoula area
1951	Timberjack		Missoula area
1951	Warpath	20th Century Fox	Billings area
1954	Cattle Queen of Montana		East Glacier
1958	Dangerous Mission		Glacier National Park
1970	Little Big Man		Virginia City/Billings
1972	Evel Knievel		Butte
1973	Route 66		Butte
1973	Thunderbolt and Lightfoot	United Artists	Malpaso/Livingston/Great Falls
1973	Winterhawk	Charles Pierce Prod.	Kalispell area
1974	The Killer Inside Me	Cyclone Productions	Butte
1974	Potato Fritz	Horizon Productions	Helena area
1974	Rancho Deluxe	Frank Perry Films	Livingston
1975	Missouri Breaks	Jack Sherman Prod.	Billings/Virginia City/Red Lodge
1975	Winds of Autumn	Charles Pierce Prod.	Kalispell
1976	Beartooth	ESI Productions	Red Lodge area
1976	Damnation Alley	20th Century Fox	Lakeside
1976	Pony Express Rider	Doty Dayton Prod.	Virginia City/Nevada City
1977	Christmas Miracle in Caulfield USA	20th Century TV	Roundup
1977	Grey Eagle	Charles Pierce Prod.	Helena area
1977	The Other Side of Hell	Aubrey/Lyons Prod./NBC	Warm Springs
1977	Telefon	MGM-Siegel Film	Great Falls
1978	Rodeo Red & The Runaway	Highgate Pictures/NBC TV	Billings
1978	The Shining	Warner Brothers	Glacier National Park
1979	Heartland	Wilderness Woman/ Filmhaus, Inc.	Harlowton area
1979	Heaven's Gate	United Artists	Kalispell/Glacier National Park/Butte
1979	The Legend of Walks Far Woman	EMI Productions/CBS	Billings/Red Lodge/Hardin
1979	South by Northwest	KWSU/Washington State	Virginia City/Nevada City
1980	Continental Divide	Universal Pictures	Glacier National Park
1982	Firefox	Warner Bros.	Glasgow/Cut Bank area
1982	Fast Walking	Lorimar Productions	Deer Lodge
1983	The Stone Boy	Roth Productions	Great Falls area
1983	Triumphs of a Man Called Horse	Sandy Howard Prod.	Cooke City/Red Lodge
1985	Runaway Train	Cannon Films	Butte/Anaconda area
1986	Amazing Grace and Chuck	Tri-Star Productions	Bozeman/Livingston/Helena
1986	Amy Grant: Home for the Holidays	NBC/Smith-Hemion Prod.	Kalispell/Glacier National Park
1986	Stacking	Nepenthe Prod.	Billings area
1986	The Untouchables	Paramount Pictures	Cascade area
1987	Powwow Highway	Handmade Films	Hardin area/Northern Cheyenne Reservation/Colstrip
1987	War Party	Hemdale Productions	Browning/Cut Bank/Choteau
1988	Cold Feet	Avenue Pictures	Livingston area

Feature Films & TV Productions, Scenes Filmed in Montana (cont.)

Year	Film	Company	Location
1988	Disorganized Crime	Buena Vista	Hamilton/Darby/Missoula
1989	Always	Amblin Entertain./Universal	Libby
1989	Bright Angel	Hemdale Prod.	Billings
1989	Montana	HBO Prod./TNN	Bozeman area
1989	A Thousand Pieces of Gold	Motherlode Prod.	Nevada City
1990	Common Ground		Columbia Falls
1990	Son of the Morning Star	Republic Pictures/ABC	Billings area
1990	True Colors	Paramount	Big Sky
1991	A River Runs Through It	Big Sky Productions/Columbia	Livingston/Bozeman areas
1991	Diggstown	MGM	Deer Lodge
1991	Far and Away	Imagine Entertain./Universal	Billings area
1991	Keep the Change	Tisch Prod./TNT	Livingston area
1991	Season of Change	Sterling Films	Bitterroot Valley
1992	The Ballad of Little Jo	JoCo Productions	Red Lodge area
1992	Josh and S.A.M.	Castle Rock	Billings area
1993	Beethoven's 2nd	Universal Pictures	Glacier National Park/Flathead
1993	Forrest Gump	Momentum Films/Paramount	Glacier National Park/ Blackfeet Reservation
1993	Holy Matrimony	Interscope Prod.	Great Falls area
1993	Iron Will	Walt Disney	West Yellowstone area
1993	The Last Ride	HKM Productions	Bozeman/Deer Lodge
1993	Return to Lonesome Dove	RHI Productions	Virginia City, Butte/Billings area
1993	The River Wild	Universal Pictures	Libby, Flathead area
1995	Amanda	Family Channel/Cinergi Pictures	Red Lodge area
1995	Broken Arrow	20th Century Fox	Lewistown
1995	The Real Thing	W. T. Entertainment	Deer Lodge
1995	Under Siege II: Dark Territory	Warner Bros.	Missoula
1997	The Horse Whisperer	Walt Disney Pictures	Big Timber/Livingston
1997	Everything That Rises	Turner Network Television	Livingston
1997	Me & Will	S & M Productions	Livingston/ Wilsall
1997	The Patriot	Interlight Pictures	Ennis area
1997	What Dreams May Come	Interscope/Poygram	Glacier Natl. Park/Blackfoot Reservation
1998	The Hi-Line	Milk River Productions	Livingston
1999	Big Eden	Big Eden Productions	Flat/West Glacier
2000	Frozen in Fear	Senta Production	Darby/Hamilton
2000	The Slaughter Rule	The Slaughter Rule Partners LLC	Great Falls
2002	Heaven's Pond	Heaven's Pond Production	Libby
2002	Hidalgo	Walt Disney Productions	St. Mary's area/Blackfeet Reservation
2002	White of Winter	Alterity Films	Bozeman, Livingston area
2002	Wolfsummer	Northern Light	Bozeman area
2003	Love Comes to the Executioner	Aura Entertainment	Butte, Deer Lodge
2003	The Music Inside	Montana Motions Picture Co-op	Bozeman
2005	Don't Come Knocking	Sony Pictures Classics	Butte

Source: Montana Film Office, Montana Department of Commerce.

The council also publishes *State of the Arts,* a bimonthly publication providing information to the Montana arts community and beyond.

Montana Arts Council
316 North Park Avenue, Suite 252
P.O. Box 202201
Helena, MT 59620-2201
444-6430
Internet address: www.art.state.mt.us

Montana Committee for the Humanities
311 Brantly Hall
The University of Montana
Missoula 59612-7848
243-6022
www.humanities-mt.org
— Presents programs, awards grants, maintains a speakers bureau, hosts reading-discussion groups and teacher workshops in history, literature, philosophy, and other disciplines.

Montana Cultural Advocacy
P.O. Box 1872
Bozeman 59771
585-9551
— A coalition of arts and cultural agencies that lobbies the State Legislature to maintain funding of cultural agencies and oversees legislation affecting Montana's cultural sector.

Montana Institute of the Arts
P.O. Box 1872
Bozeman 59771
585-9551
— Assists artists in all disciplines through educational projects, information and workshops.

Montana Performing Arts Consortium
P.O. Box 1872
Bozeman 59771
585-9551
— Supports performing arts in large and small communities; sponsors an annual conference showing performing arts; facilitates block-booking; and provides grants to rural presenters.

Very Special Arts Montana
221 East Front
Missoula 59802
549-2984
— Provides information, technical assistance, and workshops on working with people with differently-abled constituencies.

Further Reading

Center for the Applied Economic Research. *The Economic Impact of Montana Artists.* Montana State University–Billing, March 2005.

Kittredge, William, and Allen Morris Jones, eds. *The Best of Montana's Short Fiction.* Guilford, Conn.: The Lyons Press, 2004.

Kittredge, William, and Annick Smith, eds. *The Last Best Place: A Montana Anthology.* Helena: Falcon Press, 1993.

Lively Times. A monthly arts and events magazine published at 1152 Eagle Pass Trail, Charlo MT 59824; 644-2910.

Lucey, Donna M. *Photographing Montana 1894–1928: The Life and Work of Evelyn Cameron.* Missoula: Mountain Press Publishing Company, 2001.

Montana Calendar of Events. Brochure published annually by Travel Montana, 444-2654 or (800) VISIT MT (out of state). www.visitmt.com.

Montana's Cultural Treasures, The Guide to Museums, Art Galleries, Bookstores & Theaters. Brochure produced by Lee Enterprises, the Montana Arts Council, the Montana Historical Society, and Travel Montana, updated each year. (800) 366-7193. P.O. Box 8029, Missoula, MT 59807.

Newby, Rick, and Suzanne Hunger, eds. *Writing Montana: Literature under the Big Sky.* Helena: Montana Center for the Book, 1996.

Rostad, Lee. *Honey Wine and Hunger Root.* Helena: Falcon Press, 1985.

State of the Arts. Bimonthly newsletter published by the Montana Arts Council, 316 North Park, Helena, MT 59620.

Index

About the Author

Andrea (Slosson) Merrill-Maker, grew up in Anaconda, Montana, spent twenty years in Helena, and now makes Missoula her home. Her Montana ancestral roots include great grandparents who ranched in the Boulder Valley more than 110 years ago and grandparents and parents who lived most of their lives in various Western Montana counties. Ms. Merrill-Maker has a BA in Elementary Education and a master's of Education from the University of Montana. From 1981 to 1995, she served the Montana Legislature as a researcher, bill drafter, and committee staffer with the Montana Legislative Council. Andrea served as the Executive Director of the Mental Health Association of Montana for a number of years and recently retired as Missoula field representative for U.S. Senator Max Baucus. These experiences, coupled with an interest in collecting and appraising books on Montana and the West, provided the inspiration for this publication.